Nina Teichert

Innovation in General Purpose Technologies: How Knowledge Gains when It Is Shared

Innovation in General Purpose Technologies: How Knowledge Gains when It Is Shared

by
Nina Teichert

Scientific Publishing

Dissertation, Karlsruher Institut für Technologie (KIT)
Fakultät für Wirtschaftswissenschaften
Tag der mündlichen Prüfung: 16.11.2012
Referentin: Prof. Dr. Ingrid Ott

Impressum

Karlsruher Institut für Technologie (KIT)
KIT Scientific Publishing
Straße am Forum 2
D-76131 Karlsruhe
www.ksp.kit.edu

KIT – Universität des Landes Baden-Württemberg und
nationales Forschungszentrum in der Helmholtz-Gemeinschaft

KIT Scientific Publishing 2012
Print on Demand

ISBN 978-3-86644-915-2

Innovation in General Purpose Technologies: How Knowledge Gains when It Is Shared

Zur Erlangung des akademischen Grades eines

Doktors der Wirtschaftswissenschaften
(Dr. rer. pol.)

der Fakultät für Wirtschaftswissenschaften
des Karlsruher Instituts für Technologie (KIT)

vorgelegte
DISSERTATION

von
Nina Teichert, geb. Menz, M.A.

Referentin: Prof. Dr. Ingrid Ott

2012 Karlsruhe

Acknowledgements

During the course of this work I was mainly funded by the German National Academic Foundation (Studienstiftung des deutschen Volkes). Far beyond the financial support, I very much appreciated their ideal support – it shaped me to a certain extent. Preceding this scholarship, I shortly benefited from a scholarship by the Landesgraduiertenförderung Baden-Württemberg. Substantial financial support came from the Chair in Economic Policy at the Karlsruhe Institute of Technology. Moreover, parts of my work were sponsored by the evoREG project at the Bureau d'Economie Théorique et Appliquée (BETA) in Strasbourg. Last, I was funded by the Karlsruhe House of Young Scientists (KHYS), particularly for the participation in summer schools and for the stay at the London School of Economics as a visiting research student.

I would like to thank my supervisor Prof. Dr. Ingrid Ott for introducing me to the topic and for her guidance throughout the work. The completion of this doctoral thesis would not have been possible without her unrestricted support. I very much appreciated the very knowledgeable and helpful comments of Prof. Dr. Ulrich Schmoch who supported me in the final stages of this work. I moreover want to thank my colleagues, in particular Antje Schimke and Florian Kreuchauff for professional, organisational and personal support and advice as well as the fruitful cooperation on joint projects. Antje, more than that, always motivated me and literally gave me a home.

I very much appreciated the cooperation with the researchers from the Bureau d'Economie Théorique et Appliquée in Strasbourg, special thanks go to Prof. Dr. Emmanuel Muller for his encouragement and his ideas.

During my time as a visiting research student I was lucky to be a part of the inspiring environment at the London School of Economics, where Prof. Dr. Simona Iammarino acted as my supervisor. I have to thank her for the faith in me that made her invite me to the LSE in the first place. I very much benefited from our critical discussions and her honest comments.

Words of thanks are also due to my friends, who distracted and motivated when I needed one or the other. Last but not least, I owe tribute to my family. During the ups and downs throughout the whole course of this work I was wholeheartedly backed by my husband Max. Thank you for all your patience and love.

Nina Teichert

Abstract

This dissertation tackles the different aspects of the creation and transmission of (new) knowledge in the context of the characteristics of a general purpose technology (GPT). Particular emphasis is put on the role of the composition of knowledge as well as the corresponding (presumed) knowledge spillovers on the one hand and on the concrete impact of collaboration and knowledge sharing in innovator networks on the other hand. The thesis offers a coherent literature review in its first part, analysing the theoretical role of knowledge for innovation and growth as well as the role of knowledge diffusion and sharing. Although the development of GPTs is particularly knowledge- and innovation-intensive and GPTs are found to be 'engines of growth', the role of knowledge for innovation in GPTs has not been distinctive subject to investigation yet. Therefore, the two mentioned sets of research questions were tackled empirically in this thesis using the showcase example of nanotechnology. Nanotechnology is argued to be the key technology of the future, and empirical analyses in this thesis using patent and publication data provided evidence that there is sensible reason to consider nanotechnology as GPT.

The first array of research questions is concerned with the role of local knowledge composition and spillovers for the development of nanotechnology. Two different approaches capture these issues. The first one investigates how the characteristics of the regional technological nano-knowledge base as approximated (mainly) by patents influence the creation of new nano-knowledge. Panel negative binomial regression analyses are employed to disentangle the effects. The second approach captures the performance of nano-firms depending on the local endowment with knowledge as investigated by means of OLS and fixed effects panel analyses. The central finding is that the regional endowment with knowledge impacts the development of nanotechnology. Concerning the composition of the knowledge bases, evidence suggests that specialisation and diversity are positively impacting innovation in nanotechnology. More particularly both are necessary to support nanotechnology's characteristics both as high-technology and as GPT.

Focusing on the role of collaboration and knowledge sharing in networks, the second array of research questions is tackled by another two analyses. One analysis focuses on the development of the role of collaboration and networking. The means of social network analysis of German nanotechnology patents' co-contributorship networks shed light on the relationship between collaboration, the efficiency of the networks and the technological overlap (and hence the potential for cooperation) and the development of nanotechnology. The second analysis more particularly puts an emphasis on the factors that impact the generality of a patent. Therefore variables such as intensity of collaboration, access to knowledge, experience and overlap of technological background are included into fractional logit analyses. Findings include that the performance of a GPT can be enhanced through collaboration by offering efficient means for the organisation and coordination of knowledge sharing and knowledge spillovers and by fostering an increase in the technology's generality level due to knowledge sharing in teams and networks.

Keywords:
Knowledge, Innovation, General Purpose Technology, Spillovers, Networks, Specialisation, Diversity, Patents, Nanotechnology.

Zusammenfassung

Die vorliegende Dissertation beschäftigt sich mit den verschiedenen Aspekten des Entstehens und der Übertragung von (neuem) Wissen im Kontext der Eigenschaften von Querschnittstechnologien (QSTen). Der erste Teil der Dissertation enthält einen umfassenden Überblick über die Literatur, die die theoretische Rolle von Wissen für Innovation und Wachstum wie auch die Rolle von Wissensdiffusion und -transfer behandelt. Obwohl die Entwicklung von QSTen besonders wissens- und innovationsintensiv ist und QSTen gemeinhin als 'Wachstumsmotoren' betrachtet werden gibt es bis dato keine umfassende Untersuchung dieser Zusammenhänge mit QSTen. Hiermit beschäftigt sich diese Dissertation anhand des Beispiels der Nanotechnologie. Nanotechnologie wird als Schlüsseltechnologie der Zukunft angesehen, und eine entsprechende empirische Analyse in dieser Dissertation zeigt, dass Nanotechnologie durchaus zu Recht als QST betrachtet wird.

Das erste Set von Forschungsfragen analysiert den Einfluss der Zusammensetzung von (lokalem) Wissen und von Spillovern auf die Entwicklung von Nanotechnologie und wird durch zwei verschiedene Ansätze aufgegriffen. Zunächst wird untersucht, wie die Charakteristika von regionalem technologischem Nano-Wissen (abgebildet durch Patente) die Entstehung neuen Nano-Wissens beeinflusst. Eine zweite Analyse greift den Effekt von regionaler Verfügbarkeit von Wissen in Form von hochqualifiziertem Personal auf das Wachstum von Nano-Firmen auf. Zentrales Ergebnis dieser Analysen ist, dass die regionale Verfügbarkeit von Wissen und dessen Zusammensetzungen die Entwicklung von Nanotechnologie beeinflussen. Präziser sind es Spezialisierung und Diversität gleichermaßen, die das Wachstum von Nanotechnologie-Innovationen beschleunigen und die nötig sind, um den Charakteristika von Nanotechnologie als Hoch- und Querschnittstechnologie gerecht zu werden.

Zwei weitere Analysen werden durchgeführt, um die Rolle von Kooperation und gemeinsamer Wissensnutzung in Innovationsnetzwerken im zweiten Set von Forschungsfragen genauer zu beleuchten. Mithilfe der Methoden der sozialen Netzwerkanalyse wird die Entwicklung von Co-Erfinder und Co-Anmeldernetzwerken, die auf der Grundlage von Nanotechnologie-Patenten aus Deutschland konstruiert sind, evaluiert, um den Zusammenhang zwischen Kooperation, Netzwerkeffizienz und der Überschneidung technologischem Wissens zu der nationalen Innovationsproduktivität zu beleuchten. Im Anschluss wird der Fokus eingeengt auf diejenigen Faktoren und Einflussmechanismen, die die Generalität bestimmen. Dafür werden Variablen wie Intensität der Kooperationen, Zugang zu Wissen über Netzwerke, Erfahrung und Überschneidung des individuellen technologischen Wissens in Betracht gezogen und ausgewertet. Ein wichtiges Ergebnis ist, dass die Entwicklung der QST Nanotechnologie durch Kooperationen und Innovationsnetzwerke entscheidend vorangebracht werden kann, weil diese nicht nur einen effizienten Mechanismus zur Organisation und Koordination von gemeinsamer Wissensnutzung und der Effektivität von Spillovern bieten, sondern ebenfalls die Generalität und damit den (potentiellen) Effekt von Querschnittstechnologien auf das Wachstum erhöhen.

Contents

List of Figures

List of Tables

List of Abbreviations

AFM	Atomic Force Microscope
BMBF	Bundesministerium für Bildung und Forschung
CAN	Center for Applied Nanotechnology
CE	Combustion Engine
CI	Cluster Index
Coeff	Coefficients
DPMA	Deutsches Patent- und Markenamt
EPO	European Patent Office
EU	European Union
EU27	European Union with 27 Member States
GDP	Gross Domestic Product
GPT	General Purpose Technology
HHI	Hirschman-Herfindahl-Index
HP-filter	Hodrick-Prescott filter
ICT	Information and Communication Technology
INPI	Institute de la Propriété Industrielle
IPC	International Patent Classification
IPC3	3-digit International Patent Classification
IPC4	4-digit International Patent Classification
ISI	Fraunhofer Institut für System- und Innovationsforschung
ISIC	International Standard Industrial Classification
JPO	Japan Patent Office
K30	Technology concordance with 30 technological fields (Hinze et al. 1997)
KIT	Karlsruhe Institute of Technology
KIS	Knowledge Intensive Sector
LQ	Location Quotient
MAR	Marshall-Arrow-Romer
MERIT	Maastricht Economic and Social Research Insitute on Innovation and Technology
NACE	Nomenclature statistique des Activités économiques dans la Communauté Européenne
NEG	New Economic Geography
NKB	Nano Knowledge Base
Obs	Observations
OECD	Organisation for Economic Cooperation and Development
OLS	Ordinary Least Squares
OST	Observatoire des Science et Techniques
PATSTAT	EPO Worldwide Patent Statistical Database
R&D	Research and Development

RTA	Revealed Technological Advantage
RTC	Revealed Technological Compatibility
SA	Subject Area
sciNKB	scientific Nano Knowledge Base
SME	Small and Medium-sized Enterprise
SNA	Social Network Analysis
StdDev	Standard Deviation
techNKB	technological Nano Knowledge Base
UK	United Kingdom
US	United States
USPTO	Unites States Patent and Trademark Office
WIPO	World Intellectual Property Organization
WOS	Web of Science
WZ	Wirtschaftszweigklassifikation

List of Symbols

C	Watts-Strogatz Clustering Coefficient
C_B	Betweenness Centralisation
$C_B(v_i)$	Betweenness Centrality of vertex v_i
C_D	Degree Centralisation
$C_D(v_i)$	Degree Centrality of vertex v_i
COH_i	Coherence of technology i
D	Density
$d(v_i)$	Degree of vertex v_i
G_i	Generality of patent i
$\widetilde{G}_i$	Adjusted generality of patent i
g_{jk}	Number of geodesics between vertex j and k
IC_t	Innovational Complementarities in year t
l	Number of lines (edges)
L	Characteristic Path Length
N_i	Number of observed citations
n	Number of vertices
P_i	Patent count weight of technology class i
R_{ij}	Relatedness of technology i and j
SW	Small World Variable
v_i	Vertex i

Structure of the Dissertation

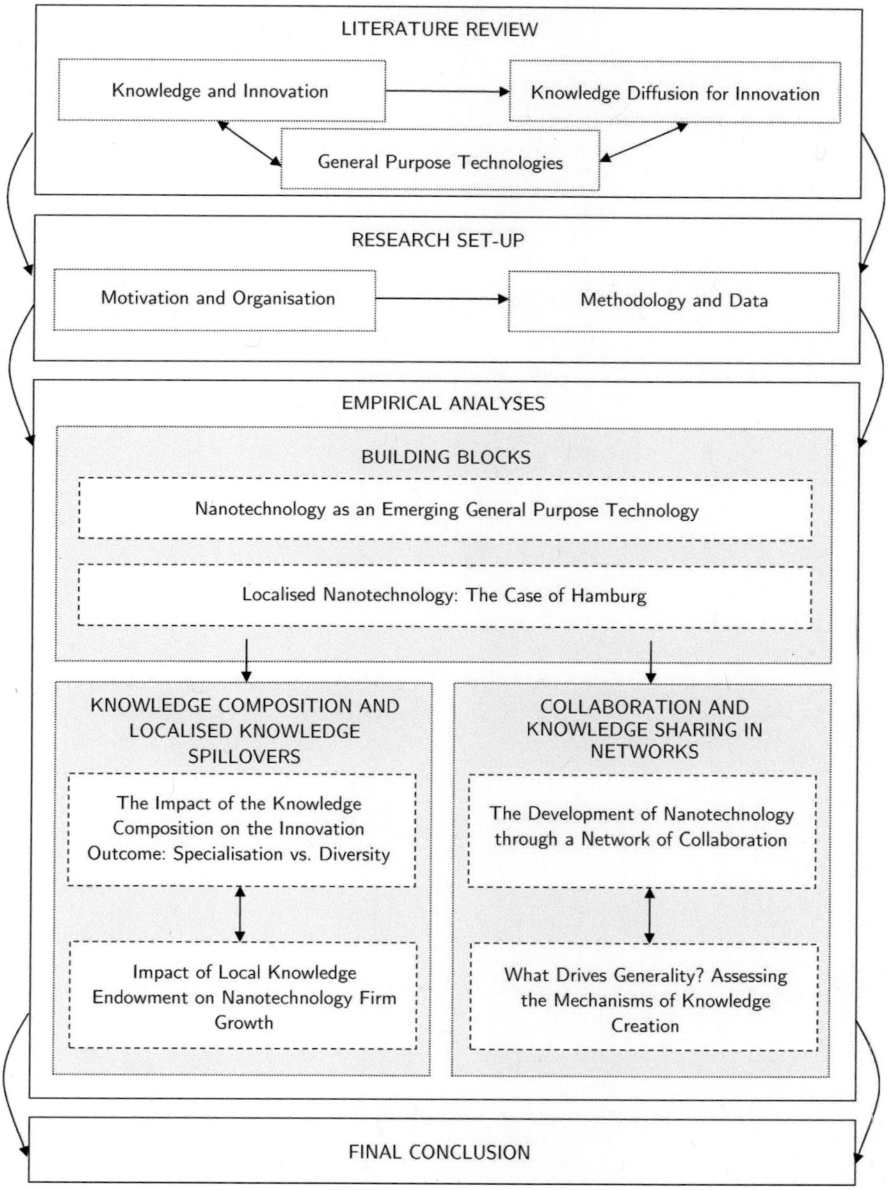

Introduction

Knowledge and innovation are nowadays the key to the wealth of nations. They ensure on-going economic growth more than labour, savings, investments or natural resources. The development of industrialised economies towards knowledge economies spotlights the role of the creation, accumulation, diffusion and transmission of knowledge for the sustainable development of innovations. The various relationships between knowledge and innovation are coined by the peculiar features of knowledge, i.e. the non-rivalry and the incomplete appropriability, or, put another way the character of being a partly public good. This property induces complex interconnected mechanisms and makes the assessment of the fundamental drivers of growth hardly tangible, elusive and difficult to measure.

The diffusion and the flow or, put differently, the transfer of knowledge is commonly recognised to be a key explanatory factor for the location of innovative activity close to other knowledge creating agents. Proximity to other sources of knowledge is accepted to heavily impact the transfer of valuable and mostly tacit, embodied knowledge that is difficult to codify: The application of knowledge created in one place for one purpose in a (completely) different context for another (additional) purpose lowers the cost and boosts the productivity of innovations. The availability of knowledge through publication, knowledge spillovers, collaboration or, generally spoken, knowledge sharing increases the stock of knowledge resources. These knowledge resources can be built on, they can be recombined to new ideas and innovations eventually, thereby impacting economic growth: *Knowledge gains when it is shared.* If one aims to understand how growth is sustained by innovation, a deeper understanding of the impact of knowledge sharing and knowledge transfers, be they spillovers, collaborations or networks of innovations, on innovative activity is indispensable.

The complexity of these relationships, and in particular the relevance of proximity, both, geographical and cognitive, as impacting innovations, does not stop at general purpose technologies (GPTs). GPTs are characterised by a wide variety of uses, technological dynamism and innovation spawning that result in innovational complementarities (Bresnahan 2010). Due to their capacity to spur a set of complementary innovations, GPTs are expected to interact with other technologies along various value creation chains and thus to serve as engines of innovation, or, more generally spoken as 'engines of growth'. Precisely due to the innovation-inducing effect of GPTs, the pertinence of knowledge, knowledge sharing, location and their impact on innovations are even multiplied. If GPTs are engines of innovation and growth, the mechanisms of knowledge creation are the prime movers of this engine. To understand how knowledge gets GPT as an engine of growth to work is the main goal of this thesis.

The central research question of this thesis is hence how the development of GPTs as engines of growth is sustained by the availability, the targeted application, the diffusion and finally the recombination of knowledge. The several research questions that are derived thereof are organised around two main working packages. One deals with the role of knowledge composition (i.e. the nature of the knowledge stock with respect to specialisation and diversity) and localised knowledge spillovers. The other takes the role of knowledge sharing and networks into account. To make these main analyses comprehensive, a preparatory working package constitutes the building block of the empirical analyses: It introduces nanotechnology as a showcase example of a general purpose technology and operationalizes the research questions by an exploratory case study. However, before these empirical analyses are accomplished, the analytical framework is built.

This thesis has a modular set-up. First, parts organise the thesis in a preparatory literature review and the description of the research set-up, followed by the empirical analyses and the conclusion. The literature review in the next part provides the theoretical underpinnings and surveys findings of former research. In particular, Chapter 1 provides an introduction into the main economic theories that elaborate on knowledge and growth. Chapter 2 broaches the issue of the diffusion of knowledge for innovation. It is subdivided in three sections, one referring to the role of spillovers for innovation and one elaborating on the impact of collaboration and networks. The intersection between the former, rather abstract and the latter, rather concrete section is constituted by the mechanisms of knowledge transfer. Then, general purpose technologies are integrated into the course of this thesis (Chapter 3). The second part derives the research gap and the correspondingly arising research questions and presents the organisation of the empirical research (Chapter 4). Chapter 5 introduces the most important data and methodology employed. It follow the part of the empirical analyses (Chapters 6 – 11), that is again unitised in three different modules in form of a basic building blocks working package and two thematic working packages. The last part concludes with Chapter 12. Note that, in order to avoid redundancies, important approaches, concepts and definitions will be introduced in the preparatory parts I (content-related) and II (methdology-related). Particularly when reading the empirical analyses chapter-wise it is hence recommended to look up unclear notions in part I and II.

The results of the analyses accomplished offer a threefold contribution: They enhance the understanding of the working principles behind knowledge, knowledge transfers and innovation in general. More particularly, the results of the analyses enrich the comprehension of how knowledge enhances innovative activity in general purpose technologies and thereby contributes to its effects on economic growth. And last, the investigation of nanotechnology as a showcase GPT in the context of the German innovation system offers a comprehensive analysis on the state of the development of nanotechnology in Germany as backed by the creation and diffusion of knowledge. This makes it possible to finally derive preliminary policy implications.

Part I

LITERATURE REVIEW

1 Knowledge and Innovation

Firms and economic entities face substantial competition leading to a dependence on innovation and technological advance in order to be able to earn – at least for a short time – monopolistic rents (Schumpeter 1946). *Innovation* in this context '[...] concerns the search for, and the discovery, experimentation, development, imitation, and adoption of new products, new production processes and new organizational set-ups' (Dosi 1988, p. 222). Put another way, innovation is the ability to blend and merge different types of knowledge into something new, unprecedented and commercialisable; it is hence a process of creating economic value on the market (Feldman and Kogler 2010). *Inventions,* by contrast, rather comprise the new idea, the concept or the new approach itself that precedes the process of commercialisation (Schumpeter 1912). However, not all inventions have to finally become innovations and result in economic value-added.

Innovations are nowadays seen as central engines of economic growth. Modern innovation theories date back to Schumpeter (1912), who was one of the first scholars who described and systematised innovative activity as process of 'creative destruction', persistently renewing the economic structure and thereby leading to economic growth. One of the most influential theories on economic growth, the neoclassical growth model by Solow (1956), however, concluded that labour and capital are indispensable to explain the growth of economies. Knowledge was brought into the economic debate again by another seminal contribution of Solow (1957) to the study of the mechanisms of growth. Having tested his earlier theory empirically in the US, he then emphasised the role of *total factor productivity* for explaining the different levels of economic growth in different economies, hence pointing to different levels of technology. A few years later, knowledge as possible determinant of total factor productivity had become implemented into production functions within several models and studies. However, these models were still neoclassical growth models, all explaining growth by assuming exogenous technological change. But knowledge does not display the typical properties of production factors and is not consistent with the neoclassical constant return to scale assumptions leading to zero compensation for the costs that are associated with creating the innovation (Barro and Sala-i-Martin 2003). Knowledge, hence, cannot be regarded as a traditional production factor. By contrast, the feature of knowledge being a partly public good makes it a peculiar economic entity. Besides the necessary distinction between knowledge and information within production contexts, which encompasses how knowledge is processed, an important and distinctive property of knowledge is the matter of knowledge externalities, also known as knowledge spillovers. These are induced by incomplete appropriability. Such 'external economies' have been described first by Marshall (1890). However, they were not systematically implemented into theoretical economic models before Romer (1986, 1990). Romer (1990), as well as Grossmann and Helpman (1990) and Aghion and Howitt (1992) used knowledge externalities to model non-diminishing returns at the macro level, thereby explaining long-run growth without exogenous technological progress and constant returns to scale in production. Modelling growth endogenously, they established the New Growth Theory. More recently, the existence of externalities played a central role in the establishment of the New Economic Geography fundamentally coined by Krugman (1991b).

1.1 Knowledge as Economic Entity

The ability to access and create new knowledge is crucial for innovation processes and technological advance and hence for economic growth, competitiveness and subsequently prosperity of (economic) regions (Cincera 2003). It is, however, difficult to give a clear definition of knowledge as there is no common one existing. By contrast, the appreciation of knowledge depends on the context it is employed in. The value of knowledge as produced and production good depends on the usability of knowledge, i.e. how it can be used, translated and converted. Although knowledge surely refers to much more than to an economic entity only, its economic properties are in the focus in this thesis. In the economic literature, knowledge is mainly seen as commodity or particular input that is used to produce value added. However, knowledge is a special factor of production as it is cumulative, that is new knowledge is produced by using the existing *stock of knowledge*, or, put differently the existing *knowledge base*, i.e. the accumulated knowledge of an individual, an organisation or a geographic space, e.g.. In contrast to common factors of production, knowledge is inexhaustible and hence non-rival in supply. This means that knowledge can, in theory, be exploited by many agents at the same time without decreasing the value of the knowledge for each of the users (Grossmann and Helpman 1991). Moreover, knowledge is only imperfectly excludable. It diffuses easily, making it impossible for the producer of knowledge to appropriate the full returns (Grossmann and Helpman 1991). These diffusion processes, given the non-rival nature of knowledge as partly public good, are focal for the consideration of knowledge as an economic entity. Knowledge created and implemented in any particular context can also develop economic value in other contexts: Knowledge processing is likely to induce *knowledge spillovers* and thereby exhibit increasing returns (Griliches 1979). The kind of knowledge that spills over is further disentangled in the literature as it is emphasised that it is mostly tacit knowledge that spills over (Audretsch 1998, Breschi and Lissoni 2001b). More particularly, knowledge has to be split up in two parts, namely a *tacit* and a *non-tacit* part. The latter refers to easily transferable, codified knowledge with an unambiguous meaning and is commonly subsumed under the term *information*, whilst knowledge in its tacit sense is difficult to codify, vague and rather difficult to transmit (if this is possible at all). This is the case although the information and communication technology's (henceforth ICT) revolution made it possible to reduce marginal cost of transmitting information to close to zero. Hence, the possibility of transmitting and processing knowledge depends on the characteristics of the knowledge: *Tacit knowledge* is in sharp contrast to information, i.e. *explicit* or *codified knowledge*. Codified knowledge can be precisely and formally articulated and subsequently transmitted easily via media in its codified form. The concept of tacit knowledge on the other hand was brought up by Polanyi (1966), referring to knowledge from a know-how-to-do perspective, i.e. knowledge that is incorporated in individuals that are capable of processing it. Tacit knowledge is highly contextual and difficult or even impossible to codify (Gertler 2003). The diffusion of tacit knowledge is thus happening mostly via face-to-face contacts and personal relations which require spatial proximity. For this distinction, Grupp (1998) more visually referred to *embodied* and *disembodied knowledge* (see Figure 1.1 for an overview on the different forms). Embodied knowledge is bound to entities and hence tacit, while disembodied knowledge is codified and can be found e.g. in traded capital, intermediate goods or services. Since the marginal cost of transmitting tacit, embodied knowledge rise with spatial and cultural distance as personal relationships become less prevalent, this kind of knowledge is no longer freely available for anyone but those proximate to its source. Therefore, knowledge that spills over is a *local* public good (Breschi and Lissoni 2001b) and knowledge in general thus a partly local public good – which is a building block in explaining localisation of innovative activity as is done in Section 2.1.[1]

During the last decades a respectable shift towards knowledge-based economies or 'the era of information' has taken place in the industrialised economies. The rise of knowledge-intensive sectors in production and in services is the main feature of this new era of capitalism (Tödtling et al. 2006). Innovation in these knowledge-based

[1] According to standard neoclassical theories that model growth externally, by contrast, knowledge is seen as a public good produced outside the economic system. Due to bounded rationality, economic agents are not capable of acting economically optimal. Hence, routines are developed that shall reduce uncertainty, particularly in the field of new knowledge creation (Nelson and Winter 1982), resulting in research close to prior existing knowledge (Boschma 2005).

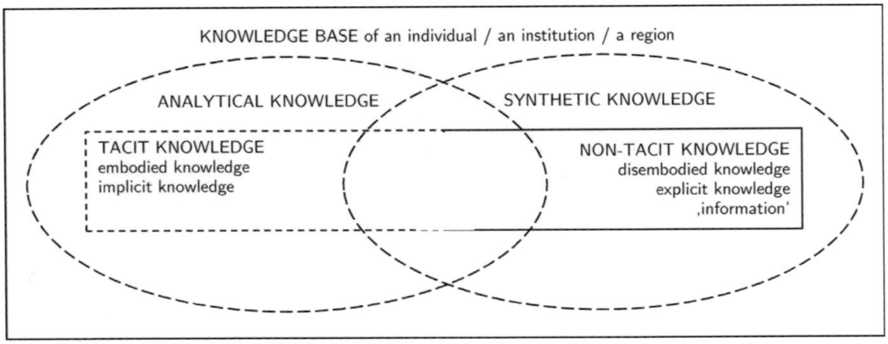

Figure 1.1: Different forms of knowledge.
Source: own illustration.

industries differs remarkably from innovation in traditional industries with respect to learning, the use, accumulation, transfer and recombination of knowledge, their links to geography and hence local economic structures (Tödtling et al. 2006). In this thesis, such knowledge-intensive high-tech industries are especially relevant. Focusing on high-tech sectors, Grupp (1994) pointed to the fact that, while innovative products are often equated with high-tech products, the high-tech phenomenon is very dynamic and cannot be captured easily. It is neither a natural nor an economic phenomenon, but rather a political or public manifestation. Notwithstanding the lack of a clear definition of what high-technology sectors exactly are, one feature is widely accepted: *High-tech* always relies on high knowledge, hence high-tech industries are knowledge-intensive, science-based industries. Grupp et al. (2000) defined high-tech as technologies which usually require an average investment in R&D of more than 3,5% of turnover and further distinguish between high-level and *leading-edge technologies*, with leading-edge referring to more than 8,5% investment shares. Science-based high-technologies are hence characterised by the importance of knowledge. In classical scientific fields, such knowledge can be considered codifiable to a large part. New knowledge is published in scientific journals and hence made explicit. In order to make use of this knowledge, experience and know-how is often needed which constraints explicitness and introduces tacitness. More particularly, leading edge technologies have to be distinguished further: While there exist a language and/or even standards on how to name, describe and handle findings in stable technologies, the situation is different in emergent technologies. Here, the field is about to be explored. Since tacit knowledge is the ultimate source of new knowledge (Nonaka and Takeuchi 1995), these fields depend on tacit knowledge. It is acquired through experience and not easily expressible in words. The articulation of such 'craftsman's knowledge' is difficult because its understanding requires high degrees of expertise in the field.[2] However, the sharing of this tacit knowledge among innovators with different backgrounds and perspectives is critical for innovation in emerging technologies. Over time, the tacit mental model can get verbalised and eventually condensed into explicit concepts (Nonaka and Takeuchi 1995). This is important for the process of the creation of knowledge, since only tacit knowledge that is made explicit through externalisation can be shared by others and become the basis for the creation of new knowledge (Nonaka et al. 2003). The less emergent and hence the more stable a technology gets, the less important the dimension of tacitness as tacit knowledge gets more and more converted into explicit knowledge. The distinction between *analytical* and *synthetic knowledge bases* (as was done by Asheim and Gertler (2005) and as presented in Figure 1.1) makes it possible to differentiate the knowledge used in rather traditional industries that particularly cope with specific problem solving and hence exhibit low levels of R&D, but high levels of learning by doing. Here, synthetic knowledge dominates. Contrariwise, analytical knowledge is crucial in industries relying on scientific inputs and tacit or embodied knowledge with formally organised knowledge production processes. Although research is done within companies in most of the cases, innovative agents rely on external knowledge spilling over from universities, public research labs and other private agents (Tödtling et al. 2006). These industries in their emerging stage are in the focus in this thesis, which puts an emphasis on the role of the sharing of tacit knowledge.

1.2 Knowledge, Innovation and Growth

The creation, accumulation, implementation and application of knowledge rely on innovation. Innovation processes, by contrast, are dynamically diverse, frequently subject to geographical concentration and imperfect competitive situations. To analyse this, traditional assumptions of perfectly competitive markets and constant returns to scale are not helpful. Standard external growth models include knowledge as costless and perfectly transferable input factor, which is in the extent of its whole stock used by rational individuals that are perfectly and at no cost informed. Knowledge is thus assumed to be a pure public good in the diffusion of which spatial distance is irrelevant. Since knowledge is non-rival, it must be produced only once. This suggests that the production of knowledge and technological advance implies large fixed R&D cost, which leads to the notion of increasing returns (Sala-i-Martin 2002). The average costs of knowledge production always exceed marginal costs. In case of perfect competition, i.e. price

[2] Döring and Schnellenbach (2006) noted that in case the process of communication of messages within an epistemic community itself is tacit (besides tacitness as an intrinsic knowledge property), benefiting from knowledge spillovers would require cognitive proximity in addition to spatial proximity. This is further disentangled in Subsection 2.3.1.

equals marginal costs, no agent will hence invest in R&D. The modelling of technological progress therefore needs the relaxation of the perfectly competitive world, which is the foundation of the exogenous growth models, and allow for imperfect competition. In Romer's first model in 1986, he avoided this problem by assuming that new knowledge was generated unpurposefully as a side product of investment. In the later 1990 model, Romer introduced imperfect competition in a Dixit and Stiglitz (1977)-model with new product variety as innovation. Aghion and Howitt (1992, 1998), by contrast, implemented innovation as improvements to existing products. The aim of innovation here was to make previous generations of products obsolete, which is why these models can be classified as Schumpeterian 'creative destruction' models.

These, and many other New Growth Theory models all have in common that they abandon constant or decreasing returns. They stress the role of technology, intellectual spillovers and knowledge externalities. The non-rival nature of knowledge allows for modelling increasing returns in competitive markets, which were needed to generate endogenous economic growth. All these theories indicate that in an endogenously growing economy with competitive markets, spillovers are a crucial feature of the economy: The technological level, or more generally knowledge, is modelled as a (partially) public or private good in this context. The know-how of the production process of a specific agent can be used by others when technology is modelled as such a partially public good. Based on the experience of other agents, an agent can develop new products by learning by doing (Arrow 1962). This affects the behaviour of other agents in turn. The technological level is considered as given and as positively dependent on the capital intensity (i.e. capital per labour unit). Now, real interests are falling with increasing capital intensity. As the technological level increases in capital intensity, this effect is countervailed by technological progress and hence diminishing returns on capital no longer prevail. This leads to positive growth of per-capita income, equal to the growth rate of capital intensity in the long-run equilibrium. Hence, the positive externality of the accumulation of capital intensity on the technological level is creating endogenous growth. By contrast and in the case in which agents can privatise the returns of their technological advance, e.g. by patenting it, innovations are characterised as rather *private* goods (i.e. knowledge becomes excludable but still, it remains non-rival in use). Successful innovations then lead to (temporary) monopoly rents which constitute incentives to invest in R&D in order to become a monopolist by innovation. This innovativeness leads to horizontal (Romer 1990) or vertical innovations (Aghion and Howitt 1992, 1998), inducing higher output and growth.

The Human Capital Theory more particularly focuses on how knowledge is processed. As discussed above, knowledge can be subdivided into explicit and tacit knowledge. Tacit knowledge cannot be formalised and is thus indivisible to the human being who possesses this knowledge. Explicit knowledge is transportable through media like books, instructions or the internet. But this knowledge cannot be activated without human beings, either. Thus, knowledge can be considered as incorporated in individuals who are able to process old and create new knowledge. This, in turn, is the principle behind the notion of human capital. The productivity of human capital is influenced by the location of the individual (Rigby and Essletzbichler 2002). Individual human capital is the amount of knowledge and skills of an individual. The level of human capital in a certain region is the sum of the human capital of all individuals living and/or working in that region (Marlet and van Woerkens 2004). Knowledge as the key driver of innovation and technological advance makes people become the motor force behind growth. Investments in human capital can be made by learning, whereas forgetting as well as knowledge that became obsolete due to technological advance depreciate the value of the human capital. Investments in human capital increase future labour productivity (Wößmann 2003). This idea was already expressed by Smith (1776) and Marshall (1890), who both pointed to the value of human capital exceeding the one of 'normal' capital. Lucas (1988) then modelled human capital and physical capital as complementary production factors where diminishing returns of each input are avoided by accumulation of the respectively complementary factor. Hence, knowledge in the form of human capital becomes a positive externality and finally results in economic growth.

More recently and more particularly Acemoglu et al. (2006) introduced an endogenous growth model where firms engage in imitation as well as innovation in technology and have access to different kinds of human capital. They argued that, vis-à-vis sources of productivity growth, innovation increases in importance relative to imitation the closer an industry[3] is to the world technology frontier. Since highly skilled human capital is indispensable for innovation (Nelson and Phelps 1966), industries closer to the technology frontier select highly skilled human capital in order to be able to pursue an innovation-based strategy. By contrast, industries farther away from the technology frontier do not only select little since they pursue an investment-based strategy. They showed that the switch from this strategy to an innovation-based one might occur at a point in time that is not optimal due to appropriability issues. In particular Acemoglu et al. (2006) suggested that the organisation of knowledge production should be dif-

[3]Their model puts an emphasis on countries, but Acemoglu et al. (2006) themselves argued that their model should be transferable to industries.

ferent in industries that are closer to the world technology frontier. The thesis at hand focuses on such industries where innovation and hence highly skilled human capital is needed and growth strategies are innovation-based.

2 Knowledge Diffusion for Innovation

Innovation tends to cluster spatially. Yet, it is highly debated in the literature whether opportunities are equally distributed across space as it is supposed by the Neoclassical Theory, assuming that production factors are frictionlessly mobile across space – or whether certain places offer a more fertile soil for economic activity. This view is supported by a short look at the map: Throughout humanity, economic and especially innovative activity has been concentrated in certain areas. And indeed and paradoxically: Despite the worldwide trend of globalising economies accompanied by decreasing costs for transport and submitting information, the importance of agglomerations increases. In contrast to some economists predicting footloose multinational corporations as a result of a 'death of distance' (Cairncross 1997), there is evidence in empirical research that exactly these multinational firms focus their innovative activity on a few particular locations. In the knowledge economy, where agents compete for differentiated performance and innovation, innovative activity as high value activity has hence not become dispersed across space. By contrast, of all economic activity it is innovation that benefits most from agglomeration (Feldman and Kogler 2010).

The following chapter sets out to introduce the discussed reasons for this relationship between proximity and productivity for the production of knowledge. Being a main rationale for the need for proximity in the context of innovation, the accessibility of knowledge is in focus in this chapter. Therefore, the investigation is split into three parts that gradually shade into each other: One focussing on knowledge spillovers, one tackling how knowledge is transferred and spilt over and the last one assessing networks and collaboration in a more particular sense.

2.1 Knowledge Spillovers and Innovation

Referring to the Human Capital Theory, Lucas (1988) highlighted the clustering effect of knowledge in cities, in which human capital and information are agglomerated. Here, knowledge spillovers are effective and ideas can move easily due to low cost levels of knowledge transfer, thereby stimulating innovation and growth.

The reason for the clustering of innovation in agglomerations in general and cities in particular can be explained by both, functional and sectoral specialisation of regions (Duranton and Puga 2005). Both of them are explored in the following. The first part of this section refers to the role of functional specialisation, i.e. the proximity-productivity relationship, knowledge spillovers in general and innovation. Subsection 2.1.2 introduces the controversy around the role of sectoral specialisation and sectoral diversity for innovation and thereby refers to the latter.

Functional specialisation within regions relies on the regional separation of management and production activities of multi-unit agents that result as a consequence of organisational change. Location costs increase with centrality and hence actors are only located at the centre of an agglomeration if the correspondingly higher costs can be justified by increased productivity, e.g. due to access to knowledge flows. Centrality is not only beneficial for headquarters and business services but also for innovation: Feldman (1994) suggested that especially innovative activities cluster spatially. Kahnert (1998) similarly found that highly knowledge intensive, innovative production facilities with high levels of necessary communication tend to be centralised in the core of agglomerations. Innovative activity is characterised by pronounced degrees of labour division, interaction and transfer of knowledge between people and institutions and can be seen as a collective learning process. Spatial proximity to other innovating actors is hence important. Therefore, a certain degree of agglomeration of innovators within a particular area is assumed to be conducive to innovation activities (Porter 1998, Fritsch and Slavtchev 2010). By facilitating flows of knowledge, agglomerations are the place where individuals crowd to learn from each other and where new ideas are developed faster, hence resulting in higher levels of innovation and growth. Feldman and Audretsch (1999) showed that there is evidence that cities are the centres of innovation, as cities are the main producers of new knowledge and new ideas. When geographic proximity enhances the transmission of information, knowledge and eventually ideas, this effect should be particularly important in dense regions. Dense regions and cities have the ability to attract human capital, thereby promoting productivity and hence inducing growth (Lucas 1988). They concentrate knowledge and the agents who are active in the process of knowledge accumulation. Jacobs (1969) and Lucas (1988) claimed that these are reasons for agents to pay significantly higher rents of production factors in cities instead of living and producing in rural areas. Localised knowledge spillovers are regarded as a key explanatory factor for the geographical concentration of innovative activity (Dahl and Pedersen 2004): It is the simple fact of being close to other agents and hence benefiting from external effects, as knowledge spillovers from other agents increase the agent's own innovative productivity (Romer 1986) and as new ideas '[...]

cross hallways and streets more easily than oceans and continents' (Glaeser et al. 1992, p. 1127). A key hypothesis is that a certain level of human capital possessing the relevant knowledge concentrated in one place generates more spillover benefits than the same level of human capital distributed across space (Martin and Sunley 1998).

In this context, two distinct kinds of externalities have to be disentangled: *Technological externalities* display direct interdependence among knowledge-producers that are not mediated by market mechanisms: A technological externality takes place when any production function implies unpaid production factors (Antonelli 2008). Put differently, they arise if an agent shares knowledge with other agents without reimbursement, be they intended or not (Grupp 1996). Such technological, *non-pecuniary* spillovers arise mainly from embodied knowledge to the extent to which the produced knowledge cannot be appropriated. Contrariwise, spillovers from disembodied knowledge are *pecuniary externalities*. These refer to an indirect interdependence. They are embodied in traded capital or intermediate goods and services and thereby affect the production, cost and revenue functions. A pecuniary externality takes place when the prices of factors and products are not equal to equilibrium values (Marshall 1890, Antonelli 2008, Fischer et al. 2009). In the following, the former case of externalities are in the focus: Technologies externalities, also known as *pure knowledge spillovers*, are elaborated upon in the New Growth Theory.[1] These deal with the role of spatial knowledge accumulation on productivity, thereby providing a rationale for location and growth patterns of industries (Henderson et al. 1995). Hence, knowledge spillovers increase the efficiency of innovations and are therefore important to regional development and growth dynamics (Jaffe 1986, Jaffe et al. 1993, Audretsch and Feldman 1996, Karlsson and Manduchi 2001, Audretsch and Feldman 2004).[2] Therefore, previously existing technologically proximate research of others might decrease an agent's own research necessary to achieve the results he intended. Caniëls (2000) emphasised the intellectual gains by exchange of information with a lack of direct compensation or at least less compensation than the value of the knowledge to the producer. Knowledge spillovers might hence be defined as 'the amount of knowledge that cannot be appropriated by the economic agent who created it' (Greunz 2003). Put another way, spillovers as positive externalities can be perceived as (unintended) results of the investments and efforts of others to create knowledge, which the local agent can benefit from without reimburse-

[1]For a detailed background reading on pecuniary externalities as implemented in Aghion and Howitt (1992) and other older models that aim at explaining the relationship between structural change and growth refer to Antonelli (2008).

[2]The theoretical importance of spillovers as a source of positive returns to scale in the aggregate production function has been stressed by Glaeser et al. (1992), Grossmann and Helpman (1991), Barro (1991), Henderson et al. (1995), Anselin et al. (1997), Keilbach (2000) and Smolny (2000), among others. For an overview see Döring and Schnellenbach (2006).

ment (Lambooy 2010). Hence from a technological point of view, spillovers constitute a positive externality that introduce increasing returns to scale (Greunz 2004), while there might be negative economic effects concerning competition and incentives to innovate. Last, knowledge spillovers are also called *dynamic knowledge externalities* since the intensity of their effects on productivity can be regarded as a function of the stock of knowledge (Henderson et al. 1995, Henderson 1997, Dohse 2001). Putting it in a nutshell, localised knowledge spillovers drive the efficiency of (regional) innovations and they are hence seen as a source of (sustainable) regional economic growth (Döring and Schnellenbach 2006).

2.1.1 Evidence for Localised Spillovers

The relevance of the geographic dimension in this context has not been obvious for a long time. Krugman (1991a) for example argued that knowledge spillovers are of such high importance that they overcome political or spatial boundaries which would limit their effects. Although significantly influencing innovation, they are moreover considerably difficult to trace (Krugman 1991b). In fact and in the age of globalisation, the possibility of transmitting information fast and at nearly no cost misleads in so far as the knowledge spillovers considered in this context rather relate to tacit knowledge than to information. The tacit dimension of knowledge, including the knowledge on how to activate information properly, cannot be transmitted by modern communication media (see Chapter 1). Knowledge spillovers are therefore not invariant to distance (van der Panne 2004, van der Panne and van Beers 2006). Geographic proximity between agents is necessary for the transmission of tacit knowledge, a fact which turns space into a determinative factor for innovation and subsequently drives the differentiation of the economic landscape (Howells 2002, Gertler 2003, Tappeiner et al. 2008). The most influential studies investigating the relationship between knowledge spillovers and geography either rely on micro-level data with patent citations and their spatial distribution or on the rather macro-level, aggregate approach estimating the knowledge production function as introduced by Griliches (1979). This approach has become a key concept of the Endogenous Growth Theory, pointing to the relevance of knowledge production for long-term productivity growth (Romer 1986, Aghion and Howitt 1992). In this context, the production of knowledge and innovation is regarded as a function of the local stock of knowledge. This stock produces, dependent on its *composition*, i.e. the nature (and not the size) of the knowledge stock (e.g. with respect to specialisation and diversity), more or less effective knowledge spillovers. Put differently, innovative outputs are modelled as a function of inputs in the innovation process, among which the most important are R&D investment and human capital.

And indeed, Jaffe et al. (1993) were the first to study the localisation of knowledge spillovers by means of patent citations and found that citations are extraordinarily localised: It is much more likely that a patent cites another patent from the same geographical region than a patent outside that region. Later, this result was confirmed with European data by Maurseth and Verspagen (2002), who found that distance between the loci of patents influences the propensity of citing negatively. The other way round, Audretsch and Feldman (1996) showed that the R&D intensity (i.e. R&D-sales ratio) of a region is positively influenced by geographical concentration of the innovative activity. Jaffe et al. (2000) again confirmed the localisation of knowledge spillovers by surveying inventors on patent citations. Knowledge spillovers are indeed mostly geographically bounded to the region they originate from and hence local. This introduces the need for proximity, which is crucial to the absorption of knowledge spillovers: The marginal transmitting cost of knowledge is lowest with frequent social interaction and communication (Venables 2006). Bottazzi and Peri (2003) found for European regions that only R&D investments within a perimeter of 300 km have a positive impact on the regional patenting activity rather than impacting uniformly across space. Anselin et al. (1997) and Malecki (2010) even found that spillovers are most effective within a range of 50 miles from the metropolitan area of origin. Other studies, however, find evidence for these effects to be time dependent: The younger the invention is, the more relevant is proximity for the inherent knowledge to spill over. Over time, the distance travelled by the knowledge increases (Keller 2002, Paci and Usai 2007). Moreover, cultural and technological proximity seem to be substitutes to geographical proximity to a certain extent: Technological specialisation between agents is shown to have a positive impact on spillovers (Peri 2002). Also, the same culture and same language of the region the knowledge originates from and the potential receiver of spillovers influence the effect on innovation (Thompson 2006, Agrawal et al. 2008). Other studies observed that knowledge spillovers are not homogeneous across firms and industries. Different knowledge production functions have been employed for smaller and larger firms (Acs et al. 1994) and for knowledge intensive, young and less complex industries (Audretsch and Feldman 1996), e.g.: Smaller firms with little or no R&D are more dependent on the appropriation of external knowledge inputs. The degree of complexity of a technology certainly determines the spatial concentration or dispersion of innovative activity (Cantwell and Janne 1999). Due to the high degree of tacitness, or, put another way, the embodied nature of knowledge, innovations in more complex technologies and fast changing, such as (particularly young) high-tech and science-based technologies tend to be geographically more concentrated as learning and spillovers are restricted within space. Audretsch and Feldman (1996) hence concluded that spillovers are more relevant in industries where new knowledge plays a crucial role.

The existing empirical research thus provides evidence that knowledge spillovers indeed can be seen as a key factor to explain spatial clustering of innovation, although their impact may differ across firms and industries. To put it in a nutshell: The investigation of knowledge spillovers within a spatial context relies on two nowadays stylised facts: Innovation is geographically concentrated (Feldman 1994, Audretsch 1998, Feldman and Audretsch 1999) and knowledge spillovers are bounded spatially (Jaffe et al. 1993, Sonn and Storper 2008). The positive effects of localised knowledge in agglomerations are therefore twofold: First, spatial proximity enhances knowledge spillovers and decreases the costs of benefiting thereof. Second, innovations cluster within agglomerations, thereby reinforcing the density and probability of spillovers. Since innovations are the main driver of technological advance, it is not surprising that economic growth in agglomerations tends to be faster than in peripheral regions. More than that, knowledge spillovers in agglomerations most presumably secure sustained economic growth due to the absence of decreasing returns (Glaeser et al. 1992, Fujita and Thisse 2002).

However, these fundamental insights into the nature of knowledge and its impact on innovation and growth have been stated in the literature without any comprehensive offer of an explanation how exactly knowledge spills over, i.e. which the working principle behind these spillovers is (Storper and Venables 2005). The evidence on localised knowledge spillovers is of indirect nature rather than definite.[3] Efforts in filling this gap by exploring and defining the mechanisms of spillovers have been done, a part of the results of which are sketched in Section 2.2.

2.1.2 Marshall-Jacobs Controversy

Marshall (1890) figured out substantial agglomeration forces which arise due to asset sharing, a market for specialised skills and positive externalities – in short: due to the aforementioned *sectoral specialisation*. In the context of innovation, knowledge externalities that arise due to the above mentioned knowledge spillovers are possibly the most important ones. Arrow (1962) contributed a formalisation of the economic implications of learning-by-doing, later picked up and refined by Romer (1986). The complementarity of these contributions on the mechanism behind inducement and exploitation of (knowledge) externalities arising within agglomerations of similar firms of the same industry was discovered by Glaeser et al. (1992), who subsumed these

[3] It is beyond the scope of this thesis to explore all shortcomings of theoretical and empirical research on knowledge spillovers. See Breschi and Lissoni (2001a), Audretsch and Feldman (2004) and more recently Döring and Schnellenbach (2006) for critical surveys on theoretical and empirical contributions to the investigation of the role of spillovers for innovation and agglomeration.

effects as *Marshall-Arrow-Romer (MAR) externalities*.[4] Traditionally distinguishing between *industry-specific* localisation economies spurred by highly specialised, dense areas and *city-specific* urbanisation economies as a result of the diversity within a given region,[5] Glaeser et al. (1992) investigated the role of the economic structure for the impact of dynamic externalities.

Industry-specificity

The basic reasoning behind Marshall-Arrow-Romer industry-specific agglomeration advantages implies that local agents within the same industry can share the same assets and benefit from goods and services provided by specialised suppliers as well as from a local labor market pool. Efficient communication as a consequence of face-to-face contacts builds up trust, promotes the development of networks, partnerships and joint projects. Thereby, it enables an easy diffusion of knowledge between the various actors involved along the value creation chain. Prevalently, the corresponding knowledge as well as the spillovers between the various actors refer to specialisation and are hence *industry-specific*.[6] By 'working on similar things and hence benefiting much from each other's research' (Griliches 1979) knowledge spillovers increase the available knowledge stock for everyone (nearby). Benefiting from these productivity gains enhances the overall income thereby leading to bigger markets, inducing labour mobility and also feedbacks to production. If the mentioned effects are sufficiently large they become self-reinforcing, thereby acting as agglomeration forces that finally lead to spatial concentration of economic activity.[7] Spatial concentration is frequently accompanied by regional specialisation and the emergence of clusters. Although there is still no overall consensus on a general definition of an *industrial cluster*, the term usually refers to a specialised network of firms and institutions thus including '[...] a geographically proximate group of inter-connected companies and associated institutions in a particular field, linked by commonalities and complementarities [...]' (Porter 2000, p. 254). Its functional principle relies on the advantages of spatial, technological, and cultural proximity and linkages across activities thereby increasing the productivity of innovation and production processes and thus triggering improved economic performance.

[4] Glaeser et al. (1992) also discussed the role of competition as 'Porter externality', but as this is not of importance in this context, it is not outlined further.

[5] Since both types of the corresponding externalities refer to a certain location and thus are localised to some extent, the notion in city-specificity and industry-specificity is preferred here.

[6] In the literature these spillovers are also summarised by the term Marshall-Arrow-Romer (MAR) or as localisation externalities.

[7] Although these basic relationships have been well-recognised for a long time, the seminal work of Krugman (1991a) has provided the theoretical basis for an entire field in economics which now is labelled as the New Economic Geography. Brakman et al. (2009) provided an excellent overview.

City-specificity

By contrast, the superior effect of specialisation on the efficiency of innovations is doubted as well. This line of argumentation bases on the concern that too much specialisation may inhibit the emergence and evolution of new technological fields. Lock-in effects are risked particularly with respect to the exchange between basically complementary, but heterogeneous knowledge (Fritsch and Slavtchev 2008). Thereby, a higher vulnerability to external shocks within a strictly localised industry is produced. This leads to the alternative estimation of the various agents' interaction and highlights the role and importance of so-called *city-specific* externalities: Already Jacobs (1969) suggested that especially the diversity of the economic structure fosters the recombination and diffusion of ideas, which is why these externalities are also known as *Jacobs externalities*.

Following this line of argumentation, the exchange of complementary knowledge across diverse firms and economic agents favours innovative activity, increases the stock of knowledge available to the individual agent and thus also strengthens productivity of a certain region in which the agent is embedded. Arguably, the most important spillovers come from outside the respective industry. Thus, particularly in the context of innovation activity, the argument of diversity and hence the importance of city-specific externalities becomes relevant. The reasoning for this is as follows: In diverse economies, the potential for an exchange of knowledge and ideas and the probability of random collisions of businesses are higher (Glaeser et al. 1992). More differentiated knowledge creates a greater variety of knowledge spillovers.

An innovation working well in one industry often can be applied, modified and/or or further developed in other industries (Wu 2005). This phenomenon of *cross-fertilisation* between basically different, but at least to some extent related technologies as well as even between (so far) unrelated technologies becomes more probable (Granstrand 1998, Suzuki and Kodama 2004, Garcia-Vega 2006). Glaeser (1996) even stated that the idea of growth resulting from the exchange of ideas points directly to the role of urban centres in triggering intellectual cross-fertilisation: It is widely accepted that multidisciplinarity and diversity of a team of highly skilled individuals can help the individual members to overcome the weaknesses resulting from being an expert in a particular field, but not being able to have an advanced overview of the possible connections of this field to other technologies. Like this, concepts to solve problems in one technology can be connected to other technologies and solve problems in those contexts as well (Schroeder et al. 1989). This underlines the relevance of diversity and indicates in the same vein that cross-fertilisation is a way in which knowledge can spill over. Agents can hence benefit from new technological possibilities, ideas and knowledge spilling over, stimulating innovative activity and preventing negative lock-in effects in one particular technology.[8]

Marshall vs. Jacobs

However, Marshall and Jacobs externalities are not mutually exclusive, which one might consider a paradox at the first glance. For instance, diversity and Jacobs economies might very well explain cross-fertilisation effects and resulting innovation but they do not exclude the additional possibility of on-going specialisation in particular industries in the very same region (see also Ibrahim et al. (2009) and Feldman and Kogler (2010)). In this vein, Henderson (1997) found that large cities (>500 000 inhabitants) are not only more diversified but also more specialised, particularly in new industries, compared to medium-sized cities.

So far, the overall impact of industry-specific and city-specific externalities on regional development or, put differently, the question whether regional growth benefits most from Marshall or Jacobs externalities, is still an unresolved puzzle. Previous analyses do not provide an unambiguous solution to whether specialisation or diversity in a region better stimulates knowledge production and innovation activities. While Feldman and Audretsch (1999) found that diversity rather than specialisation is important and Duranton and Puga (2000) supported this view for the US, Paci and Usai (1999) found ambiguous results for the case of Italy, where both externalities played a role in the innovations processes, with a tendency to more relevant specialisation effects. Fritsch and Slavtchev (2008) concluded that specialisation is important but only to a certain degree, further emphasising the ambiguity. Meanwhile, van der Panne and van Beers (2006) argued that both externalities affect technological development but at different stages of the innovation process with specialisation at the beginning and diversification rather at later stages. They hence contemplate that dynamics are relevant in this context as well. Also, diversity and specialisation might account for different kinds of innovation, the former potentially favouring rather radical innovations, the latter rather incremental ones (Schumpeter 1946). This is also supported by recent research. Frenken et al. (2007) expected industry-specific externalities to rather spur incremental and process

[8] Besides the diversified industrial structure, the advantages of city-specific urbanisation economies also include more benefits arising from the density and size of a region, mainly in form of static externalities: market sizes, availability of suppliers and numbers of customers increase and the public infrastructure endowment improves (Combes 2000). Moreover, fiscal and environmental externalities are relevant and might come as negative externalities as well (e.g. pollution, congestion) (de Groot et al. 2008). One might argue that all of these could be industry-specific as well, in this context, however, city-specific effects will always outreach industry-specific ones.

innovations and hence to increase productivity, while they found city-specific externalities to rather induce radical innovation by facilitating the recombination of knowledge from different sectors (see also Döring and Schnellenbach 2006, Feldman and Kogler 2010). Hence, which kind of spillover is more beneficial might eventually depend on micro-level, i.e. sectorial and firm-level conditions (Porter 1990), while a possible answer might be one of composition. However, while it is not clear which industrial structure is preferable to innovations, this debate emphasises that it is not only the stock of knowledge that affects growth, but also its precise composition in a qualitative sense (Frenken et al. 2007).

In this context, the speed of knowledge diffusion through knowledge spillovers has been subject to investigation as well (Verspagen and Schoenmakers 2000, Mariani 2000, Maurseth and Verspagen 2002). There is evidence that knowledge diffuses faster (and hence develops new value in other context faster) in regions with higher productivity and larger knowledge stocks. This is a striking support for the cumulative nature of knowledge creation: new knowledge can be better employed when necessary complementary knowledge is available. More particularly, the diffusion between regions that exhibit similar specialisation patterns is more likely and faster. Döring and Schnellenbach (2006) argued that this is a support for the conjecture that spillovers are more likely (to be effective) if source and recipient are similar in terms of knowledge needed and knowledge acquired. Following these studies, intra-industry spillovers should spread faster than city-specific spillovers, since the heterogeneity of recipient and source does not seem to be driving knowledge diffusion. Summing up, these findings support the role of the compatibility of new knowledge to existing knowledge for the pace of innovations.

Recent research hence elaborates on a variety of complex relationships, emphasising knowledge as a particular and in importance increasing input in an interplay with agglomeration forces and proximity (de Groot et al. 2008). Moreover, the respective industrial structure characterised by specialisation and diversity is also considered important when investigating the impact on location, innovation, productivity and eventually (regional) economic growth.

2.2 Mechanisms of Knowledge Transfers and Spillovers

Having unravelled knowledge, or, put differently, human capital as a cornerstone for innovations and technological change, economic growth theories yet treat knowledge as spreading easily throughout the economy due to its nature as intangible good. This assumption, however, neglects the fact that knowledge *does not* diffuse this easily and frictionlessly. It is by far not obvious how knowledge is spread most efficiently. There is, by contrast, agreement that frictionless roaming of ideas even within geographic proximity remains exceptional (Martin 2011). While geographical proximity might increase the exposition to knowledge spillovers, it is by far not a sufficient precondition for the transmission of knowledge or at least for a granted access to this knowledge. More particularly, although knowledge spillovers are widely accepted as a diffusion channel for technological (tacit) knowledge (Jaffe 1986, Krugman 1995, Nooteboom 2000, Breschi and Lissoni 2001a, Breschi et al. 2003, Henderson 2007), the precise nature of spillovers and the mechanisms of transfer are much less clear. The transmission of explicit knowledge, by contrast, can be mediated by market mechanisms (Breschi and Lissoni 2001a, Baumol 2002).

On purpose, this section hence tackles both, knowledge transfers and knowledge spillovers. Knowledge spillovers indeed are a form of knowledge transfer. In the models of the New Growth Theory, the main focus is on the stock of knowledge and its non-rival, non-exclusive features on the *aggregate* level (Romer 1986, Lucas 1988). In these models, the concept of spillovers refers to a non-specified mechanism of transfer and is therefore appropriate. But, being concrete, what are these spillovers exactly? Veugelers (1998) and Lambooy (2010) considered spillovers as intended and non-intended knowledge transfers ('leakages'). Fallah and Ibrahim (2004), by contrast, distinguished between transfers of tacit knowledge and spillovers. While transfers imply that knowledge is transmitted intentionally, spillovers happen beyond the intended boundary. However, they also argued that as soon as knowledge is exchanged, it can be used in any other context. Hence knowledge sharing could result in spillovers and other knowledge externalities. Thereby, Fallah and Ibrahim (2004) also very strongly connected transfers and spillovers. Lambooy (2010) argued that the concept of knowledge transfers is better than the one of spillovers, since the latter is too general and too difficult to measure (see also Krugman 1991b). The former, by contrast, makes its possible to capture and investigate both, intended transfers and unintended spillovers – both as externalities.[9] To operationalize spillovers and make them tangible, the approach of knowledge transfers in a broad sense is employed in this thesis as well in order to capture knowledge spillovers in particular. Since the transfer of tacit in contrast to explicit knowledge can be assumed to be different with respect to the relevant mechanisms, the next section only focuses on the form of knowledge that is most relevant in the context of innovation and spillovers; hence on the tacit form as highlighted in Figure 2.1.

[9] Pure unintentional spillovers, Lambooy (2010) argued, should rather be reserved for the investigation at the aggregate level where only the output of knowledge investments is interesting.

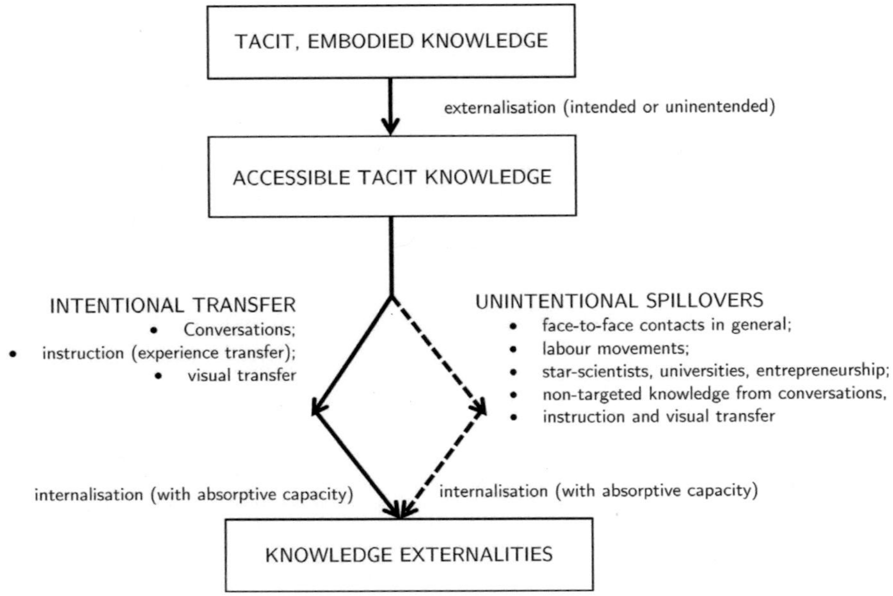

Figure 2.1: Diffusion of tacit knowledge and knowledge externalities.
Source: own illustration.

2.2.1 Preconditions

First of all, tacit – embodied – knowledge is tied to persons. This is why relational structures and contexts should be stressed (Bathelt and Glückler 2005). In this vein, a common knowledge and competence base, i.e. a *cognitive proximity*, is often seen as a prerequisite for bringing people together and enable them to learn interactively. Put another way, an *absorptive capacity* as complementary asset is required to be able to identify, interpret and exploit new knowledge (Cohen and Levinthal 1990). The recipient of knowledge, as it is argued, has to be cognitively able to employ the available knowledge. This capability refers not only to a common knowledge and competence base, but also to the individual's willingness to incur the costs of learning on how to implement the new knowledge. Bernstein and Nadiri (1988) for example showed that own knowledge spreads and new, externally gained knowledge is received quite differently across agents working in different industries. Therefore, Singh (2008) proposed that the reception of new knowledge in form of spillovers needs informal mechanisms promoting knowledge integration as well as learning across locations.

Boschma (2005) argued that *organisational arrangements* coordinate the exchange and transfer of knowledge. Furthermore, economic relations are to some extent always embedded in social contexts that affect the economic outcome. Above all, trust enhances the exchange of tacit knowledge. *Institutional proximity* refers to a system of norms and rules that is indispensable to the unhampered flow of knowledge between agents. Only finally Boschma (2005) emphasised the role of geographic proximity, as this defines the extent to which positive knowledge externalities are effective at all.[10] Geographical and at least a certain degree of cognitive proximity are sufficient (but not necessary) for interactive learning, while all other dimensions of proximity may strengthen or substitute these.[11] I.e. a certain degree of overlap coinciding with a certain extent of complementarity of the accumulated knowledge of two agents, or, put another way, their individual knowledge bases and geographical co-location are sufficient for knowledge spillovers to occur. Too much distance, e.g. between two very different knowledge bases with a very small overlap might entirely suppress knowledge transfers by prohibiting communication and/or lowering the absorptive capacity. By contrast, too much proximity might inhibit the positive effects of knowledge transfers, as no additional and complementary knowledge can be added, hence no innovation can be produced. Thus, Boschma and Iammarino (2009) proposed that it is neither regional diversity nor regional specialisation (both referring to the optimal distance between knowledge (bases)), but *related variety* that is most conducive to effective knowledge transfers and spillovers for innovation. It triggers innovation by nourishing absorptive capacities through the low level of distance between platform sub-fields.[12]

Malmberg and Maskell (2006), by contrast, assumed interactive learning processes, and hence the creation of the capabilities necessary to process the new knowledge, to occur along the dimensions of learning by interaction and by monitoring. This is often unintentional rather than mediated by market mechanisms, encompassing frequent face-to-face interactions, local institutional and organisational embeddedness and a (social) system of norms and rules creating a *local buzz* (Storper and Venables 2005). Yet, in the context of increased competition as a result of globalisation, global pipelines must not be underestimated. Searching for global knowledge is much more planned and conscious (Bathelt et al. 2002). Long-distance collaboration is therefore certainly a part of new knowledge creation, although it can be assumed that this global knowledge connects to the core competencies of the searcher, hence offering less opportunities to benefit (unintendedly) from a very different but somehow complementary knowledge. Often, this long-distance collaborations even reflect prior co-location and hence mirror (past) geographical patterns (Bercovitz and Feldman 2011).

[10] A feature inherent in all kinds of proximity is the reduction of uncertainty and the solving of coordination problems (Boschma 2005).
[11] See Boschma (2005) for further details on proximity, as well as Feldman and Kogler (2010).
[12] Cooke (2009) directly related this to 'general purpose innovations'.

However, given the absorptive capacities, related varieties or local buzzes, knowledge transfers and spillovers can happen through different channels. The extent to which knowledge can effectively be transferred depends on the features of the knowledge good (Cincera 2003). However, the notion of the local buzz (Bathelt et al. 2002, Storper and Venables 2005) emphasises that knowledge externalities can become effective without any concrete interaction. But still, most frequently face-to-face contact is argued to be a critical medium for the efficient transmission of knowledge, which points to both, geographical and cognitive proximity (Storper and Venables 2005).

2.2.2 Actual Transfers and Spillovers

Marshall (1890) already underlined the relevance of direct and unplanned contact between economic agents. Lucas (1988) also pointed out that knowledge accumulation, being a social activity, works through face-to-face interaction. By face-to-face contacts, diversity and cosmopolitanism exhibit their positive effects (Storper and Venables 2005). Following von Hippel (1994), 'sticky', i.e. highly contextual, uncertain knowledge is best transmitted by frequent face-to-face contacts. One might even go one step further and contend that face-to-face contacts are indeed necessary to exchange tacit knowledge (Lawson and Lorenz 1999). After all, tacit and embodied knowledge is bound to the individual and transfers of such knowledge compellingly require the involvement of the individual. This must not, but in the most cases does, refer to direct interpersonal contacts in form of face-to-face interaction. Lucas (1988) modelled knowledge accumulation as such a social activity: Highly educated individuals interact face-to-face and hence increase both, their own and each other's knowledge. This process of interpersonal knowledge exchange can then be subdivided into intentional and unintentional transfers (e.g. of unprotected, unvalued knowledge or knowledge that is non-excludable in personal interactions), the latter ones referring to spillovers in the classical sense (see Figure 2.1 for a visualisation). In any case, face-to-face contacts build up a platform of communication, trust and exchange. No matter if inter- or intra-industry knowledge transfers, both happen via face-to-face communication. As Nelson and Winter (1982) and Feldman and Audretsch (1999, p. 412) similarly pointed out, a basis for interaction, such as the proximity of the new knowledge to the individual's prior knowledge base facilitates the exchange of old and the generation of new ideas via face-to-face contacts. But even if the individuals interacting have completely different backgrounds, face-to-face contacts can help to develop a common language that makes coordination between different key concepts possible and opens opportunities for inter-industrial spillovers without a common knowledge base (Desrochers 2001). This need for face-to-face contacts indicates why human capital accumulation works better in dense cities than in rural areas and that a given amount of human capital in turn yields more benefits stemming from knowledge externalities (Marlet and van Woerkens 2004). Dahl and Pedersen (2004) examined the role of face-to-face contact driven informal networks for the development of regional agglomeration and found that such networks are the main drivers of knowledge transfers between agents. The value of these contacts partly even converges to more formal trading of information (von Hippel 1987). The concept of 'good' face-to-face contacts is closely related to that of 'know-who', which involves information about 'who knows what' and 'who knows to do what'. This particularly includes the social capability to establish relationships to specialised groups with the experience one can best profit from (Lundvall 1996). With the best knowledge transfers one can get, absorptive capacity is highest which in turn accelerates the diffusion of knowledge.

2.2.3 The Realisation of Face-to-Face Interaction

A typical mechanism for realising such face-to-face contacts is interfirm movement of highly skilled labour (Breschi and Malerba 2001, Breschi and Lissoni 2001a,b). Knowledgeable workers who move between firms enhance the absorptive capacity and the ability of firms to recombine knowledge to new ideas, to make use of good ideas spilling over and to improve the productivity of their innovativeness (Storper and Venables 2005). The circulation of workers brings their previous know-how into a new context. Thereby, different combinations of knowledge might bring up new ideas. Another important aspect in this context is the employment of university graduates, constituting a mechanism for knowledge transfer from university to industry (Dasgupta and David 1994). Moreover, Zucker et al. (1998) argued that 'star-scientists' embody highly relevant and large amounts of knowledge. These scientists tend to enter in contractual arrangements with existing firms or start up their own firm in order to extract the supra-normal returns from their human capital. Localised intellectual capital which is embodied in such star-scientists is hence a key to the development of new technological start-up firms (see also Audretsch and Feldman 2004). The skills and knowledge of these scientists are, in addition, another mechanism by which knowledge spills over from universities to firms applying the universities' research results (Knudsen et al. 2007). Star scientists thereby shape the importance of spatial proximity, as they are more likely to be located in the same region the firm is located in when the transfer of new (economic) knowledge is involved. More generally, research laboratories of universities provide one source of knowledge that is accessible to private firms and can be exploited commercially. Hence knowledge created in universities induces spillovers and thereby contributes to the generation of innovations by industrial firms (Feldman and

Desrochers 2003). Researchers in private enterprises that have had an idea for an innovation would, if it is not valued enough in their company, leave the firm and build-up their own firm. Since the knowledge was generated in their old firms the new start-up is a spin-off from the existing firm. Such start-ups normally do not have a large R&D laboratory, but they are able to benefit from exploiting the knowledge and experience they gained in their previous firms (Audretsch and Feldman 2004).[13]

Summarising, the literature assessing the transmission and diffusion of tacit knowledge emphasises the importance of face-to-face interactions (Cowan and Jonard 2004). There might exist other channels of diffusion of knowledge in innovation contexts, but the personal one seems, by definition, the crucial one for the exchange of embodied knowledge. The role of collaboration and particularly the role of corresponding networks are therefore explored further in the next section.

2.3 Collaboration in Networks and Innovation

As argued above, the diffusion of knowledge happens mostly interpersonally. Particularly in these cases, geographical and cognitive proximity are accepted to improve the efficiency of knowledge transmission since more geographically and cognitively proximate individuals more easily establish interpersonal contacts. Consequently, knowledge is not equally accessible and not equally diffused across innovators, regions or (technological) innovation systems. In this context it is an important observation that the knowledge production in science and technology over the last decades was characterised by an increasingly collaborative nature (Meyer and Bhattacharya 2004, Wagner and Leydesdorff 2005). This indicates that researchers need to collaborate in order to continue contributing to state of the art knowledge production (Autant-Bernard et al. 2007, Hoekman et al. 2009). Since collaboration in innovations is a process involving both tacit and codified knowledge exchanges (Gao et al. 2011), this also points to the increasing role of face-to-face interactions for innovation efficiency. Face-to-face interactions within the boundaries of a region or a technology can be considered as networks of collaboration: If tacit knowledge is diffused by means of face-to-face contacts, the investigation of this diffusion must take explicit account of the structure of connections between agents (Cowan and Foray 1997), since these networks constitute an important mode for knowledge transmission. Evidence from empirical research indicates that most industries have well-established informal networks through which knowledge is exchanged and traded (von Hippel 1987, Schrader 1991, Hicks 1995, Cowan

[13] See Feldman (1999) and Breschi and Lissoni (2001a) for more complete overviews of spillover mechanisms.

and Jonard 2004). The analysis of such networks plays a crucial role to understand the dimension of the relationships between social entities in fostering the exchange of knowledge for innovation.

The increasing complexity of technologies and the accordingly shifting research frontiers highlight the role of very specialised researchers with an in-depth knowledge on the field. On the other hand, the convergence of classical disciplines in many novel high technologies considerably challenges the knowledge bases of individual researchers or even research teams within an organisation: In these branches, only a few innovators, i.e. single actors, are capable of innovating on their own since this means that they have to have access to a huge amount of specialised and at the same time heterogeneous and diversified knowledge. It is hence not only the sheer amount and specialised depth of knowledge that is essential to innovations, but also the complementarity and novelty of knowledge. This is needed in order to be able to exploit and recombine existing knowledge and develop new ideas out of it. The need for targeted and in-depth, but yet to a certain extent diverse knowledge results in a significant trend towards multi- and interdisciplinary research, triggering collaboration between researchers (Calero et al. 2006). Particularly in novel and complex fields, research tends to become a collective effort encompassing diverse actors, competencies and capabilities. Allen (1983) introduced the concept of 'collective invention' pointing to the phenomenon of exchange and availability of (tacit) knowledge within social networks of – even competing – agents that results in faster diffusion and accumulation of knowledge conducive to the innovation processes. Agents hence enter networks and collaborative alliances with other agents to gain advantages they lack when operating independently. Innovation-seeking agents need sources of expertise and knowledge that lie beyond their scope. The organisational institutions that connect individual researchers and their research institutions are therefore discussed to play a crucial role (Laredo 2003). Still, local teams constitute the basis for successful research, but emphasis is also put on the broad cooperative elements that actually reflect reality in the scientific processes nowadays. Therefore, not only the direct knowledge dimension focusing on *which* knowledge has to be developed, but also indirect dimensions of knowledge pointing to organisational aspects of *how* knowledge diffuses in such networks have to be considered.

When different individuals jointly work on R&D projects in order to develop innovations, knowledge transfers are obviously occurring. In these cases, spillovers are considered to be at least partly voluntary. Thus, partners in R&D collaboration networks can improve on the knowledge transfer among them (Veugelers 1998). Thereby, knowledge is exchanged directly as well as as a side-product and hence in form of spillovers.

Through such networks of collaboration, R&D partners can gain access to implicit as well as only partly accessible explicit knowledge (Schmoch 2003). In any case, collaboration of this kind enhances not only the exchange of tacit know-how, but also mutual learning, cross-fertilisation, unintended spillovers and thereby finally exponentiates the value of each individual's knowledge.

For such collaborations to be established, it is crucial that agents expect the relationship to be reciprocal regarding the quality and quantity of knowledge that would be exchanged; otherwise agents would refuse to be a source of knowledge spillovers. The more spillovers there are to be expected, the higher the levels of cooperative R&D (Veugelers 1998). Collaboration, hence, can be seen as an integral foundation for trust, which allows sharing tacit knowledge and thus encourages the diffusion of knowledge and thereby fosters innovation (Almeida and Kogut 1999, Singh 2005). Moreover, knowledge assets are not only incorporated in people, but are also often embedded within relationships between people or organisations. As Ranft and Lord (2000) pointed out, a significant share of knowledge might be located in formal and informal networks of relationships within and across organisations (see also Nelson and Winter 1982). Döring and Schnellenbach (2006) interpreted this as emphasis on the importance of social networks for the fast diffusion of knowledge. This is confirmed by a number of studies on the role of networks in innovating regions, among them the prominent example of Saxenian (1996), who found that networks are important for innovating actors in Silicon Valley and the Boston Area and very recently Meyer et al. (2011) and Schiffauerova and Beaudry (2012) who showed the same for nanotechnology in the UK and Canada.[14] Schrader (1991) empirically showed that the frequency of R&D collaboration has a positive impact on innovativeness. In the industrial organisation literature it is moreover argued that, in the absence of cooperation, knowledge spillovers are considered unintended. Eventually this results in lower R&D investment levels. Cooperation, instead, enables agents to internalise such spillovers and increase efficiency (Kamien et al. 1992, de Bondt 1996, Amir et al. 2003).[15] It has hence become widely accepted that cooperation between (regional) actors an important channel for knowledge transfer and spillover (Fritsch and Franke 2004) and that agents who are integrated in a network of inter-agent relations exhibit a better innovative performance (Gilsing

[14]Cowan and Jonard (2003) introduced some documented historical examples for collective inventions and innovative networks already in the early 1800s and showed that, contrary to Allens conjecture of the decrease of the importance of collective invention with the rise of the industrial R&D lab (Allen 1983), rapid and free distribution of knowledge is an important input to innovations today . The most important proof for the crucial role of collective invention they contended the internet and emerging developer communities in projects such as LINUX.

[15]The role of R&D cooperation has been more extensively treated in the competition policy literature, among others Katz (1986), Katz and Ordover (1990), Jorde and Teece (1990) and Vonortas (1994).

et al. 2008). Consequently, innovation-related collaboration is also discussed by policy makers who increasingly implement network promotion policies. They thereby follow scholars stating that suboptimally low R&D investment might not only be due to appropriability problems, but also due to a lack of coordination of actors (Bresnahan and Trajtenberg 1995, de Jong and Freel 2010). By contrast, the focus on the role of proximity has also been questioned in the literature. Empirical work that points to a higher incidence of extra-local linkages over local linkages in the innovation context suggests that it is not only spatially proximately originating, external knowledge that supports innovative activity, but also knowledge stemming from other geographical scales such as international cooperations (de Jong and Freel 2010).

In the contexts of the range of knowledge diffusion in networks, Callon (1997) put forward the difference between different states of networks. *Emergent configurations* of networks rather consist of research laboratories, where huge investments are necessary in order to make knowledge accessible and applicable. Moreover, embodied knowledge is in this stage not substitutable through codified knowledge. Tacit knowledge hence dominates (see Chapter 1): Mechanisms to externalise the newly created tacit knowledge do not yet exist. This limits the range of the knowledge and the necessity of sharing tacit knowledge for innovation and for the applicability of the newly created knowledge as a source for future innovations (Nonaka et al. 2003) points to the role of face-to-face interactions as transmission mechanism. With the expansion of the emergent network towards a *stable configuration*, the specific knowledge in the networks becomes more and more general. The public good character of the knowledge in the network develops and it becomes non-exclusive in the networks it circulates in. Codified knowledge dominates in stable networks, actors are mostly private firms. Emergent networks hence do not produce any conflict between appropriation and knowledge sharing since the use and replication of the knowledge requires a costly infrastructure. Networking is perceived as 'strategy of interessment' (Callon 1997, p. 17) in order to rouse interest and acceptance for research results. Stable configurations, by contrast, are characterised by a homogeneous set of actors with the same knowledge bases and the same expectation. Networking persists because costs and risks are seeked to be shared and own positions shall be stabilised. However, both configurations are not expected to be found in their pure forms, as intermediate configurations are the most common ones (Callon 1997). Rather, a given configuration has to be regarded as a snap shot of the same dynamics which points to the progressive development of a network (Schmoch 2003). This approach can be put forward to account for the development of networks, particularly between science and industry and particularly if the emergent phase is long enough in order to establish relations (Schmoch 2003).

To sum up, collaborations and the corresponding networks are assumed to play a more and more important role in innovation activity. Particularly the increasing complexity of emerging, science-based technologies reveals a necessity for joint research and collaboration on the field (Haagedorn 1993). Thereby, different, but potentially complementary knowledge can be exchanged resulting in the (faster) generation of new knowledge induced by mutual learning. Subsequently, networking potentially fosters the diffusion and the exchange of knowledge and thereby drives innovative activity. The motivation to form network relations, however, depends on the actors' need for access to knowledge and thereby on the state of the network itself.

2.3.1 Geographic and Cognitive Systems of Innovation: Which Network to Consider

There is a large body of literature dealing with *national* or *regional innovation systems* (Lundvall 1992, Cooke 1992). Within such a geographic system of innovation it is a central assumption that actors do not innovate on their own but in collaboration and cooperation with other agents. The concepts hence rely on the mechanisms of learning and the exchange of knowledge (Lundvall 1996). These approaches refer to the border of a geographic region as border of the innovation system (i.e. national or regional borders), within which the respective policies (such as property rights and funding, e.g.) influence innovative activity. More particularly, the requirement of direct interaction for the transmission of tacit knowledge points to the relevance of spatially bound innovation networks: Geographical proximity reduces the cost of establishing and maintaining face-to-face interactions. Innovative networks most presumably hence do not stretch across national or regional boundaries and are often relatively stable once they have been established (Wilkinson and Moore 2000). Actors in these innovation systems are public and private, large and small. The important point about innovation systems is how these actors are interrelated, how they are formally and informally connected to each other and how knowledge is processed in this system of innovation in order to eventually produce innovation (Meyer et al. 2011).

Cognitive systems of innovation, by contrast are not defined by national but sectoral or technological borders. The distinctive element is constituted by the idea that innovation patterns differ drastically across the technologies they rely on. Such a cognitive system consists of a distinctive knowledge base, a defined set of inputs, certain key technologies, and a corresponding demand for its innovations (Malerba 2002). As a particular subgroup, technological systems concentrate on general purpose technologies with their widespread applications across different industries (Bresnahan and Trajtenberg

1995, Meyer et al. 2011). However, it is mainly the borders, i.e. the perspective of investigation that distinguishes this approach from the geographical ones. The core of a technological system of innovation is still how the actors jointly advance the technology. For instance, this approach has been used in the past in order to study the development of specific technologies. As Meyer et al. (2011) pointed out, similar analyses could be particularly interesting for policy-makers that aim at designing instruments to support emerging technologies.

Both approaches are not capable of explaining technological change alone; more particularly it is very difficult to disentangle between the systems: Innovation is not taking place in one region only – irrespective of the scale taken there is most presumably always an 'outside' that is important. On the other hand, innovation cannot be seen isolated from regional conditions only in the context of their technological underpinning (Oinas and Malecki 2002). Hence to completely display how innovation is processed in networks one has to consider both, the technological and the regional dimension.

2.3.2 Knowledge Diffusion for Innovation in Networks

Both streams of research, however, emphasise the role of cooperation and collaboration of actors to gain access to external knowledge. And indeed, cognitive proximity combined with geographic proximity is found to culminate in more effective knowledge transfer (Sorenson and Stuart 2001, Owen-Smith and Powell 2004). It was only recently that attention in the economic literature was drawn to the properties of networks processing the knowledge needed for innovations and the corresponding impact on knowledge diffusion and rate of innovation (Cowan and Jonard 2003, Cowan et al. 2004, Cowan and Jonard 2004, Cowan et al. 2005, Schiffauerova and Beaudry 2009, Chen and Guan 2010, Schiffauerova and Beaudry 2012). Notwithstanding the kind of possible organisational arrangements that constitute collaborations for innovation, physical interaction finally takes place between people, i.e. between inventors. Interpersonal networks of inventors, constructed on the basis of face-to-face interaction are hence systems of channels for the flow of knowledge (Zucker et al. 1998). Sorenson (2004) found evidence for an increase in importance of networks between agents the more complex the knowledge base the inventors rely on. Moreover, this complexity also affects the distance this knowledge can travel. Studies elaborated on the role of the embeddedness of agents in order to find out how and which kind of collaboration drives innovative performance. Moreover, studies at the network level have also been conducted, pointing to the properties of the alliances as affecting innovation: Direct as well as indirect ties and their redundancy (i.e. the frequency of the collaboration with the same partners) are relevant for the innovative performance of an agent (Ahuja 2000, Baum et al. 2000, de Jong and Freel 2010). The diffusion potential, i.e. the principle of alliances being inter-agent channels for knowledge transfers is seen as the main cause for this.

Knowledge for Exploitation

When knowledge, ideas and inventions are predominantly exploited, actors collaborate because they can gain access to complementary know-how (Teece 1986) and/or speed up the innovation process when they understand and elaborate on the same issues and hence use a similar underlying knowledge base. This concept is strongly related to the principle of absorptive capacity (Cohen and Levinthal 1990). Empirical studies have indeed shown that the knowledge transferred and implemented becomes less with decreasing similarity of the different actors' knowledge bases when the innovative goal is an exploitative one (Mowery et al. 1998, Fleming and Sorenson 2001).

Knowledge for Exploration

Exploration, by contrast, is a more radical part of the process of innovation since it refers to the abandoning of old and the development of new ideas. Therefore, exploration is a much more uncertain exercise with unforeseen outcomes. It is hence reasonable to argue that is not the main function of transferring similar complementary knowledge that makes networks relevant in this context. Contrariwise, networks are relevant in their function as transfer mechanism of new knowledge, which is indispensable for the creation of novelties. Here, it is not the similarity but the complementarity of knowledge bases that constitutes an incentive to cooperate (Gilsing et al. 2008).

Putting these arguments together, innovating agents face a dual task: In order to be able to develop new ideas, they have a strong need of heterogeneous and diversified knowledge as potential sources of novelty. Obviously, this diversified knowledge requires disintegrated network structures, i.e. continuous opportunity to get in touch with new actors with diverging and novel knowledge bases. However, once valuable novel knowledge is accessed it has to be processed and absorbed in order to create value within the organisation. Therefore, the embeddedness in a dense and more homogeneous, redundant network providing access to complementary knowledge can be seen as beneficial (Hansen 1999, Cowan and Jonard 2003, Cowan et al. 2004, Gilsing et al. 2008).

2.3.3 Network Structure Properties

The advantages of agglomeration economies and geographical proximity have been addressed in a prolific literature. Many different forms of knowledge transfers in close proximity generate territorial externalities, or, put differently, localised knowledge spillovers, such as informal knowledge flows, interactive learning, face-to-face contacts and network intensity (Storper and Venables 2005, D'Este et al. 2011). Recently, Social Network Analysis (SNA) has proved to be a suitable tool for the analysis of innovation networks. SNA is an interdisciplinary methodology, mainly developed by sociologists and mathematicians. Due to the formal techniques employed to measure relationships among interacting units, this approach has become interesting for many other disciplines as well (Wassermann and Faust 2009). In economics and geography, the literature around regional and national innovation systems claims the possibility of fundamental contributions to the field, disentangling the interaction of local institutions and agents in the innovation process more systematically. Thereby, information on how these agents are connected, and at which spatial levels, is analysed (Ter Wal and Boschma 2009). Network analysis, however, is not confined to social contacts in their basic sense: Any proximity that relates two social entities with each other can be used to build a network. However, the networks that are analysed by means of SNA typically consist of agents and relational ties between these agents, possibly constituting different clusters again: Direct relationships between two agents are modelled with a relational tie. These may also exist between groups of agents sharing the same characteristics, e.g.. Within SNA the terminology from graph theory is adopted, and hence agents constitute the *nodes* or *vertices* of a network, while the linkages between the actors are employed as *lines* or *relations* connecting the vertices, more particularly as *arcs* (directed) or *edges* (undirected), which altogether constitute a *graph*. The kind of linkage is dependent on the underlying data; a link might display pure knowledge, friendship or collaboration. A network consists of a graph and additional information on the vertices or the lines of the graph (de Nooy et al. 2008).

Given the assumption that a network improves its members' accessibility of knowledge, the impact of the network structures on the flow of knowledge is assessed several times throughout this thesis. Therefore, as already mentioned, the approaches of SNA and the corresponding assessment of network structure properties are useful.

The most basic measures of SNA are shortly introduced here and put into context in order to provide the overview of the basic network structure properties necessary for the grasp of the discussed concepts. These would structurally be subsumed under 'methodology' and should consequently be tackled in Chapter 5. However, they are essential for the discussion of the literature on efficient knowledge diffusion in networks, which is why they are advanced in the course of this chapter.

Ego-centred Indicators

A network, of course, is characterised by the number of *vertices* n, each of which can have $n-1$ *relations* to the other vertices in the network (resulting in $\frac{n(n-1)}{2}$ possible connections in the whole network). The actual number of lines a *vertex* v_i is incident with is the *degree* $d(v_i)$ of the vertex. This measure is not comparable since it does not relate to the size of a network. Therefore, *degree centrality*, the normalised degree, can be employed:

Degree centrality

$$C_D(v_i) = \frac{d(v_i)}{n-1}, \quad C_D(v_i) \in [0,1]. \tag{2.1}$$

A higher degree centrality displays the relative number of connections a vertex has. However, this measure has to be treated with care: Degree centrality does not (necessarily) identify the most important vertex in the network – the importance of a vertex for the knowledge flow in a network is also determined by the quality of the connections, for instance a vertex might be the single connection between important *components* of the networks and hence all knowledge flows via this vertex. A component is a subnetwork with the maximum number of vertices that are all directly or indirectly connected by links (Wassermann and Faust 2009). Assuming that the connections in the networks, or, put differently, the social relations are the channels that transmit information and knowledge between people, central vertices are those who either have good access to the knowledge flowing in the network or who are able to control the flow of knowledge (de Nooy et al. 2008).

In order to measure the importance of a single vertex, the *betweenness centrality* indicator is employed. In this sense, a vertex is more central if it is more often located on the knowledge chains between other vertices. Knowledge chains are modelled as geodesics, i.e. the shortest path between two vertices; the number of geodesics between vertex j and k is g_{jk}. The betweenness centrality $C_B(v_i)$ is then the proportion of geodesics between pairs of other vertices that include the vertex, $g_{jk}(v_i)$:

Betweenness Centrality

$$C_B(v_i) = \sum_{i=1}^{N} \frac{g_{jk}(v_i)}{g_{jk}}, \quad C_B(v_i) \in [0,1], \tag{2.2}$$

Thereby, it is assumed that each of the geodesics is equally likely to be chosen for the flow of knowledge. High betweenness centrality indicates that a vertex acts as important intermediary in the network of knowledge flows. Therefore, not only its access to knowledge is better, but also its control over knowledge or, put differently, the vertex is important for bringing together knowledge from different loci in the network.

Socio-centred Indicators

The so far introduced indicators are all *ego-centred,* i.e. they focus on the role of an individual vertex. They also exist on the level of a network and hence as *socio-centred* indicators. The basic measure corresponding to the pure degree is captured in the indicator of the *density* of a network, which measures the *structural cohesion* within a network. Density is the number of *lines* l in a simple network, expressed as a proportion of the maximum possible number of lines:

Density

$$D = \frac{2l}{n(n-1)}, \quad D \in (0;1). \tag{2.3}$$

Most intuitively, a tighter network contains more connections resulting in a more cohesive structure of the network and a value closer to the maximum value of density which is 1 (with the lower limit of 0).

For the rest of the indicators, the idea behind the network level measures is always relying on *centralisation*. Network centralisation is higher if it contains very central and very peripheral vertices at the same time. This can be computed by comparing all centrality scores in a network: More variation in the scores (i.e. a larger difference between the maximum score and the individual scores of each vertex) corresponds to a higher centrality (de Nooy et al. 2008). All indicators hence yield values between 0 and 1, where a centralisation index close to zero displays a network where all vertices are equally central and an index value close to one identifies a strong centre-periphery structure. The calculation of indicators is taken from Wassermann and Faust (2009).[16]

[16]Proofs for the simplification of the formulas were conducted by Freeman (1979).

Referring to degree centrality, *degree centralisation* can hence be computed the following way (with $v*$ as the respective maximum value):

Degree Centralisation

$$C_D = \frac{\sum_{i=1}^{n}(C_D(v*) - C_D(v_i))}{max\sum_{i=1}^{n}(C_D(v*) - C_D(v_i))} = \frac{\sum_{i=1}^{n}(C_D(v*) - C_D(v_i))}{(n-1)(n-2)}, \quad C_D \in [0,1]. \tag{2.4}$$

Referring to betweenness centrality, *betweenness centralisation* can similarly be constructed, relying on betweenness centrality:
Betweenness Centralisation

$$C_B = \frac{\sum_{i=1}^{n}(C_B(v*) - C_B(v_i))}{max\sum_{i=1}^{n}(C_B(v*) - C_B(v_i))} = \frac{2\sum_{i=1}^{n}(C_D(v*) - C_D(v_i))}{(n-1)^2(n-2)}, \quad C_B \in [0,1]. \tag{2.5}$$

2.3.4 Network Structure and Knowledge Diffusion

This subsection now turns from the focus on the relevance of collaboration and networks to concrete network structures that support the diffusion of knowledge. Therefore, the *efficiency* of a network structure in these respects is evaluated. A network is, in these respects, regarded as more efficient if knowledge diffuses more easily thereby increasing the productivity of innovations. Put differently, networks structures are evaluated in terms of their creation of *social capital*. Social capital can be described as a set of different entities that consists of social structures and that facilitate certain action of actors (Coleman 1988). Cowan et al. (2004) showed that the existence of such efficient network structures impacts the growth of knowledge positively in the long run by influencing the diffusion of knowledge and thereby an agents' innovative potential. This was also confirmed by Fleming et al. (2007), who argue that an inventor's past collaborations increase subsequent innovative productivity.

Structural Cohesion

Schiffauerova and Beaudry (2012) argue that efficient knowledge transmission takes place in cohesive networks. *Structural cohesion* refers to the connectedness of innovators. The closer innovators are connected, the better the knowledge transfer should work and the more positive should the impact on innovative activity be. The larger the network, the more possible connections there are and the more probable is actual collaboration. One would hence expect an increase in density causing an increase in the productivity of the system. However, as Morrison et al. (2011) put it, a successful networks need always external linkages in order to ensure the inflow of new, complementary knowledge into the network, thereby avoiding lock-in effects.

Fragmentation

More efficient networks in terms of knowledge diffusion mechanisms, moreover, should experience a lower level of fragmentation compared to less efficient networks. The largest component's size, for instance, goes beyond pure density by taking into account the direct and the indirect contacts an innovator has in the network. It implies that innovators can access knowledge not only through direct interaction but that they can also benefit from knowledge that is available and transmitted from one innovator to another through intermediaries who act as a 'broker' of knowledge (Burt 1992, Walker et al. 1997, Martin 2011, Schiffauerova and Beaudry 2012). Being embedded in a component hence provides innovators not only with access to knowledge of directly connected partners, but also to knowledge they are (via the connections of their partners) indirectly connected to (Gulati and Gargiulo 1999). Consistently, Fleming et al. (2007) found that larger components are correlated positively with the number of innovations. They pointed to the necessity of the aggregation of components, i.e. the process of integrating previously unconnected components or *isolates* (i.e. vertices that are not connected at all), for improved innovativeness. Aggregation supports the flow of new knowledge within the network and smaller components as well as isolates will gain access to the knowledge produced in other components (Fleming et al. 2006). Network aggregation also promotes cross-fertilisation between so far isolated groups in different fields (Hargadon 2003, Burt 2004). A larger (relative) size of the largest component hence should provide a better environment for innovations. Last, lower levels of fragmentation can be seen as bridging geographical distance.

Centrality and Centre-Periphery-Structure

Agents with central positions in broad networks tend to benefit better from the network advantages than more peripherally located agents. The centrality at the convergence of multiple, tightly bounded channels within the network is more likely to enable access to the knowledge flowing within the network. The more central an agent is positioned, the more he becomes a passage point for the knowledge spilling around (Owen-Smith and Powell 2003). Moreover, even first mover advantages can be gained by agents when they get the relevant knowledge early. There are hence incentives to not only join networks with a high and relevant knowledge potential but also to collaborate actively in order to gain central positions.

Furthermore, the network position also determines the extent of possible non-redundant collaborations, which are seen as potentially generating novel ideas. Central agents are faster and better informed of what is going on within the network and hence their opportunities to initiate new, non-redundant collaborations are better than those of more peripheral agents (Gilsing et al. 2008). This is true for firms as well as for public research institutes and universities, who can, given a strong and central position, improve their reputation and stimulate the research activity within their network by letting their knowledge diffuse within the network. This kind of technology transfer can indeed be socially significant (Bergmann and Maier 2009). A dense network structure with central agents as 'connecting interfaces' hence could improve the region's innovativeness and counteract the common market failures in the innovation process.

Concerning the network structure as a whole, the efficiency in knowledge transmission and diffusion is supported by a centralised structure that induces fast knowledge transmission (Schiffauerova and Beaudry 2012). Both in regions and in sectors, innovation networks shaped such that there exists a core as well as a periphery are found to be more productive in terms of innovations (Graf and Henning 2009, Ter Wal and Boschma 2009). Innovators with leading-edge or relatively interdisciplinary knowledge are usually positioned in the core, while innovators that are rather specialised and/or produce incremental innovations are rather to be found in the periphery. Centralised networks, in contrast to decentralised networks, are less homogeneous which enriches new knowledge creation due to the possibilities of selection and synthesis of knowledge from different clusters or parts of the network (Scheidegger 2008). Centre-periphery-structured networks are hence less redundant in knowledge provision than decentralised networks. This implies that access to the same amount and diversity of knowledge in such a network is less time consuming and therefore more efficient. A centralised structure supports hence fast transmission of knowledge and should therefore induce higher innovation levels (Schiffauerova and Beaudry 2012). However, it has to be kept in mind that strongly centralised networks, as they are coined by a few very centralised individuals, bear the risk of becoming disrupted once knowledge diffusion through central actors is disturbed.

Small Worlds

A more integrated approach to assess efficient network structures is the concept of a 'small world'. It is a common observation that people seem to have relations to comparably similar subsets of other close people, although the overall population on earth is very large: Meeting a complete stranger happens as often as finding out that one has at least one friend in common, which often results in the finding that the 'world is small'. Milgram (1967) was the first to tackle this phenomenon empirically and Granovetter

(1973) developed a rationale for these short paths within a given social network: The people I am friends with are likely to be friends with each other which results in a dense network of friends. Although many of the connections are redundant, there are also some few people that connect different groups of friends that are not connected to each other. The connecting vertices (or 'weak ties') are important vertices in the network since they open opportunities of knowledge flows between different groups. This is the background for the small world graph introduced by Watts and Strogatz (1998) and Watts (1999). Figure 2.2 depicts the particularity of small world networks: These networks are coined by short distances between agents (i.e. so called *short path lengths*) and high degrees of *clustering* (Cowan and Jonard 2004, Morone and Taylor 2004).[17] Clustering, also known as *cliquishness*, refers to the likelihood that two vertices that are both connected to a particular third vertex are also connected to one another. While the spectrum exists from regular to random connections, small world networks are in between. In regular networks, the path length (which is the mean geodesic, i.e. the mean of all lowest numbers of intermediary vertices needed to reach any other vertex) increases with the number of vertices and the level of clustering is high. The other extremum, a random network, exhibits a low degree of clustering since path length only increases logarithmically with the number of vertices and hence path lengths are way shorter. In this network, inventors would be as likely connected to remote inventors as to proximate ones. In small world networks, short paths lengths are possible due to the introduction of cross-connections that provide short-cuts to distant vertices, which keeps the degree of clustering high but makes isolates possible as well. This property is found in many different networks, such as social networks but also networks in biology and physics. Most importantly, small world networks accelerate knowledge diffusion due to a high transmission capacity resulting from high degrees of clustering (Burt 2001). Such structures thereby support knowledge creation in innovation processes: Clustering increases the absorptive capacity of a network and facilitates quick flows of knowledge, supports the creation of trust and opens opportunities for collaboration between inventors (Schilling and Phelps 2007). This clustering by contrast, is also found to have negative effects on innovative productivity, since the knowledge exchanged often is redundant (Cowan and Jonard 2004, Fleming et al. 2006). Since new knowledge is crucial to innovation success, indirect relations and 'weak ties' between different subgroups of inventors are substantial and a comparably low number of intermediaries (i.e. short path lengths) secures fast dissemination. Decreased path length should hence improve innovation due to easier transfers of new knowledge. High clustering and short path length in combination hence increase the creation and dissemination of knowledge, in particularly complex, tacit knowledge (Baum et al. 2003, Uzzi and Spiro 2005,

[17] See Watts and Strogatz (1998) for a more detailed discussion of this network structure.

Schilling and Phelps 2007, Breschi et al. 2009, Gao et al. 2011). It is hence sensible to assume that more innovation occurs in small worlds, allowing the coexistence of dense relationships for trust and close collaboration with more diverse ones that allow the access to new knowledge (Fleming et al. 2006).

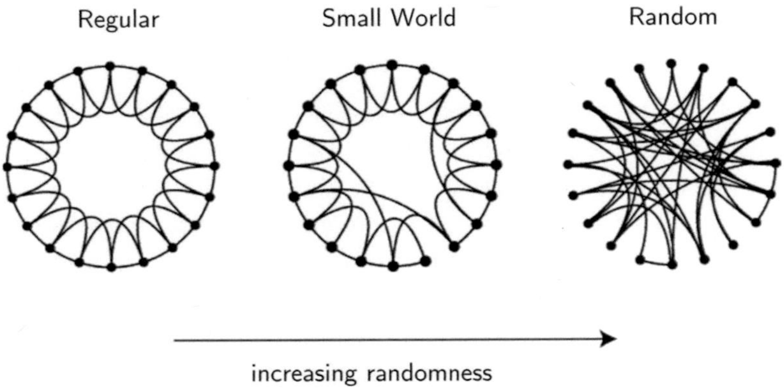

Figure 2.2: Network topologies, small world.
Source: Watts and Strogatz (1998, p. 441).

Several studies find that knowledge flows best in networks with these so called 'small world properties' (Kogut and Walker 2001, Baum et al. 2003, Cowan and Jonard 2004, Verspagen and Duysters 2004, Uzzi and Spiro 2005, Schilling and Phelps 2007, Chen and Guan 2010). Newman (2001) found that networks constructed by means of co-authorship of scientific publications often exhibit this clustered structure. By contrast Balconi et al. (2004) proposed, based on a study using co-inventorship data included in patents, that inventor-networks in industrial research are often highly fragmented. In line with Newman (2001), academic inventors are found to be more central than non-academic inventors which might suggest that academics cooperate more (Balconi et al. 2004). However, Fleming et al. (2007) found ambiguous results of small world properties of regional co-inventor-networks on innovative performance.

A key question in the context of innovativeness and hence competitiveness and eventually growth of economies is not only how the current network structure influences knowledge flows and innovative productivity but also how the configuration of a network evolves over time, and which mechanisms might be held responsible for that. This helps to assess future innovativeness and identify necessary policy measures. However, while there has been an increased interest in the dynamics of networks (Snijders 2001, Baum et al. 2003), virtually all existing empirical research on innovation networks has investigated the network properties from a static perspective, examining the network at a certain point in time (Ter Wal and Boschma 2009).

For the dynamics of knowledge networks, *preferential attachment* is argued to be a possibly relevant factor (Barabasi and Albert 1999, Ter Wal and Boschma 2009). Preferential attachment explains how central agents tend to become more central over time, while agents in the periphery stay peripheral. First empirical evidence supports this argumentation: Orsenigo et al. (1998) found that core-periphery structures of collaboration networks are fairly consistent. Studying the innovation networks in Jena, Cantner and Graf (2006) moreover found that agents on the periphery exit the region while new entrants rather locate proximate to the core. They conclude that the network develops towards an increasing focus on core competencies or core technologies. This is then supposed to lead to an increasing specialisation of the regional innovation system within these technologies. Moreover, geographical proximity is assumed to affect network evolution, while the impact of proximity for the networking decisions might be influenced by the respective relevance of tacit or explicit knowledge in the industry or technology life cycle (Cowan et al. 2004). However, these are mainly suggestions based on sparse empirical studies or theoretical argumentation only. They hence need thorough empirical validation, in which the methods of social network analysis might play a helpful role.

3 General Purpose Technologies

The idea of the rise, implementation and evolution of technologies that can be applied in many different contexts is as old as the analytical study of economics. Smith (1776, p. 11) already referred to the capability of 'philosophers' being able to combine the most distant and dissimilar objects, i.e. to apply a given technology to different sectors. Stigler (1951) referred to 'general specialities', David (1990) quoted 'general purpose engines'. Bresnahan and Trajtenberg (1995) formalised these ideas in their seminal contribution. 'General purpose technologies' (henceforth GPTs) potentially provide explanations for long-run macroeconomic growth eras. Each era can e.g. be characterised by long waves of economic development caused by a single drastic innovation and followed by many incremental innovations (Schumpeter 1912, Kondratieff and Stolper 1935). Emerging GPTs, such as the steam engine, the electric motor or computers, can possibly induce such cycles of pervasive technological progress. In sharp contrast to the assumption of technological change occurring at a constant rate throughout the economy in the Neoclassical Growth Theory, GPTs are discussed as hardly predictable – inducing major break-through innovations at any point in time (Lipsey et al. 2005). The fact that GPTs can act as engines of growth is, by contrast, a direct implication of the New Growth Theory, as there exist scale economies in invention (Bresnahan and Gambardella 1998). Moreover, GPTs might also be interesting when studying the microeconomics of technological progress at different levels of value creation chains and at different stages of the development process. However, the most important insights might be gained when combining these two perspectives, offering explanations for macroeconomic growth already on the micro-level, investigating incentives and interdependencies (Bresnahan 2010).

3.1 Characteristics of General Purpose Technologies

Bresnahan (2010), relying on Bresnahan and Trajtenberg (1995), defined a GPT by three characteristic features: A GPT is (1) widely used, exhibits (2) scope for ongoing technological improvement and (3) spurs innovation in applications sectors.[1] *Innova-*

[1]These characteristics are highlighted in a similar way also by other scholars, see e.g. Lipsey et al. (1998) or David and Wright (1999).

tional complementarities combine feature (2) and (3) and point to a *dual inducement mechanism* introduced by innovational complementarities: Innovations in the GPT sector raise the return to innovations in each application sector and thereby the incentives to innovate. These incentives then feed back vice versa. GPT models are capable of explaining sustained aggregate growth, as GPTs with an economy-wide scope exhibit increasing returns that are a necessary condition for permanent growth (Romer 1986, Bresnahan 2010).

3.2 Innovation Processes in GPTs

While breakthrough innovations frequently are a result of the invention of a GPT and of the ensuing successive technological generations, equally economically important innovations result from the complementary invention of applications. As Bresnahan (2010) emphasised, a GPT is characterised by horizontal inducement as well as innovative complementarities between upstream and downstream sectors. These complementarities are fundamental. While the GPT extends the frontier of possible innovations for the whole economy, innovation in the application sectors changes the production function of the respective sectors. The innovative activity in the application sectors exponentiates the innovations induced by the GPT and at the same time increases the size of the market for the GPT – e.g. by inducing new application fields themselves. Meanwhile, the productivity and return on investment of GPT-related innovations in the various sectors increases by mutual innovation. This process of mutual innovations can be maintained since through further development at every level of the value creation chain, the GPT may be improved continuously. When the quality of the GPT is improved, the downstream application sectors in turn benefit of a better quality of the GPT as an intermediate input. As private returns on investment in R&D are increasing with the GPT's quality, the downstream sectors have an incentive to improve their technology as well. These interdependencies arise along the entire value creation chain. Moreover, the use of the GPT becomes profitable for other sectors and thus the GPT's range of use is widened. This process of innovation works upwards the value creation chain as well, as a wider range of use or a better downstream technology provides scope for improvement and commercial opportunities as incentives to innovate in the GPT sector, thus displaying a market size effect. Profits in the GPT sector are in the same way dependent on the application sectors' technologies, leading to higher investments in R&D when a downstream technology is improved. These feedback effects describe the aforementioned innovational complementarities: Profits from innovations in the downstream sectors rise when the GPT is improved and vice versa, both as a result of an increased productivity of R&D in the respective sector (Bresnahan and Trajtenberg 1995). These dynamic feedback mechanisms hence induce at best a long-term dynamism, triggering investments in R&D throughout the economy and having large positive effects on private and social rates of return (for a formal derivation see Appendix A).

3.2.1 Social Increasing Returns and Externalities

Due to innovational complementarities, technical progress in the GPT sector hence increases the incentive for innovators in the application sectors to invest in their technological level. This, in turn increases the incentive of GPT innovators to invest in their quality. These increasing differences can overcome diminishing returns to innovation over a wide range of applications and improvements (Bresnahan 2010). Particularly, all the different, heterogeneous sectors and production processes of an economy are relevant for the GPT consideration: The innovation costs of a large, heterogeneous economy can decrease if there exists a way of exploiting the results of innovation in a particular sector in others sectors as well. For instance, the construction of airplanes and the improvement of medical endoprotheses are very heterogeneous fields at the first glance. However, this illustrates how the technological progress of nanotechnology (which will later be considered as GPT) combined with co-inventions in both of these fields can spread across a wide variety of industries. As Bresnahan (2010) put it more generally, the central assumption in considering GPTs as engines of growth is that intermediate inputs can be made less resource intensive due to continuous technological improvements as they may become useful in a wide range of sectors. Pointing to the features of knowledge as economic entity (see Section 1.1), the main point is that there are, at least at the aggregate level, no marginal cost of reusing knowledge in different contexts and hence knowledge may produce additional value at no additional cost. By using co-inventions in application sectors, diminishing returns can be avoided. Thereby, GPTs create social increasing returns at a high level. However, there are also externalities immanent in this dual inducement mechanism (see Figure 3.1.

The positive *vertical externality* arises due to the feedback loops between up- and downstream sectors' profits. Because of the innovational complementarities, their payoffs are interdependent, resulting in appropriability effects in both directions: An innovating sector, no matter if GPT or application sector, fails to appropriate the returns of its investments in innovation entirely because all other sectors of the value creation chain profit from higher productivity of innovation investments. What follows is a bilateral moral hazard problem: Neither up- nor downstream sectors have an incentive to invest in innovations in a range that would be socially optimal (Bresnahan and Trajtenberg 1995).

The positive *horizontal externality* is a product of the interdependence between the different application sectors in combination with the generic function of the GPT: With an increasing number of application sectors, the opportunities for the GPT sector to realise profits increase as well. This is also true for a higher technology level of the application sectors as a result of investment in R&D. Consequently, these are incentives for the upstream sector to innovate, the quality of the GPT will thus increase. Suppose only one application sector invests in R&D, enhancing a growth of the aggregated technology level of the application sectors and in consequence of the GPT's quality. Not only the productivity of the innovating sector, but the productivity of all non-innovating application sectors will improve, too. Thus at least a part on the return of the investment of the innovative sector is a social return. As a result, innovation activity in application sectors is lower than in the social optimum due to arising free rider behaviour, or, put differently, another moral hazard problem.

This is why the quality of the GPT as well as the aggregate technology level of all application sectors can be characterised as a partially public good (Bresnahan and Trajtenberg 1995). A bilateral moral hazard problem and corresponding free ride behaviour occur and in equilibrium neither the upstream nor the downstream sectors have enough incentives to innovate. Hence the quality of the GPT as well as the overall technology level of the application sectors is lower than in the social optimum.

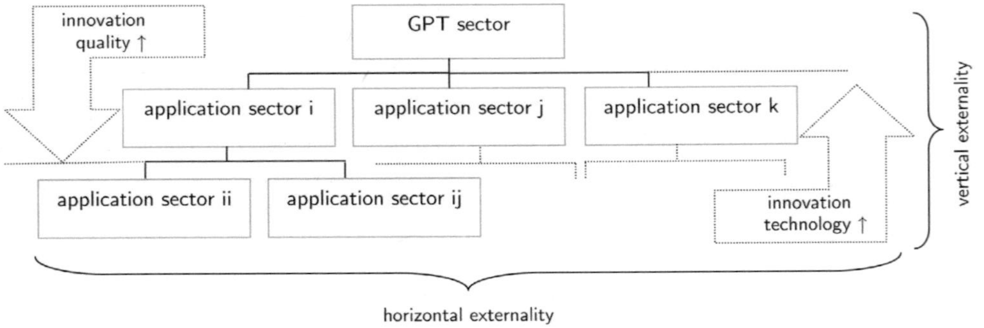

Figure 3.1: Linkages and externalities in the innovation processes of a GPT.
Source: own illustration.

3.2.2 Dynamics of a GPT

Assume a profit-maximising GPT sector and (for simplicity) only one application sector with a certain quality of the GPT as well as a certain technology level of the application sector at a given point in time t. Let the adaption period one sector needs to adapt its technology to the innovation made by the other sector in the precedent period be of ever the same length. To develop this adaption, the quality or technology level at time t is thus relevant. Hence in each sector the quality/technology level remains constant for a length of time of two adaption periods: From t to $t+1$ the GPT sector develops a certain improvement to the quality level of the GPT, from $t+1$ to $t+2$ the application sector adapts its technology to this GPT. Then, from $t+2$ to $t+3$ the GPT sector adapts the quality of the GPT to this technology level, in turn from $t+3$ to $t+4$ the application sector responds with the development of an adaption of the technology level and so on (see Figure 3.2). Over time, each agent in each sector maximises payoffs discounting with the discount factor δ. This discount factor can be considered as the anti-proportional measure for the difficulties of forecasting technological developments in the respectively other sector.

This means that increasing difficulties of anticipation (thus decreasing δ) induce lower values for the levels of quality/technology, respectively, for every point in time and subsequently for the long-term equilibrium. In the extreme case of absolute uncertainty ($\delta = 0$) innovations would be disrupted entirely. Bresnahan and Trajtenberg (1995) assume that, presumed there is coordination, knowledge exchange or flow of complementary knowledge (and thus less uncertainty), a part of the R&D for the adapting innovation can already be done while the other sector has not finished its technology improvement yet. Consequently, the innovation period (=double adaption period) could be shortened. If there is no coordination at all, the innovation period is of maximum length, which effectively results in a decelerated innovation rate (Bresnahan and Trajtenberg 1995). Uncertainty, besides the externalities, can thus be seen as another market failure in the innovation process of GPTs. It has to be pointed out, however, that uncertainty is a market failure inherent in innovation process in general and thus not exclusive to GPT innovation processes. Notwithstanding, the impact of uncertainty on innovation processes in GPTs is particularly strong due to the mentioned dual inducement mechanism and the inherent feedbacks.

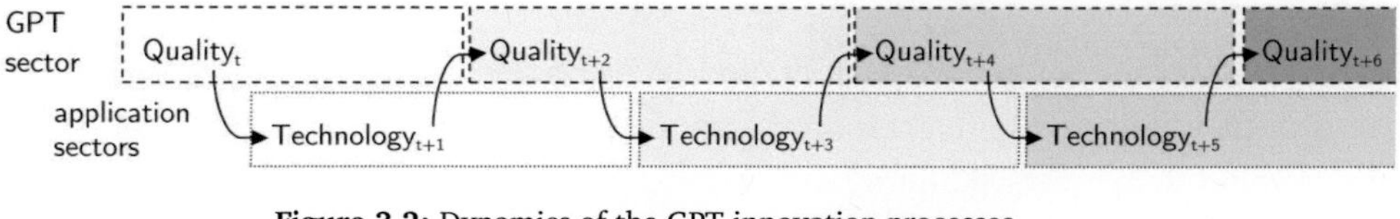

Figure 3.2: Dynamics of the GPT innovation processes.
Source: own illustration.

To sum up: General purpose technologies introduce two main market failures in the innovation process. Due to innovational complementarities and the resulting appropriability effect, returns on investments in innovations cannot be appropriated completely (positive vertical externality) which leads to too little investments. The same problems occur on the horizontal level: Raising the technological level of all application sectors by investments of a single application sector in R&D makes all application sectors better off, which leads to a free-rider-symptomatic and results in too few application sectors, each of them innovating too little. Hence externalities as well as uncertainties decelerate innovations and lower the long-term equilibrium level of the GPT's quality and the application sectors aggregate technology level. Overcoming the moral hazard problems, e.g. by coordination, however, would lead to a positive feedback loop, trigger incentives to innovate at a certain sector in the system first and then – by increasing private incentives – in the whole GPT innovation system (Bresnahan and Trajtenberg 1995).

It is hence not the idea that GPTs are important for growth because of the actual importance of a particular GPT innovation alone. Due to the combination of technological advance in the GPT sector as well as in other complementary sectors, innovations are triggered by the GPT innovation that then feed back, thereby creating a cycle of innovations and potentially large amounts of economic value.

3.3 GPTs, Diffusion and Aggregate Growth

Attempting to understand the benefits of coordinated inventions in the GPT as well as the application sectors in order to understand how GPTs eventually impact macroeconomic growth needs to understand the timing of innovation: The economic impact of a GPT is driven by technology diffusion.

GPT theories refer to the distinction between GPT and application sectors when modelling the delay between the technological invention and the final aggregate productivity growth. Indeed, many empirical studies of past GPTs showed that diffusion of these technologies was slow at the beginning and accelerated later on (e.g. for electricity, steam and ICT) (David 1990, Jovanovic and Rousseau 2005, Bresnahan 2010). Possible reasons for the delay and then the acceleration of diffusion are manifold, including supply constraints (such as profitable adoption requiring the price of the technology to fall below or the quality exceed a certain threshold), demand constraints (the large group of low value demanders adopting later) and adjustment cost (learning in adoption) (Bresnahan 2010). These constraints, however, are not exclusive to GPT innovation processes and they are subject to diminishing returns. In GPTs, by contrast, the feedback mechanism provides another reason for the S-shaped (i.e. slowly at the beginning, accelerating later on) diffusion path and therefore the diffusion might even last longer: A newly introduced GPT creates a new system of innovation that is, at the beginning, limited in relevance by a low technological level of the GPT on the one hand and the existing older solutions on the other hand. This lowers the extent to which the GPT triggers innovation. However, the early adoption and complementary innovation in an increasing number of application sectors endogenously enhances the incentives to innovate over time. The rapid adoption, steep part of the S-shape is reached once there is a sufficient number of adopters making the system switch to the second wave of dual inducement (Helpman and Trajtenberg 1998a). Slow diffusion is hence sustained by an additional force which is constituted by the need for co-invention and hence the two waves in which the innovation feedback cycle takes place. This delayed rapid adoption is impacting wide fields of the economy. Due to the inherent dual inducement mechanism in GPT innovations, this happens even if coordination among the agents works perfectly fine (Bresnahan 2010). Hence, the innovational complementarities lead to a divergence between social optimum and the individual optima of chosen technological expenses which occurs for all arms-length market mechanisms.

But when does aggregate economic growth finally occur? Helpman and Trajtenberg (1998b) were the first to model cycles of macroeconomic growth induced by the diffusion of GPTs, followed by many others (among them e.g. Jovanovic and Rousseau (2002), Carlaw and Lipsey (2006)). The common feature of all these models is that the reallocation of resources towards R&D in the field of the newly arrived GPT initially may cause a productivity slowdown due to delayed research output and the missing corresponding payoff. The phase of economic growth arriving once the research efforts translate into economic returns of the GPT, however, outweighs the initial losses and results in positive aggregate economic growth (Jovanovic and Rousseau 2005), reaching its peak when all application sectors went through the phase of investment without returns and subsequently contribute positively to aggregate economic growth.

Part II

RESEARCH SET-UP

4 Motivation and Organisation

The previous Chapter 3 introduces GPTs as 'engines of growth' which induce a bulk of follow-up innovations which are speeded up by feedback mechanisms that provide ongoing incentives for innovation along various value creation chains. As elaborated in the preceding Chapters 1 and 2, the central input for innovation is knowledge. Knowledge, in turn, incorporates all the assets and drawbacks that have been discussed in the same vein. Issues arising in the context of knowledge and innovation, such as the diffusion and spillover of knowledge determining the degree of productivity of innovations are expected to be even more relevant in the context of GPTs since they are particularly intensive in knowledge and innovation. The accessibility of knowledge can, without exaggeration, be seen as a drive mechanism of the growth-engine GPT. Even more so, the coordination of knowledge creation processes is instanced as a potential remedy for the occurring market failures that are found to reduce the levels of innovative activity in GPTs. Hence, the peculiar characteristics of knowledge might be cause and cure for the lower-than-socially-optimal innovation levels in GPT: On the one hand, knowledge as partly public good induces the problem of appropriability and hence the externalities in the innovation processes of a GPT that lower the level of innovations beyond the social optimum. On the other hand the non-rivalry of knowledge offers a potential remedy for this market failure, as these might be internalised through coordination in form of collaboration and sharing of knowledge. The central questions arising in this context hence refer to how the characteristics of GPTs influence the creation and diffusion of (new) knowledge, or put differently, innovations on the one hand and how the supply of knowledge on the other hand feeds back on innovations in GPTs. It should be the aim to finally derive (policy) measures to trigger, support and align knowledge creation processes, increase their efficiency and hence strengthen a GPT's positive impact on growth.

4.1 Research Gap and Research Questions

The most important aspects about GPTs for innovation and growth are the induced complementary co-inventions in conjunction with the wide variety of uses. These constitute the main features of a GPT. Co-invention lowers overall innovation costs by opening the opportunity to reuse and recombine knowledge in the many different fields the GPT is applied in. Complementary inventions moreover trigger an increase in innovation incentives resulting in the dual inducement mechanism. This mechanism, on the other hand eventually and fundamentally influences the diffusion and growth process and hence the scope of GPTs. Occurring externalities and uncertainties, however, lower the extent to which a GPT triggers innovations below the level that is socially optimal. Coordination was brought up as a central solution to overcoming these problems already in the seminal contribution by Bresnahan and Trajtenberg (1995).

Yet, the effects of the GPT characteristics, most prominently expressed in the dual inducement mechanism, on the creation, accumulation and diffusion of knowledge and vice versa, as well as the proposed coordination of research efforts has to the author's knowledge not been investigated in more detail. On the one hand, the mechanisms of a GPT's diffusion and its impact on the economic development were modelled as detailed in Section 3.3 and empirical studies aimed at identifying former and present GPTs, such as conducted by Lipsey et al. (1998, 2005), Jovanovic and Rousseau (2005) and Youtie et al. (2008). On the other hand there has been a vast amount of literature assessing the role of knowledge for innovation as elaborated in Chapters 1 and 2. And yet, there has been no structured attempt to connect the role of knowledge for innovation with GPTs as not only engines of growth but particularly 'engines of innovation'. On the one hand, the general findings on knowledge creation, diffusion and exploitation for innovation should also hold true in the context of a GPT. On the other hand, given the peculiarities of GPTs, the composition of knowledge bases as well as the nature of collaboration and re-utilisation of knowledge in different contexts is pointed out to be of outmost importance for the optimal development of these technologies: As elaborated, the optimal employment of knowledge reduces the (aggregate) costs for innovation and opens opportunity for cross-fertilisation, which might be particularly important in the context of a GPT: Cross-fertilisation describes the employment of knowledge from one context into a completely different one which, at the end, benefits innovation in both fields. Moreover, by targeting the diffusion of knowledge, coordination can take place in many different ways: Through cross-fertilisation, in form of localised knowledge spillovers and particularly through collaboration and hence in networks. These knowledge diffusion mechanisms therefore might provide a promising remedy to overcome occurring market failures at least partly. Thereby, the inherent innovation processes of GPTs could be increased and speeded up. This would add to the 'normal' positive effect on innovation collaboration is found to have.

The central research question of this thesis is hence which role the creation and the diffusion of knowledge play for innovations in GPTs with respect to their character as engine of growth. Hence, the focus is put on how knowledge translates into innovations, how this relates to the central characteristics of a GPT and how this might impact technological and subsequently economic development. Given the state of the art and the presented existing research (see Chapters 1 - 3), two arrays of questions are to be answered in this context:

4.1.1 Knowledge Composition and Localised Knowledge Spillovers

This array refers to the role of knowledge bases, their composition and their potential to trigger different forms of knowledge spillovers. In this context, spillovers are treated in a quite abstract way, similarly as it is done in most of the literature on spillovers. No concrete mechanisms, but rather the potential for spillovers is subject to investigation. The arising questions are:

> **What is the role of the composition of knowledge bases and the resulting potential for spillovers for the development of GPTs?** In which (regional) knowledge contexts are GPTs developed? Which composition of (regional) knowledge supports the development of the 'engines of innovation' best? How does the development of GPTs feed back to the development of the knowledge bases? Do knowledge spillovers occur? What kind of spillovers is particularly conducive to GPT innovation? Given a GPTs multipurpose on the one hand and its nature of a leading-edge technology on the other, which role do diversity and specialisation of knowledge play? How does the interdependence of innovation processes along the value creation chain, e.g. due to innovational complementarities impact the processing of knowledge and subsequently overall innovativity? (How) do agent-specific and location-specific characteristics interact and influence the growth processes in a GPT? What is the impact of regional specialisation in this context? Which characteristic of the GPT predominates in the context of firm growth: its character as a high technology or the very GPT features?

4.1.2 Collaboration and Knowledge Sharing in Networks

The second set of questions tackles, more concretely, the role of collaboration and the resulting networks as a diffusion channel for knowledge and a concrete mechanism for spillovers on the one hand and as a potential remedy for occurring market failures in the innovations processes of a GPT on the other hand.

Which role does collaboration and networking play for the innovation processes of a GPT? Which role does external knowledge play for an innovator in a GPT context? What is the current role of collaboration in the R&D processes of a GPT? Is there a pre-defined development path of collaboration? How does collaboration impact the development of a GPT? Is there a difference between national and international collaboration? Are these processes of knowledge-sharing efficient? Which network structure prevails? What are the potentials for knowledge sharing in such a widespread technology? How can they be used? Which innovators cooperate most productively for the development of a GPT? How is knowledge shared between innovators? What about the often mentioned technological proximity - is it a blessing or a curse for the development of a *general* purpose technology? How do specialisation and diversity influence the network? What is the effect of collaboration on generality? What is the impact of the access to (new) knowledge on generality? Are experienced inventors enhancing team performance? Is experience supporting the (productive) recombination of knowledge? What is impact of technological relatedness in a team on the generality of purpose (and hence the main feature of a GPT?

4.2 Research Organisation and Contributions

The empirical part of the research in this thesis is organised in three working packages. The first of them is the building blocks-package. It describes the current state, marks the fundament for educated extrapolations into the future, explores relevant issues and tests indicators as well as hypotheses. Generally spoken, it constitutes the building blocks for the following analyses. The second working package is concerned with the impact of the composition of knowledge (i.e. the nature of the knowledge with respect to, e.g., specialisation, diversity and compatibility) and localised knowledge spillovers and hence with the first array of the derived research questions, while the third working package particularly tackles the role of collaboration and knowledge sharing in networks. Figure 4.1 depicts this organisation of working packages while Table 4.1 summarises the derived and investigated hypotheses in detail.

4.2.1 Building Blocks – Working Package 1

To operationalize the research approach of this thesis, nanotechnology was chosen as a showcase example for a particularly knowledge intensive and widely spread technology with an enormous growth potential for the future. **The first analytical Chapter 6**

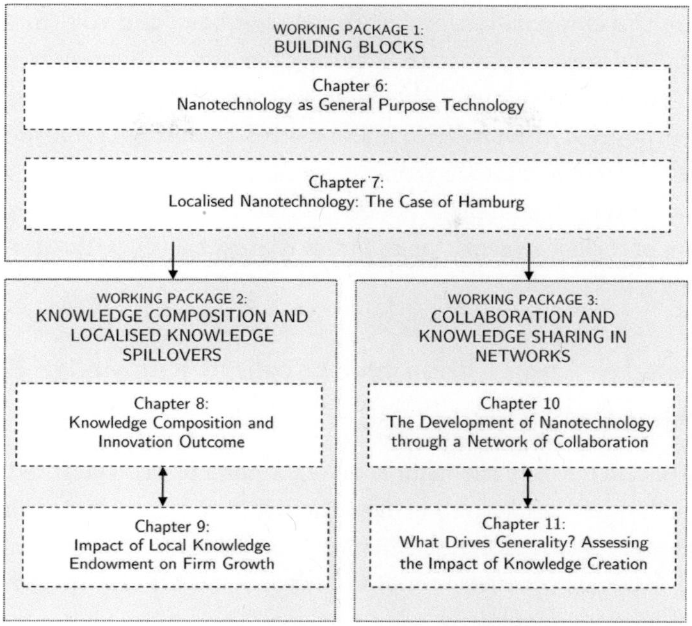

Figure 4.1: Organisation of the empirical analyses in working packages. Source: own illustration.

tackles the question whether nanotechnology can indeed be considered as a general purpose technology. Furthermore, the character of a merging technology, i.e. feature of nanotechnology as merging different disciplines, is assessed in depth, since this, similarly to the GPT character in general, directly connects to the challenges that come along with nanotechnology and the handling of diverse knowledge. This chapter mainly relies on the theoretical derivations from Chapter 3. It contributes to the current scientific debate around the appropriate classification of nanotechnology and its characteristics. Thereby, the character of nanotechnology as GPT is tested with patenting and publication data from the whole world as well as for Europe in particular. The focus lies on a comprehensive analysis of existing indicators (a survey of already existing studies is provided) and the development of new ones. Most importantly, the performance of nanotechnology is structurally compared with benchmark technologies. Finally, the analysis validates the choice of the example of nanotechnology as GPT showcase and thereby constitutes a building block for the following analyses.

The next chapter forms the other part of the empirical building block. The analytical approach relies on a case study of the development of nanotechnology in a particular (regional) context. **The aim of this Chapter 7 is to identify relevant aspects concerning the interrelationship between the development of nanotechnology, the access**

to knowledge, the composition of the knowledge base and the (local) economic development. This is accomplished by exploring the issues around the two main arrays of research questions, i.e. around the role of collaboration and knowledge sharing as well as the composition of knowledge and localised knowledge spillovers. Chapters 2 and 3 provide the theoretical underpinning for this explorative analysis. The main contribution to the current state of the art is, besides the provision of an in-depth case study, the exploration of further relevant topics in this context as well as the development and testing of analytical indicators.

4.2.2 Knowledge Composition and Localised Knowledge Spillovers – Working Package 2

This working package within the main analyses is particularly concerned with the first array of research questions derived above. The issues chosen to be investigated follow from the case study accomplished in Chapter 7. It hence tackles question around the impact of the (regional) composition of knowledge and the corresponding (potential for) localised knowledge spillovers.

The analysis in Chapter 8 focuses on the potential role of the anchorage of nanotechnology into the regional specialisation pattern and even more prominently on the role and dynamics of specialisation and diversity for innovation. A panel of 34 German nano-regions covering the local nano-patenting activity during the time period from 1990 to 2009 is exploited for this scope. The nano-patenting activity is used to construct the local nano-knowledge bases. The main assumption this analysis relies on is that the propensity of industry- or city-specific externalities in form of knowledge spillovers is relative to the degree of specialisation and diversity, respectively, of the local nano-knowledge bases. Panel negative binomial regression analysis is then employed to evaluate the impact of regional compatibility, specialisation and diversity on future innovativeness. Thereby, this chapter contributes to the Marshall-Jacobs debate tackling the role of specialisation and diversity (externalities) for innovation.

The next chapter also deals with the array of research questions around knowledge composition and spillovers. Yet, the approach is significantly different to the one followed in Chapter 8 since the analysis is zooming in: The focus is laid on the influence of the indicated issues on employment growth in firms processing nanotechnology. **Chapter 9 investigates the contribution of location-specific characteristics and knowledge endowment to firm growth in nanotechnology with a particular focus on the role of specialisation.** Therefore, a unique panel of 245 German firms covering the time period from 2007 to 2010 is exploited. This data-set is the result of an online-survey exclusively conducted for this purpose. The empirical analyses apply two regression techniques, a simple OLS regression and a fixed effects model. This chapter contributes to the literature in two ways: First, it investigates the knowledge-processing characteristics and interrelationships in nanotechnology firms for the first time. Second, it advances the knowledge about the role of location for firm growth: While current research only elaborates on the influence of the accessible stock – and hence the quantity – of local knowledge, the analysis is extended to the composition and hence the quality of the local knowledge base, thereby pointing to issues such as the role of Marshallian knowledge spillovers.

4.2.3 Collaboration and Knowledge Sharing in Networks – Working Package 3

This third working package within the main analyses focuses on the second array of research questions derived above.

Collaboration and innovation in networks are assumed to play an increasingly important role for the efficiency of innovation in leading-edge technologies. This and the corresponding theoretical underpinnings from Chapter 2 are the basis for the following analysis. Particularly the increasing complexity of nanotechnology as a merging general purpose technology (which directly connects to Chapter 6) reveals the urgent necessity for joint research and collaboration in order to be able to contribute to leading edge research. Notwithstanding the elaborated relationship, research on nanotechnology networks still lacks a comprehensive analysis of collaboration in innovation and corresponding networks. **The analysis in Chapter 10 hence sets out to explore the evolution of collaboration and (efficient) networking coming along with technological advance and most presumably influencing subsequent innovative activity.** The empirical research is organised around three main questions. These tackle the role of collaboration and networks in general, the evolution of an efficient network of knowledge sharing and the cooperation potential in terms of cross-fertilisation possibilities in a network of technological overlap. Therefore, the analysis was restrained on the German nanotechnology networks from 1980-1984 to 2003-2007, built through co-contributorship as indicated in patent data. Indicators from similar and totally different contexts were employed, adapted and developed further for the scope of deciding on the derived hypothesis. The contribution to the empirical literature consists in a stock-taking of the state of development and its ex-post dynamics, but it shall also offer the basis for extrapolations into the future and provide insights into how important (efficient) collaboration is for the development of a GPT. Last, the analysis evaluate how potentials for collaboration are/can be exploited, particularly vis-à-vis the important role of coordination for solving the occurring market failures in a GPT's innovation processes.

The last empirical analysis shall consist in a catch-all-analysis, at least as far as possible. Having elaborated on the role of knowledge, knowledge spillovers and knowledge sharing, the last chapter picks up relevant issues from each of the preceding analyses, still having the main focus on intended collaboration. **Chapter 11 assesses the knowledge- and cooperation-related factors that influence the generality of a nanotechnological invention.** The aim is to shed light on how the generality of an invention develops and how it can be increased. Albeit alone not a sufficient feature, the generality of purpose is certainly the most striking feature of a GPT. It ensures the possibility to employ, adopt and adapt a GPT throughout the economy. Without exaggeration, the formation of a set of extremely general inventions can hence be seen as not only driving the development of the GPT itself, but also impact aggregate economic development positively. The potential issues explored in this analysis concern the impact of collaboration, the access to new knowledge (both directly picking up the findings from Chapter 10), (individual) experience and technological background (both relating to the role of the composition of knowledge and hence to Chapters 8 and 9). The German nanotechnology patenting data from 1980-2005 were once again the basis for the fractional logit analyses that investigated these factors. This research adds to existing research as it, to the best of the author's knowledge, is the first analytical empirical analysis of knowledge-related factors influencing the main feature of a GPT as 'engine of innovation'.

As the description of the working packages has made obvious, nearly all of the empirical analyses rely on the use of patent data. There are even more data and methodological approaches that are employed more than once. In these cases, data and methodology are introduced beforehand in Chapter 5 in order to improve readability and avoid redundancies. Yet, for the scope of comprehensiveness, redundancies cannot be totally avoided either.

Chapter	Research Question	Hypothesis	Expectation
6	Is nanotechnology a GPT?	Pervasiveness (H6.1)	Nanotechnology is pervasive.
		Scope for Improvement (H6.2)	Nanotechnology exhibits scope for improvement.
		Innovation Spawning (H6.3)	Nanotechnology spurs innovations.
		Innovational Complementarities (H6.4)	Nanotechnology features innovational complementarities.
	Is nanotechnology a merging technology?	Knowledge Mergence (H6.5)	Nanotechnology merges knowledge from several disciplines and technologies.
7	Is knowledge shared?	Knowledge Sharing (H7.1)	Knowledge sharing occurs in the context of nanotechnological knowledge creation.
	How does nanotechnology fit into the region?	Compatibility (H7.2)	Nanotechnology is advanced according to regional specialisation.
	Which role do specialisation and diversity play?	Composition of the NKB (H7.3)	Both specialisation and diversity of the NKB may be observed.
	How does nanotechnological knowledge develop?	Feedbacks over Time (H8.3)	(a) Specialisation deepening and widening occur. (b) The importance of specialisation decreases; importance of diversity increases.
8	How does nanotechnology fit into the region?	Compatibility to Local Structures (H8.1)	Nanotechnology is advanced according to regional specialisation.
	Which role do specialisation and diversity play?	Specialisation and Diversity (H7.3)	(a) The specialisation of the regional NKB is conducive to its growth. (b) The diversity of the regional NKB is conducive to its growth.
	How does the impact of specialisation and diversity develop dynamically?	Dynamics (H8.3)	As the NKB evolves, the importance of specialisation decreases whereas the importance of diversity increases.
	Which effect has the composition of the sciNKB?	Diffusion (H8.4)	(a) The size of the scientific NKB has a positive influence on the growth of the technological NKB. (b) Specialisation of the scientific NKB hampers the growth of the technological NKB. (c) Diversity of the scientific NKB stimulates the growth of the technological NKB.
9	What is the role of local knowledge endowment for the development of nanotechnology?	Local Knowledge Endowment (H9.1)	Location characteristics do influence the employment growth of firms in nanotechnology.
	What is the role of specialisation?	Impact of Local Specialiation (H9.2)	Local specialisation impacts the employment growth of firms in nanotechnology.
	Are the results robust?	Robustness (H9.3)	Specialisation effects that are related to average employment growth are the same as those that are related to a year-to-year consideration of employment growth.
10	How does collaboration develop?	Collaboration Pattern in General (H10.1)	(a) Collaboration increases. (b) International collaboration decreases in importance. (c) Collaboration occurs particularly where actors are geographically and cognitively proximate.
	How does efficiency develop?	Efficiency of the Innovation Network (H10.2)	The efficiency of the innovation network of nanotechnology increases with its development and over time.
	How do specialisation and diversity influence the network?	Technological Overlap (H10.3)	The network of technological overlap develops towards a center-periphery structure.
11	What is the impact of collaboration on generality?	Role of Collaboration in General (H11.1)	Generality increases with collaboration.
	What is the impact of the access to (new) knowledge on generality?	Impact of the Access to (New) Knowledge (H11.2)	Generality increases with centrality in the network.
	What is the impact of the inventors(') experience on generality?	Impact of Experience (H11.3)	Generality increases with experience and hence absorptive capacity.
	What is the impact of the inventors(') technological background on generality?	Impact of the Technological Background (H11.4)	Generality decreases with relatedness.

Table 4.1: Overview of research questions and hypotheses.
Source: own composition.

5 Methodology and Data

While the basic theoretical framework and the main research questions derived thereof are introduced in the preceding chapters, this chapter introduces the data, as well as some of the main tools and indicators on which the empirical analyses rely. Note that this chapter shall not be a complete introduction of all methodology employed in this thesis, but rather an introduction to the most important concepts, approaches and data (i.e. normally those that is used more than once in the analyses to come).

Jointly considering technological development, innovation, new knowledge and location, which is done throughout this thesis, the industrial cluster concept is frequently referred to. Instead of focussing on this narrower framework, this thesis assesses knowledge production in the basic framework of regional knowledge bases as a broader concept. Knowledge bases have a stock character and hence a knowledge base has a self-reinforcing feature, as the existing knowledge can be used to create new knowledge and innovations out of it, thereby contributing to the growth of the current (local) stock of knowledge. Knowledge bases hence account for the peculiar characteristics of knowledge (see Chapter 1) as well as for the knowledge production function approach with respect to its (regional) conceptualisation (see Subsection 2.1.1). Yet, particularly when investigating tacit knowledge it should be mentioned that not all components of this particularly intangible good can be described appropriately (Nesta 2008). Instead, only indirect trails of tacit knowledge can be analysed. As a proxy for this regional (tacit) knowledge base it is referred to two essential parts: The *scientific* or *analytic* knowledge roughly serves as a measure for scientific research outcomes and innovations and is proxied by publications. By contrast, the *technological* or *applied* knowledge, as proxied by patents, reflects more applied research and development results. Thereby, the directly measurable outcome that constitutes a knowledge base always also includes the intangible amounts of tacit knowledge that are directly related to it and that are not codifiable and measurable. In particular when one is concerned with high technologies where tacit knowledge is the most important ingredient to innovation one hence has to accept such proxies in order to operationalize the subject of investigation at all.

Due to the complexity and for the scope of brevity, the discussion of knowledge production and innovation indicators in general is set aside. Nowadays there is a wide range of commonly accepted indicators, among which are patent- and publication-based indicators. Because these are the main data sources for the following analyses, Sections 5.1 and 5.2 discuss only these, but in more detail.

Besides the creation of innovation through the accumulation of knowledge, the diffusion of knowledge has been derived as a central mechanism for the productivity and finally success of innovative activity. Innovation networks have been discussed in their relevance for the accessibility of knowledge for inventors and the creation of innovations. Section 5.4 introduces the network construction based on patent data.

5.1 Patents as Resource for Innovation Analysis

Patents, very generally, are property rights that are granted for inventions and their corresponding commercial use. A patent hence constitutes a temporal monopoly awarded to the inventors for the commercial use of their invention (Trajtenberg et al. 1997). Moreover, patents also have an information function. By disclosing patents, the technological state of the art is published and knowledge diffusion is amplified. In order to be patentable at all, an invention has to fulfill three patentability criteria. (i) It has to be *novel*, less evident it has also to be (ii) *non-trivial*, i.e. it shall hence not be obvious for specialists in that particular field or, put differently, the invention must reach a particular quality – the inventive step. Last (iii) it has to be *useful*, i.e. it shall have potential commercial value. A patent is published together with detailed information on the exact technology of the inventions, the inventor, applicant and owner of the patent and (frequently also) their addresses as well as the invention's potential fields of use. Moreover, prior art, either added by the assignee or by the patent examiner, in form of technological antecedents (which may be patents or non-patent literature) is documented in form of (backward) citations. Objections and forward citations, hence such patents that cite the patent under consideration, are included as well (Fischer et al. 2009).

In the field of innovation research, patent data provide a fruitful and important source of information for the study of innovation and technological change, since they are detailed, highly standardised, very well available and, most importantly, have a very close – though imperfect – link to innovational activity. These data include not only information on the invention itself, but also relevant information on the applicant and inventor, prior and subsequent art and corresponding technological areas in form of IPC classes. Within the system of innovative activity, patent count is therefore a commonly used measure reflecting the *innovative output* of (mainly industrial) R&D activity, especially within the framework of the knowledge production function (Grupp 1998). However, Griliches (1990) and Trajtenberg (1990) and others claimed that patents only measure an intermediate output in the entire innovation process since they incorporate differences in efforts and hence are not a direct indicator of innovation output. They subsequently also propose patents to be employed as a measure of *inventive input*. Most importantly for the scope of this thesis, patent data is assessed with the limitation that the tacit knowledge is not directly but rather indirectly captured by the patent itself. A patent hence stands for a certain amount of tacit knowledge necessary for the realisation of that very invention. However, more standard limitations and assets shall be discussed in the following, since most of the analyses constituting this thesis rely on patent data.

5.1.1 Benefits and Shortcomings of Patent Data

The use of patents as innovation indicator has important limitations. First, patents reflect innovative (and not just inventive) activity since they are applied for during the whole development and commercialisation process (Pavitt 1985). Second, by far not all innovative activity is patented or even patentable. This is e.g. due to the costs a patent application process incurs, due to the necessary publication of the inventions or due to the characteristics of the invention itself, such as process innovations that are hardly patentable. Subsequently patent analyses cannot capture these. Patentable inventions or innovations hence constitute only a subset of all R&D outcomes. Third, patenting often is a strategic decision as well, with the result that not all patentable inventions actually become patented (Fischer et al. 2009). As a result, patents are not equally frequently used in all sectors – by contrast, the propensity to patent varies significantly across different sectors and industries (Pavitt 1985). Additionally, it has also to be considered in a very general manner that larger firms tend to patent more than smaller ones, mainly due to cost effects and the fact that intellectual property has to be published during the patent application process. This might spoil technological and hence competition advantages of smaller firms, which might therefore prefer alternative protections, such as secrecy. Furthermore, there is a wide range of values of patents from a technological and economic point of view: Many patents actually have nearly vanishing effects, while some patents protect break-through inventions that are, in addition, easily commercialisable (Schankerman and Pakes 1986). To face this problem, patent citations that are seen as proxy for value are often used to estimate the impact of patents. Last, patent analyses over time face the problem of other influences impacting patenting activity, such as changing intellectual property rights, changing industrial landscape, and not to forget changing patenting behaviour – a biases that has to be kept in mind when analysing such data (Pavitt 1985).[1]

However, in many cases patent data has proven to highly correlate with R&D activities and hence to be a good proxy for (overall) innovative output (Griliches 1990). Moreover, these shortcomings lose their relevance at all, when patents are used as proxy for competencies and the underlying knowledge instead of innovative performance (Nesta 2008) – which is the way patents are employed in this thesis. Patent data therefore is very promising data for analyses on technological and innovational dynamics and the geography of innovations in the short as well as in the long term (Grupp 1990, Griliches 1990). The detailed information about the locus of invention and the relationships to other patents as captured by citations give rise to patents becoming the central resource for analysing the spatial extent of knowledge spillovers (Fischer et al. 2009). Especially in nanotechnology and other emerging technologies, patent data offers a basis for analysis where other data is only scarce. Patent analysis is therefore a valuable approach for the investigation of technology development from the analysis of strategy at a national level to modelling specific emerging technologies (Bengisu and Nekhili 2006). Although very few of these patents eventually become highly valuable in terms of commercialisation opportunities, most of them are technically significant because they induce further developments in technology (Ashton and Sen 1989). The detailed information provided in patent documents permits the investigation of the development of the field in different regions, the identification of agents active in the field, the mapping of technology clusters, the construction of innovator-networks and much more (OECD 2009).

With citation references, patents also point to the use of prior art. This provides a basis for tracing back knowledge flows and map the diffusion of previous inventions. While patent citations are references from one patent to another patent, non-patent literature citations mainly refer to scientific publications or e.g. manuals. These can be used as a proxy for knowledge spillovers between the different patent applicants and inventors (Jaffe et al. 1993, OECD 2009). However, the character of this proxy has to be emphasised as it is not standard, in contrast to references in scientific publications, that the inventor or applicant add the citations themselves. Although, when filing a patent at the USPTO inventor and applicant have to point to prior art by providing references to the technology underlying their invention, this is not needed when applying at other important patenting offices, such as EPO, WIPO, DPMA or JPO. At these offices, patent

[1]Pavitt (1985) further discussed possibilities and problems of patent analyses. In particular, he instanced a number of different biases of the corresponding data with regard to international comparisons, comparisons amongst industrial sectors or technical fields and comparisons amongst industrial firms. For the scope of brevity, the interested reader is referred to his article.

examiners or attorneys add the relevant prior art during the examination process or later to the patent documents. Patent citations hence do not (directly) display which existing knowledge was used by the inventor, but only what *could have been known* by the inventor. When using patent citations in economic analyses, it is, by contrast assumed that the citations reflect knowledge spillovers. To be exact, this is not necessarily the case. However, patent citations are still a proxy for the knowledge that could have been spilling over or eventually might still spill over (Thompson 2006). The fit of the proxy is emphasised by Jaffe et al. (2000), who found through a survey of inventors that the knowledge represented by the cited patent is known by the inventors of the patent citing. However, the patent citation approach is not useful to investigate the concrete mechanisms of local technological spillovers, let alone tacit knowledge (Breschi and Lissoni 2001a, Döring and Schnellenbach 2006, Huber 2011).

Depending on the aim of the analysis, patent data provide fundamental information on the dynamics, development and geography of technological inventions. According to the perspective, however, different pieces of information from the patent document are particularly useful. Figure B.1 in the Appendix B provides an example of a patent application including different kinds of information.

5.1.2 Using Patents as an Indicator

Identifying the Appropriate Patents

When aiming at analysing how particular technological fields evolve, develop or perform the International Patent Classification (IPC) system is moreover especially helpful. It is an internationally recognised patent classification system corresponding to which patents can be classified by the applicants and patent office's examiners according to technology groups. These groups refer to the technological area(s) in which a patent is relevant. The IPC is a hierarchical system, distinguishing between eight sections that constitute technology as a whole. Each section is again divided into classes, subclasses and groups. Yet, since the intention of the IPC is to make it easier to retrieve patents, IPC classes do not display industrial sector classification. However, using the IPC classes, it is possible to identify different technological sectors a patent is relevant in. Therefore, concordance tables are useful (see Tables B.1 and B.2 in the Appendix, for instance). Several different approaches exist that link IPC classes into different industrial classification systems. For instance, Verspagen et al. (1994) developed the MERIT concordance table ISIC–IPC, Hinze et al. (1997) developed the OST/INPI/ISI concordance and Schmoch et al. (2003) developed the NACE/ISIC concordance. Despite this classification system, patent identification is a tricky task – above all in emerging technologies. It is, for every technology, nearly impossible to cover all relevant patents since they might be classified into very diverse (technological) contexts (Hinze and Schmoch 2004). For statistical purpose it is hence the aim to identify as much relevant patents as possible, thereby including as few inappropriate as possible. In emerging fields it is, more particularly, not seldom that there does not even exist a common definition of the novel technology, not to talk about the implementation of the technology into the IPC system. Patent identification in these fields is most frequently done by using keyword queries, searching in abstracts and patent titles (Daim et al. 2006, Bengisu and Nekhili 2006). Yet, Hinze and Schmoch (2004) emphasised that keyword searches in patent documents published by national patent offices are not as productive as desirable due to less strict legal requirements of disclosure with regard to titles and abstracts.

Choosing the Appropriate Time Scale

When investigating patents as an indicator for the development of a technological field, one has to carefully distinguish between the different dates that become relevant during a patent application process. While the *application filing date* refers to the date when the application is handed in to the patent office, the *publication date* is the date when the patent application – and hence the invention – is published. At most of the patent offices this date is 18 months after application. However, the date the closest to the actual invention is the *priority date* (Hinze and Schmoch 2004). This date is the first date of filing of a patent application anywhere in the world. Normally during a period of one year (the priority year), the applicant can apply for patenting the very same inventions at other patent offices as well. However, during this period, the priority date is always used to determine the novelty of the invention. Inventions made after the priority date but before the date of additional filing will not peril the novelty of the invention to be patented (OECD 2009). The *grant date* has to be after the publication date. The length of an application process differs heavily between 2 and 8 years. However, which date is chosen for the analysis of time perspectives depends on the scope of the analysis itself. Most frequently, application or priority dates (which coincide in case of one application only) are chosen as they are closest to the invention. Within this thesis, the priority date is considered. As patents are above all regarded as newly created knowledge in the field, the priority date is suitable since it is the date closest to actual invention (Hinze and Schmoch 2004).

Choosing the Appropriate Geographic Origin

Patent data, moreover, are a valuable source for the study of geographical influences of an on the invention processes, as the regional allocation of patents is possible. This is most frequently done by using either the office of priority application or the address data of applicants and/or inventors (Hinze and Schmoch 2004). The choice of patent authorities as entity of geographical analysis is often misspecified, as international applicants to national patent offices do not display the innovative activity within the respective national borders. However, it does make a difference whether the location of the applicant or the one of the inventor is chosen as determinant of the geographical allocation of a patent. The patent inventor is the one that actually developed the invention to be patented. The applicant, by contrast, is the one that, in case of a grant, will own the patent as legal right. While inventor and applicant can be the same person, they often are not, as the applicant most frequently is the company or organisation employing the inventor. When determining the location of an invention one has hence to decide whether one wants to know where the invention was created or where the legal rights are located. Patent counts can be allocated to inventor or applicant locations in different forms. A patent may be assigned to a location if at least one of the associated persons is located in this region. However, as Hinze and Schmoch (2004) remarked, it has also become common to refer to the first person only or to use fractions to avoid double counting.

Choosing the Appropriate Office of Reference

Patents are national legal rights, i.e. patent protection is limited to the country where a patent is filed (Hinze and Schmoch 2004). Frequently, though not always, applicants tend to file at their national offices first, resulting in the 'domestic advantage' effect, i.e. the overestimation of the home nation when using national data (Schmoch et al. 1988). On the other hand, patents from different national patent offices are hardly comparable to each other because of different national patenting policies, leading to different patent breadth, patenting costs, approval requirements, citation practices and enforcement rules across different patenting offices (see Pavitt (1985) and more recently (Fischer et al. 2009)). Therefore, international patent data often is preferred to data from national patenting offices, as comparability of data is better due to relatively higher homogeneity and value of patents, which corresponds to the same (higher) costs of patenting and one policy during the application process, which is not influenced by national legislation. Yet, and as a direct result of higher costs and efforts on the international level, many smaller firms and less valuable inventions tend to file only at the national level. Hence, international patenting data again only constitutes a subset of all patenting data (Grupp et al. 2010). Although Hinze and Schmoch (2004), pointed at the domestic advantage at national patent offices to be a major problem in patent analyses, this can be confined to analyses that aim at comparing the performances of different countries.[2] Concerning the use of patents as an indicator for the very basic underlying competencies and knowledge, the argument of comparability is hence not valid, since one is not aiming of assessing the value of an innovation but the existence of the novel idea in a very basic sense.

Peculiarities of GPTs and Patenting

The more general an invention is with respect to its potential applicability, the more likely is it to become patented: With increasing numbers of applications, (potential) demand for the technology also increases as it may be useful in a multitude of industries. Also, the propensity of this technology to be used in somewhat unrelated and distant applications increases, which makes it more attractive for the owner of the invention to patent it because the licensee might be in a fairly remote final market and the potential competition could be weaker. From a more theoretical perspective, Bresnahan and Gambardella (1998) argued that more general purpose technologies induce a greater vertical specialisation in the industry as well as the formation of upstream technology specialist firms, which license the technology to several manufacturers in different industries (Gambardella et al. 2007). However, when considering a distinctive technology, problems of different propensities to patent only arise to a limit extend: Griliches (1990) argued, that the propensity to patent varies across the industries. Although GPTs are by definition relevant in a number of different industries, GPTs are, to some extent, merging the classic disciplines (see Chapter 6 for more details). Therefore, this might only be a minor problem in the context relevant for this thesis.

5.1.3 Patent-Databases used in this Thesis

Given the possibilities and problem introduced above, the following basic set-up is chosen for all the patent databases employed in this thesis.

Although Feynman pointed at 'plenty of room at the bottom' already in 1959, it was

[2] In order to be able to compare innovative performance and technological developments between different countries, one has to finally overcome the well-known home advantages of domestic applicants and unequal market orientations of different patenting offices. After is has been popular for a long time to use the triadic approach, i.e. to only include inventions filed for patents at USPTO, JPO and EPO simultaneously (so called triadic patent families) (Grupp et al. 1996), Frietsch et al. (2008) nowadays propose, due to changed impact of the corresponding countries within R&D, to instead chose transnational patents, i.e. patents that are filed at WIPO within the PCT application process or at the EPO (for a modification see also Frietsch et al. 2011).

not before 1980 that the electronic force microscope was developed, which would then make it possible for scientists to begin working at the nano-scale. The focus in this thesis is therefore on the development of nanotechnology during the 30 years subsequent to the AFM discovery. Hence for the following analyses data of priority patents with priority application year between 1980 and 2009 were extracted from the 'EPO Worldwide Patent Statistical Database' (PATSTAT), version September 2010. This database encompasses information about published patent applications (regardless of whether they were granted later in the application process or not) filed at 81 patent authorities worldwide. PATSTAT contains nearly complete information about these applications,[3] e.g. information on applicants and inventors, filing dates, IPC classes, citations, delivered in an easily accessible and aggregated raw format. PATSTAT consists of 18 relational database tables (see Appendix B.2) containing information on about 66 million patent applications. Enriching the analyses accomplished in this thesis, the database was enhanced with additional information and cleaned datasets.[4]

In order to allocate the patents in the database of this thesis to Germany (respectively to German regions), the country (region) of the inventor was chosen (if not stated otherwise). Since it is not intended to compare the performance of countries but to account for competencies and knowledge, no fractional counting was applied.

Given that the scope of this thesis is never to compare the technological performance of different countries, the 'domestic advantage' problem does not apply here. In order to catch as much experience and knowledge in the field as possible, priority application from every patent office in the world for which data is contained in PATSTAT is included. Weighing pro against contra arguments for this approach, the most relevant one it shall be avoided that a patent (and more important the corresponding knowledge) is not included because the authority it was filed at is excluded.

Nano-Patent-Database

To identify relevant nano-patents, a validated search strategy is used that is based on an approach merging keywords proposed by Mogoutov and Kahane (2007), Glänzel et al. (2003), Noyons et al. (2003) and Porter et al. (2008); the keywords can be found in the Appendix B.3.1. Abstract and title of all applications were then searched for these keywords. In the literature, the search for nanotechnology patents is carried out

[3]For instance, legal information (i.e. information on objections and renewals, e.g.) are not included.

[4]Note that, throughout the following work, patent-related analyses are always based on this data and for the scope of legibility, the terms 'patent' and 'patent application' are used synonymously, both referring to the application of a patent as contained in the PATSTAT database.

through two methods: lexical queries (i.e. search terms based on keywords) and patent classes. The problem with patent classes is that since nanotechnology is an emerging technology and the corresponding patent classes are still young, older patents have to be reclassified by professional examiners which is not (fully) done yet. Therefore, lexical queries are the most popular search methodology used in the literature to identify nano-patents (Huang et al. 2010). However, nanotechnology is very cross-disciplinary and its boundaries are not defined in a comprehensive way (Porter et al. 2008). Huang et al. (2010) provided a detailed comparative overview on different search strategies and find that the queries and their results commonly used only differ to a very limited extent since they all share the same set of core keywords. This core set is hence used in the following analyses as well. And still, mainly due to the ill-defined boundaries of nanotechnology, but also resulting from limitations inherent in keyword searches, the database of nano-patents underlying this thesis can be assumed to contain *silence* and *noise* (besides all other limitations of patent data treated above): While not all actual nano-patents can be retrieved (silence), some patents that are included in the nano-database actually do not protect a nano-invention (noise). By excluding patents that only contain very common keywords (such as 'nano-metre' or 'nano-second'), the noise can be reduced but never fully eliminated. By contrast, Bawa (2004) even pointed to the common assignee practise of 'hiding' nano-content in the patent-document in order to inhibit knowledge diffusion to competitors or the explicit use of nano-terms for marketing reasons, which also contributes to silence and noise, respectively. Figure 5.1 summarises what the nano-database underlying the empirical analyses in this thesis catches and what is does not.

Comparative Databases

For the scope of comparison, the development of other technologies, namely information and communication technologies (ICT) as commonly accepted, present GPT (e.g. Jovanovic and Rousseau 2005) and the combustion engine technology (CE) as distinct non-GPT (Graham and Iacopetta 2009) is also considered in this thesis. The basic ICT- and CE-patent databases are constructed similarly to the nano-database. For the scope of comparison, the same period of time is considered. However, both rely on IPC classes and not on lexical queries. In the case of ICT a set of different IPC codes was scanned for in the IPC classes of each first or priority patent application (see Appendix B.3.2). In the case of CE only on IPC class, 'F02', was used to identify relevant patents (Graham and Iacopetta 2009). Further information on the range of comparativeness is given in the respective sections were this is relevant.

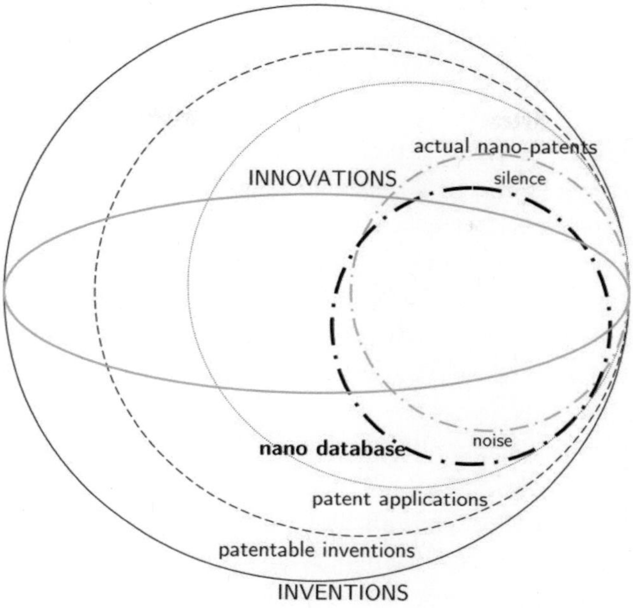

Figure 5.1: Inventions and innovations in the nano-database.
Source: own illustration based on Grupp (1998).

5.2 Publication Analysis

In analogy to patents, scientific publications display the output of the (public) research system. In contrast to patent data, which capture applied R&D used downstream the value chain, publication data are taken as a measure for R&D activities closer to basic science. Since they are subject to peer-review, there is a quality control as well.

5.2.1 Benefits and Shortcomings of Publication Data

Like patent data, publication data cover various scientific fields and are easily available over long time periods. Publication databases are more easily accessible than patent databases, but in contrast to the patenting system publications are more random and their publication process is less standardised. Yet, publications contain a huge variety of information, such as authors, their affiliations, their addresses, sometimes even the authors' technological background. Moreover, besides the fulltext, the classification of the journal itself, the abstract, the title and the subject help to find relevant publications and to classify them. Yet, the lack of a standardised publication procedure translates to the databases as well, as different technological indexing systems are used by different databases instead of an analogously to the IPC system constructed common technological classification system. Last, publications in common databases also include backwards citations (commonly known as 'references') and also forward citations, i.e. publications that cite the publication of interest.

Again, the mere number of publications as indicator of value can be misleading since quantity does not necessarily reflect quality. Consequently, value indicators such as numbers of citations are often included in analyses since they proxy the quality and the usefulness of a scientific publication of the community (Hullmann 2007). Moreover, publication data is biased in favour of English-language journals. And, similar to the limitations of patent data, only published scientific outcome is covered, still the uncodified knowledge is not publishable and still, the propensity to publish in form of scientific papers varies significantly across the different disciplines (Palmberg et al. 2009). The structures of the individual disciplines often vary distinctly (Schmoch et al. 2012).

Yet, as scientific performance is as difficult to measure as is the innovative output that shall be caught by patents, scientific publications are a commonly used and appropriate indicator for measuring scientific excellence by quantifying the output. Similarly conducted statistical analyses of publications are regarded as meaningful if they are accomplished with regard for the methodology employed (Schmoch et al. 2012). Citations and connections to scientific fields, moreover, provide a paper trail of the structural relationships between and the diffusion of scientific knowledge (Palmberg et al. 2009).

5.2.2 Using Publications as an Indicator

There are some methodological issues that should be considered when using publication data. Yet, these issues are similar, yet not as complex as when using patent data, which is why this section is intentionally kept short.

Identifying the Appropriate Publications

To identify appropriate publications from the database basically two ways exist. One possibility is to rely on lexical keyword searches as proposed for patent data. The other way would be to rely on the classification system of the database employed, i.e. to use their subject classes or journals dedicated to particular subjects.

Choosing the Appropriate Time Scale

Since there is only one date involved in the process of publishing, i.e. the publication date the choice of the appropriate time scale is rather straightforward. However, it should be mentioned in this context that the Web of Science as one important database recently substantially extended the coverage of journals (the number of journals covered in the database increased between 2000 and 2008 by 29%, the number of papers even by 34%, (Schmoch et al. 2012)). Schmoch et al. (2012) advised against comparing absolute publication numbers when accomplishing country comparisons as the real increase is difficult to determine. Specific growth structures in a given field or shares should rather be taken into account (Michels and Schmoch 2012, Schmoch et al. 2012).

Choosing the Appropriate Geographical Origin

Similar to the time scale, the appropriateness of the choice of geographical origin is not as complex as in patent analysis since there is no difference to be made between authority, inventor or applicant: Authors are affiliated to their research institutions and hence have one address. At most, fractional count is also applicable when there are several authors.

5.2.3 Publication-Databases used in this Thesis

The publication analyses in this thesis are conducted on the basis of the Web of Science (WOS) publication database provided by Thomson Reuters. This database covers highly cited journals, which can be seen as a quality indicator similar to the examination process in the patent filing process (Schmoch et al. 2012). Since all searches conducted refer to natural, medical and engineering and life sciences, the coverage in Thomson Reuters WOS can be regarded as suitable, whereby the English language bias should not be a problem either since most German authors in these fields already publish in English (Schmoch et al. 2012).

Nano-Publication-Database

As dedicated journals still only exist to a limited extent, emerging science fields such as nanotechnology are about as hard to identify as are nano-patents. This is the case although nano-publications are larger in numbers than are nano-patents since basic research still plays a major role in the development of nanotechnology. Subsequently, nano-publications have to be identified in the same way as nano-patents are identified: By a keyword search algorithm, based on the one used for the identification of patents (see Appendix B.4 for more details).

The considered nano-related publications are indexed in the Thomson Reuters 'Web of Science' database. Here, it is relied on the period between 1980 and 2009. Again, a

Boolean search term is used in order to identify nano-related publications by searching for certain keywords and excluding other keywords in the topic of the paper. Again, the search term is based on a combination of different search queries, as proposed by Glänzel et al. (2003), Mogoutov and Kahane (2007), and Porter et al. (2008) but, due to technical restrictions, way shorter than the patent search term. The exact query can be found in the Appendix B.4.1. Referring to publications, however, the distinction of technological fields (parallel to the IPC system in the patenting system) is based on the definition of Thomson Reuters subject areas assigned to the publication by the Web of Science. These are the basis for measuring the publication indicators, well keeping in mind that this classification system is not as reliable as the IPC classification system.

Comparative Databases

Concerning CE and ICT as benchmark values for publications the search terms were self-developed due to the lack of existing work. For CE publications a lexical query was developed, while for ICT publications all publications that were in the Thomson Reuters subject areas 'Computer Science' and 'Telecommunications' were extracted, since a good description via keywords seems to be impossible for this field (Schmoch 2011, personal communication) (see Appendices B.4.2 and B.4.3).

5.3 Analysing Spillovers: An Approach Based on the Knowledge Production Function

In line with previous research attempting to investigate the nature of spillovers (such as Feldman and Audretsch (1999) and Paci and Usai (1999)) the theoretical framework of the knowledge production function is employed where spatial agglomeration of knowledge depends on the characteristics of the already existing knowledge (see Subsection 2.1.1). The presence of spillovers implies hence that a distinction must be made between the sum of innovative effort of each individual agent and the effective knowledge base (Veugelers 1998). The knowledge base represents the total amount of knowledge accessible for agents in the region. As a proxy for this existing regional knowledge base this is split into two essential parts: the *scientific* knowledge that roughly serves as a measure for basic research outcomes and which is represented by the accumulated publications whereas the *technological* knowledge reflects more applied research results and is approximated by the accumulation of patents. Innovations and hence new knowledge are captured by newly published scientific or patented technological knowledge (as argued above), whereas the stock of existing and potentially newly combinable knowledge consists of innovations (i.e. patents and publications) of the last periods.

Other than tracing knowledge spillovers directly, as e.g. done by Jaffe et al. (1993) and many others after them, another approach to address the effects of spillovers is hence pursued: By looking at the composition of the knowledge base on a regional level and relating this to the creation of new knowledge, thereby indirectly measuring spillovers. Former studies also implementing the knowledge-production-function-based approach for analysing knowledge spillovers (such as e.g. Jaffe (1989), Audretsch and Feldman (1996), Henderson et al. (1998), Feldman and Audretsch (1999), Audretsch et al. (2005), Fritsch and Slavtchev (2007)) have, in general, hardly paid attention to the exact mechanisms behind these spillovers. This leads ineluctably to a lack in disentangling market-mediated exchanges of knowledge and true knowledge spillovers (Breschi and Lissoni 2001a, Massard and Mehier 2010). By contrast, these studies measured the potential for localised spillovers that occur relying on various different transaction mechanisms of knowledge (Breschi and Lissoni 2001b, D'Este et al. 2011). When this approach is employed in the following (i.e. in Chapters 7 and 8), the focus is on the composition of the knowledge base and the kind of the most presumably resulting spillovers. Thereby, the concrete mechanism of the knowledge transfers is neglected and the (admittedly strong) assumption is made that knowledge transfers just occur. Operationalising the importance of the nature and composition of knowledge spillovers, it has hence to be kept in mind that the approach of investigating the knowledge production function and hence the potential for spillovers overlooks the actual transport mechanisms.

5.4 Patents (and Publications) as a Source of Network Data

Besides using the knowledge production function to approach the composition and kind of spillovers, concrete mechanisms of knowledge transfer is subject to investigation as well. Chapters 10 and 11 analyse collaboration and innovation networks as channels for the diffusion of knowledge. This is accomplished by means of social network analysis (see Section 2.3.3). In the context of this thesis, networks are considered as a way of simplified knowledge diffusion, improving the accessibility of knowledge to their members (see Section 2.3). The agents and their relational ties in focus are therefore innovators, i.e. contributors to the innovation process, and their relational ties are mainly constituted by collaboration or, more basically, knowledge assumed to flow between them. For the scope of building these networks, patent data proved to be fruitful. The analysis of networks from patent data has the striking advantage that it rather assesses the role of relations between individuals in which knowledge is embodied and between

which the knowledge is assumed to be exchanged. The problem of the measurability of the intangible is hence avoided by assessing relations rather than stocks.
Patent data as relational data has been used as secondary network data since first employed by Jaffe et al. (1993), who traced knowledge spillovers by patent citations and by Breschi and Lissoni (2003), who were the first to use the data as relational data and build a network thereof. In terms of co-contributorship networks, either inventor or applicant can then be used as nodes in the network to be constructed, which one to choose depends on the intention one has. Figure 5.2 schematises and illustrates an example of such networks and shows the differences. Most frequently, regional network analyses use inventors as nodes in order to appropriately allocate patents as this corresponds to the reality where personal relationships between inventors are said to be a central mechanism of knowledge transfer. Inventors who are assigned to the same patent are seen as related, assuming that they got to know each other, as for example done by Breschi and Lissoni (2004, 2005) and Fleming et al. (2007). Such relationships then constitute the social network of inventors. In these cases, redundant collaboration is regarded as redundant knowledge flowing and does, unless stated otherwise, not change neither the relationship between the inventors nor the network structure. The advantage of using the inventors' addresses moreover is that applicants often are multi-establishment companies. Hence, patents most frequently are assigned to the company's headquarters which does not necessarily display where the knowledge behind the patent has been produced. By contrast, taking the inventor's address most probably displays where the knowledge actually comes from (Verspagen and Duysters 2004).

Yet, the boundaries of the organisation that appears as applicant are not considered in these networks. When aiming at displaying the organisational level, links are established either via co-patenting of applicants or via multi-applicant inventorship (Ter Wal and Boschma 2009). Co-patents are patents that are applied for by more than one actor. This option is not frequently chosen. Although more than 20% of patents result from collaborations with external organisations, only 3.6% of all patents are co-patents. This approach hence leaves much silence in the relation of actual to observed collaboration (Ter Wal and Boschma 2009).[5] Multi-applicant inventorship occurs when one inventor is assigned to patents applied for by different organisations. This is widely interpreted as a result of labour mobility, another acknowledged mechanism of knowledge transfer. However, this is not always the reason for multi-applicant inventorship, particularly not if patents are applied for at the same time. For instance, the reason not to co-patent brought up above and hence to split up patents that resulted from a joint

[5]This might be due to the legal complexity of co-patents, which is why splitting of the right to patent co-inventions between the partners of a joint R&D project (Ter Wal and Boschma 2009).

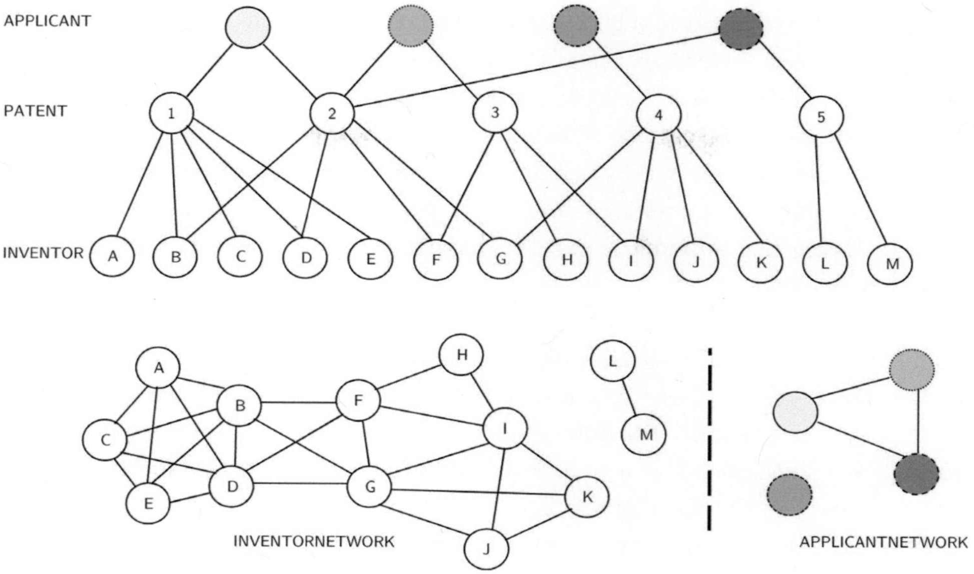

Figure 5.2: Bipartite graph of applicants, patents and inventors (top) and corresponding one-mode projections of co-contributorship-networks of inventors (bottom left) and applicants (bottom right).
Source: own illustration based on Breschi and Lissoni (2005).

research project might result in multi-applicant inventorship and hence indicates cooperation as well. Another reason for multi-applicant inventorship might be that the right to patent an invention was sold by the developing organisation; then applicants change but inventors remain the same (Ter Wal and Boschma 2009). While such networks, no matter how they are constructed, might not all show past cooperations, they all display knowledge flows.

However, patent-data-based networks have a number of shortcomings as well. They, first of all, only capture cooperative relationships that led to a patent, hence not all successful relationships can be displayed. Moreover it has to be considered that patent data always refer to cooperation and knowledge flows that connect applied, technological knowledge, whereas scientific and hence more fundamental knowledge cannot be patented. Lastly, the shortcomings of patent data in general apply with the consequence that the analyses of such networks have to be handled and interpreted with care (Ter Wal and Boschma 2009). Since they constitute a relevant and easily accessible source of data on knowledge diffusion in the innovation process, the advantages and the potential of these kinds of analyses outweighs their shortcomings. Particularly due to the fact that the results of scientific research are most frequently not displayed in patents but rather in publications – and that nanotechnology is in a very young stage of development that relies to a huge extent on scientific research – it would have been desirable to extend the construction of networks to co-authorship as displayed in (scientific) publications. This is, in theory, very well possible. However, the data that was accessible for this thesis did not allow for such analyses, which is why co-publication networks are neglected here. The results obtained for patent data based networks may, however, be helpful to get an idea of how collaboration in nanotechnology in general works and opens opportunities to make educated guesses how networking in scientific research might work.

The networks built and analysed in this thesis hence all rely on patent data from the PATSTAT database. The data was then processed and analysed with free software such as BIBEXCEL[6] and PAJEK.[7] The timespan a network connection is assumed to be valuable (i.e. valuable knowledge is transferred without renewing the relationship in form of a new joint patent application) amounts to five years, which is consistent with a commonly assumed annual depreciation rate of patents around 20% (Leten et al. 2007).

[6]Developed by Olle Persson. Available for free download at http://www8.umu.se/inforsk/Bibexcel/. Persson et al. (2009) provide a good introduction into its application.

[7]Developed by Vladimir Batagelj and Andrej Mrvar. Available for free download at http://pajek.imfm.si/doku.php. de Nooy et al. (2008) provide an excellent manual.

Part III

EMPIRICAL ANALYSES

Part III.a

Working Package 1: Building Blocks

6 Nanotechnology as an Emerging General Purpose Technology

It is widely accepted that nanotechnology is one of the most important technology of the future. Nanotechnology is interdisciplinary and combines a lot of classical basis technologies. This is what makes it so difficult to find a clear and common definition.[1] To quote the US National Nanotechnology Initiative

> 'Nanotechnology is the understanding and control of matter at dimensions of roughly 1 to 100 nano-metres, where unique phenomena enable novel applications. Encompassing nano-scale science, engineering and technology, nanotechnology involves imaging, measuring, modelling and manipulating matter at this length scale.'

The European Patent Office, which just recently introduced a classification system for patents protecting nanotechnology inventions comes to a similar definition:

> The term nanotechnology covers entities with a controlled geometrical size of at least one functional component below 100 nano-metres in one or more dimensions susceptible of making physical, chemical or biological effects available which are intrinsic to that size.' (European Patent Office 2011).

The term nanotechnology stemming from and being applied in different fields thereby refers to most different types of analysis and processing of materials which have one thing in common: Their small size. Nanotechnology makes use of the special characteristics that nano-structures do not only depend on the original material, but very much also on their size and shape, which is used and manipulated by purpose in order to obtain novel functions.[2]

---

[1] Palmberg et al. (2009, p. 19f) provide an overview on the definition of nanotechnology by various actors.

[2] In this context, it could even be discussed whether nanotechnology encompasses too many different technologies 'only' having the small size and the corresponding purposeful manipulation with respect to new functionalities in common. In this case, it would be sensible to employ 'nanotechnologies' only in the plural form. Yet, since nanotechnology is treated as (possible) GPT in the following, the convergence of technologies within the range of the term of nanotechnology is assumed and subsequently the singular form is employed.

The expectations held of nanotechnology are impressively emphasised by market forecasts and the correspondingly steeply increasing public R&D investments throughout the world (see Figure 6.1): In fact, hardly any other technology field has benefited from similarly extensive public support in a similarly short time (not even considering private sector investments). The investments promise to pay off as future market size has been estimated to up to as much as 3 trillion USD in 2015, corresponding to a job creation of around 2 million globally (see Figure 6.2) (Hullmann 2007, Lux Research 2008, Palmberg et al. 2009).[3]

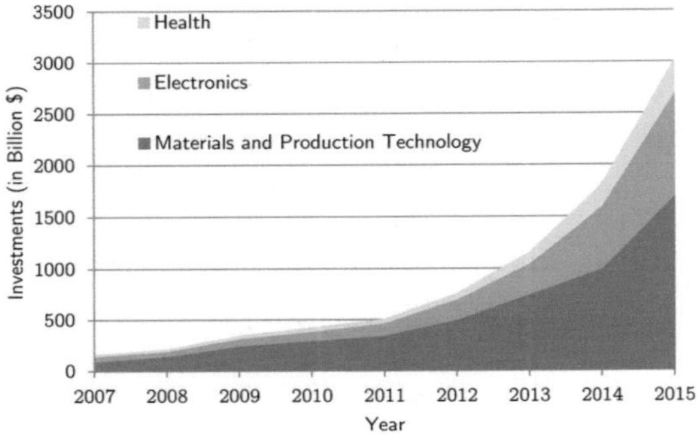

Figure 6.1: Global public R&D investments in nanotechnology
Source: Roco (2007).

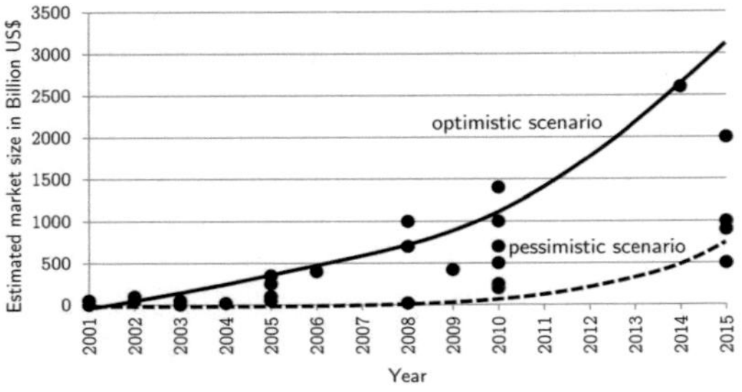

Figure 6.2: Expected world market of nanotechnology. Scenarios based on the basis of 17 sources.
Source: Hullmann (2006).

However, as can easily be seen, nanotechnology still is in an early stage of its development. It can therefore be described as *emerging technology* (Wong et al. 2007, Youtie

[3] Note that these figures were exemplarily chosen in order to point to the enormous expectations in nanotechnology. For a summary of market forecasts see BMBF (2009), Palmberg et al. (2009), Aschhoff et al. (2010), Schmoch and Thielmann (2012). These forecasts rely on studies of private consultancy firms since no official statistics exist due to the lack of a clear cut definition. These firms, however, tend to forecast positively and hence numbers might be too optimistic. See particularly Schmoch and Thielmann (2012) for a recent discussion.

et al. 2008, Palmberg et al. 2009, Schultz and Joutz 2010, Finardi 2011). By definition, information diffusion is incomplete about emerging technologies (Saha et al. 1994): In the early stages of its diffusion, only a subset of scientists and producers develop, or even are aware of the new technology. This is also true for nanotechnology, as research in this field is still mostly basic research (Jansen et al. 2007) with huge shares of public research fundings and hence a resulting involvement of public research institutions in the course of its development. Moreover, uncertainty about the future development of nanotechnology is comparably large and technology forecasting is correspondingly difficult, which results in a limited comprehension of the whole technology ecosystem (Daim et al. 2006). Examples for such bottlenecks were put forward by Schmoch and Thielmann (2012): They noted a lack of complete understanding of many effects in nanotechnology arising due to the enhanced surface to volume ratio. In terms of commercialization they pointed to the high cost of industrial production, i.e. of producing large quantities of nanomaterials that would limit the wide range of potential applications. Moreover, missing information on the potential hazards of nanomaterials could produce a negative image of nanotechnology in the public and thereby inhibit its further development. Last, Schmoch and Thielmann (2012) emphasised nanotechnology's character as enabling technology, processed in vague value creation chain where the current technology push needs to be considered alongside the complementary demand pull.

While it might not be clear to what extent these huge expectations hence will indeed become true, many scholars emphasise that nanotechnology is not only *one important* but *the* GPT of the coming decades. In contrast to other important technologies spurring innovations and hence tackling economic growth, the effect of GPTs for economic growth does not mainly stem from the invention of the GPT as such, but the economic value is created by the pervasive mutual inducements and complementarities of joint inventions in GPT and application sectors, yielding wide and continuing impacts for the whole economy during a whole era (Bresnahan 2010) (see also Chapter 3).

There is a vast literature examining whether past technologies could have been such a GPT, e.g. Lipsey et al. (1998) review potential candidates, Moser and Nicholas (2004) examined whether electricity was a GPT, Jovanovic and Rousseau (2005) compared the impact of IT and electricity and so forth. However, it is considerably more difficult as well as more important to investigate whether currently emerging technologies have the potential to become a GPT. It is more difficult because ex-ante even an exact definition of emerging technologies is difficult, not talking about ways to measure their impact. Youtie et al. (2008) doubted that the kinds of tests proposed in the literature are made for ex-ante analyses of emerging technologies because of the need of a considerable amount of (historical) data. It is important, because GPTs provide large potential effects for economic growth, but the inherent innovation processes also are subject to market failures and hence innovations are assumed to arrive too late and to a too little extent (Bresnahan and Trajtenberg 1995), hampering their positive effects on economic growth. However, these theories rely on stable situations and not on emerging technologies. Hence, if nanotechnology can be identified as young, but emerging GPT, important policy implications could be derived in order to avoid potentially occurring market failures or resolve them in parts. The identification of nanotechnology as possible (future) GPT therefore constitutes the first building block within the main analysis of this thesis. This chapter offers a threefold contribution to the existing literature: First, existing studies are surveyed. Then, the investigation of nanotechnology as possible GPT is conducted using EPO-data and thereby shifts the focus from the US to Europe as well as the world. Last, the investigation is systematised, indicators are modified and novel indicators, such as technological coherence and innovational complementarities come to use.[4]

6.1 Derivation of Hypotheses

As introduced in Chapter 3, Bresnahan and Trajtenberg (1995), who coined the term GPT, characterised them as enabling technologies, offering a generic function which can be productively used in a wide range of application fields. A GPT features three distinctive characteristics: it is (1) widely used and pervasive, (2) exhibits scope for on-going technological improvement and (3) spurs innovation in application sectors. Innovational complementarities result from feature (2) and (3), pointing to the dual inducement process: Innovations in the GPT sector raise the return to innovations in each application sector and thereby the incentive to innovate and vice versa (see Chapter 3 for further details).

GPT models are capable of explaining sustained aggregate growth, as GPTs with an economy-wide scope exhibit increasing returns which are a necessary condition for permanent growth (Romer 1986, Bresnahan 2010). However, this positive effect on productivity and growth does not arrive immediately with its emergence. By contrast, Helpman and Trajtenberg (1998b) theoretically showed that the need for the development of a certain threshold level of complementary inputs before the GPT can become

[4]This chapter relies to a large part (investigation and discussion of hypotheses H6.1 – H6.4) on joint work with Florian Kreuchauff, research assistant at the Chair in Economic Policy, Karlsruhe Institute of Technology. The jointly achieved findings are, however, presented in an own form. Needless to say, all remaining mistakes are entirely the author's.

effective induces an initial phase of below average growth. David (1991) found empirical evidence for this time lack. However, once this threshold is reached, the benefits of an advanced GPT manifest themselves and the GPT can become an effective engine of growth (see Section 3.3).

Nanotechnology seems to qualify as GPT because it potentially features the three characteristics argued for as typical for general purpose technologies: Pervasiveness of use (1) is ensured by the generality of purpose, stemming from the possibility to arrange nano-scaled structures encompassing new material properties for literally countless applications in nano-medicine, atomically precise manufacturing, fuel cell electro catalysis, organic photovoltaic cells etc.. The scope for improvement in nanotechnology (2) is provided by the possible reduction of size and costs and increasing complexity. For instance, nano-applications in semiconductor manufacturing technology resulted in a remarkable reduction of processing size in recent years (Graham and Iacopetta 2009). Hints for nanotechnology to spur innovation in application sectors (3) are given by the existence of a nano-oriented value chains with basic, intermediate and downstream innovations (Youtie et al. 2008). It is hence proposed that nanotechnology is a general purpose technology and subsequently the following hypotheses shall be tested.

Hypothesis 6.1 *Pervasiveness*
Nanotechnology is a widely used, pervasive technology.

Hypothesis 6.2 *Technological Improvement*
Nanotechnology exhibits scope for ongoing technological improvement.

Hypothesis 6.3 *Innovation Spawning*
Nanotechnology spurs innovation in applications sectors.

Hypothesis 6.4 *Innovational Complementarities*
Nanotechnology features innovational complementarities.[5]

Although not referring directly to the GPT character of nanotechnology, the debate around converging technologies shall be picked up as well in this context. Wood et al. (2003) pointed to the fact that many of the novel applications arising from nanotechnology indeed are the result of the convergence of several (basis) technologies within the field of nanotechnology. Put differently, nanotechnology is interdisciplinary and combines various basic technologies thereby merges up to now mostly isolated disciplines,

[5]Technically speaking, innovational complementarities can be derived from H6.2 and H6.3 (Bresnahan 2010). However, finding evidence for innovational complementarities on their own provides further evidence for nanotechnology being a GPT. This is why they are listed as proper hypothesis.

e.g. physics, chemistry and biology. Since this feature, however, might heavily influence the processing of knowledge within the innovation processes of nanotechnology (for instance for issues such as cross-fertilisation, the complementarity of knowledge bases, cognitive proximity etc.), the investigation of this hypothesis seems sensible. The investigation of mergence serves a dual scope. First, the convergence of knowledge used to create new knowledge in a certain technology might later translate into high levels of generality of purpose. Therefore, the level of convergence might serve as an indicator for the potential generality. Second, this merging of technologies indicates the need for multidisciplinarity and emphasises the potential benefits of cross-fertilisation. Since the knowledge base, on the basis of which new knowledge and subsequently innovation is created, is of major importance for the rest of this thesis, the investigation of the merger characteristics indeed is of interest here.

Hypothesis 6.5 *Knowledge Mergence*
Nanotechnology merges knowledge from several disciplines and technologies.

6.2 Methodology and Data

The key question is hence whether nanotechnology already provides empirical evidence for being considered as GPT. There are two main paths tackling the investigation of this question and the correspondingly derived hypotheses. First, focusing on the early stage's productivity loss, macroeconomic measures can be defined to identify the impact of nanotechnology on an economy's development. This approach is strongly output-oriented, since a sufficient number of commercialised products in various application sectors is needed to trace (nanotechnological) assets, R&D investments as well as complementary organisational, social and cultural efforts which may cause productivity slowdowns, while costly restructuring and adjustment of whole parts of the economy take place (Aghion and Howitt 2009). Jovanovic and Rousseau (2005) therefore defined the start of a GPT-era as the point in time when the GPT has achieved a one-percent diffusion in the median sector, e.g. measured by shares of total horsepower generated by the main sources in manufacturing and shares of computer equipment and software in the aggregate capital stock, regarding electricity and ICT respectively. Quite obviously, a considerable amount of time will have to pass, until nanotechnology's core inventions emerge visibly in similar measures (Nikulainen 2007).

The second pathway is to find evidence for the peculiar characteristics of GPTs in nanotechnology. Essentially considering the aforementioned early stage of development this can be done either by looking at R&D expenditures displaying the overall input effort or turning to patents and scientific publications as the resulting output. The R&D approach has a major drawback as well, considering the limited available data on public R&D expenditures (attributable to nanotechnology) due to the lack of common statistical definitions (Palmberg et al. 2009). Private expenditures are even harder to account for. By contrast, patents and publications as indicator – yet, encompassing a number of shortcomings as well – provide an accessible and rather complete insight into the existing output of nanotechnology nearly up to present times. Taking these output indicators and the corresponding citation structures allow insights into the technological links between different inventions (Bresnahan 2010) and hence constitute a basis for investigations of the manifold characteristics of the underlying technological advances (see Chapter 5 for a detailed discussion of these indicators).

Nanotechnology patent and publication data have recently been used in order to identify economic trends in these emerging technologies. Heinze (2004) studied the development of nanotechnology based on publications and patent applications pointing to its worldwide expansion. Hullmann (2007), for instance, examined the state of the art of nanotechnology by analysing data on markets, funding, companies, patents and publications finding that nanotechnology easily has the potential to overtake the traditional biotechnology and even reach the level of the current situation with ICT concerning economic impact. The study by Wong et al. (2007) using USPTO-nanotechnology patents to investigate the evolution of application areas found that the focus formerly was on instrumentation (which is necessary for its development), whereas today more application-based developments dominate the field. Meyer (2007) emphasised the integrating and field-connecting characteristics of instrumentation within nanotechnology. These results again point to the generality of purpose of nanotechnology. Palmberg et al. (2009) gave a detailed overview on the development of nanotechnology, mainly based on indicators using patent and publication data. Their publication data highlight the broad-based and interdisciplinary nature of scientific advances that are conducive to nanotechnology developments. Their findings on nanotechnology patenting include dynamically increasing distribution across a broad range of sub-areas and application fields. This emphasises the multiplicity of applications and a certain generality of purpose. Though not systematically investigating this issue, these lines of research all point to the direction of nanotechnology being an emerging GPT.

There are also studies that directly assess the general purpose technology characteristics of nanotechnology using patent data. First attempts to uncover GPTs alike were made by Hall and Trajtenberg (2006). They suggested measures of GPTs, such as generality, numbers of citations and patent class growth for the patents themselves and for the patents that cite the patents. First attempts to investigate whether nanotechnology might be a GPT were made by Palmberg and Nikulainen (2006). However, they do not apply common indicators or other measures to test their hypotheses systematically. These were explored by Youtie et al. (2008), who tested indicators for generality and highlighted evidence for nanotechnology being as pervasive as GPTs like ICT. Moreover, they developed further indicators for innovation spawning. This finding is confirmed by Graham and Iacopetta (2009), who also tested for these two features. Schultz and Joutz (2010) also assessed this topic, finding that interdisciplinary nanotechnology is quickly expanding, while they discovered a few very general nano-fields with the potential for wide economic impact *and* nano-fields that experience a more focused development path. Most recently, Shea et al. (2011) analysed a sample of USPTO patents of the first 25 'nano-years', looking for early evidence that nanotechnology is a general purpose technology, assessing all three characteristics. Table 6.1 provides a compiliation of the existing studies investigating how a technology – in particular nanotechnology – might be discovered as a GPT, focusing on the indicators that were used for this purpose.

Hence, the literature *suggests* that nanotechnology might be a GPT as it is employed in a wide variety of applications and first approaches to investigate GPT features within nanotechnology *systematically* have been developed. However, these were all based on patent applications and all were investigating USPTO data. In the following chapter it is attempted to further systematise the existing approaches, particularly with respect to the indicators measuring the three GPT features and extending the analyses to publication data. More particularly, although nano-activity has been subject to investigation by the OECD in recent years (Palmberg et al. 2009), to the best of the author's knowledge there have not been any examinations of broadly accepted measures of GPT-characteristics identified in scientific literature within the EU27 yet. This is also done in the following.

In order to tackle the five hypotheses, distinct indicators for the validation of each hypothesis is identified first. The calculation is always based on the nano-patent and nano-publication database introduced in Chapter 5. To be able to compare the absolute values of the indicators for nanotechnology to other technologies, namely a GPT and a non-GPT, calculations of the same indicators were also done for ICT and CE respectively (see Subsections 5.1.3 and 5.2.3 for further details). ICT can be found implemented in almost every industrial sector or consumer product in electronics since semiconductor elements have become extremely important and of general purpose, e.g. in desktop PCs, notebooks, tablet PCs, cell phones, automobiles and many more. Moreover, fast and timely information and communication have become increasingly important, sky-

study	database	indicators and expected outcomes			comparison
		pervasiveness	scope for improvement	innovation spawning	
Palmberg/Nikulainen 2006	-	(i) diffusion of nano-patents across many industries (ii) widening of application fields	accelerating growth of nano-patents	(i) existence of top-down approaches (ii) new start-ups and university spin-offs	biotech
Hall/Trajtenberg 2006	not nano	(i) high generality index (ii) high generality index of citing patents	(i) high within class growth in patenting (ii) high within class citations	(i) growth in citing patent classes (ii) longer citation lags	-
Youtie et al. 2008	1983-2005 USPTO	high generality index		(i)longer citations lags (ii) higher citation counts	drugs, computers
Graham/Iacopetta 2009	1975-2006 USPTO	high generality index	high forward citation rates	knowledge dissemination curves of patent citation patterns	IT, CE
Schultz/Joutz 2010	1978-2008 USPTO	high generality index	qualitative evidence		-
Shea et al. 2011	1971-2004 USPTO	(i) wide spread across 3-digit IPC classes (ii) wide spread across industry sectors (iii)high citation rates outside nanotechnology (iv) high generality index		(i) rapid growth in patenting (ii) increasing share of nano-patents (iii) high citation rates	-

Table 6.1: Overview on different indicators used in studies investigating GPT characteristics.
Source: own compilation.

rocketing the need for high level ICT accordingly. First, computers revolutionised data processing and automation, then personal computers invaded people's lives and eventually the Internet has again changed economies. Combustion engines, by contrast, have the rather specific function of producing mechanic energy by moving a physical component (e.g. pistons) via pressure changes within a combustion chamber. Therefore, this technology lacks the highly generic type of function that is responsible for application in multiple industrial sectors and was argued in Section 3.1 to be the core element of a GPT. Notwithstanding CE constituted a major technological breakthrough and has also been carefully investigated as being a possible GPT by some (Jovanovic and Rousseau 2005, Lipsey et al. 1998), it can still be seen as a regular type of (radical) technological breakthrough, constituting the lower benchmark level for comparative scope. Note the fact that nanotechnology is still an emerging technology and the chosen benchmark technologies ICT and CE are not emerging anymore. However, the time period investigated is the same for all three technologies (i.e. 1980-2008 and not the respective time periods when ICT and CE were still emerging) and in order to test a possibly emerging technology against an existing, stable GPT and a stable non-GPT.

6.3 Analyses and Results

6.3.1 Pervasiveness (H6.1)

For a technology to be(come) pervasive, it has to be widely applicable already at an early stage of its development, thereby using different diffusion channels and strengthening its impact on the whole economy with increasing maturity. Potential pervasiveness should hence become obvious is the technological characteristics of a (future) GPT. Finding evidence for nanotechnology being a future GPT hence includes finding linkages of nanotechnology to a broad variety of different industries and technologies.

There is indeed qualitative evidence for the pervasiveness of nanotechnology. The generality of purpose, stemming from the possibility to rearrange atoms encompassing new properties, particularly creates this potential. Nanotechnology can be processed in arbitrary levels of the value creation chains, but given its potential for the improvement of old processes, materials and products (top-down approach) it is mainly applied at the beginning of a value creation and should therefore tend to exhibit high diffusion rates. The respective technological fields can be entirely different, as nanotechnology can be employed, for instance, in making airplanes lighter without loss of stability, in drug delivery systems or in new generation solar cells. By contrast, bottom-up innovations, i.e. completely new products developed with nanotechnology, are not that present yet.

Diffusion

Nikulainen (2007) found that nanotechnology is linked to a variety of industries, and in particular to industries with higher than average R&D intensity. Examining diffusion rates as one possible indicator of pervasiveness, one might consider the share of nano-patents/publications to total patents/publications in the respective portfolios of the most innovative firms and research institutes, as here diffusion is assumed to be fastest. Therefore, this first quantitative measure exemplarily is applied to the TOP25 firms in the European R&D Investment Scoreboard 2010[6] for patents and to the TOP25 publishing institutions in Europe (as extracted from the WOS) for publications. The TOP25 institutions were chosen to ensure to get the most innovative institutions within the Scoreboard, i.e. the top 2,5%. However, since nanotechnology still is in a nascent phase and not all GPT characteristic can be assumed to be developed yet (even if it will become a GPT eventually), the trend rather than the absolute level is of central interest. It is therefore expected that the diffusion rate increases steeply with tendency towards the one of ICT with proceeding time (and hence maturity of nanotech). The CE level of diffusion rates should thereby serve as lower benchmark.

Figure 6.3 shows the shares of ICT-, CE-, and nano-patents of the Top25 firms in the European R&D Investment Scoreboard 2010 over the past three decades.[7] As the trend indicates, the fraction of ICT-patents in innovative companies shows only a slight increase over the past 20 years.[8] It thus seems that there is a quite constant output rate of new codified knowledge in ICT, so the growth follows a linear pattern. This is not only true for these 25 chosen companies, but for the overall observations of patents as well, as is shown in Subsection 6.3.3. While the share of patents of the non-GPT proxy CE appears constant as well (around 7% percent for the last 20 years), the fraction of nano-patents seems to rise with a remarkable increase setting in about 1997. Nanotechnology inventions thus appear to gain in importance regarding their proportion of R&D-output. But even in the observed companies with higher than average R&D intensity nanotechnology is still far away from outmatching the share of countable results in CE related research, not to mention the comparison to ICT. Nevertheless, the trend

[6]'The 2010 EU Industrial R&D Investment Scoreboard', released in October 2010, presented information on the top 1000 EU companies and 1000 non-EU companies investing in R&D in 2009. (...) The data for the Scoreboard are taken from the companies' latest published accounts, i.e. the 2009 fiscal year accounts and indicate the R&D invested by companies' own funds, independently of the location of the R&D activity.' (see http://iri.jrc.es/research/scoreboard_2010.htm).

[7]Taking into account the fact that not every of those firms has attributable R&D-Output at the beginning of the observation period, the data is clearly biased. Nonetheless, the shown trends seem to be robust when reducing the sample to the firms for which patents can be found within the whole panel.

[8]It is worth noting that interpreting patent developments demands caution regarding the last years, since patent filing and publishing takes its time. Data collection was therefore stopped 2008 (with a database ranging till September 2010) due to this lag.

points to a realignment of research activities with a considerably strong effort on nanotechnology.

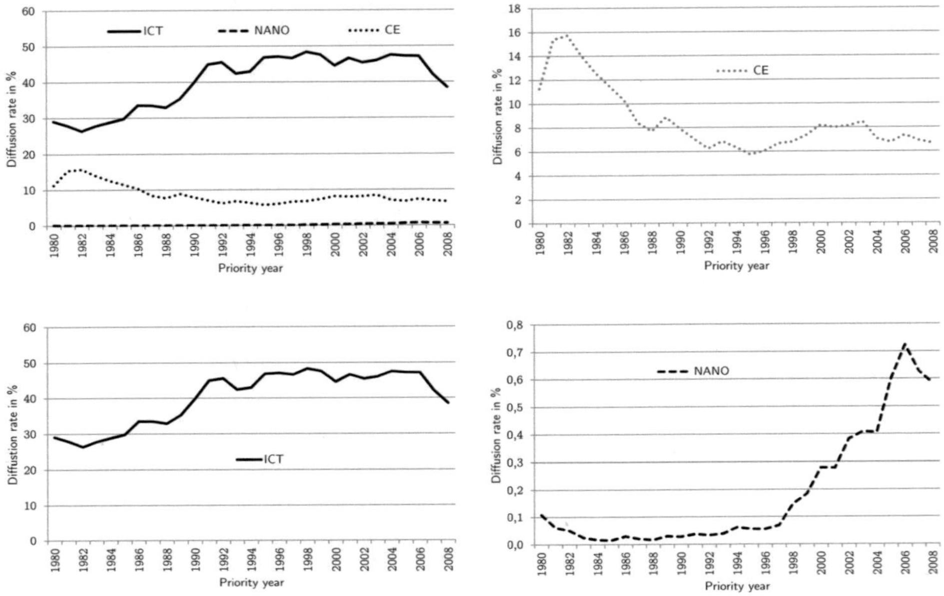

Figure 6.3: Diffusion rates based upon patents of Top25 firms' R&D.
Source: PATSTAT, own searches and calculations.

Scientific publications, though, are often associated with the more fundamental research, and nanotechnology evidences this quite clearly, as Figure 6.4 depicts: While patent diffusion rates for the Top25-sample in patenting do not nearly conquer either ICT or CE, shares of nano-related scientific literature around 6.5% can be observed within total publications of the Top25 publishing institutions worldwide, with an unbowed trend pointing to further growth in years to come. ICT shares of these publications linger around 3%, with only a 1% increase in two decades. Hence ICT in general reveals a focus on applied research (as marked by patents), while nanotechnology is still primarily a matter of the scientific debate. This is what could have been expected due to the still largely nascent stage of nanotechnology in general. Moreover, this is almost the same for the whole sample, as becomes obvious in Subsection 6.3.3.

With regard to these results measuring the pervasiveness of nanotechnology, a strong and intensifying concentration concerning efforts of highly innovative firms and the leading scientific institutions (chosen on the basis of high expenditures on R&D and publishing output respectively) was expected. Although the pervasive character of nanotechnology based upon the proposition of Nikulainen (2007) is not to be seen in patents yet, it is already visible within publications – arguably the upstream complement to patents. After all, there is no reason to doubt that the pervasive character obvious within publications can be observed in their technological (and downstream and hence later) counterparts patents soon, since the growth of nanotechnology in both indicators shows the anticipated courses without any signs of weakening.

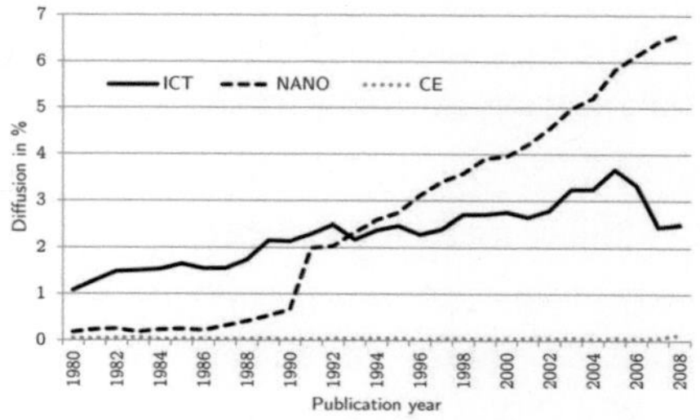

Figure 6.4: Diffusion rates based upon publications of Top25 publishing institutions. Source: WOS, own search and calculations.

Generality

Already within their seminal paper, Bresnahan and Trajtenberg (1995) pointed to the possibility of identifying valuable inventions by patents that are cited by a wide range of different industries. To measure this, Trajtenberg et al. (1997) employed the Hirschman-Herfindahl index which was further developed by Moser and Nicholas (2004) and Hall and Trajtenberg (2004) as generality index G_i,

$$G_i = 1 - \sum_{j}^{n_i} s_{ij}^2, \quad G_i \in [0,1] \tag{6.1}$$

where s_{ij} denotes the percentage of citations received by patent i assigned to patent class j, out of n_i technological classes. Thus, if the knowledge of an invention benefited subsequent inventions in a wide range of technological fields, this measure will be close to one, whereas if most citations are concentrated in a few fields it will be close to zero. This measure is not only useful with respect to patents and the corresponding IPC classes on different levels, but can also be computed across technological fields in concordance to the ISIC system. Hence, the underlying classes n_i can consist of n-digit patent IPC class or classifications by main technological fields (e.g. following the NACE/ISIC Concordance developed by Schmoch et al. (2003), see Subsection 5.1.2). This index is not even restricted to patents. As publications display the output of the public research system and hence the scientific ideas and inventions, publication data and a corresponding classification system (such as the Subject Areas (SAs) in Thomson ISI Web of Science) can be used similarly. Yet, an only small forward time window in the field of new and emerging technologies poses difficulties in calculating sensible Generality indices, and hence s_{ij} is biased downwards as not all the citations are yet observed, which constitutes a 'lag' effect. Correcting this bias is possible e.g. by using

$$\widetilde{G}_i = \frac{N_i}{N_i - 1} G_i, \quad \widetilde{G}_i \in [0,1] \tag{6.2}$$

with $N_i =$ being number of citations observed (Hall 2002). This indicator, $\widetilde{G}_i$, is hence calculated for nano-patents with respect to IPC classes and technological fields as well as for nano-publications and subject areas for forward in order to test whether nanotechnological inventions exhibit the feature of pervasiveness. This is then compared to the respective ICT and CE values. Due to resource constraints, only Top10 cited patents are included. Hall and Trajtenberg (2006) argued that distribution of patent importance is highly skewed and only very few are highly important, a characteristic that is commonly accepted to reflect in patent citations. True GPT patents should be among those patents, and hence the Top10 patents are chose as the tail of this skew distribution here. K30, i.e. the allocation of IPC classes into the concordance of 30 technological fields was chosen because less distinguishable classes reflect higher generality if a patent scores high. This is the case because fewer classes provide a higher accuracy of discrimination between pervasive technologies and those of which the citation structure refers to a more limited number of fields.

Figure 6.5 shows the yearly average forward generality indices of the Top10 cited patents of each year according to the K30 technology classification (see Table B.1 in the Appendix for the IPC Concordance).[9] The average generality values of the lower benchmark CE are almost everywhere considerably smaller than those of ICT and nanotechnology, as was expected.[10] To clarify the interwoven curves of nanotechnology and ICT a Hodrick-Prescott filter was employed ($\lambda = 100$ for yearly data) on the right hand side (see Figure 6.5). The separation of the cyclical component with respect to time allows a disconnected view of the data at hand and the levels of ICT, nanotechnology and CE respectively become more distinguishable (at the cost of a cyclical outcome that is at least arguable). Anyhow, by concentrating on the pure levels now ICT's generality is

[9]Note that for the CE values were calculated for 5-year-intervals only since the employed amount of data was intended to be kept at a reasonable level. All other values are interpolated. However, there is no reason to expect robustness problems by extending the data set.

[10]Note again, that the last around 4-5 years within the observation period are not to be overrated, now even more in the context of forward citations that underlie this measure.

visibly above the one of nanotechnology, indicating the grown pervasive character of the upper benchmark is yet to be reached. This interpretation has to be taken with caution, since for many years in the sample, nanotechnology's average generality is clearly exceeding the one of ICT and the t-test results also do not indicate a significant difference between the two technology's generality values (see Table 6.2). A significant difference can only be found for the generality values of CE against both groups of ICT and nanotechnology (see Table 6.2). The t-tests indicate that nanotechnology outperforms the non-GPT by far in terms of forward generality and does not show any significant difference between nano and ICT. Hence, although the t-tests do not account for the trend but compare the means of the generality values (and hence neglects the fact that nanotechnology is still an emerging technology), nano can be regarded similarly general as ICT. The fact that the t-tests do disclose any significant difference between European and worldwide generality values and hence the regional comparison does not reveal any contradiction only supports this fact.

A more sophisticated measure which allows for more distinctive scores that qualitatively account for the perceived cognitive distance between the fields is desirable though, which is why the technological coherence indicator is employed in the next subsection.[11]

	Obs	Mean	StdDev	ICT	CE	EU27[1]
			WORLD			
NANO K30	29	0.5339	0.1144	-0.0403	3.7965***	-0.9671
ICT K30	29	0.5351	0.1109		3.9159***	-0.3279
CE K30	29	0.3482	0.1241			-0.1561
			EU27			
NANO K30	29	0.5353	0.1145	-0.2821	6.7428***	
ICT K30	29	0.5425	0.0754		8.7179***	
CE K30	29	0.3539	0.0888			

Table 6.2: t-Tests (unpaired) of forward average generalities for ICT-, Nano- and CE-patents in the world and in EU27 over time.
[1] Paired t-Tests between WORLD and EU group values.
***Indicates significance at 0.01.
Source: own calculations.

Technological Coherence

Hall and Trajtenberg (2006) confined the extent of the validity of the generality measure they introduced, since they suffer from the fact that every pair of technologies is

[11] Results of the publication generalities are not discussed here since they offer no additional information. Moreover, classification within Thomson ISI subject areas is subject to minor objectivity, which results in hardly distinguishable average generality indices (see Figure C.2 in the Appendix).

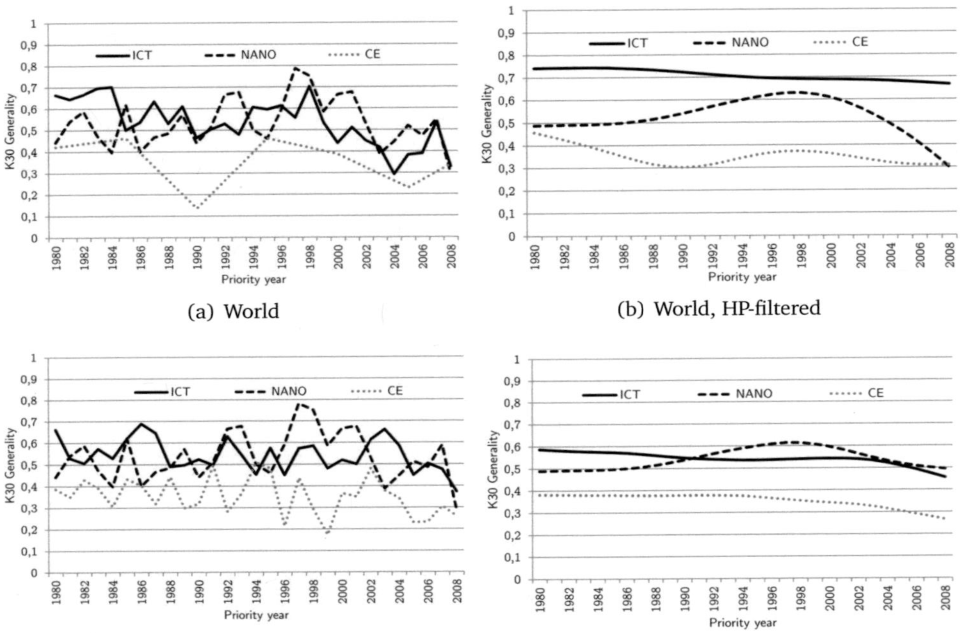

(a) World

(b) World, HP-filtered

(c) EU27

(d) EU27, HP-filtered

Figure 6.5: Forward average generalities of Top10 cited patents p.a. (K30).
Source: PATSTAT, own search and calculations.

treated as equally 'distant' or 'similar' once they are in different technological classes. This assumption is not as close to reality as it should be with the result of possible over- or underestimations of the generality value. They propose the introduction of a weighted generality measure. For this scope, the measure of technological coherence shall be introduced.[12] Technological coherence, in this context, is defined as the extent to which inventions (i.e. patents) in a technological area share the same underlying knowledge, i.e. the extent to which the technological underpinnings of the patents are similar. This technological coherence can reasonably be assumed to be higher the more specialised a technological field is. New inventions in a highly specialised technological field are expected to be somewhat more *coherent* than are inventions in the field of a general purpose technology. By definition, GPT related inventions can be found in a wide range of application fields and therefore the technological coherence of these inventions can be expected to be considerably smaller. Technological coherence has already been used and calculated in other contexts, for instance in studies examining the role of spillovers, diversity and related variety by using patent data. However, it has

[12]However, this is not a direct advancement of the generality measure since it does not rely on the Herfindahl index.

never been used to identify or measure GPTs. It is hence be employed for the first time in this context.

To calculate the relatedness of a patent portfolio a measure of the degree of relatedness has to be determined for each pair of technology classes. Commonly, as e.g. done by Breschi et al. (2003) and Leten et al. (2007), this measure is constructed using co-occurences of technological classes that are associated (directly or via citations) to a patent. This measure is not recalculated, but the technology relatedness matrix constructed by Leten et al. (2007) is used instead.[13] Following their approach, two technology classes are considered as technologically related if patents associated to one technology class often cite patents classified in the other technology class and vice versa.

The technological relatedness matrix (see Table C.1) is hence used to calculate the technological coherence of (i) nano-patents applied for within one year and (ii) forward citations of nano-patents, again within one year. These shall display how the technology itself is developed by different fields and how it is applied. Benchmark values are calculated for CE and ICT patents. Coherence is then defined as the average technological relatedness of all technologies associated to the patents, weighted by the patent counts. Therefore, the weighted average relatedness COH_i of technology i to all other technologies relevant in the considered year is calculated for each technology, displaying

$$COH_i = \frac{\sum_{i \neq j} R_{ij} \times P_j}{\sum_{i \neq j} P_j} \tag{6.3}$$

where P_j is the patent count weight.[14] The overall coherence measure of nanotechnology patents by year is then calculated as the weighted average of all the COH_i measures:

$$COH = \frac{\sum_i P_i \times COH_i}{\sum_i P_i}, \quad COH \in [0;\infty) \tag{6.4}$$

With the technological coherence, the measurement of the extent to which patents in a technological area share the same underlying knowledge is put into focus. The more

[13] The measures are based on EPO and USPTO cited patens by EPO patents applied for between 1990 and 2003 and granted before 06/2005. Concerning the technological classes the OST/INPI/ISI concordance is used, developed by Hinze et al. (1997). Since the time period as well as the patent authorities of the patents to calculate this matrix were filed at are also covered by the nano-patent database all further calculation rely on, the use of the matrix for the purposes of this thesis is justifiable. For a more detailed description on how this measure is constructed see Leten et al. (2007) or the Appendix C.1.

[14] See the Appendix C.1 for the derivation of R_{ij}.

specialised a technology is, the higher should be its technological coherence since it reflects the relatedness of the technological classes a patent is classified in (or cited by). The coherence measure for nanotechnology as an emerging GPT was therefore expected to be lower than for the non-GPT CE. Figure 6.6 shows that this is indeed the case. The GPT-proxy ICT and nanotechnology shape a narrow side-by-side course with visible distance to the CE coherence values. To verify the significance of this offset, a two sample location t-test was performed (see Table 6.3). The results are robust across the EU27 as well as the WORLD sample and also when taking the technology classes of citing patents instead of the cited patents technology classes themselves (see right hand side of the Figure).

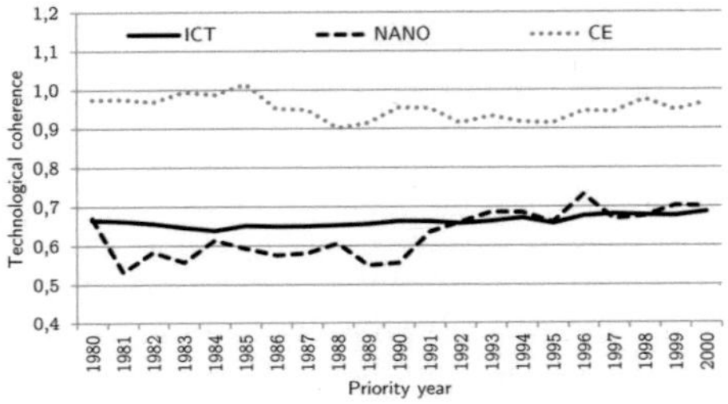

(a) World, patent applications

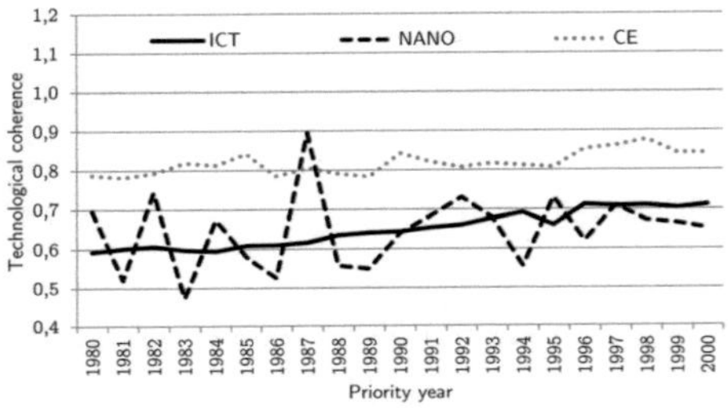

(b) World, forward citations

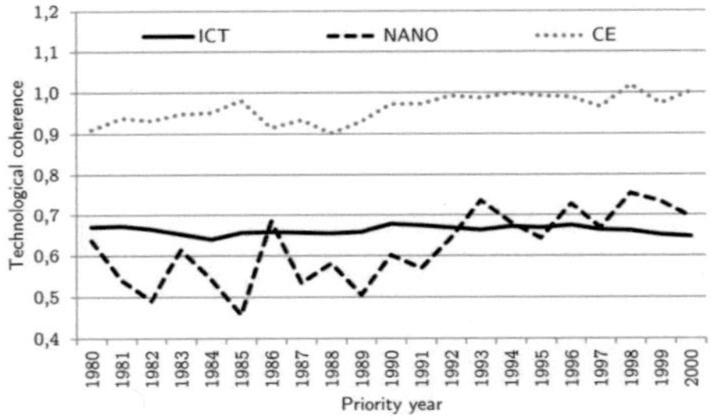

(c) EU27, patent applications

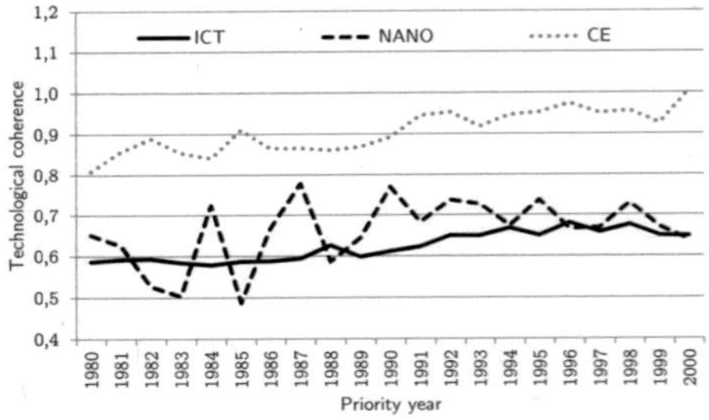

(d) EU27, forward citations

Figure 6.6: Technological coherence of ICT-, Nano- and CE-patents p.a..
Source: PATSTAT, own search and calculations.

Hence, with this new measure it becomes clear that pervasiveness is undoubtedly much stronger for the ICT and the GPT-candidate nanotechnology. Both show a visible distance to the lower benchmark technology CE, ICT with a smoother line due to the clearer basis in the categorisation system, nanotechnology with soft swings around an *almost* stationary level. This is visible in the results of the t-tests as well: Nano and ICT seem to be pretty similar in terms of technological coherence when compared to CE:

	Obs	Mean	StdDev	ICT	CE	EU27[1]
			WORLD			
NANO	21	0.6305	0.0595	-2.4374**	-22.0292***	0.8630
ICT	21	0.6628	0.0131		-39.9758***	0.4385
CE	21	0.9514	0.0304			-1.0831
NANO fw	21	0.6624	0.0811	-0.1871	-7.9591***	-0.9516
ICT fw	21	0.6490	0.0435		-14.9552***	7.5255***
CE fw	21	0.9067	0.0512			-10.4017***
			EU27			
NANO	21	0.6200	0.0871	-2.1688**	-16.8209***	
ICT	21	0.6614	0.0096		-39.7650***	
CE	21	0.9619	0.0333			
NANO fw	21	0.6448	0.0955	1.9996*	-11.6696***	
ICT fw	21	0.6239	0.0351		-20.8685***	
CE fw	21	0.8177	0.0279			

Table 6.3: t-Tests (unpaired) of coherences of ICT-, Nano- and CE-patents and forward citing patents over time.
[1] Paired t-Tests between WORLD and EU group values.
***Indicates significance at 0.01.
Source: own calculations.

They exhibit statistically significantly lower values of technological coherence across all different samples and indicators (see Table 6.3). In pairwise comparison, the set of nano patents is even a little bit less coherent (significant on the 10% level) than the ICT patents. These results are less clear when considering the set of forward citations. Yet, a slight increase in coherence of nanotechnology might be found after 1990, the starting point of a significant rise in the number of nanotechnology patents, possibly due to a related small gain in concentration among technology classes. The comparison of the WORLD sample against the EU27 again does not disclose any difference for the patents themselves. However, the coherences of the forward citations of ICT and CE are significantly lower in the EU27 than in the world. Since this does impact the described relationship within the EU27 this is, finally, not a contradiction to the general support for nanotechnology being similarly general as ICT. All in all, technological relatedness seems to keep the promise of adding valuable information to current pervasiveness measures.

After all, the above derived results show that nanotechnology indeed exhibits a level of pervasiveness that exceeds or at least levels the one of the non-GPT CEs. From the upper benchmark's ICT view, nanotechnology values are getting close(r). Generally spoken, the above findings hence support hypothesis 6.1, at least in terms of a trend towards the level of the ICT-benchmark: Nanotechnology develops with (increasing) pervasiveness.

6.3.2 Scope for Improvement (H6.2)

In nanotechnology the vast potential to further reduce cost, size or, e.g. improve other characteristics of nano-enhanced material, such as the increase of stability of nanomaterial is given at present. This displays the large scope for improvement.

Increase of Nano-Inventions

A very simple measure of scope for improvement was suggested by Palmberg and Nikulainen (2006) in form of accelerating growth of nano-inventions. Thereby, the pure number of patents was observed and an accelerating growth pattern shaping nanotechnology's development over recent years was expected. Figure 6.7 illustrates this course strikingly. The number of nano-patents evolves noticeably, though it is still far from reaching that of CE (not to mention ICT), a result strongly related to the contemporaneous lack of countable applications for the emerging technical feasibilities.[15]

As already found for diffusion rates, publications again underscore the fundamental theoretical work that has been done for nanotechnology in the past two decades. With the pure numbers of publications surpassing those of ICT around the year 2000, nanotechnology has clearly become an object of scientific interest of the new century. Although, as Schmoch et al. (2012) remarked, publication count data shall not be taken for trend analyses because of the increasing coverage of the WOS and the resulting artificial growth of publications, this indicator might be used when comparing technologies, since they all are subject to the database enlargement. Hence, although growth effects might be partly due to database extension, nanotechnology still outperforms CE and even ICT, on what level whatsoever. Its scope for on-going improvement is unbowed. Considering scientific as well as crescent public excitement related to the countless technological possibilities, there is no reason to expect any attenuation within the next years. One can only guess how many of those theoretical technological advancements might transfer into applicable results manifested in patents soon.

Forward Citation Rates

In order to be characterised as GPT, a technology must undergo continual technological improvements. Schultz and Joutz (2010) proposed later work citing the original invention as an indicator for this development. Following hypothesis 6.2, nano-patents are hence expected to have many citations indicating a pattern of cumulative innovation (Hall and Trajtenberg 2006), an expectation which can easily be transferred to

[15]Again, the last few years within the observation period are not to be overrated.

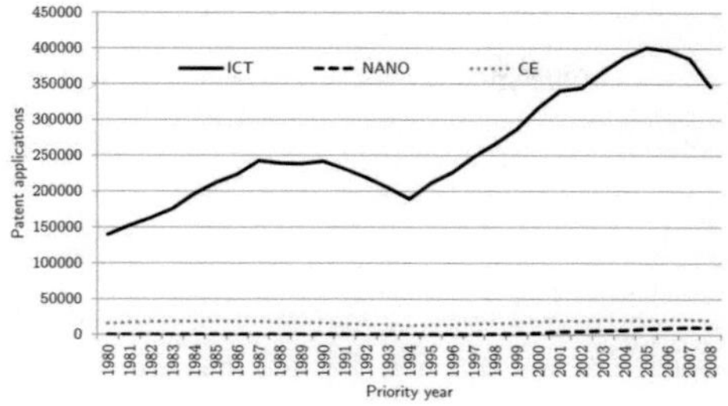

(a) World

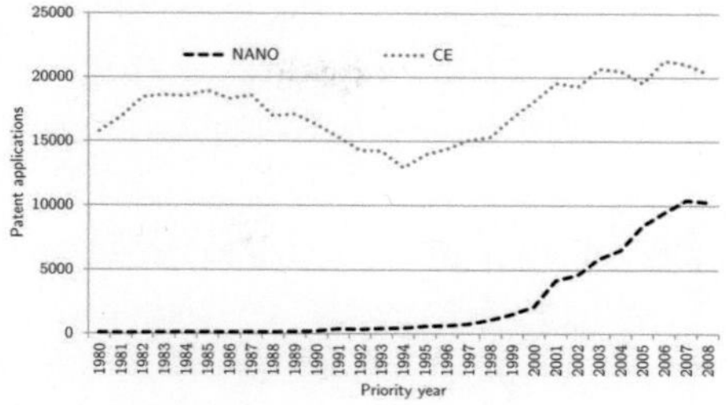

(b) World, comparison Nano to CE

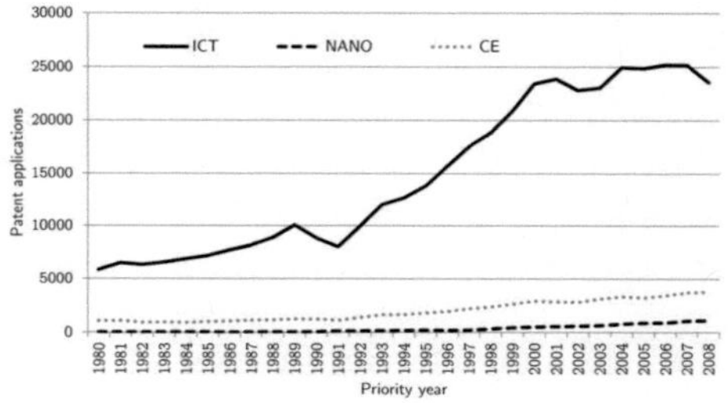

(c) EU27

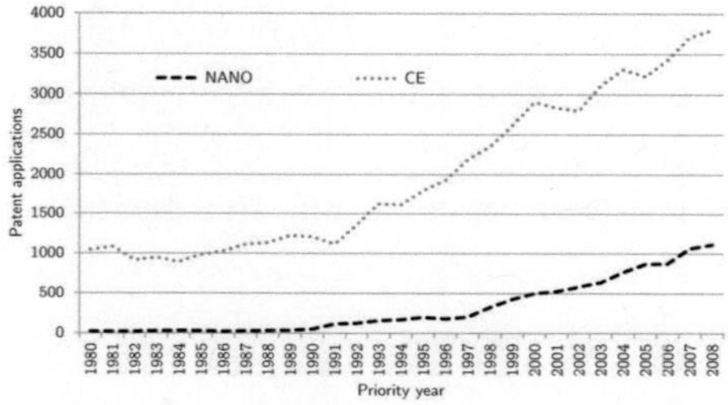

(d) EU27, comparison Nano to CE

Figure 6.7: Numbers of ICT-, Nano-, and CE-patents p.a..
Source: PATSTAT, own search and calculations.

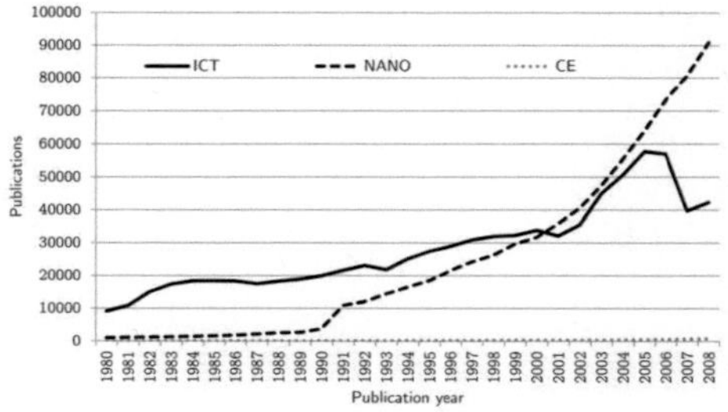

(a) World

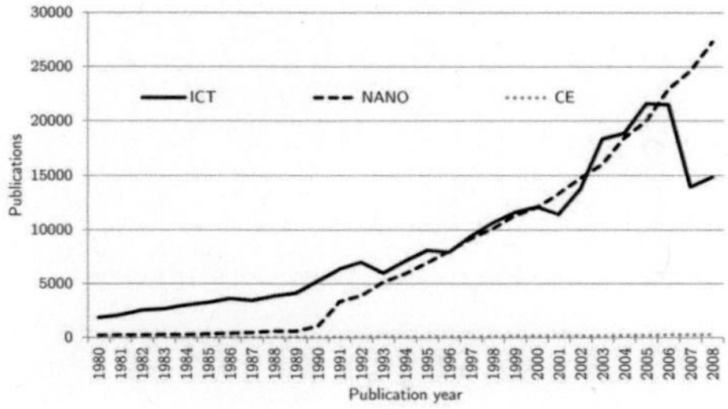

(b) EU27

Figure 6.8: Numbers of ICT-, Nano-, and CE-publications p.a.
Source: WOS, own search and calculations.

publications. Hence, citation rates for nano-patents as well as nano-publications are computed. Citation rates are expected to be between those of ICT and those of combustion engines. However, the trend is again considered relevant since nanotechnology as emerging technology is still at the beginning of its development process. Moreover, citation rates are anticipated to increase and develop into the direction of ICT citation rates.

In fact, nanotechnology was found to produce patent citation rates even above those of ICT as Figure 6.9 reveals. For nanotechnology a small absolute number of core patents produce comparably large numbers of references. And these core technology founding patents seem to stem from outside Europe, since the nano-patents found in the European Union have considerably smaller citation rates (see Figure 6.9(b)). Publications should not be affected that much by borderlines, and as expected European publications show high nanotechnology-related citation rates again.[16] This indicates that the continuing technological improvements associated with nanotechnology are even more impressive than expected. The significance of these findings is supported by the t-tests performed between the different technologies' citation rates which can be found in Tables 6.4 and 6.5.

H6.2 can hence be confirmed in general means: Nanotechnology is a technology offering a large scope for improvement. Although the absolute numbers in overall nanotechnology patenting are unexpectedly low compared to ICT and CE, the steep increase in nanotechnology-patents and hence the trend indicates the large potential of nanotechnology, particularly as emerging technology. This trend is also supported by the strong numbers in nano-publications. Also, the results for the forward citation measures outperforming ICT and CE similarly support the hypothesis.

[16] As pointed out in Section 6.2, available data is restricted to European publications for this citation measure, which does not affect the interpretation here anyway. For worldwide publications similar citation rates should be expectable.

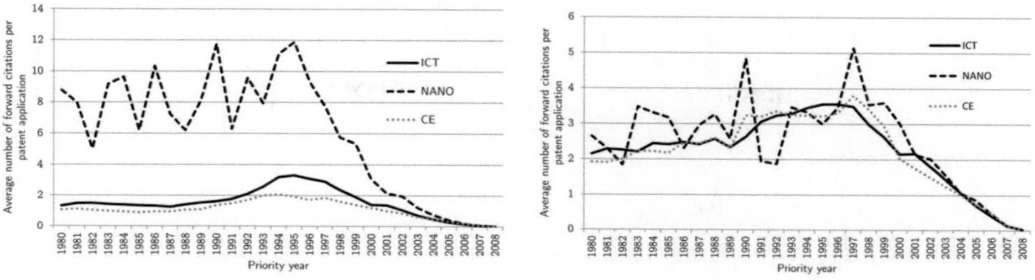

(a) World (b) EU27

Figure 6.9: Forward citation rates of patents p.a..
Source: PATSTAT, own search and calculations.

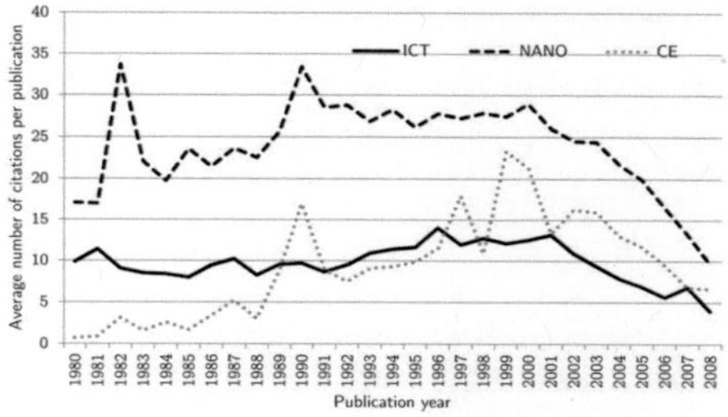

Figure 6.10: Forward citation rates of publications in the EU27.
Source: WOS, own search and calculations.

	Obs	Mean	StdDev	ICT	CE	EU27[1]
			WORLD			
NANO	29	6.0445	3.8381	6.1676***	6.8659***	6.2011***
ICT	29	1.5283	0.9045		2.1711**	-11.5856***
CE	29	1.0983	0.5651			-11.2240***
			EU27			
NANO	29	2.5303	1.2504	0.9271	1.0510	
ICT	29	2.2552	0.9957		0.1564	
CE	29	2.2135	1.0357			

Table 6.4: t-Tests (unpaired) of forward citation rates of ICT-, Nano- and CE-patents in the World and in EU27 over time.
[1] Paired t-tests between WORLD and EU group values.
***Indicates significance at 0.01.
Source: own calculations.

	Obs	Mean	StdDev	ICT	CE
NANO	29	23.9221	5.5554	12.6820***	9.4701***
ICT	29	9.7372	2.3275		0.3342
CE	29	9.3283	6.1649		

Table 6.5: t-Tests (unpaired) of forward citation rates of ICT-, Nano- and CE-publications in the World over time.
***Indicates significance at 0.01.
Source: own calculations.

6.3.3 Innovation Spawning (H6.3)

The last of the three necessary features of a GPT is tested with Hypothesis 6.3, stating that innovations which build on nanotechnology will themselves spawn many new innovations.

In the field of nanotechnology innovation spawning could be found in the existence of nano-enhanced value creation chains, consisting of initial, intermediate, and downstream innovations. Carbon nanotubes, embodied in nano-enhanced coatings and finally employed in a variety of final products, such as airplanes, nano-enhanced clothes, self-cleaning windows, oxidising organic matter, rotor blades or electronic displays can be identified as such (Lux Research 2006, Youtie et al. 2008). In combination with technological dynamism, this characteristic is the main driver of innovational complementarities (see H6.4).

Dynamism of Nano-Invention Activity

The dynamism that goes beyond the pure increase of nano-inventions constitutes a meaningful indicator: An increasing share of nano-inventions can be used as an indicator for the innovation spawning characteristic of nanotechnology, as well as the mere volume of citations to inventions (nano/non-nano) might serve as an indicator evidencing nano to be a GPT (Shea et al. 2011, Hall and Trajtenberg 2006).

For the most part, trends for the diffusion rate of nano-, ICT-, and CE- patents worldwide as displayed in Figure 6.11 are similar to the Top25 firm sample (see Figure 6.3). The share of CE patents appears to decrease below 1.5% in recent years, at least for world data (by contrast, an almost constant share for the Top25 firm sample around the last 20 years was found). On the other hand, ICT-patents made up the majority of patents within R&D intensive firms with up to almost 50% for two decades. Although worldwide shares constitute a 20% smaller ICT-patent share, this ratio has been quite constant for this 20 year period as well. Again, this does not hold for Europe: For ICT and CE likewise, there is a positive trend indicating strong research efforts on catching up with Silicon Valley for ICT and gaining supremacy for CE respectively.

Nano-patents evolved the same way it was observed for the firm sample, which might seem surprising: The shares within the Top25 firm sample could have been expected to outweigh those of all patents. Nonetheless, while it was constituted that pervasiveness with respect to diffusion measures was not to be seen yet (since nanotechnology is still far away from outmatching the share of CE patents), the growth pattern anyhow indicates the high innovation spurring character of a GPT. As argued before, a remarkable increase of the nano-patent proportion statistics can be observed. This manifests the gains in importance regarding R&D-efforts into this new technology. For nascent, emerging drastic technological advancements such as nanotechnology as potential GPT, with most of the research efforts made in basic research, these efforts are naturally much more apparent in publications, where nano-related scientific output has already surpassed that of ICT, as Figure 6.12 depicts.

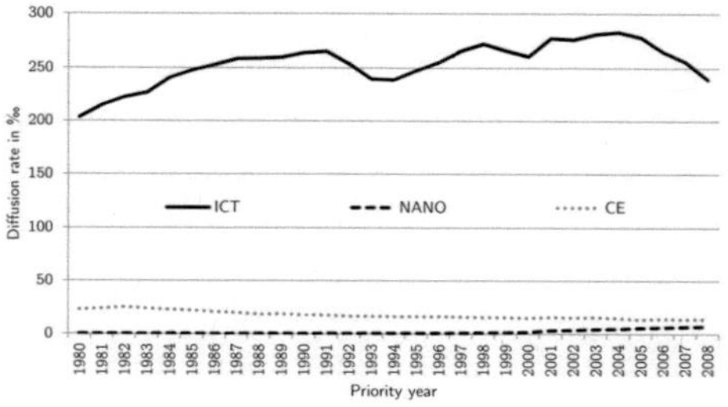

(a) World

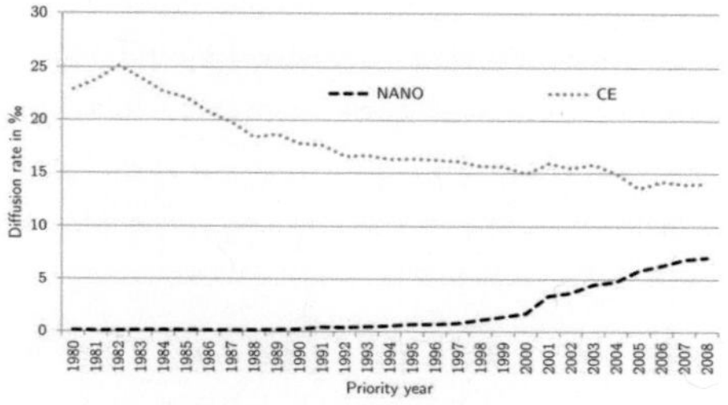

(b) World, comparison Nano to CE

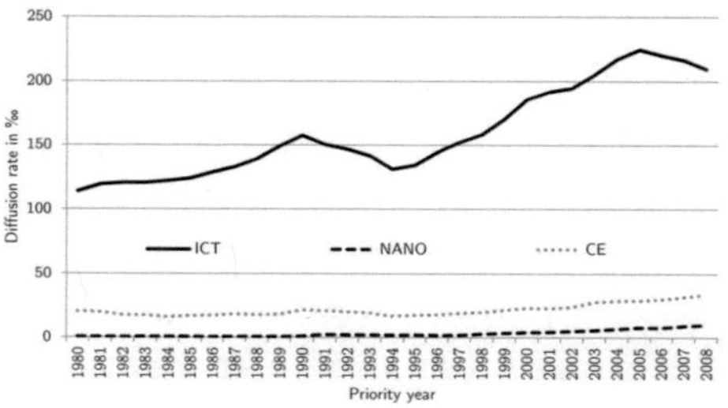

(c) EU27

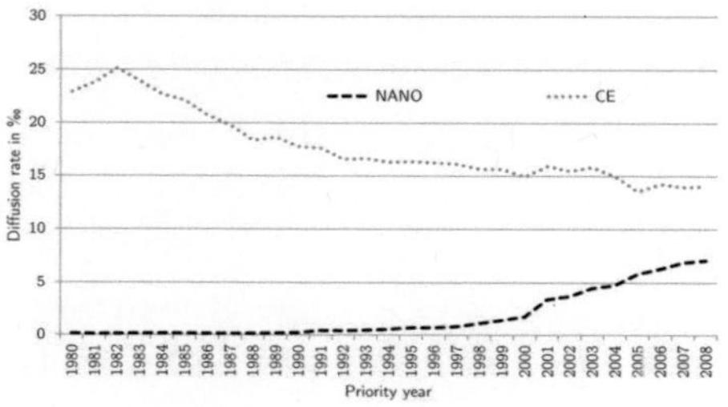

(d) EU27, comparison Nano to CE

Figure 6.11: Diffusion rates of ICT-, Nano-, and CE-patents p.a..
Source: PATSTAT, own search and calculations.

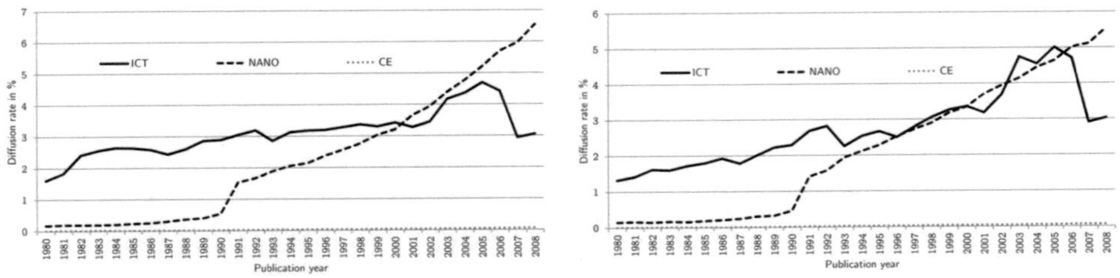

(a) World (b) EU27

Figure 6.12: Diffusion rates of ICT-, Nano-, and CE-publications p.a.
Source: own calculations.

Growth in Citing Technological Classes

If H6.3 can be supported, nano-patents-citing technologies could be subject to a burst of innovations because complementary goods are developed (Hall and Trajtenberg 2006). A proxy for innovation spawning can hence also be the growth of the technological classes that cite such a technology as was proposed by Hall and Trajtenberg (2006). When nano-innovations are indeed spurring innovations, a way to see this in the data could be to investigate the growth of the technological classes that cite nanotechnology, assuming that innovations that refer to nanotechnology are increasing in numbers. Therefore, nanotechnology patents and publications should show high citing technological class growth.

Technological classes (or subject areas, referring to publications) that harbour nano-citing patents were expected to show an above average growth. The top ten citing classes were chosen according to their numbers of references. Similarly, the top ten subject areas were identified according to a score system that accounts for the Top25 cited publications and the occurrence of their citations in these different subject areas.[17] In the resulting development diagram 6.13 the time before 1988 is cut, since just a few classes in the beginning of the evolution of nanotechnology were observable, of which excessive average growth would lead to the false impression that nanotechnology's trend was decreasing. Values later than 2002 were cut as well, since with declining overall citation rates (remember Figure 6.9) the average class growth becomes much less conclusive. Especially in highly complex technological areas (including unde-

[17] No European data was collected for this measure, since the immediate question arises how this categorisation could be implemented. Restricting the underlying cited patents to European ones would incorporate citations from everywhere, which would invoke a misleading interpretation of the outcome, as would covering only European citations for worldwide patents instead. Finally, employing European patents with European citations does not yield any additional information of particular value, and even if so, is out of all proportion to collecting the underlying additional data.

niably the three technologies compared, i.e. ICT, nano and CE) citations and therefore continual advancements take their time. So while not willing to conceal an observed below average class growth for all of these three technologies after 2002, one has to point out that the choice of classes is biased through the declining observable citations. Thus with time, other classes might become more meaningful as predictor for an above average class growth. Reselection of classes every year would lead to incomparability though, which is why being careful in interpreting the years after around 2000 is mostly without alternative.

For the observation period left, nano and ICT both prove to be outstanding in their innovation spawning character. Almost without exception (1997 nano, 1993 ICT) citing class growth is found to be above average. The results of the performed t-tests, however, indicate that only ICT values are significantly above average (see Table 6.6). Admittedly, the lower benchmark CE does not perform too bad for this indicator either (however, again, not significantly different from the average), which is not surprising however: Though CE is not considered as GPT here, its ability to spawn innovation within a less pervasive set of technological classes is unquestionable. Finally, regarding publications as supporting indicator, the results are pretty similar – which can be seen in Table 6.7: While ICT displays significant above average values for this indicator, the other technologies perform fairly like the average.[18]

In overall terms, nanotechnology can hence be seen as technology inducing as many innovations as should be expected from a GPT. The medium support of patenting diffusion and the strong support of publications diffusion outweigh the missing support from the citing class growth indicator – or at least clearly prevent a rejection of H6.3.

[18]However, a straightforward explanation for the significantly above average unweighted CE values is yet to be found, but one might guess that the method chosen to select the top subject areas (with the above mentioned score system) could be responsible for that outcome.

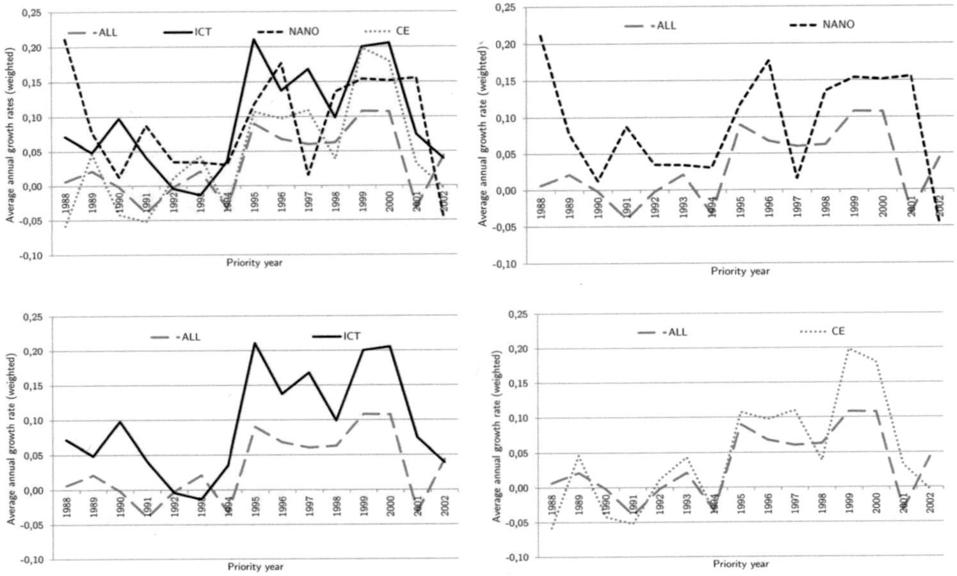

Figure 6.13: Average annual growth rates (weighted) of top citing classes, ICT-, Nano- and CE-patents in the world.
Source: PATSTAT, own search and calculations.

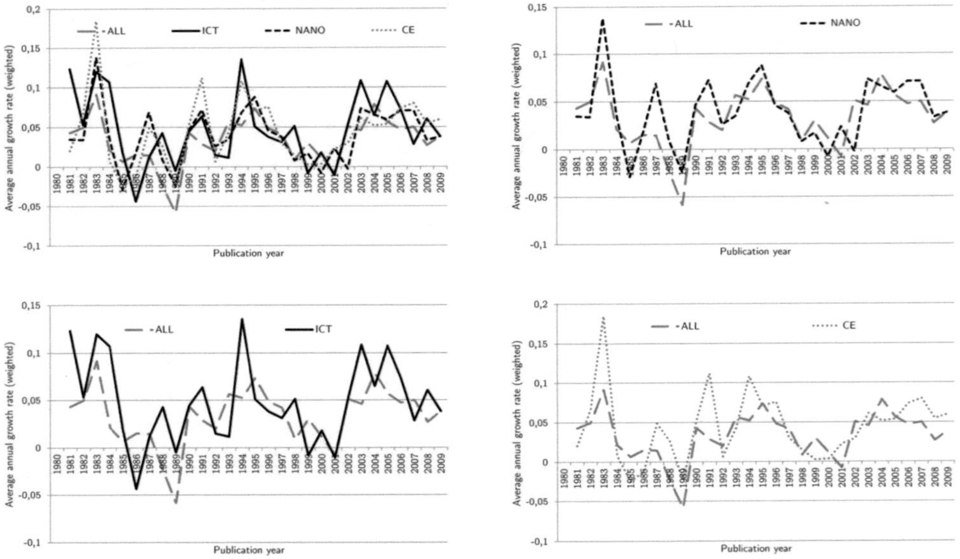

Figure 6.14: Average annual growth rates (weighted) of top citing subject areas, ICT-, Nano- and CE-publications in the world.
Source: WOS, own search and calculations.

	Obs	Mean	StdDev	ICT	CE	ALL[1]
ALL	28	0.0207	0.0587			
NANO	28	0.1011	0.2818	0.7634	1.3519	1.5593
ICT	28	0.0571	0.1153		1.1243	2.3013**
CE	28	0.0246	0.1005			0.2918
NANO w	28	0.0832	0.2292	0.6424	1.5860	1.5186
ICT w	28	0.0525	0.1070		1.6071	2.1767**
CE w	28	0.0086	0.0973			-0.8766

Table 6.6: t-Tests (unpaired) of average within class growth rates of ICT-, Nano- and CE-patents' citation's technology classes, unweighted and weighted (w).
[1] Paired t-tests between NANO, ICT, CE and ALL, respectively.
***Indicates significance at 0.01.
Source: own calculations.

	Obs	Mean	StdDev	ICT	CE	ALL[1]
ALL	28	0.0332	0.0313			
NANO	28	0.0400	0.0364	-0.5677	-0.5318	1.3604
ICT	28	0.0461	0.0433		0.0307	1.7682*
CE	28	0.0457	0.0437			2.0139*
NANO w	28	0.0404	0.0363	-0.7189	-0.3311	1.449
ICT w	28	0.0482	0.0451		0.3598	1.9729*
CE w	28	0.0439	0.0441			1.7012

Table 6.7: t-Tests (unpaired) of within class growth of ICT-, Nano- and CE-publications' citation's subject areas, unweighted and weighted (w).
[1] Paired t-tests between NANO, ICT, CE and ALL, respectively.
***Indicates significance at 0.01.
Source: own calculations.

6.3.4 Innovational Complementarities (H6.4)

H6.4 refers to a GPT's innovational complementarities and the mutual inducement processes that Bresnahan and Trajtenberg modelled in 1995. They introduced two distinct externalities, a vertical one between the fundamental research sector and various application sectors, and a horizontal one across application sectors (Bresnahan and Trajtenberg 1995). The vertical one follows from innovational complementarities while the horizontal one is an immediate consequence of generality of purpose (Bresnahan and Trajtenberg 1995, p. 94). Innovational complementarities can indeed be found anecdotic evidence for in nanotechnology. Electronic microscopy first made research on and progress with nanotechnology possible and is now an application sector of nanotechnology itself (Palmberg and Nikulainen 2006, Youtie et al. 2008): Nano-components are applied to augment the visibility of nano-scale effects based on digitally constructed pictures, relying on the use of such microscopes and hence the inherent computers. The storing capacity of computers doubled every one and a half years (known as 'Moore's Law'). This reaches its physical boundaries when the laws of solid state physics do no longer hold. At this point, nanotechnology can enhance and still miniaturise the storing chips using the laws of quantum physics. Consequently, technological progress in nanotechnology is a precondition for future innovations in micro technology, itself triggering innovations in nanotechnology (Geng and Zhou 2005, Ott et al. 2009). Empirically, this relationship is attempted to become detected in the data as well.

Innovational complementarities are a result of innovation spawning and the technological dynamism inherent in GPTs. Yet, since they constitute a very important characteristic for the further assessment of the economic implications of GPTs (see e.g. Chapter 3), this feature shall be explored in more detail in this section. Therefore, the ratio $IC_{i,t}$ is calculated. Given the original patent is from technology i, the first generation citation is a citation by a patent stemming from technology j, $IC_{i,t}$ is calculated as follows

$$IC_{i,t} = \frac{c_{i,t}}{c_{j,t}}, \quad IC_{i,t} \in [0,\infty), \tag{6.5}$$

with c referring to the number of second generation patent citations, i standing for the technology under consideration, here nano, ICT or CE, respectively and j all other patents that are not referencing to this technology and t referring to the year the original patent was filed. Put differently, this indicator hence calculates the share of patents that triggers a mutual innovation process from the original technology to a technology from another field back to the original technology. Here again, the trend is interesting concerning the expectations (since absolute values of this ratio should rise with the number of original patents): The share of such innovational complementarities in nanotechnology is assumed to rise in the direction of the ICT values, which is expected to be significantly higher than the CE indicator.

For ICT the number of patents is high. Moreover, the generality of purpose leads to a broad applicability in a variety of tech-fields, with concentration among those fields tending to be low. Thus, within this broad base of high diversity, it is admissible to assume that the *IC*-indicator might show only slight increases over time, since the technology has already emerged from its nativity phase. Hence, high but almost time-invariant values for ICT can be expected using this first-step measure. The lower benchmark CE on the other hand is expected to have a highly concentrated but small basis, so associated patents should be located in only a few technology fields with a high degree of specialisation. Given these circumstances, CE might as well produce high values for this measure even without being considered as GPT. Second-generation citations with a 'CE-NonCE-CE'-like path are not that unlikely: One might think of an engineer enhancing the performance of an engine by altering materials and thereby inducing further advancements in material sciences in the following years, with results eventually being adopted by engineers again. So the share of those 'homecoming' advancements should be quite high as well, while an increasing value of this measure is not expected either. The first-step *IC*-indicator is thus best suited for emerging GPTs in a very early stage, such as nano, where an initially small number of patents within a growing basis of technology fields should facilitate the traceability of an increasing mutual-inducement trend, which is of high interest concerning the expectations of future developments. In the light of these expectations for the proposed indicator, a second step is performed, taking into account the breadth and magnitude of diversity for the three respective candidates. The final measure is then computed as follows

$$IC_{i,t}(weighted) = ln\left(p_i \frac{1}{HHI} IC_{i,t}\right), \quad IC_{i,t}(weighted) \in [0,\infty), \tag{6.6}$$

where p_i is the patent count weight. The additional expression 'weighted' refers to the reflection of the number of patents and their spreading amongst technology fields (measured by a reciprocally entering Herfindahl-Hirschman-Index) as a weight for the shares of 'homecoming' citations computed in the first step. These adjustments should yield a measure which still incorporates the emerging trend of nanotechnology but gives credit to the insight that an emerging GPT's growing number of patents and the corresponding pervasiveness exhibit a great scope for improvement as well as innovation spawning in various application fields, both of which are the foundation for those innovational complementarities Bresnahan and Trajtenberg originally thought of, and for the measurement of which the two-step indicator represents a first approach.

When investigating technologies through patents (and publications) it is no simple task to distinguish between fundamental and applied research. One could argue that patents on the whole have to be associated with development processes leading to marketable products and are hence altogether results of applied research, but thinking of carbon nanotubes for instance reveals that very fundamental research is obviously patentable as well. Separating fundamental from applied research *within* patents is ultimately a contentious decision and (even worse) not feasible for the amount of patents it is dealt with in this thesis. The proposed indicator is hence to be seen as an indirect measure and hence as proxy for innovational complementarities based upon citation patterns *between* different technologies, incorporating patent growth and the magnitude of diversity of each respective technology. It might thus be seen as a first approach to conquer both horizontal and vertical externalities, catching the latter one – and thereby the object of interest: complementarities between up- and downstream – 'incidentally'.

Figure 6.15 shows a comparison between the IC-indicators over time.[19] The first-step measure provides inside on the consideration of emerging GPTs: ICT has a broad base of patents throughout the observation period and is clearly confined, though very pervasive as seen before. A huge fraction of second generation citations stems from ICT-patents (referring to non-ICT patents that are originally based upon an ICT-point of departure). This is quite the same for CE, with both technologies showing an almost time-invariant share of those citations. Besides that, nanotechnology as an emerging GPT in its very early stage of development is the only technology with an increasing path of this measure. Since the number of patents as well as their diversity among tech-fields is growing, possibilities for innovation spurring across technological field borders increase likewise. Weighting the first-step-measure with this basis-growth, as done in Figure 6.15(b), therefore incorporates the idea of an increasing chance of within-technology vertical externalities. This addition does not affect the general patterns of ICT's and CE's development, but makes the trends more obvious. The results of the performed t-tests that investigate differences in means over the observed time period (and hence not a trend), however, point to the weak performance of nano in general (Table 6.8): Innovational complementarities are significantly more prevalent in ICT and CE. There is anecdotic evidence for innovational complementarities to exist and to improve. This trend ist particularly interesting since nanotechnology is not a fully matured technology yet and hence a stable situation is to be reached. The positive trend hence points to its potential. Therefore, and since H6.4 is supported by the confirmation of H6.2 and

[19]Note that due to the need for patents to obtain second generation citations in order to obtain sensible results, the calculation of the IC indicator stops after the year 2000. This allows 4 years for each generation of forward citations to occur (2008 is the last year the underlying dataset can be considered complete).

H6.3, H6.4 can at least not be rejected and should be confirmable with the indicator employed within the next couple of years.

With view to all the shortcomings mentioned, the proposed indicator offers only a first attempt to catch innovational complementarities in patent data. Yet, the employed measure of IC shows higher values for ICT than for CE, indicating the goodness of fit of this indicator referring to the relationship of ICT as upper and CE as lower benchmark.

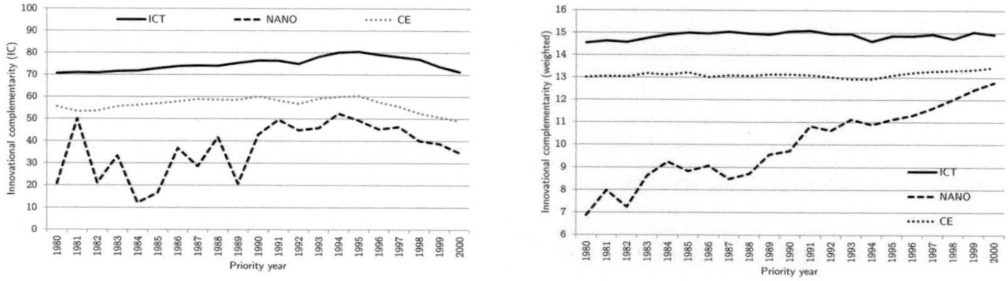

(a) unweighted (b) weighted

Figure 6.15: Innovational complementarities p.a..
Source: PATSTAT, own search and calculations.

	Obs	Mean	StdDev	ICT	CE
NANO	21	9.9595	1.6859	-13.2914***	-8.5998***
ICT	21	14.8733	0.1676		36.7705***
CE	21	13.1338	0.1376		

Table 6.8: t-Tests (unpaired) of weighted innovational complementarities of ICT, Nano and CE.
***Indicates significance at 0.01.
Source: own calculations.

6.3.5 Knowledge Mergence (H6.5)

Finally, H6.5 intends to investigate the mergence character of nanotechnology. Since a technology based on a variety of different core sciences and technologies might indicate large ranges of possible uses (Nikulainen 2007) and since this potential of different uses is an important and assessable characteristic, particularly when aiming at finding ex-ante GPT-evidence in a young technologies' life cycle, one could not only focus on forward, but also on backward citations of nanotechnology patents.[20] While forward citations refer to the diffusion of nano-knowledge into later work, backward citations indicate the use of a wide range of different core sciences and technologies, prior art

[20]Due to data restrictions, this is not possible for publications though.

that, the more general it is, indicates a converging character of GPTs. To exploit this, the generality measure introduced above is also calculated for backward citations. In line with the assumed mergence character of nanotechnology, a similar value of backwards generality of nano-patents is to be expected compared to ICT values and a higher one compared to CE results. As a second measure, the coherence of the patents that are cited by nano (CE, ICT)-patents is investigated, in strong analogy to the measure developed above to index pervasiveness. The less coherent, and hence the less cognitively proximate the set of backward citations is, the more the technology can be seen as convergent.

The results of the comparison of the generality of backward citations show that the values of this indicator for nanotechnology lie significantly in between the values for CE (lower) and ICT (higher), as Figure 6.16 and the results of the t-tests for K30 in Table 6.9 display. Since IPC4 is a much more granular level and high generality values are reached fast (see above), the K30 results are more meaningful. Nanotechnology's level of mergence is not significantly different from the level found for ICT as upper benchmark. Yet, its level is significantly higher compared to the non-GPT CE. Moreover, this relation holds true for both, patents from all over the world and patents from Europe, although the levels of generality in Europe are significantly lower across all considered technologies (see Table 6.9, EU27 t-tests). This overall lower level of backwards generality indicates that inventions stemming from Europe are generally less convergent than patents from anywhere in the world.

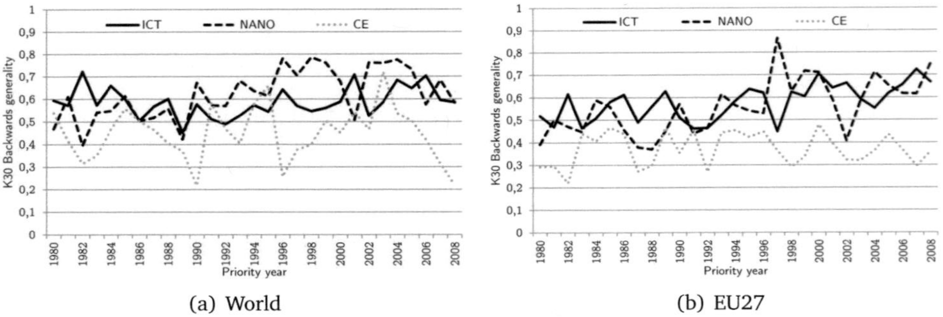

(a) World (b) EU27

Figure 6.16: Average generalities (K30) of backwards citations of ICT, Nano- and CE-patents p.a.. Source: PATSTAT, own search and calculations.

	Obs	Mean	StdDev	CE	ICT	EU27[1]
			WORLD			
NANO K30	29	0.6210	0.1108	5.6814***	1.4343	3.0054***
CE K30	29	0.4482	0.1207		- 5.4273***	3.1864***
ICT K30	29	0.5867	0.0658			0.5694
			EU27			
NANO K30	29	0.5581	0.1221	7.0727***	-0.7068	
CE K30	29	0.3710	0.0734		-10.3424***	
ICT K30	29	0.5771	0.0782			

Table 6.9: t-Tests (unpaired) of backwards average generalities (K30) for Nano, ICT and CE in the World and in EU27 over time.
[1] Paired t-tests between WORLD and EU group values.
***Indicates significance at 0.01. Source: own calculations.

The confirmation of H6.5 is also supported by the findings for the backwards coherence, i.e. the technological coherence of backward citations of patents. This measure constitutes a rather qualitative indicator for the similarity in terms of cognitive proximity of the origins of the knowledge implemented in newly developed patents in the respective technology. A high level of similarity therefore refers to a lower level of mergence of knowledge. Although the backwards coherence of nanotechnology is significantly higher than the backwards coherence of ICT patents, it its way lower than the backwards coherence of CE patents, as can be seen in Figure 6.17 and Table 6.10 similarly for the world and for Europe. The difference between nano and CE is several times larger than the difference between nano and ICT, which nearly vanished in the most recent years. This might be interpreted as a trend towards the level of non-coherence of ICT and towards an even more converging character of nanotechnology in the future. Again, coherence in the world in general is significantly lower (except for nanotechnology) compared to Europe, supporting the findings from backwards generality. It might therefore be stated that nanotechnology has is indeed merging knowledge from different fields, similar to the one of ICT as present GPT and significantly differing from the less converging character of CE as lower non-GPT benchmark.

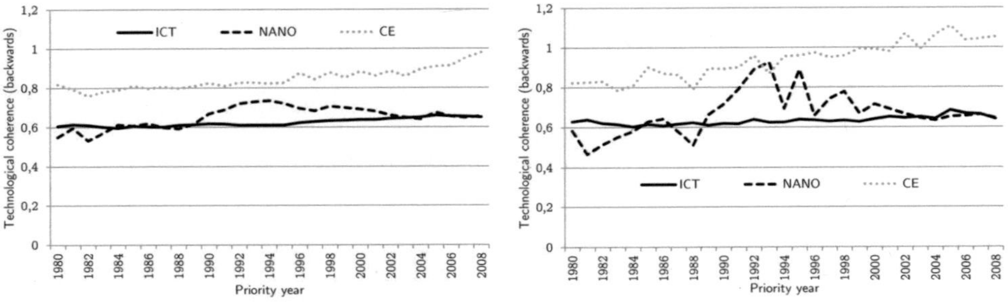

(a) World (b) EU27

Figure 6.17: Technological coherence of backward citations of ICT, Nano- and CE-patents. Source: PATSTAT, own search and calculations.

	Obs	Mean	StdDev	CE	ICT	EU27[1]
			WORLD			
NANO	29	0.6511	0.0538	-13.8240***	2.5625**	-1.4573
CE	29	0.8441	0.0525		21.2079***	-9.4439***
ICT	29	0.6239	0.0192			-4.8558***
			EU27			
NANO	29	0.6705	0.1092	-10.0539***	1.7958*	
CE	29	0.9359	0.0910		17.5107***	
ICT	29	0.6335	0.0192			

Table 6.10: t-Tests (unpaired) of technological coherences (backwards) for ICT, Nano and CE in the World and EU27 over time.
[1] Paired t-Tests between WORLD and EU group values.
***Indicates significance at 0.01.
Source: own calculations.

6.4 Conclusion

Stating that nanotechnology is widely considered as *the* general purpose technology of coming decades yields huge promises regarding consequent impacts on long-term economic growth. A GPT's three constituting characteristics, namely pervasiveness, high technological dynamism and innovation spawning in various application fields have therefore been subject of many studies. This chapter contributes to this research by extending the underlying data to scientific publications, regarding Europe as additionally examined region for the very first time, adding up new measures such as technological coherence and a first approach towards innovational complementarities as a composed feature of technological dynamism and innovation spawning and, last, systematising the investigation with respect to indicators and benchmark levels. With an upper and lower benchmark technology, ICT and the CE respectively, comprehensive counterparts are provided, which prove to be useful comparisons indeed. In addition to testing the traditional three characteristics only, the analysis is extended to testing the direct results of technological dynamism and innovation spawning, namely innovational complementarities for the first time. Finally, the knowledge mergence character is subject to investigation, a feature not constituting a GPT but assumed to be correlated with the nature of a GPT.

Hypothesis	Indicator	Result of Nanotechnology	Support
H6.1 Pervasiveness	Diffusion TOP25	PAT: way below ICT & CE, pos. trend	weak
		PUB: above ICT and CE	strong
	Generality	Nano roughly between ICT and CE	strong
	Technological Coherence	Nano and ICT way below CE	strong
H6.2 Scope for Improvement	Increase of Nano-Inventions	PAT: way below ICT & CE, pos. trend	medium
		PUB: way above CE, surpassing ICT	strong
	Forward Citation	PAT: way above ICT and CE/ALL (W)	strong
		PUB: way above ICT and CE/ALL (EU27)	strong
H6.3 Innovation Spawning	Diffusion	PAT: way below ICT, trends tw. CE (W)	medium
		PUB: way above CE, surpassing ICT (EU27)	strong
	Citing Class Growth	PAT: average, below ICT, similar to CE	weak
		PUB: average, below ICT, similar to CE	weak
H6.4 Innov. Complementarities	IC weighted	below ICT and CE, positive trend	medium
H6.5 Knowledge Mergence	Backwards Generality	above CE, close to ICT	strong
	Backwards Tech. Coherence	way below CE, minimally above ICT	strong

Table 6.11: Overview of results supporting the hypotheses.
Source: own compilation.

The results indicate what was expected: From an economic point of view (but driven clearly from technological data) there is no substantial reason to doubt that nanotechnology will evolve as GPT, as predicted by both scholars and practitioners. While it remains unclear if nanotechnology will yield similar potential as ICT has shown in the past two decades, the development of nanotechnology regarding its unbowed continual advancement is undisputabley as promising. As summarised in Table 6.11 the first three major hypotheses could be regarded as supported – or at least not as rejected. Despite the fact that nanotechnology is still an emerging technology and despite the corresponding difficulties in the forecast of its development, the indicators that are employed here seem to suggest that nanotechnology already satisfies at least the most important feature of a GPT, namely that of generality, already. The other features convince at least in their potential for development and with respect to the infancy of this technology this is already an insightful achievement. Regarding the early stage of the technology's development, a clearer confirmation in the future may be reckoned. Moreover, the additional two hypotheses underlining the impact of the first three hypotheses, i.e. the one for innovational complementarities and the one tackling knowledge mergence, could also not be rejected. Hence, to put it in a nutshell: Notwithstanding its early stage nanotechnology can, from today's point of view, reasonably be seen as a pervasive, technologically dynamic and innovation spawning technology, or, put differently, as a general purpose technology. It has nonetheless to be noted that a development in another direction than in the one of a full GPT is still possible.

Certainly, the incorporation of R&D expenditures representing the input side would enable important insights when combining these two perspectives, offering explanations of macroeconomic growth already on the micro-level by investigating incentives and their interdependencies (see Bresnahan 2010). This enrichment should facilitate the political discussion regarding emerging GPTs, especially as soon as country-level data reveals catching-up potentials. Furthermore, by adding impact measures of national (or for instance European) and institutional technological leverage capabilities, inference statistics could provide a more holistic view on nanotechnology and even more, on GPTs altogether.

This means that, for the rest of the thesis to follow, nanotechnology is employed as a showcase-example for a GPT, including all chances and opportunities as well as the risks and problems associated with this kind of technology – and keeping in mind that it still is considered as a an *emerging* instead of a *stable* GPT: Hence the results to come are not deterministic.

7 Localised Nanotechnology: The Case of Hamburg

Since the last chapter provides strong evidence for nanotechnology to be an (emerging) GPT, the rest of this thesis further investigates the consequences of the corresponding effects and the peculiar economic aspects. For this scope, this chapter exemplarily explores the issues related with 'nanotechnology localised': The particular, local setting of nanotechnology in the German city state of Hamburg, which is chosen as a level of analysis due to the property of being a city state, which is easily manageable but thereby not less informative than for a broader regional setting, shall be introduced in depth in a case study with the aim of identifying relevant aspects and hypotheses concerning the interrelationship between the development of nanotechnology and the local economic development, thereby constituting the second of the building blocks in the main empirical analyses of this thesis.

In order to get a better understanding of the advancement of a GPT in general and nanotechnology as emerging GPT in particular, one has to deal with the derived and discussed characteristics of the technology (see Section 3.1). Thereby, one has to emphasise how the technology is embedded within the existing research and production environment: Within a regional context, agglomeration economies such as spillovers that result from the non-rivalry of the knowledge produced can have a positive impact on innovations. Knowledge spillovers trigger increasing returns but they are limited by geographical distance (see Section 2.1). As nanotechnology as GPT entails a great variety of innovations (see Chapter 6) it is reasonable to assume that they act as agglomeration forces in sectors already showing a tendency to cluster. However, the impact of different kinds of knowledge spillovers on innovativeness and regional development is still an unresolved puzzle. The following questions are therefore tackled in this chapter: In which contexts is nanotechnology in Hamburg developed and how does this feed back to prevailing specialisation patterns? What is the role of diversity of the local nano-knowledge base as immediate consequence of the pervasiveness of nanotechnology in contrast to its specialisation? How does the importance of specialisation and diversification evolve over time? What happens if innovation processes along the value creation chain are linked and hence interdependent, e.g. due to innovational complementarities?[1]

7.1 Derivation of Hypotheses

In the literature around national and regional innovation systems, evidence was found that scientific and technological development as well as innovational activity show a tendency to cluster (Feldman 1994, Zitt et al. 1999). More particularly and more recently, this has also been confirmed for nanotechnology. In this field a strong regional concentration of scientific and technological activity can be observed: Publications and patents often are obviously concentrated in a few regions (Noyons et al. 2003). For instance, Mangematin and Errabi (2012) found that only 200 clusters account for 70% of the worldwide scientific publications in nanotechnology. Moreover, since nanotechnological knowledge is generated using the existing knowledge bases in parent sciences, such as physics or chemistry, the development of nano-knowledge bases (henceforth NKBs) depends on previously existing and presumably regional structures. Such regions, where nano-knowledge concentrates are often called *nano-districts* in the literature. While Shapira and Youtie (2008) observed a concentration of nano-activity in US metropolitan areas, Zucker et al. (2007) investigated the reasons for this concentration and find that regional growth of nano-knowledge is of cumulative nature, i.e. it is stimulated by the regional stock of existing knowledge across all (not only nano) fields. Moreover, it is important to the development how this knowledge is transferred between the local actors. The importance of cooperation between actors has also been pointed out by Robinson et al. (2007). Meyer et al. (2011) emphasised the potential role of the overall knowledge production capabilities of a region in this context. They moreover underlined that, while there surely is a stimulative effect of regionally concentrated knowledge on the development of nanotechnology, it should not be overseen that links to other sources of non-local (but technology-specific) knowledge is indispensable as well. There are many different (local and non-local, nano- and non-nano) knowledge stocks that are assumed to be influencing the development of nanotechnology, the composition of the regional nano-knowledge base has hence to be set into focus.

Tacit knowledge and spatially bound knowledge spillovers are conducive for local collective learning processes (see Section 2.1). Put differently, proximity enhances the ability to exchange ideas, to sense new developments, to induce learning processes, to

[1] An earlier version of this chapter has been published together with Ingrid Ott as KIT Working Paper No. 18, 2011 under the title: 'On the role of general purpose technologies within the Marshall-Jacobs controversy: the case of nanotechnologies'. However, it has been modified a lot since. Needless to say, all remaining mistakes are entirely the author's.

reduce uncertainty and to align R&D activities. This facilitates the generation and diffusion of innovations, thereby also feeding back along the value creation chain. Between proximate actors, the marginal transmitting cost of knowledge is lowest due to frequent social interaction, hence communication and knowledge spillovers arise much more frequently than between remote ones (Venables 2006). Hence, innovation activities locate where knowledge sharing and knowledge spillovers reduce R&D-costs and increase the productivity of innovations. It can hence be assumed that

Hypothesis 7.1 *Knowledge Sharing*
Knowledge sharing occurs in the context of nanotechnological knowledge creation.

Moreover, regions with specialised economic structures tend to be more innovative in that particular industry. The specialisation of an industry in a region can stimulate R&D cooperation between firms or institutions sharing similar knowledge bases and thus induce a high level of MAR knowledge spillovers between them and between others (Mowery et al. 1998). This also applies to knowledge-intensive industries in general where technological spillovers are crucial since they are a major driver of innovative activity. More particularly, the diffusion between regions that exhibit similar specialisation patterns is more likely and faster (see Subsection 2.1.2). This is argued to emphasise a more probable and more effective diffusion of spillovers if source and recipient are similar in terms of knowledge needed and knowledge acquired. Hence, intra-industry spillovers from regional specialisation should spread faster and thereby support innovative activity particularly. These findings suggest an important role of the compatibility of new knowledge to existing knowledge vis-à-vis the pace of innovations. Callon (1997), furthermore, pointed to the mostly tacit knowledge in technologies that are characterised by emergent configurations: Here, particularly, the knowledge range is limited and its composition is of rather specific nature. Since a certain degree of specialisation is moreover also required to achieve sufficient expertise for improving the state of the art of any technology, it is quite reasonable to develop an emerging GPT along already existing specialisation patterns.

Hypothesis 7.2 *Compatibility*
Nanotechnology is mainly advanced in the context of already existing specialisation patterns.

But such foci essentially come at the cost of a limited number of application fields. Moreover, considering the GPT's feature of pervasiveness, this restriction is not compulsory: Instead, it is the multipurpose of uses that induces continuous technological improvements thereby allowing for an even wider range of applications and thus exponentiating the GPT's inherent productivity effects. An increasing number of application sectors leads to higher innovation incentives in both the (upstream) GPT sector and the other(downstream) application sectors. Due to innovational complementarities, the innovation processes along the value creation chain are interdependent, horizontal and vertical linkages between the various actors arise, and successful innovation hence feeds back in both directions (Bresnahan and Trajtenberg 1995). Basically, aside from the invention of new products and applications, the development of the GPT may also lead to an overlap between so far unconnected fields, e.g. via cross-fertilisation that is most probably realised by effective Jacobs externalities. Ideas and innovations that firstly have been developed for a particular use are presumably applicable in a broad variety of different fields as well (see e.g. Csikszentmihalyi (1997), Berkun (2007) and Desrochers and Leppälä (2010)). Besides, GPTs entail a great variety of innovations and may become a relevant agglomeration force in those sectors that already show a tendency to cluster but where concentration is not yet prevalent. Thus, restricting the development of a GPT in the context of already existing specialisations neglects the technology's inherent potential. It may even decrease the region's overall productivity of innovations elsewhere if feedback effects with other sectors and thus further innovations are impeded. This leads to the hypothesis that

Hypothesis 7.3 *Composition of the NKB*
Both specialisation and diversity of the NKB may be observed.

Hence over time, specialisation alone cannot be the optimal development pattern of nanotechnology in regions, as diversity in the sense of broad applications promises respectable growth effects, too. Put differently: If specialisation and diversity are both assumed to be conducive to the development of nanotechnology by innovations in this field, hence if MAR and Jacobs externalities are basically relevant, how can these externalities successfully be exploited? Given a prevailing regional production structure, how does the regional nano-knowledge base develop over time?

In this context, it has to be set into focus how the given regional structure, on the one hand, influences the development of nanotechnology and how this structure is shaped by this development due to feedback effects on the other hand. Basically, two scenarios are imaginable over time: The development of nanotechnology as a GPT begins with already existing specialisation patterns that firstly are enhanced, e.g. by feedback loops or bigger market opportunities. In this sense, nanotechnology is a source of *specialisation deepening*, i.e. the strengthening of existing specialisation patterns. At the same time, as the NKB increases it is natural that it also becomes broader. But then already existing but different specialisations in the region might get tied together through the common use of the GPT and inherent cross-fertilisation opportunities. This provides another source of specialisation deepening within already existing regional specialisations. Furthermore, due to the generality of purpose and the various vertical and horizontal linkages along the value creation chain, bigger advancements of the innovation may also have an impact on other and so far unrelated applications. This could induce the development of new regional specialisations that extend the existing regional specialisation patterns, e.g. via cross-fertilisation. Since the amount of specialisation within one region increases, this phenomenon hence describes a specialisation widening - mainly referring to diversification in line with specialisation. Both seem to be likewise plausible and relevant in such a complex technology like nanotechnology. Consequently, both specialisation and diversification of relevant nano-knowledge must be assumed to be important determinants of the development of nanotechnology, but the time dimension has to be considered. Finally, knowledge spillovers within the region would be expected to particularly arise along related sectors and only to a small degree among unrelated sectors, in analogy to economies of scope at the firm level. Jacobs externalities are hence argued to increase with the extent of related variety among sectors in a region, while the extent of local unrelated variety constitutes a custody against the negative lock-in effects and possible asymmetric shocks (Frenken et al. 2007). Nanotechnology as GPT might – in this context – be thought of as interface converting unrelated to related sectors.

Hypothesis 7.4 *Feedbacks over Time*
(a) With the development of nanotechnology, specialisation-deepening occurs as well as specialisation-widening/diversification.
(b) Over time and with an evolving NKB, the importance of specialisation decreases while the importance of diversity increases.

7.2 Methodology and Data

In order to find out how innovative activity in nanotechnology might be shaped by specialisation and diversity, how this would respond to the regional economic structure and how the importance of specialisation and diversity change over time, a case study on the role of nanotechnology and on its development was accomplished in the city state of Hamburg, Germany, in 2011.

7.2.1 Data Collection

As introduced in Section 5.3, the following analysis mostly relies on the knowledge-production-function-based approach to analyse the composition of the knowledge base and the (potential) spillovers that result thereof. Notice hence that the discussion refers to the NKB itself rather than the concrete transfer mechanisms. For the analysis of the technological NKB, data of nano patents applied for between 1995 and 2008 was obtained from the PATSTAT database (see Section 5.1 for further information on the data). For the period 1995-2008, 164 patents related to nanotechnology, which were either applied for or developed by different actors located in Hamburg, were identified. Both invention and application of nano-patents refers to local nanotechnological competence. The further analysis also considers how each patent is assigned to one or more patent classes according to the IPC system.

Referring to the NKB, a publication analysis was moreover conducted to gain information about the dynamics of the *scientific* knowledge. The considered nano-related publications are stemming from Hamburg and are indexed in the Thomson-ISI WOS database. Again, the investigated is 1995 to 2008. 1878 publications with at least one contributor who is located in Hamburg were identified (see Section 5.2 for further information on the data). Instead of information on IPC classes, subject areas (SAs) were used in order to assess the disciplinary background and application.

To get a deeper understanding of Hamburg's nano-scene as well as to better interpret the publication and patent data, archival and documentary data, including websites and analyses of the Hamburg chamber of commerce as well as of the Senate of Hamburg were used, expert interviews and a telephone survey were carried out, and the specialisation pattern was investigated. Besides, some analyses of data of the official statistics are included.

For the following analysis, however, the specialisation pattern in general as well as the development of the city state's nanotechnological knowledge base in particular is in the focus. Several indicators to measure specialisation and diversification of the NKB as well as their impact on the development of new knowledge are developed and applied in the following.

7.2.2 Case Description: Nanotechnology in Hamburg

Hamburg is Germany's second biggest city and a relatively economically prosperous metropolis with a GDP/capita of about 50 000 Euros in 2008 (Statistische Ämter des Bundes und der Länder 2008). The city state's economic structure is characterised by a developed industrial and a well-developed tertiary sector. The harbour ensures access to the world market which is especially important for industrial production. It reflects first-nature geography advantages thereby providing the basis for specialisation in maritime industries. Other specialisation advantages in the secondary sector refer to aerospace industries and life sciences[2], while specialisation in the tertiary sector relies mostly on media.[3]

Basically there exist various indicators to measure concentration or specialisation according to a given context.[4] Table 7.1 provides an overview on the recent economic structure in the city state of Hamburg as represented by relative employment shares resulting in location quotient (LQ) and cluster index (CI). The LQ calculates the ratio between regional and national employment shares. The CI is calculated by Runkwid and Christ (2011) employing relative industry concentration and specialisation indicators weighted by the size of the industry, again on the basis of employment data.[5] The results for selected branches that are distinguished according to the German Wirtschaftszweigklassifikation (WZ), a classification system that is similar to the international standard industry classification (ISIC), are displayed.[6] The left column in Table 7.1 highlights how the various branches may be assigned to the already well-established clusters media, aerospace industries, maritime industries, and life sciences. An $LQ > 1$ indicates that employment in the respective branch is above national average thus displaying regional specialisation, while a $CI > 1$ indicates above average cluster characteristics, a hint for cluster tendencies, while values of $CI > 64$ identify a NUTS3 region as proper industry cluster on the level of 3-digit WZ classifications.

The nano-scene in Hamburg is shaped by protagonists which include private firms (11 SMEs and 8 large companies), 11 different university research departments, and 4 research institutes. Moreover, there exist also explicit nano (research) networking institutions, that somehow act as coordinating point: One of the central nano research institutions in Hamburg is the Center for Applied Nanotechnology (CAN) that focuses its

[2]Notice that there is no clear cut delineation of life sciences within the official statistics. However it is broadly accepted that life sciences encompass biotechnology, pharmacy, cosmetics and medical engineering.

[3]These clusters are also promoted by the regional economic policy (see e.g. Handelskammer Hamburg (2006) or http://metropolregion.hamburg.de/karte-clusterinitiativen).

[4]For instance, Paci and Usai (1999), Beaudry and Schiffauerova (2009) and Palmberg et al. (2009) mention some indicators that are relevant in the context of nanotechnology.

[5]The cluster data used in this text was calculated for the research project "Die Bedeutung von Innovationsclustern, sektoralen und regionalen Innovationssystemen zur Stärkung der globalen Wettbewerbsfähigkeit der Baden-Württembergischen Wirtschaft". See Runkwid and Christ (2011) and Hagemann et al. (2011) for further details.

[6]For further information on the WZ classification see http://www.destatis.de/. More information on ISIC can be found on http://unstats.un.org/. Notice that according to the LQ and CI more specialisations could be identified for the city state of Hamburg. Within this chapter the discussion is restricted to those specialisations that to the author's understanding refer to nanotechnology. A recent and exhaustive overview of specialisation in the city state of Hamburg is presented by Boje et al. (2010).

Specialisation	Branch of Economic Activity	WZ	LQ	CI
Media	– reproduction of recorded media	182	2.05	58.4
	– retail sale of cultural and recreation goods in specialised stores	476	1.61	
	– publishing activities	58	2.32	66.0
	– motion picture, video and television programme production, sound recording and music publishing activities	59	3.04	105.3/ 43.3[1]
	– television broadcasting	602	0.46	18.7
Aerospace Industries	– manufacture of air and spacecraft and related machinery	303	8.94	189.1
	– air transport	51	1.54	33.7/ 228.5[1]
Maritime Industries	– fish processing	102	1.28	12.1
	– manufacture of refined petroleum products	192	4.36	204.4
	– building of ships and floating structures	301	3.57	144.0
	– water transport	50	11.93	1668.5/ 58.1[1]
Life Sciences	– manufacture of medical and dental instruments and supplies	325	0.67	16.1
	– manufacture of soap and detergents, cleaning and polishing preparations, perfumes and toilet preparations	204	3.19	35.8
	– manufacture of other chemical products	205	1.36	26.9
	– manufacture of pharmaceuticals, medicinal chemical and botanical products	210	0.28	1.1
	– manufacture of irradiation, electromedical and electrotherapeutic equipment	266	5.22*	
	– veterinary activities	75	0.44	3.0
	– human health activities		0.82	9.1
Aerospace Industries, Maritime Industries, Life Sciences	– R&D in science, engineering, agricultural science and medicine	721	0.95	17.5

Table 7.1: Existing specialisations in Hamburg, as per LQ (2010) and CI (2008) and their assignments to the specialisations media, aerospace industries, maritime industries and life sciences.
Source: Bundesagentur für Arbeit (Statistik der sozialversicherungspflichtig Beschäftigten), March 2010 (*data from December 2008), own calculations. Branches according to the German Wirtschaftszweigklassifikation (WZ2008 for LQ and WZ2003 for CI) and matching to the existing clusters.
[1] Two values are due to restricted compatibility between WZ2003 and WZ2008. In case of two merged WZ2003 classes in WZ2008, both values of the original classes are given.

activities on nano-applications in life sciences. It has been co-founded as a public private partnership by industrial enterprises in 2005.[7] Since then, the CAN is concerned with life science topics in three (of altogether four) foci: Cosmetics, medicine and pharmacy; partnerships with private firms exist with enterprises that are also strongly related to life sciences[8]. Another important nano institution in Hamburg, namely the interdisciplinary nanotechnology center Hamburg (INCH) strongly focuses on basic research and states its key activity likewise as the connection of nanotechnology and life sciences. Besides, the nano-industry is often considered as being part of the virtually existing life science cluster (Handelskammer Hamburg 2006). However, since nanotechnology is still in a nascent phase, most of the nano-knowledge produced is still basic research and obviously stems from the two universities in Hamburg, which are the University of Hamburg and the Technological University Hamburg-Harburg and their institutes, particularly physics, chemistry and medicine. Therefore, nanotechnolgical knowledge in Hamburg has to be described as being in a rather emergent configuration and therefore not yet stable (Callon 1997). This indicates that the technological development in Hamburg is coined by uncertainty.

7.3 Analyses and Results

Figure 7.1 illustrates how the technological and scientific NKB in Hamburg has grown during the years. The large technological dynamics inherent in the development of nanotechnology induces innovation spawning and is hence mirrored by an immense increase of the NKB within the last years. This pattern displays at a regional level the development of nanotechnology that might be observed across all industrialised countries (for a comparison of (international) dynamics see Palmberg et al. 2009).

7.3.1 Knowledge Sharing (H7.1)

The transfer of knowledge through face-to-face collaboration is one of the well-known mechanisms of knowledge spillovers (see Section 2.2). Aiming at showing the potential for knowledge spillovers in the city of Hamburg, the collaborative patterns of the players in the nano-scene are hence traced. While it is difficult to trace collaboration between the above mentioned institutions directly with patent data[9], it is possible to

[7]Further information can be found at www.can-hamburg.de/company/background.php.

[8]Industrial partners are Beiersdorf AG, Eppendorf AG, Merck KGaA and BODE Chemie GmbH, see www.can-hamburg.de/company/network.php.

[9]This difficulty is due to the fact that the institutions mostly appear as applicants on patents. Patents with two different applicants (so called co-patents) are, however, not very frequent (for details see Subsection 5.1.2).

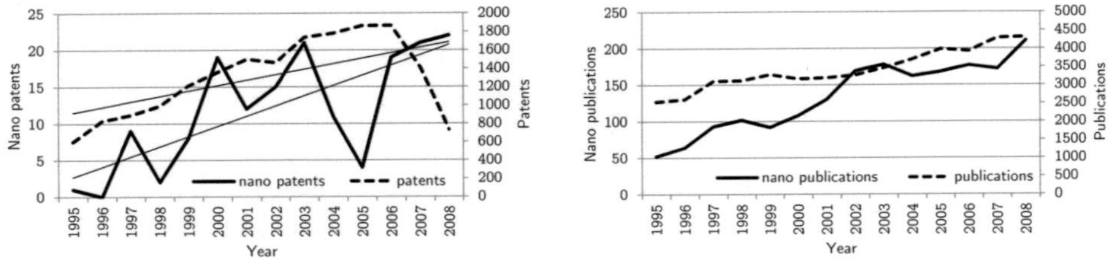

(a) Technological NKB

(b) Scientific NKB

Figure 7.1: Development of the NKB in Hamburg compared to overall knowledge base development. Source: PATSTAT, own search and calculations.

show that there is cooperation between the different actors by means of mapping the inventor-inventor (patent-based) network and the co-author (publication-based) network over time. Inventors who are assigned to the same patent (authors on the same publication) are seen as related, assuming that they got to know each other and knowledge spillovers became effective via face-to-face interaction (see Subsection 5.4). These relationships then constitute the social network of inventors.[10]

The co-inventor network in Figure 7.2 only includes inventors who live in Hamburg or in commuting distance. The vertices represent the inventors, their size refers to their patenting activity. As can easily be seen, inventors are connected quite densely, although there are isolated inventors and although not all vertices are indirectly connected. The density, i.e. share of actual to possible connections is 0.028. The average degree, i.e. the average number of connections one inventor has is 2.31. Due to technical restrictions, the co-author network shown in Figure 7.3 includes all, not only local authors. As is obvious, the network is extremely dense, i.e. authors are highly connected as well. Comparing the network measures to those of the co-inventor network this network is less dense, but the authors have more connections on average: Density amounts to 0.02, average degree is 10.6. These findings on the relevance of (local) collaboration in nanotechnology are also confirmed by Meyer et al. (2011). They showed for the UK regions that collaboration is stronger the more proximate the actors are to each other. However, this analysis shows that collaboration plays an important role in the development of new nano-knowledge. This indicates to confirm H7.1. Based on the co-inventor

[10]Note that the boundaries of the organisation that appears as applicant are not relevant in these networks, which is why it is also shown that there is cooperation between the different institutions. However, due to the low rates of reported applicant-applicant collaboration on patents compared to actual collaborations, this is only given for the sake of completeness and only built of nano-patents that were applied for with reference to Hamburg; since an applicant-applicant network that only includes within-Hamburg collaboration does only show very few collaborations.

network, Figure 7.4 highlights how Hamburg's inventors are connected to the periphery of Hamburg (nodes on the inner circle), to other German regions and to regions in other countries (nodes on the outer circle). Knowledge stemming from outside the region's local knowledge base seems to be employed as well. Hence, extra-regional knowledge flows occur as well. However, these analyses do not offer a full picture of the relevance of collaboration for nanotechnological knowledge creation. They rather indicate that collaboration occurs, thereby constituting an opportunity for knowledge spillovers.

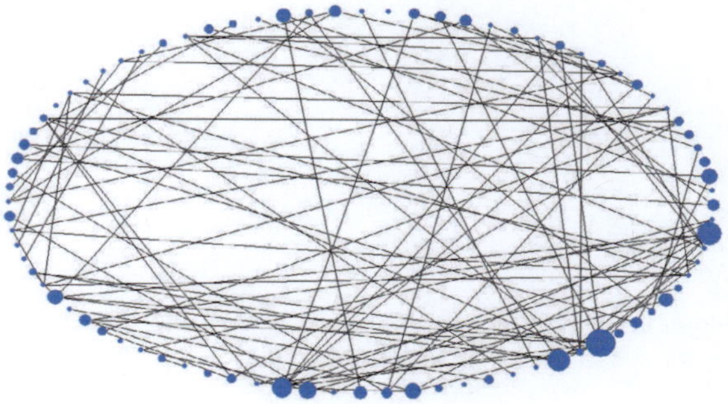

Figure 7.2: Co-inventor network Hamburg, only local inventors. The vertices are randomly distributed across the circle. Size of vertices proportional to patent count. Density: 0.028, average degree: 2.31.
Source: PATSTAT, own search, calculation and illustration.

Figure 7.3: Co-author network of collaboration on publications with at least one contributor from Hamburg. The vertices are randomly distributed across the circle. Size of vertices proportional to publication count. Density: 0.02, average degree: 10.6.
Source: WOS, own search, calculation and illustration.

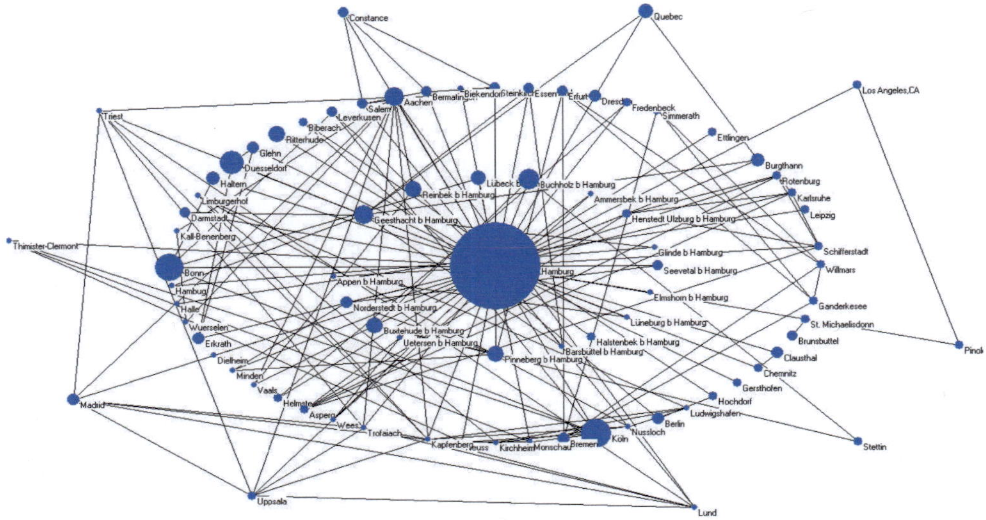

Figure 7.4: Interregional collaboration on patents with at least one contributor from Hamburg.
Size of vertices relative to patent count.
Source: PATSTAT, own search and calculations.

7.3.2 Compatibility (H7.2)

As argued before, nanotechnology is still a very young technology and its development is promoted by various actors. It was derived above that it is reasonable to assume that during the advancement of the technology the actors tie in – at least to some remarkable extent – with the existing economic structure. Recall that hypothesis 7.2 is discussed with respect to the NKB. Other information on the nano-scene were incorporated to interpret the results.

The specialisation of the economic structure as presented by the LQs and CIs within Table 7.1 also mirrors the recent economic policy of Hamburg that supports clusters in the fields of life sciences, maritime as well as aerospace industries, and media. Among these clusters, life science is by far the most important application field of nano-activated products, including nano-materials, nano-tools or nano-particles in general. Hence one might observe not only specialisation of nanotechnology activity but one might assign this activity to an already existing cluster.

Figure 7.5 displays the distribution of patents and publications into the most relevant 25 IPC4 classes/SAs. In order to make the classes more comprehensive, the concordance developed by Hinze et al. (1997) is employed grouping these IPC4 classes into industrial fields (see Subsection 5.1.2). These fields are again classified into 18 macro-disciplines, an adaption of the classification Porter and Rafols (2009) developed for WOS categories. Publications and their respective TOP25 WOS categories are classified into the same system. This has the advantage to make IPC4 classes and WOS categories comparable concerning their contents. First of all it can clearly be observed that the scientific knowledge base is mainly constituted by knowledge in the basic fields physics and chemistry, while material science as interdisciplinary field seem to be important as well. However, the few applications advanced within the scientific NKB are biomedical science, relating to the life sciences cluster, and engineering science and technology, most presumably a connection to basic applications in the aerospace and maritime cluster. This connection to existing clusters becomes even more obvious regarding the re-classification of patents. Here applications in biomedical science and technology as well as the connection to the basic applied knowledge from materials science and chemistry (both still open for multipurpose-applications) and transport (civil engineering) play a major role.

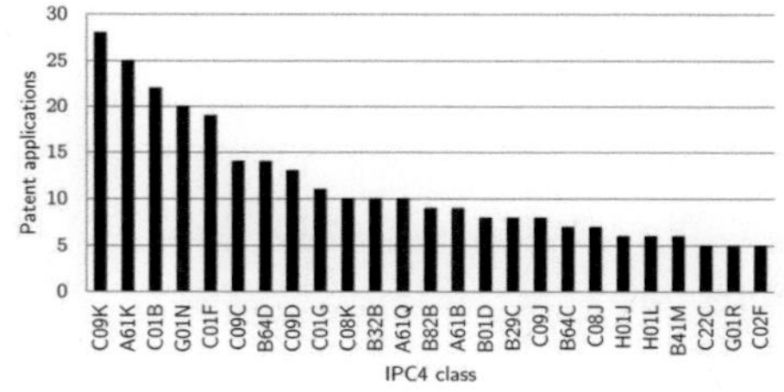

(a) Distribution of patents across TOP25 IPC4 classes

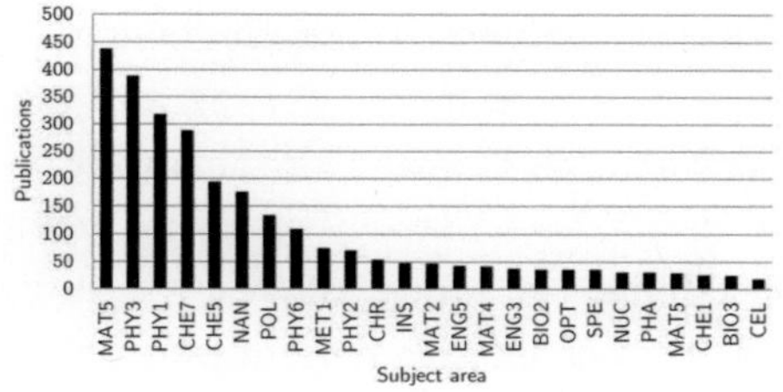

(b) Distribution of publications across TOP 25 SA areas

Figure 7.5: Distribution of patents and publications across fields. See the Appendices D.1 and D.2 for the codification. Source: PATSTAT/WOS, own search and calculations.

This aspect can also be assessed by measuring the compatibility of nanotechnology to overall technological and scientific knowledge, which leads to the calculation of the so called Revealed Technological Compatibility (RTC) index: The RTC index is adopted from the Revealed Technological Advantage (RTA) index which is frequently used to measure specialization within trade theory (Almeida 1996). Similarly to the LQ, the RTC index calculates the ratio of the share of the number of nano-patents (nano-publications) in the respective 3-digit IPC class[11] (WOS SA) relative to the overall number of patents (publications) in this IPC class (WOS category) in Hamburg and

[11] Since concordances, which connect IPC4 classes and ISIC classes, are not employed here, IPC3 classes are chosen to ensure the caption of distinct technological fields.

the respective shares in Germany:

$$RTC = \frac{P_{d,i} \ / \ \sum_i P_{d,i}}{\sum_d P_{d,i} / \sum_d \sum_i P_{d,i}}, \quad RTC \in [0, \infty), \tag{7.1}$$

with P patent (publication) count, i region and d technological field. It hence displays to which degree nanotechnology publications and patent applications from Hamburg across different technological fields correspond to the city state's overall scientific and technological specialisation profile. Figure 7.6 illustrates the respective index values for the top 15 IPC classes quoted by patents filed from Hamburg. A value close to unity indicates that the considered field in nanotechnology application fields is similar to the overall technological specialisation. This hence reflects links to locally existing research and development structures. RTC values significantly larger than 1, by contrast, indicate application fields towards which much research activity is directed. This might suggest that the actors expect important future markets in this field. Obviously, this is the case for the WOS categories PHY2 (physics, atomic, molecular & chemical) and CHE5 & 7 (chemistry multidisciplinary & physical) as well as for most of the IPC classes concerned with more basic/general matters (in contrast to those already focused on particular application fields). For micro-technology, this index value supports the thesis that nanotechnology opens up new opportunities towards miniaturisation and the sustainment of Moore's Law, for materials science this hints to the relevance of nanomaterials as intermediary for the overall development of nanotechnology. Hence high RTC values might also be a slight indicator for future emerging specialisation fields. Figure 7.6(b) highlights that about one half of the scientific top nano-applications in Hamburg coincide with the existing specialisation pattern. The picture drawn by Figure 7.6(a), which highlights compatibility of the technological knowledge, is differing from this observation. However, in most of the application fields directly related to a focused application rather than more general, multi-purpose fields RTC values are still closest to one.[12] Yet, the qualitative evidence as well as the employment of the RTC index in general suggest that pre-existing scientific as well as technological specialisation patterns significantly shape the relevant application fields of GPTs. This is especially true for the existing cluster structure in Hamburg, shaping the regional development of nanotechnology. Nanotechnology advances hence in the context of already existing specialisation

[12]However, over half of the values are largely exceeding unity. Yet, while this large exceedance might be a hint to the recognition of the high potential of nanotechnology at the first glance, the structure of the patent data is a large problem for the calculation of this indicator: The underlying PATSTAT database does not always report addresses of persons. While all data on nano-patents was manually cleaned and hence more address data entries could be gathered, this procedure is way too time-consuming for all entries of the database. Therefore, the RTC indicator can be assumed to be biased towards overshooting and hence only tendencies and relative relationships can be interpreted reasonably.

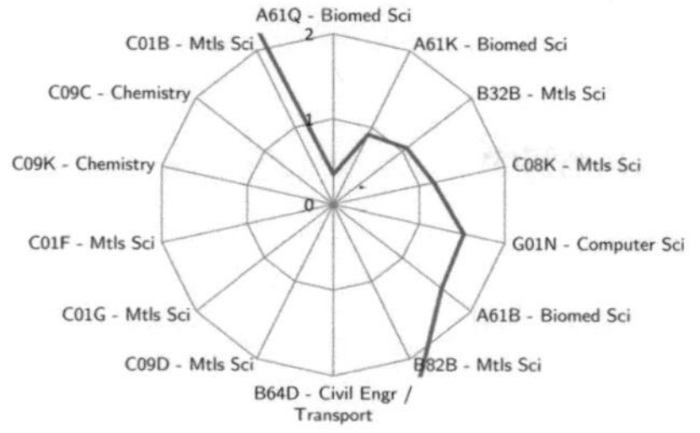

(a) Compatibility of patents with respect to TOP15 IPC classes (4-digit)

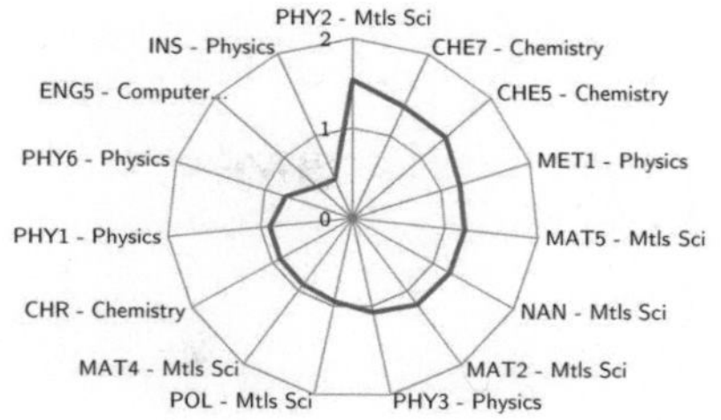

(b) Compatibility of publications with respect to TOP15 SA areas

Figure 7.6: Compatibility of patents and publications w.r.t. fields.
Source: PATSTAT/WOS, own search and calculations.

patterns, which strongly supports H7.2. With respect to Hamburg it becomes obvious that not all clusters are equally affected by the development of nanotechnology, but that there is a strong bias in favour of life sciences.

7.3.3 Composition of the NKB (H7.3)

Taking a closer look at the composition of publication and patent fields, it becomes obvious that both specialisation and diversity of the NKB may be observed (see Figure 7.5(a)): In total, the 164 patents refer to 85 different IPC4 classes and thus cover a large variety of application fields – hence displaying diversity. If one also considers multiple assignments of one patent to various IPC classes these sum up to a total quotation of 396 IPC classes for the 164 patents, again highlighting the feature of diversity. But at the same time one might observe specialisation. For instance, it becomes obvious that 28/396 and hence 7% of patents quote one single IPC class. Thus, specialisation has two dimensions: Among the 28 patents quoting IPC class C09K, for instance there are patents exclusively assigned to C09K and patents that quote other IPC classes as well. This can also be observed for publications, where 437/1878, i.e. 23% are assigned to 'multidisciplinary material science', again not hampering diversity of different classes. Figure 7.5(a) clarifies for the 25 most cited IPC4 classes that both issues of specialisation and diversity may be observed: There is a large number of mentioned IPC classes which displays breadth/diversity, but at the same time one might also observe concentration in some of them. An analogous result arises in the context of publications, where again each single publication may be assigned to various WOS categories (see Figure 7.5(b)). The 1878 nano publications stemming from Hamburg cover altogether 74 different WOS categories areas, thus reflecting very diverse fields. But one might again observe that there are only a few subject areas where most of the publications concentrate. Again both features of specialisation and diversity become prevalent.

One might conclude that these findings basically support H7.3 since both features of specialisation and diversification may be observed.

7.3.4 Feedbacks over Time (H7.4)

Figure 7.7 stylises a technology tree for nanotechnology in Hamburg and thereby depicts, how nanotechnology as a GPT relies on the existing clusters life sciences, maritime and aerospace industries.[13] This figure also includes the slightly observable cluster of renewable energies which yet is important within the metropolitan area of Hamburg but not within the city state.[14] Moreover, it illustrates the already huge variety of interdependencies of actors along the value creation chain and displays both horizontal and vertical linkages among the various upstream and downstream industries. These connections have manifold impacts on the specialisation patterns: (i) already existing specialisations are strengthened in the context of isolated clusters (specialisation-deepening as a consequence of MAR externalities), (ii) cross-fertilisation induces interaction between so far isolated specialisation fields, which also deepens existing specialisations (specialisation-deepening as a consequence of Jacobs externalities), and (iii) cross-fertilisation also enables the development of new specialisations (specialisation-widening or diversification as a consequence of both MAR and Jacobs externalities).

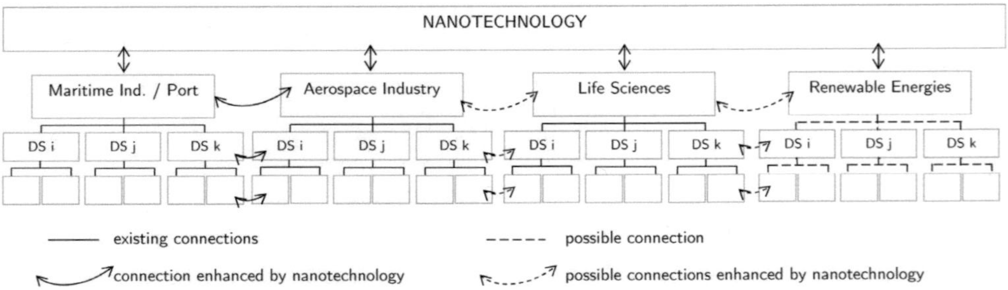

Figure 7.7: Technology tree of nanotechnology in Hamburg, displaying the relationship of nanotechnology to the economic structure. DS= Downstream Sector.
Source: own illustration based on Bresnahan and Trajtenberg (1995).

[13]Within Figure 7.7, the cluster 'media' is neglected since there is no obvious link to nanotechnology at this stage of technology development.

[14]This is why no LQ values for renewable energy industries are available yet.

Composition and Compatibility over Time H7.4(a)

Since H7.2 could be supported in general and hence the development of nanotechnology anchors into the already existing specialisation pattern, it is now investigated, whether specialisation-deepening and diversification indeed emerge.

The existing degree of nanotechnological specialisation in the life science sector in Hamburg is presumably needed in order to achieve the expertise that is necessary when aiming to improve the state-of-the-art techniques in such a complex technology (Garcia-Vega 2006). Anecdotally, it can be stated that the application of nanotechnology in this field hence deepens the existing regional specialisation pattern while contrariwise the specialisation on life sciences at this stage of development surely drives the innovative activity within nanotechnology. This reflects the feedback effects between upstream and downstream sector and also provides an example for specialised innovation spawning which leads to specialisation-deepening from the viewpoint of a single specialisation field. Moreover, there exists a second dimension of specialisation-deepening, as nanotechnology as connecting interface is also a starting-point of possible cross-fertilisation effects, for instance in the development of nano-particles for different applications (Henn 2008). The application of nanotechnology across different fields may hence also lead to an overlap between so far unconnected specialisation fields which then have the same 'very upstream sector' of nanotechnology in common (as is illustrated in Figure 7.7) and can possibly benefit of cross-fertilisation effects. The research on nanomaterials in Hamburg, for example, is not only interesting for applications in life sciences. Composites that, thanks to nanotechnology, combine old with new features (like stability and lightness with conductivity) are not only interesting in medicine (like for artificial replacements), but also for the endowment of airplanes (Airbus S.A.S. 2007). Nano-particle research could be used as platform, originating nano-particles with partly the same and partly differing features, depending on the later application. An improvement of quality and technology levels of nano-materials as well as nanotechnology in general (based on the feedback mechanism of innovational complementarities) is due to increased research activity, learning and cross-fertilization effects. Besides, the joint use of structures in several specialisation fields at the same time opens specialisation advantages for other application sectors, in total exponentiating the positive effects for the development of nanotechnology. In Figure 7.7 this effect of cross-fertilisation between so far unconnected specialisation fields is indicated by the dashed arrows.

The possibility of cross-fertilisation is not easily made visible. However, Figures 7.8 and 7.9 provide some evidence that there are several actors in Hamburg that apply for nano-patents with reference to the same technology fields, although stemming from different industries.[15] Hence, actors with a background in life sciences as well as in aerospace and materials all file nano-patents in materials processing. Therefore, one should assume, that there exists at least the potential for the actors in all fields to benefit from each-others knowledge since the fields they are working in are considerably different, but share at least the application of nanotechnology within materials processing. Figure 7.9 illustrates such relationships more systematically. It depicts the applicants of patents with at least one connection to Hamburg. Edges display the potential for cross-fertilisation; this relationship is constructed when two applicants file nano-patents on the same technology field. Given their cognitive and geographical proximity, mutual learning is very likely to occur once these applicants connect somehow (which might happen trough collaboration, but also through labour movements or other mechanisms of knowledge transfer). This is not only another hint to the multipurpose of nanotechnology, but this overlap could also be a possible originator of cross-fertilisation: When actors of different industries apply nanotechnology in the same technological field it is most likely that the technological underpinnings are the same and actors could learn from each other.

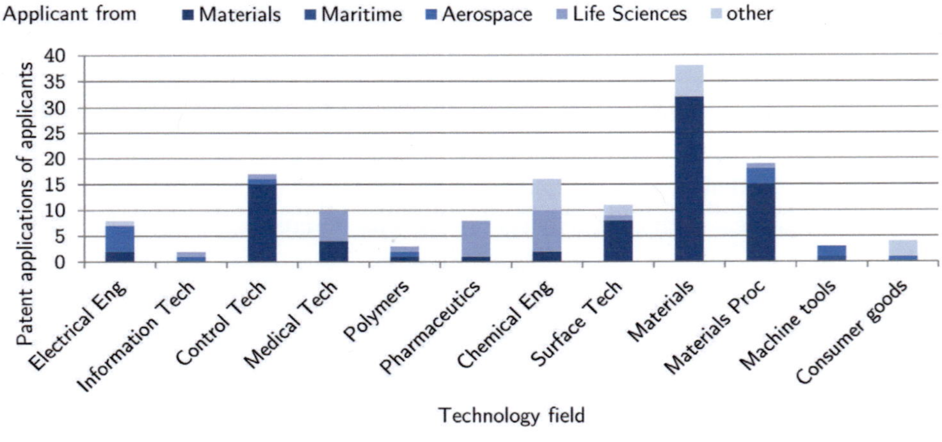

Figure 7.8: Overlapping technology fields of applicants as possibility for cross-fertilisation. Source: PATSTAT, own search and calculations.

Finally, nanotechnology as a GPT could possibly enhance connections to other potential clusters in Hamburg, as its generality of purpose makes them applicable virtually everywhere and subsequently strengthens developments there. The opportunity of cross-

[15] Since actors focusing on 'materials' are very frequent, this category was included as well as the three main industry clusters in Hamburg and the category 'others' for actors from all other industries. Since there are only very few university patents, universities were excluded here.

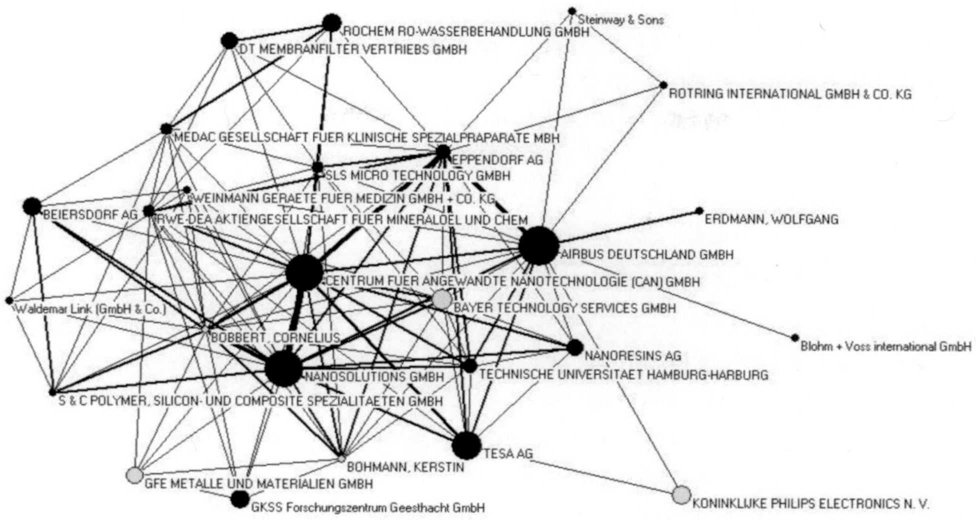

Figure 7.9: Network of potentials for cross-fertilisation due to technological overlap. Size of vertices is relative to filed nano-patents, width of edges refers to the number of overlapping technology fields. Applicants without headquarters in Hamburg are coloured grey.
Source: PATSTAT, own search, calculation and illustration.

fertilisation for instance also exists for renewable energies, where another kind of the mentioned composites could be used in rotor blades of wind wheels (NEWMEX Consulting GmbH 2004, Hessen Agentur 2008). To quote another example, employing nano-materials, new solar cells could be developed by utilising nano-tubes in combination with quantum dots which has already been tested at Hamburg's research institutes (Bürgerschaft FHH 2008). These quantum dots were afore applied in pharmaceutical applications. By improving the opportunities and shaping the structures of an emerging field of regional specialisation, nanotechnology is potentially able to induce a specialisation-widening of both, the regional economic structure and the application fields of nanotechnology. This interplay of existing and new structures and nanotechnology is finally implemented in figure 7.7 by mentioning also the cluster of renewable energies.

This presumed (future) structure is developed due to rather qualitative findings on the pattern of nanotechnological competencies and development in Hamburg. Although there is not enough sensible qualitative neither quantitative evidence yet that could support H7.4(a), there is not enough evidence to reject it either. However, these anecdotal results do emphasise the role of the regional economic specialisation pattern: Nanotechnology is specialised where Hamburg's regional industry is specialised, conveying compatibility of nano-specialisations and the existing production as well as research and development structure. Furthermore, existing specialisation gets strengthened with the development of nanotechnology, also since so far isolated fields, such as e.g. aviation and maritime industries, possibly get related via nano-applications. Specialisation-widening seems to be plausible with respect to renewable energies.

Impact of the Composition over Time H7.4(b)

H7.4(b) is very closely related to H7.4(a) since it considers the other side of the feedback mechanism. While H7.4(a) focuses on how nanotechnology development might influence regional development, H7.4(b) points to the feedback of the regional characteristics on nanotechnology. H7.4(b) hence refers to the relative decline of the importance of the specialisation of the nano-knowledge base for its future growth, while diversity is assumed to become relatively more prevalent and growth-influencing with evolving time. While, at the beginning, the anchorage into the general regional specialisation pattern determines the composition of the regional knowledge base and thereby evokes specialisation (H7.2), the development of nanotechnology as GPT in interaction with the regional specialisation pattern is assumed to cause a diversification of the NKB.

This is investigated by developed indicators, which have at most marginally been applied to regional contexts – they are mostly borrowed from other contexts of the literature, e.g. industrial organisation or international trade. The argumentation is most closely linked to the discussion of Avenel et al. (2007), who analysed NKB at the firm-level. Again, the regional NKB which sums up all publications and patents stemming from Hamburg serves as basis for the analyses. In order to identify specialisation, the well-known concentration measure of the Hirschman-Herfindahl Index (HHI) is used. It is constructed as

$$HHI = \sum_j \frac{N_{ij}}{N_i}^2, \quad HHI \in [0,1], \tag{7.2}$$

where N_i refers to the overall count of assigned IPC classes (subject areas) in year i, N_{ij} is the count of the specific IPC class j. Applied to this analysis, specialisation thus measures to which extent publications (patents) are concentrated within subject areas (IPC classes). Higher levels indicate higher degrees of specialisation. In what follows the corresponding variable is employed as $DEPTH$. In contrast to this is an indicator that measures diversity or $BREADTH$. Notice that breadth is not just the opposite of depth but is represented by an additional indicator that provides information on how many SAs (IPC classes) are assigned per publication (patent) on average:

$$BREADTH = \frac{\#\ of\ assigned\ technological\ fields\ in\ Hamburg\ in\ year\ t}{\#\ of\ nano-publications/patents\ in\ Hamburg\ in\ year\ t}, \quad BREADTH \in [1,\infty) \tag{7.3}$$

The resulting values are equal to or exceed unity with higher values indicating more breadth since then a single publication/patent becomes more useful in more fields or applications.

	Variable	Obs	Mean	StdDev	Min	Max
	Publications	13	140.46	44.57	64	211
scientific NKB	*DEPTH*	14	0.07	0.02	0.06	0.12
	BREADTH	14	2.45	0.92	1	4.42
	Patents	13	12.54	7.63	0	22
technological NKB	*DEPTH*	14	0.18	0.25	0.04	1
	BREADTH	14	1.57	0.26	1.02	1.85
control	*GDP/Capita*	14	43.77	3.53	38	48.7

Table 7.2: Descriptive statistics.
Source: own calculations.

The goal of the following part of the analysis is to better understand how the NKB in Hamburg develops, not only with respect to time and size but with respect to its composition, in this context assessed by breadth and depth.[16] In doing so, an empirical analysis for the period 1995–2008 is carried out, estimating the following regressions:

$$Publications_t(Patents_t) = \alpha + \beta_1 DEPTH_{t-1} + \beta_2 BREADTH_{t-1} + \beta_3 GDP/capita_{t-1} + \varepsilon \tag{7.4}$$

Recall that the development of the size of the NKB is already illustrated in Figure 7.1. Table 7.2 gives an overview on the parameters *DEPTH* and *BREADTH* for both scientific and technological knowledge as respective independent variables and the employed control variable *GDP/capita*, which shall catch up overall yearly economic effects. Since the aim is to investigate how depth and breadth influence the development of the NKB, publications and patents are chosen as dependent variables and regress the respective lagged explanatory variables on them. Like this, the *DEPTH* and *BREADTH* of the precedent year's NKB are modeled to impact the actual NKB development. Moreover,

[16]Alternatively it is possible to calculate breadth and depth at the firm level. This does not allow for a proper analysis of how the values evolve over time as individual firm's NKB are too small (yet).

different models are estimated for both the scientific and the technological NKB in order to account for the time effect. Therefore, the period is split into the 'early' (1995-2001) and the 'later' (2002-2008) stage of the NKB in Hamburg. A correlation matrix can be found in the Appendix D in Table D.3. It shows that variables in the same model do not suffer from multicollinearity; except for the partly high values of the control variable. Since the dependent variables are count data and suffer from overdispersion (variance exceeds mean), a negative binomial regression model is employed, the results of which are displayed in Table 7.3.

	Scientific NKB - PUBLICATIONS					
	OVERALL		early stage		later stage	
DEPTH	3.0000*	(1.8109)	4.9337*	(2.9072)	3.0368	(2.4928)
BREADTH	0.2787*	(0.1490)	0.0911	(0.1990)	0.3032	(0.3293)
GDP/Capita	0.0887***	(0.0108)	0.1372***	(0.0241)	0.0507**	(0.0228)
constant	0.3934	(0.4512)	-1.4793	(0.9675)	2.1106*	(1.1689)
Obs	13		7		6	
Log likelihood	-48.2409		-23.0354		-21.5833	
LR chi2	38.76		21.16		6.63	
	Technological NKB - PATENTS					
	OVERALL		early stage		later stage	
DEPTH	-3.6111*	(2.0902)	-6.0529**	(3.0812)	2.9033	(4.0230)
BREADTH	-0.0128	(0.2286)	-2.1448***	(0.7520)	0.8848	(0.5449)
GDP/Capita	0.0805	(0.0695)	1.4034***	(0.5038)	0.3625*	(0.1869)
constant	-0.5437	(3.5376)	-49.6929***	(19.1114)	-16.2313	(9.9301)
Obs	12		6		6	
Log likelihood	-36.2707		-10.7496		-18.8761	
LR chi2	12.16		17.91		3.49	

Table 7.3: Negative binomial regression results. *PUBLICATIONS/PATENTS* as independent variable. Standard errors in parentheses.
***Indicates significance at 0.01.
Source: own calculations.

Figures 7.10(a) and 7.10(b) illustrate how *DEPTH* and *BREADTH* evolve over time in both the technological NKB and the scientific NKB, with the former rather increasing and the latter decreasing. However, this only points to their prevalence. Table 7.3 presents the results of the regression analysis investigating whether specialisation and diversity indeed impact the subsequent development of the NKB. As one can easily see from the results of the regressions, specialisation and diversity (i.e. *DEPTH* and *BREADTH*) are both relevant for the overall development of the scientific NKB. However, when separating the analysis for the time perspective, it becomes clear that *DEPTH* is only significant in the early stage of the development, while *BREADTH* shows no influence at all. While the influence of specialisation in the early stage is in line with the expectations, the non-

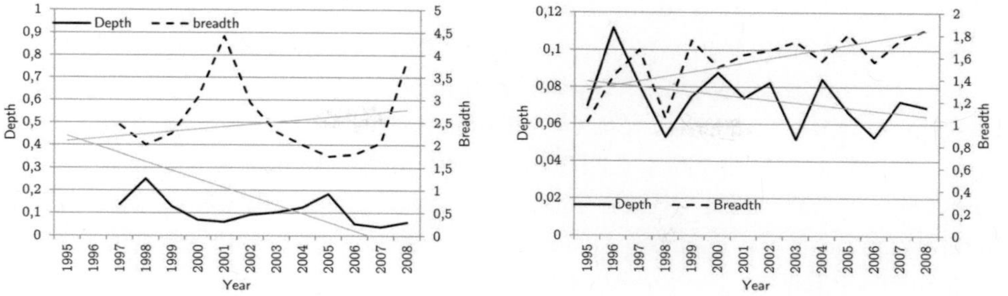

(a) Technological NKB (b) Scientific NKB

Figure 7.10: Development of the characteristics of the NKB in Hamburg w.r.t. depth and breadth. Source: PATSTAT, own search and calculations.

significance of diversity does not support the assumptions. Causes might be seen in the very low number of observations or the still early stage of development from an overall perspective. For the technological NKB the results point completely into another direction: The specialisation (*DEPTH*) of the knowledge has a significantly negative influence on the overall development, particularly in the early stage. This might indeed point to the fact that the mere concentration into a few technological fields (in terms of IPC classes) restricts the technological innovativeness in the field. In contrast to scientific achievements, technological innovations in form of patents benefit extraordinarily from a multitude of applications in terms of monetary revenue. The negative sign of *BREADTH* in the early stage, by contrast, contradicts this possible explanation, since diversity hence seems to be negatively influencing further development as well. However, since there are only very few observations and since there is only one single case investigated, these findings might not be reliable nor are they representative, which is why they rather serve to test the appropriateness of hypothesis and measures. Therefore, the assessment of this hypothesis is picked up again in the next Chapter 8. However, for the moment H7.4 cannot be confirmed.

7.4 Conclusion

The results obtained within this introductory case study confirmed many of the suggested hypotheses concerned with (local) aspects influencing the development of nanotechnology. However, it has to be said that nanotechnology is an emerging technology and hence all relevant activity must be assumed to define an emergent configuration (see Section 2.3 and Callon (1997)). This implies that a stable situation is yet to be reached and a constant change of the situation in Hamburg is expectable. Having said this, it can be stated that nanotechnological competence in Hamburg emerges and develops where the existing regional economic structure already exhibits specialisation advantages, such as effective MAR-externalities. This is neither obvious nor compulsory because nanotechnology as GPT is potentially applicable in virtually every industry. In the context of the Marshall-Jacobs controversy, the results hence suggest that the role of specialisation and diversity for technological development is not only to be asked within the context of the given technology (such as (potential) GPTs) but also has to be investigated in the light of prevailing regional economic structures. In Hamburg, for instance, it has become obvious that nanotechnological specialisation is compatible to the corresponding regional specialisation, which is mainly supported by sticking to the life science cluster's specialisation. This specialisation is the starting point of any investigation of occurrence of specialisation and diversity within the NKB. The NKB in Hamburg indeed shows signs of both, specialisation and diversity at the same time. However, aiming at finding evidence for mutual feedbacks (i.e. nano-innovation system in Hamburg to overall industrial structure to nano-innovation system...), there was found anecdotal evidence for nanotechnology to (potentially) influence the industrial structure in Hamburg. Specialisation deepening is evidenced by a rather natural result from compatibility, namely the strengthening of competencies in the respective field, but also by the fact that the development of nanotechnology relates fairly unconnected, but in themselves specialised fields via cross-fertilisation of possible nano-applications in these diverse fields. This cross-fertilisation might also become the driver of specialisation (advantages) in additional fields by the mere application of nanotechnology in this field, opening opportunities to benefit from existing knowledge. This diversification of specialisations in Hamburg, for instance, seems plausible with respect to renewable energies. The last hypothesis, i.e. the relevance of the specialisation and/or the diversity of the knowledge base as a cause of the development of new innovations, could, by contrast not be confirmed.

While this points to a central weakness of the case study approach (i.e. lack of comparability, the few numbers of observations and, also, the lack of systemised operationalization of the investigation such as hypothesis testing by anecdotal evidence), the attention to detail in this case study was necessary to gain awareness and important insights into relevant aspects of the development of nanotechnology within the context of a location.

The most important finding of this Chapter 7 for the rest of the analyses is that the development of nanotechnology has to be analysed in the context of location: The underlying regional economic structure significantly shapes the development of nanotechnology – and these feed back on the regional economic structure. Splitting this main point into its parts, relevant results of this case study in the course of this thesis are the following starting points for further in-depth (and non-case based) analyses within two main fields of investigation (which is tackled in two more working packages to follow):

Knowledge Composition and Localised Knowledge Spillovers (WORKING PACKAGE 2)

The development of nanotechnology is assumed to anchor into existing industrial specialisation patterns; it should therefore be investigated whether and how this influences innovativeness in nanotechnology. Specialisation and diversity and with them the Marshall-Jacobs controversy are indicated to be an important and non-neglectable aspect in the context of the (localised) development of nanotechnology. Their influence shall therefore be assessed further.

Collaboration and Knowledge-Sharing in Networks (WORKING PACKAGE 3)

Collaboration occurs, which, being a central mechanism for knowledge transfer bears the very probable possibility of positive knowledge externalities to become effective. Moreover, networks of collaboration (might) contribute to the diffusion of knowledge. It is therefore of central interest how collaboration is organised and how it influences innovativeness in GPTs and how mutual learning and cross-fertilisation can become effective.

Part III.b

Working Package 2: Knowledge Composition and Localised Knowledge Spillovers

8 The Impact of the Knowledge Composition on the Innovation Outcome: Specialisation vs. Diversity

The role of the knowledge composition and the nature of knowledge spillovers is derived as an open issue in Chapter 7. This chapter and Chapter 9 set out to investigate the impact of the composition of knowledge on innovativeness. When the relevance of agglomeration economies on economic growth has been assessed in the past, a focus was laid on the analysis of innovation and the corresponding knowledge base within regions. The central question discussed in this context is displayed within the Marshall-Jacobs controversy and weighs whether specialisation or diversity generate more and more efficient knowledge spillovers. Specialisation and diversity have been indicated to be important and non-neglectable aspects in the context of the (localised) development of nanotechnology as well (see Section 7.4). Moreover, there is evidence that the development of nanotechnology anchors into existing industrial specialisation patterns. This chapter hence tackles how the compatibility with the respective regional industrial structure as well as specialisation and diversity of nanotechnological knowledge influence the development of nanotechnology as GPT.

8.1 Derivation of Hypotheses

Since this chapter mainly takes up the hypotheses under investigation in the smaller context of the case study of Hamburg accomplished in Chapter 7, the derivation of hypotheses in this chapter is held shorter without omitting any main points.

First, the anchorage of a nanotechnology into the regional industrial structure was indicated to influence its development. Geographic and cognitive proximity (in the sense of the use of similar knowledge bases in the same regions) of agents in the same industry generate intra-industrial (MAR) knowledge spillovers and other specialisation advantages (Jaffe 1986, Boschma 2005). In order to benefit from these advantages that regional specialisation of knowledge in some fields offer (such as asset sharing, access to a qualified labour market and infrastructure) and in order to be able to catch up to and advance the state of the art, is is reasonably assumed that nanotechnology as an emerging GPT, although being applicable in nearly all fields of the local industry is advanced along and benefits from already existing local specialisation patterns. Remember also that Callon (1997) pointed to the specificity of knowledge bases in emergent configurations and the necessity of huge investment in technology platforms in order to be able to advance the technology (see Subsection 2.3). It can be presumed that the accessibility of existing local structures in similar fields hence drives the development of a technology.

Hypothesis 8.1 *Compatibility to Local Structures*
The development of nanotechnology in the context of regionally existing technological patterns is conducive to the innovativeness in nanotechnology.

However, the advantages of specialisation are not the only factors conducive to innovation. Pure specialisation of the regional knowledge-base, for instance, essentially comes at the cost of a limited number of application fields within the context of a GPT. This hampers its development in two ways. On the one hand, the incentives to innovate increase with the number of application sectors across the whole value creation chain, mainly due to innovational complementarities (see Section 3.2). On the other hand, the relative cost of producing the new knowledge are higher: The more sectors actually employ nanotechnology, the more can the newly produced knowledge in this sector become valuable in different contexts downstream – the fruits from innovation can be shared. More differentiated knowledge potentially creates a greater variety of knowledge spillovers: The more diverse the application, the higher the potential for an exchange of knowledge and ideas and for random collisions of businesses (Glaeser et al. 1992). An innovation working well in one industry often can be applied, modified and/or further developed in other industries (Wu 2005). This phenomenon of cross-fertilisation between superficially different, but to some extent related technologies as well as even between (so far) unrelated technologies becomes more probable (Granstrand 1998, Suzuki and Kodama 2004, Garcia-Vega 2006). Griliches (1998, p. 258) even pointed out that 'true spillovers are ideas borrowed by research teams of industry i from the research results of industry j', thereby directly pointing to the relevance of inter-industrial spillovers and the resulting possibilities of cross-fertilisation. Agents can hence benefit from new technological possibilities, ideas and knowledge spilling over that stimulate innovative activity and prevent negative lock-in effects in one particular technology. Thereby, this issue directly tackles the Marshall-Jacobs controversy (see Subsection 2.1.2).

Hypothesis 8.2 *Specialisation and Diversity*
(a) The specialisation of the regional nano-knowledge base is conducive to its growth.
(b) The diversity of the regional nano-knowledge base is conducive to its growth.

The coexistence of specialisation and diversity is not a contradiction, since the existence of multiple specialisations, for instance, might constitute diversity. However, there is a fine line between specialisation and diversity due to several specialisations and diversity without any specialisations. Given the presumed importance of MAR and Jacobs externalities, it is of relevance how the corresponding possible externalities can successfully be exploited regarding their innovation-supporting effects. Nesta (2008) investigated the role of specialisation and diversity of knowledge bases of firms: Specialisation, i.e. the depth of large firms' knowledge bases would be conducive to innovation most importantly in the short run. In the longer term it would be rather diversity, i.e. the breadth of their knowledge bases that drives innovative activity. Conveying this to the aggregate regional nano-knowledge bases (regional NKBs, i.e. the aggregate regional knowledge in nanotechnology) and to their general purpose character, the initial adaption to the overall regional specialisation pattern and the corresponding depth of small NKBs might trigger intra-industry knowledge spillovers and enhance the organisation of innovations and the formation of strong knowledge to rely on later. With a growing regional NKB and hence enough 'architectural' knowledge, i.e. the knowledge of how to incorporate diverse and multi-disciplinary knowledge (Zhang et al. 2007), is built up in the region. Then, the diversification of the NKB might become conducive to its further development, particularly as the breadth of the NKB potentially exponentiates innovation incentives within the context of the diffusion of a GPT and triggers knowledge spillovers across industries.

Hypothesis 8.3 *Dynamics*
As the NKB evolves, the importance of specialisation decreases whereas the importance of diversity increases.

Last, empirical research has found evidence that scientific knowledge has a strong influence on the process of shaping new knowledge and innovation in high-technologies (Plum and Hassink 2011). Put differently, technological knowledge needed for the development of applications is based on the basic scientific knowledge. It can therefore be assumed that the scientific nano-knowledge base and its characteristics do have an influence on the development of the technological nano-knowledge base. However, as it is most presumably not the specialised in-depth scientific knowledge at the edge of the research frontier in a specific subject (and far away from application) that can be transferred into marketable inventions, specialisation of the scientific knowledge base might be counterproductive for the development of technological applications thereof. By contrast, diversity of the scientific knowledge might be the characteristic that drives the development of applications in various different fields, thereby augmenting patenting activity.

Hypothesis 8.4 *Diffusion*
(a) The size of the scientific NKB has a positive influence on the growth of the technological NKB.
(b) Specialisation of the scientific NKB hampers the growth of the technological NKB.
(c) Diversity of the scientific NKB stimulates the growth of the technological NKB.

8.2 Methodology and Data

This chapter focuses on the impact of local knowledge characteristics on the development of nanotechnology. Therefore, the perspective is restricted to a regional level, thereby ignoring the knowledge flow into (and out of) the region by non-intra-regional collaborations.[1] In particular, different agglomerations of nanotechnological knowledge across Germany are investigated. The analysis focuses on the determinants of the growth of the respective NKB. Again, the NKB can be split up into a *scientific* and a *technological* part. The technological NKB can be measured by the number of nano-patents (see Section 5.1.3 for detailed information on the underlying database of nanotechnology patents). The regional NKB that is assumed to influence subsequent innovation activity is constructed by using a moving time window of 5 years. Hence, the relevant regional NKB in year t consists of the cumulated patent applications of the prior five years stemming from that region. This makes a reliable measurement of compatibility, diversity and specialisation possible, which are all calculated as average values over the last 5 years. It has been found that a moving window of 4 to 5 years is an appropriate time frame for assessing technological impact in high-tech industries. This is consistent with the depreciation rate of patents close to 20% (Leten et al. 2007). The scientific knowledge base is approximated by publication records. Characteristics of the regional NKB are studied in this chapter and publication data is not as nearly as standardised as patent data, the classification scheme is by far not as objective and valuable. Therefore, the focus here is laid on patent data and the technological NKB. This NKB is appropriate as is encompasses nearly the whole value creation chain of nanotechnology: Patents, protecting marketable inventions, are employed throughout the whole value creation

[1]Yet, these are possible sources of novel and complementary knowledge that can be absorbed by local agents. Similar to the relevance of the composition of the local knowledge base, the kind of knowledge flowing in might very well be of importance: When it is related to the regional knowledge base, it might enhance local learning and growth (Boschma and Iammarino 2009).

chain with an increasing number of patenting research institutions. By contrast, it is mostly in the very upstream basic research sector where publications dominate and prevail. Yet, Jansen et al. (2007) found that Germany universities describe 75% of nanotechnological research as basic. Still, nanotechnology is an emerging technology. Therefore, the scientific NKB shall not be neglected here. Eventually and carefully, publication data is employed in this very function, as constituting the very upstream sector's knowledge, in order to be able to trace a diffusion pattern of knowledge in H8.4. For publication as well, the moving time window approach to assess the impact of new scientific knowledge in form of publications.

The relevant nano-agglomerations that are included in the panel are exclusively German clusters to avoid the influence of country-specific differences. Identified nano-regions are listed in the Micro/Nano-Atlas of Germany, published by IVAM (2010). A nano-region identified very in size between more than 90 and less than 10 actors. The very small regions have been defined either because there are very intense research activities or because they are the only regional concentration in their respective federal state (IVAM 2010). This resulted in 38 nano-regions in Germany, each of which was classified in subgroups according to its size. However, when data on patent and publication activity in the field was collected, substantial nanotechnological knowledge output could only be found in 34 of these regions. The data on these regions now constitutes the investigated panel data set. The regional distribution of these clusters across Germany is displayed in Figure 8.1.

Then, data of nano-patents applied for between 1990 and 2008 and being localised to the regions considered were extracted from the PATSTAT database (for further details on the nano-database see Section 5.1). The considered nano-related publications are stemming from the respective regions and are indexed in the Thomson-ISI WOS database (for further details see Section 5.2). Here the analysis relies on the period between 1995 and 2008.

8.2.1 Variables

Dependent Variable

This chapter considers the growth of the regional NKB, i.e. newly produced knowledge, and not the performance of the given regions but the productivity in terms of innovativeness in nanotechnology is in focus. The productivity of the region is displayed by its scientific and technological knowledge output, which are regarded in the context of the knowledge production function again. Since only the development of the technological

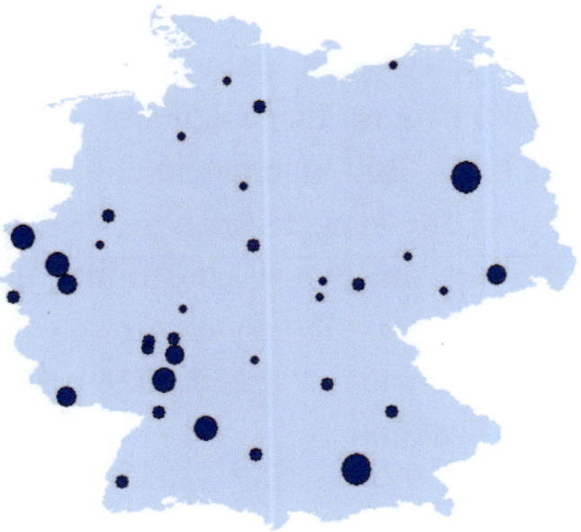

Figure 8.1: Considered nano-agglomerations in Germany.
Size of circles proportional to nano-patent-output of the regions.
Source: own compilation.

knowledge is investigated, *PATENTS* serve as dependent variable, counting the absolute number of patents applied for in the considered year in the considered region (for the database see Subsection 5.3.1).

Explanatory Variables

Knowledge production is seen as a function of the stock of knowledge, which, dependent on its composition produces more or less useful knowledge spillovers. The concrete mechanisms of such transfers and spillovers are not subject to investigation, but rather the theoretical possibilities of certain kinds of knowledge flows triggered by a certain composition of the knowledge base. The variables catching these characteristics are introduced in the following. Note that all explanatory variables are employed with a time-lag, i.e. the explanatory variables are calculated for the 5-year period preceding the year t, in which the dependent variable is measured. Like this, the effect of the prior characteristics of the NKB on actual patenting in t can be caught.

Compatibility Displaying the degree of fitness of the NKB with the given regional structures, the compatibility of the developed NKB to the specialisation profile of the region's overall KB, the so called Revealed Technological Compatibility (henceforth *RTC*) index is included. The *RTC* index is adopted from the Revealed Technological Advantage (*RTA*) index which is frequently used to measure specialisation within trade theory (Almeida 1996). The *RTC* index calculates the ratio of the share of the number of nano-patents (nano-publications) in the respective IPC 4-digit class (subject area) in a region relative to the overall number of patents (publications) in this IPC class (subject area) in the given region and the respective shares in Germany:

$$RTC = \frac{P_{d,i} \; / \; \sum_i P_{d,i}}{\sum_d P_{d,i} / \sum_d \sum_i P_{d,i}}, \quad RTC \in [0, \infty), \tag{8.1}$$

with P patent count, i region and d technological field. The co-domain is $[0, \infty)$, where values close to 1 for an application field display a specialisation profile of the nanotechnology application field close to the overall specialisation profile of the regional NKB country or economic region. Since deviating values in both directions indicate non-symmetric deviations from this overall profile (Palmberg et al. 2009), straight-forward implications are not easily drawn. Therefore, the following normalisation is employed:

$$RTCN = \frac{1}{\left| \frac{RTC-1}{RTC+1} \right|}, \quad RTCN \in [1, \infty). \tag{8.2}$$

This normalised index ($RTCN$) with co-domain $[1, \infty)$ increases with increasing compatibility. Then, the average $RTCN$ value of the top 5 of most frequently assigned subject fields is taken as the indicator for compatibility $COMP$. This is done because not all fields, but the most important fields are assumed to be relevant in terms of 'fitness' of the nano-knowledge to the regional specialisation pattern. Following hypothesis 8.1 hence, growth is tested to be increasing with $COMP$.

Specialisation In order to identify specialisation, the already mentioned Revealed Technological Advantage (RTA)[2] index is employed. The RTA index calculated here by contrast is used to assess the relative advantages of region i in a patent's technological field d. It is calculated by the ratio of the share of patents of this region in a given nanotechnology application field, divided by the total share of patents in this very field in the whole country.

$$RTA = \frac{P_{d,i} / \sum_d P_{d,i}}{\left(\sum_i P_{d,i} / \sum_{d_i} P_{d,i} \right)}, \quad RTA \in [1, \infty) \tag{8.3}$$

This index is commonly used as a measure for specialisation and the possible existence of Marshallian externalities (Paci and Usai 1999, Palmberg et al. 2009). It equals unity if the region holds the same share of nano-patents in one technological field, as total patents exists in that area in the whole country, and is below (above) one if there is a relative weakness (strength). Regarding the co-domain and the interpretability, similar problems as described for the RTC occur. Moreover, this index is constructed as relative specialisation index for one technological field and therefore not yet employable as index for the specialisation extent of the NKB of a whole region. The following re-

[2]In conjunction with the use of employment data, this index is also known as locations quotient, LQ.

construction is accomplished for this purpose: For the same top 5 assigned IPC classes k on a 4-digit level[3] as used for the calculation of the $COMP$ variable, the square root of the mean of the squared RTA_k value is taken for each of these IPC classes. In order to make this new indicator symmetric, it is normalised using the formula $\frac{RTA-1}{RTA+1}$. This yields a symmetric co-domain of $[-1;1]$ with increasing values indicating increasing specialisation and zero displaying average specialisation. I.e. the specialisation index ($SPEC$) employed here is constructed as

$$SPEC = \frac{\sqrt{\frac{\sum_k RTA_k^2}{k}} - 1}{\sqrt{\frac{\sum_k RTA_k^2}{k}} + 1}, \quad SPEC \in [-1,1]. \tag{8.4}$$

Being designed like this, under-average specialisation contributes negatively and a higher level of specialisation in a few fields is more relevant than a lower level in more fields, which displays the focus on specialisation in form of depth. According to hypothesis 8.2b, a positive relationship between specialisation and the growth of the NKB is hence expected.

Diversity First of all, note that diversity is not just the opposite of specialisation. By contrast both can coincide. Therefore, diversity is represented by two additional indicators. In order to identify diversity, the inverse of the well-known concentration measure of the Hirschman-Herfindahl Index $1 - HHI$ is used. It is calculated as

$$DIV = 1 - HHI_k = 1 - \sum_{i=1}^{N} \frac{p_{ik}}{P_k}, \quad DIV \in [0,1], \tag{8.5}$$

with i representing the IPC class[4], k the overall region and P the number of patents. Applied to this context, diversity thus measures to which extent patents are distributed across IPC classes and hence how universal nanotechnology is. This index yields values within the interval of zero and unity with higher levels indicating higher degrees of diversity. Diversity is expected to be positively related to the yearly record counts, as stated in H8.2a.

Size and Experience Above all diversity, but also opportunities to specialise within one field depend on the size of the knowledge base. It is natural that larger NKBs are more diverse than smaller ones, as more actors can process more and more different knowledge. Moreover, larger NKBs are offering more possibilities of recombination.

[3] For the analysis of the last hypothesis, PUB_SPEC, specialisation for the scientific NKB is calculated on the basis of subject areas.

[4] For the analysis of the last hypothesis, PUB_DIV, specialisation for the scientific NKB is calculated on the basis of subject areas.

This leads to a larger propensity of the actors who have access to it to eventually produce new knowledge and hence absolute counts of new knowledge will be higher.[5] It should therefore be controlled for the size of the NKB in terms of patent (or publication) counts over the respective period. In this context, another aspect is important:

Tacit knowledge, being an important ingredient to innovation, frequently can only successfully be acquired through lengthy experiences of individuals and learning-by-doing. However, since experience and the corresponding tacit forms of knowledge are so difficult, costly, and time-consuming to obtain, these might be a relatively strong and lasting source of competitive advantage in what concerns the creation of new knowledge and innovation within a region.[6] This aspect shall be accounted for by including an experience variable into the regression. On the one hand, it can be accounted for the experience by including the size of the total stock of nano-patents gained within a region, which is the lagged accumulated number of patents over the past 5 years $SIZE\_NKB$, assuming that behind every patent a considerable amount of tacit knowledge is gained as well. The lagged size of the NKB is expected to have a positive influence on NKB growth as also detailed above.[7] Moreover, the local stock of highly educated human capital also proxies the amount of – admittedly less focused – experience. Therefore, the variable HQ, displaying the local share of highly educated employees (i.e. those holding a university degree) in the precedent year $t-1$ is included into the regressions as well to improve the fit of the regressions and act as a control variable.

Year dummies To control for time specific factors that are likely to affect the number of new patents, the model also includes year dummies. Such factors might include the overall growing relevance of nanotechnology and the associated changes in these technological fields as well as, for instance, economic fluctuations.

8.2.2 Descriptive Statistics

Descriptive statistics of the dependent and explanatory variables are provided in Table 8.1. The mean number of new patent applications per region is 14, mean lagged share of highly qualified employees is 10% and the mean size of a region's knowledge base amounts to 69 patents. Technological specialisation of this knowledge base is 0.84 in mean, whereas compatibility amounts to 1.71 and diversity to 0.74. As expected, these

[5]By contrast, relative growth rates are likely to be smaller since the denominator of the growth rate is larger.

[6]Ranft and Lord (2000) detail this aspect for firms, but this might be particularly true for regions as well.

[7]However, since knowledge might become obsolete after a certain amount of time, once again only the knowledge stock of the 5 last years is included.

numbers already reveal that the regions examined here are specialised in their main nano-application fields as well as diversified across a wider range of fields. Table E.1 in the appendix displays the correlation coefficients between the variables (except for the year dummies). The size of the NKB correlates highly with the rate of new patent applications. This is also true, as expected, for the specialisation indicator with patents and the size of the existing knowledge stock. Keep this in mind for the interpretation of the results.

Variable	Description	Obs	Mean	StdDev	Min	Max
PATENTS	Number of patents applied for in t	385	14.10	22.69	0	149
PUBLICATIONS	Number of publications applied for in t	396	158.90	155.52	0	951
SPEC	Specialisation of the techNKB in $t-1$	367	0.84	0.12	0.45	0.99
COMP	Compatibility of the techNKB in $t-1$ to the overall regional structure	367	1.74	1.46	1.02	20.72
DIV	Diversity of the techNKB in $t-1$ to the overall regional structure	367	0.74	0.21	0	0.97
SIZE_NKB	Patent count over the whole 5-year period in $t-1$	385	69.07	95.55	0	642
HQ	Local share of highly educated employees in $t-1$	351	10.31	2.71	4.1	17.9
PUB_SPEC	Specialisation of the sciNKB in $t-1$	396	0.48	0.22	0.09	1.00
PUB_COMP	Compatibility of the sciNKB in $t-1$ to the overall regional structure	396	22.53	31.25	1.15	206.80
PUB_DIV	Diversity of the sciNKB in $t-1$ to the overall regional structure	396	0.80	0.10	0.21	0.90
PUB_SIZE_NKB	Publication count over the whole 5-year period in $t-1$	396	622.27	629.48	3	3909

Table 8.1: Descriptive Statistics.
Source: own calculations.

8.2.3 The Model

Since the growth of the regional NKB is investigated, which is nothing else than how much new knowledge is produced *given* the existing stock of knowledge and its composition, the knowledge production function approach is employed. It points to the relevance of knowledge production for long-term productivity growth (Romer 1990, Aghion and Howitt 1992). In this context, the production of knowledge is regarded as a function of the stock of knowledge, which, dependent on its composition produces more or less useful knowledge spillovers. Hence observable knowledge, i.e. patents, is linked to observable regional characteristics of the stock of knowledge within the knowledge production function and likewise determinants of the knowledge production shall be examined. The knowledge production function employed in this context is of the form

$$PATENTS_{i,t} = \alpha + \beta_1 SPEC_{i,t-1} + \beta_2 DIV_{i,t-1} + \beta_4 COMP_{i,t-1}$$
$$+\beta_5 SIZE\_NKB_{i,t-1} + \beta_8 HQ_{i,t-1} + \sum_{i=9}^{16} \beta_i YEAR + \varepsilon, \tag{8.6}$$

which is adapted for the different models and scopes. When the dependent variable is employed as a count variable, it only takes non-negative integer values (the number of patents applied for from actors of a particular region in given year). Therefore, the assumption of an underlying Gaussian distribution, as for instance used in OLS models, is misleading. By contrast a Poisson regression approach provides an appropriate model for such data (Vanhaverbeke et al. 2007, Grimpe and Patuelli 2008), but as count data is likely to suffer from overdispersion (variance exceeds mean) – which is the case for this data as well – the assumption of this model is violated. This is particularly relevant in case of (time-invariant) unobserved heterogeneity, which might be a problem here. Being able to better control for unobserved heterogeneity, i.e. the possibility that identical regions according to the measured variables still differ with respect to unobserved features, a fixed effects negative binomial regression model is used. This is very similar to the Poisson model but accounts better for heterogeneity problems. Moreover, the employment of the size of the NKB in the precedent 5 years as control variable has the effect of an instrument, further controlling for unobserved heterogeneity (Heckman and Borjas 1980).

8.3 Results and Interpretation

In the following, the investigation of the hypotheses stated above is accomplished step by step and is directly discussed.

8.3.1 Compatibility (H8.1)

In this chapter, the focus is laid on the influence of the characteristics of the existing knowledge on the development of new knowledge in nanotechnology. It is hypothesised in H8.1 that new knowledge is developed in the context of regionally existing technological patterns. To test this, the characteristics of the technological NKB were included into the regressions as well as some control variables testing the overall impact of knowledge. The results of the fixed effects negative binomial estimation of the relationship among the growth of the NKBs (i.e., the number of new patent applications, *PATENTS*), diversification *DIV*, specialisation *SPEC* and compatibility *COMP* are presented in Table 8.2. Model 8.I includes all variables. As can be clearly seen, *COMP* is positively statistically significant, but, however economically only weakly influencing the technological development. Yet H8.1 can generally be seen as supported. Hence, the compatibility of the NKB, i.e. its fitness into the region's overall specialisation profile appears to have indeed a positive influence on the further development of the NKB. However, different clusters in different stages of development are examined over a relatively long period, particularly in relation to the young stage. Therefore, even though the compatibility does not show a strong effect over this whole period of time it might very well have been more important for the first few initial years. Hence, it might be simply the given setting that produces the low impact. This result is thus relevant since it becomes obvious that the anchorage into the regional system of industries does have a (even if only a small) mid-term effect on the development of nanotechnology in German regions. Moreover, as was elaborated in Chapter 7, the compatibility of nanotechnology might have an impact on the development of structures of the region itself. However, this is not evaluated in this chapter.

	Model 8.I - ALL	
SPEC	1.3991*	(0.8374)
DIV	0.9643*	(0.5234)
COMP	0.0869**	(0.0411)
HQ	0.1442**	(0.0586)
SIZE_NKB	0.0022***	(0.0007)
year dummies	yes	
Const	-17.3657	(917.0516)
Obs	329	
Number of Groups	34	
Log likelihood	-822.7665	
Wald chi2	185.17	

Table 8.2: Results of negative binomial fixed effects panel data analysis of *PATENTS*. ***Indicates significance at 0.01. Standard errors in parentheses. Source: own calculations.

8.3.2 Composition of the NKB (H8.2)

Advancing to a more detailed consideration of the composition of local technological NKB, hypotheses 8.2 state that diversity and specialisation are conducive to the development of new nano-knowledge. For the discussion of H8.2 Table 8.2 again displays the results to be discussed. The results are in line with previous findings in other technological contexts such as Paci and Usai (1999) and van der Panne and van Beers (2006), and partly also with Mangematin and Errabi (2012). Concerning the Model 8.I, the share of highly qualified employees and the size of the lagged nano-knowledge base have the expected positive signs and are significant, using conservative two-tailed tests.

This points to the relevance of the old knowledge for producing new knowledge on the one hand, and to the importance of access to qualified employees that are able to process this knowledge, on the other hand. The year-dummy coefficients indicate an overall, although not monotonic, increase in patent applications across the years. As expected and stated in H8.2, both, specialisation and diversity have a significant and positive influence on the growth of the technological NKB. Remember that specialisation and diversity are not regarded as being mutually exclusive: A knowledge base can be seriously specialised in certain fields (namely in this case, as is taken into account in the employed specialisation measure, the most frequently cited technological fields) and at the same time be diversified, producing and obviously reemploying diversified knowledge. In this special case of nanotechnology as GPT, this result was expected: In order to develop high-tech knowledge needed to radically and basically advance the GPT, leading edge and highly specialised knowledge and the corresponding knowledge spillovers are necessary. On the other hand, in order to make a high technology become a GPT and to open up opportunities to unfurl its whole potential, options must be proposed to employ the GPT in different, widespread application fields and to potentially benefit from city-specific Jacobs externalities, such as cross-fertilisation. While simultaneous specialisation and diversity might be counterproductive on the firm level by producing a difficulty to cope with trade-off between exploitation and exploration (Abernathy 1991, Benner and Tushman 2003),diversity and specialisation at the regional level do not trigger such a trade-off or even dilemma – by contrast, they seem to be stimulating simultaneously.

8.3.3 Dynamics (H8.3)

Coming to the dynamic impact the characteristics of the existing knowledge base, i.e. the extent of the impact specialisation and diversity have on the development of new nanotechnological knowledge, remember that H8.3 expresses the conjecture that the importance of specialisation decreases, while the importance of diversity increases with the size of the NKB. To advance this conjecture, it is distinguished between the dynamics of specialisation and those of diversity. In order to be able to sketch the different development stages, different sizes of agglomerations are considered separately. The SMALL Group refers to agglomeration with a cumulative NKB below the average and hence to relatively more emergent configurations, while the LARGE group refers to a local NKB above the average which proxies a more developed knowledge and hence a later stage of nano-development and hence to relatively more stable configurations.

As the results of the t-test in Table 8.3 clearly indicate, there are significant[8] differences in the mean values of specialisation and diversity across these groups: While the specialisation is significantly higher in smaller regions compared to regions with larger NKBs, this relationship is the other way around for diversity. However, these results do not tell us anything about the role of diversity and specialisation for the further development of nanotechnology.

Group	Obs	Mean	StdDev	t-Value
			SPEC	
SMALL	169	0.9143	0.0433	-13.4563***
LARGE	198	0.7797	0.1237	
			DIV	
SMALL	169	0.6032	0.0957	14.133***
LARGE	198	0.8569	0.2304	

Table 8.3: Independent group t-test of specialisation and diversity across size of agglomeration. ***Indicates significance at 0.01.
Source: own calculations.

Table 8.4 displays all results of the four different models employed in order to test whether these difference do indeed influence the development of new patents on a year-to-year basis. The results show that specialisation has a significant negative impact on the patent activity in small clusters and a significant positive impact on the development of larger clusters. This is the opposite to what is expressed in H8.3. Moreover, diversity does not seem to have an impact any longer once the models are split up. Therefore, H8.3 cannot be confirmed. Trying to interpret these results, the negative impact of specialisation in small clusters might be a result of the specific characteristics of nanotechnology: Nanotechnology as GPT is assumed to profit from specialisation as well as diversity. The employed indicator of specialisation in this context, however, is higher when specialisation is stronger. This focus on stronger specialisation might be the reason for this negative effect as a strong focus might hamper the positive effects from diversity and multipurpose right from the beginning. Mangematin and Errabi (2012), for example, also find that certain kinds of (scientific) specialisation in certain fields hamper the growth of the clusters. In larger clusters, however, specialisation is more stimulating. This result is, by contrast, in line with the (firm-level) literature on exploration and exploitation of a technology, for instance. March (1991) distinguishes between exploration and exploitation as two basic strategies for firms that aim to acquire new knowledge, thereby adapting to technological advance. The former can be related to searching, flexibility and radical innovation, while the latter rather encom-

[8]The t-value can be considered as significant if a limit of 2.0 is exceeded at a confidence level of 0.95 and a degree of freedom of at least 5. This holds true for the tests accomplished here. Hence, a significant difference between two mean values is given and the null hypotheses can be rejected (Bosch 1998).

passes refers to refinement, production and incremental innovations (see also Subsection 2.3.2). While for the exploration and radical innovation phase, in which young nano-regions surely are, diversity and creativity is assumed to be more relevant, specialisation becomes stimulating later when incremental innovations and exploitation becomes important (Dittrich and Kijkuit 2004). Perhaps these findings are more relevant for the development of nanotechnology as GPTs than assumed before, where the focus was laid on the need for specialisation in small settings with respect to advancing high-tech research. This however seems to become more relevant in cases where the regional nano-knowledge bases are larger. Yet, the diversity of the NKB does not show any positive influence. This might have several reasons: It can be interpreted as diversity only being particularly stimulating when there is a simultaneous influence of specialisation like in Model 8.I. However, referring to the argumentation that led to the formulation of the hypothesis and the literature on exploration and exploitation, the reasoning is diametric. If both effects were relevant, this could lead to a mutual cancellation of effects. However, these results can also be interpreted as diversity not being particularly relevant for any distinct size, but likewise for all sizes (see Model 8.I).

	Dynamics of Specialisation				Dynamics of Diversity			
	MODEL 8.II - SMALL		MODEL 8.III - LARGE		MODEL 8.IV - SMALL		MODEL 8.V - LARGE	
SPEC	-5.0416*	(3.0357)	1.4135*	(0.7429)				
DIV					0.76120	(0.6546)	-1.0287	(0.7045)
HQ	0.0520	(0.1049)	0.0773	(0.065)	0.10926	(0.1014)	0.0425	(0.0632)
SIZE_NKB	0.0011	(0.0093)	0.0022***	(0.0007)	0.00305	(0.0091)	0.0017**	(0.0007)
year dummies	yes		yes		yes		yes	
Const	-9.7298	(757.2158)	-3.1471***	(1.1172)	-14.6705	(527.81)	-0.6518	(1.0512)
Obs	149		180		149		180	
Number of Groups	16		18		16		18	
Log likelihood	-270.1009		-537.2057		-270.70728		-538.0078	
Wald chi2	50.28		136.84		49.24		133.57	

Table 8.4: Results of negative binomial fixed effects panel data analysis of *PATENTS*.
***Indicates significance at 0.01. Standard errors in parentheses.
Source: own calculations.

8.3.4 Diffusion (H8.4)

Finally turning to H8.4, it is assumed that (a) the size of the scientific NKB has a positive influence on the growth of the technological NKB and moreover (b) specialisation of the scientific NKB hampers the growth of the technological NKB while (c) diversity of the scientific NKB stimulates the growth of the technological NKB. In order to test these hypotheses, the characteristics of the scientific NKB have been calculated in analogy to the characteristics of the technological NKB. Keep in mind that due to different qualities of the classification systems, results have to be treated with care, which is why they are taken as a hint here, not a definitive result. Table 8.5 presents the results for this Model 8.VI. The results indicate that H8.4 can be confirmed here, at least in parts: The size of the regional scientific NKB has a significant and positive influence on the count of newly filed patents. Yet, although the effect is statistically significant on the 10% level, the economic significance is to be doubted due to an extremely small coefficient. However, at least in tendency the amount of regionally existing scientific nano-knowledge, contributes to the development of technological innovations. It can easily be interpreted as being in line with the pure mathematical fact that the mere amount of pre-exiting knowledge increases the opportunities of re-combination as well as being in line with previous findings that scientific knowledge diffuses at an early level of the value creation chain and is then employed in inventions in the fields of technological application. Given this relationship, however, the small coefficient has to be mentioned again. This part of the diffusion pattern is frequently referred to as technology transfer and points to the relevance of basic research (i.e. most presumably university-industry knowledge flows). Moreover, the results also show that while scientific diversity does not have a significant influence on the development of the technological NKB, scientific specialisation does not only not positively contribute, but indeed significantly hamper the growth of the technological NKB. While scientific specialisation might advance the scientific NKB, this highly contextual knowledge is only seldom directly marketable and therefore obviously not useful for commercial applications in the short and medium run. This would explain a non-significance. The negative sign might be a hint that even the knowledge transfer suffers from this specialisation. Once stated that scientific knowledge stimulates technological inventions, a weakly existing knowledge transfer hence would even hamper the development of new applied nano-knowledge. Diversity, by contrast, does again not show any positive impact on the creation of new technological knowledge in nano. This is why H8.4a can be weakly and H8.4b can be strongly confirmed, H8.4c cannot be confirmed.

8.4 Conclusion

Nanotechnology as GPT has the inherent potential to foster radical and widely spread innovations that result in remarkable growth. Subsequently, it seems to be of significant importance that regions create an environment for innovation that is conducive to the development of such future technologies in order to benefit from the growth potentials. In many regions, such policies have already been set in place in form of nano clusters or science parks. However, nanotechnology is not only a knowledge intensive technology, but also a general purpose technology. Therefore, not only the extent and the efficiency

	Model 8.VI	
PUB_SPEC	-1.3684***	(0.5261)
PUB_COMP	0.0012	(0.0012)
PUB_DIV	1.0780	(1.1366)
PUB_SIZE_NKB	0.0003*	(0.0002)
HQ	-0.0187	(0.0612)
year dummies	yes	
Const	-12.60152	(397.4815)
Obs	341	
Number of Groups	34	
Log likelihood	-848.5509	
Wald chi2	188.28	

Table 8.5: Results of negative binomial fixed effects panel data analysis of *PATENTS*. ***Indicates significance at 0.01. Standard errors in parentheses. Source: own calculations.

of knowledge spillovers, but also their composition is of particular importance. This chapter thus investigates, which circumstances support the technological development and hence its competitiveness within the fast growing field of nanotechnology. The empirical analysis in this chapter employs new patent filings in different German regions to regress the characteristics of the previously existing nano-knowledge bases (constructed as a 5-year-window of patent filings) on them.

First and most basically, it is found that the previously existing regional scientific and technological nano-knowledge has a positive influence on the creation of new knowledge. Given the cumulative nature of knowledge, this result is not surprising but yet of fundamental importance for the development of NKBs in regions. This does not only point to a path dependent creation of new knowledge given the existing *regional* knowledge stock. Although nanotechnology is a high technology advanced in a worldwide race for innovation, everything that so far happened locally is highly influential, emphasising the role of local knowledge spillovers. Development paths cannot be changed quickly since they rely on knowledge acquired in the past few years. This has to be considered by policymakers aiming to set up any kind of supportive policies.
Second, and prolonging the first point, not only the amount of precedent nanotechnological knowledge, but the composition of the past nano-knowledge bases influences present innovations. As found here, specialisation and diversity of the technological NKB both have a significant and positive influence on the growth of the technological NKB. Not being mutually exclusive, these results are highly interesting within the Marshall-Jacobs-controversy, debating on whether specialisation or diversity externalities stimulate innovations (better). In the case of nanotechnology, both seem to positively impact innovation activity which is assumed to be particularly due to the GPT

nature of nanotechnology: While specialisation is needed to advance the technology incrementally at the edge, diversity stimulates the application in various (new) fields, thereby opening opportunities for cross-fertilisation and exponentiation of innovation incentives.

However, concerning the dynamics of specialisation and diversity, the results obtained are contrary to what was expected. For the two different cluster stages no difference in the impact of diversity was found (in contrast to the expectation that diversity would rather be important in later stages of development). By contrast, specialisation shows a significantly negative impact on innovation in smaller clusters and a significantly positive influence in larger clusters. Assuming that the size of an agglomeration in terms of the NKB reflects a time-dependent level of development, this is in contrast to what was formulated in H8.3. As already argued above, this is in line with firm-level literature on different innovations strategies. Sensibly assuming that, in general and hence on a regional level, the exploration stage is prevalent before the exploitation phase, specialisation would become more relevant in more advanced clusters. Diversity, however, has no particular time-dependent effect, which might be due to its stage invariance or due to mutual cancelation of the mentioned effects.

In what concerns the diffusion of scientific knowledge in direction of application within the technological NKB, one can clearly state that the scientific knowledge base has a positive impact on the growth of the technological knowledge base. Put another way, this is a hint to active technology transfer. With respect to the composition of the scientific knowledge base, results are again ambiguous: While specialisation of the scientific NKB has a highly significant negative impact on technological innovations, which is likely to be a hint to problems of technology transfer and and the marketability of basic research results, scientific diversity – again – has no significant effect on innovations in application.

Yet, for all these results it has to be pointed to the emerging character of nanotechnology and hence to regional configurations that are not yet stable. This implies that changes in the investigated relationships have to be expected. Hence, all the insights gained have to be regarded as a snapshot for this point in time. To put these in a nutshell: Locally existing nano-knowledge is an important ingredient to the development of new knowledge in the field. Therefore it can reasonably be assumed that knowledge transfers and respective spillovers are effective. Contributing to the Marshall-Jacobs-controversy it has been investigated which characteristics of the local NKB contribute to innovations in nanotechnology and how. The underlying central assumption was that the characteristics of the knowledge stock are in direct relationship to the kind of spillovers that are at work. Generally spoken, both, specialisation effects and diversity effects, are found to be stimulative for innovation in nanotechnology as GPT. However, when it comes to the consideration of dynamics of diffusion effects, results change and are dependent on the stage of development. Given the importance of GPTs for economic growth and these results in the light of the still small sample and short period of time investigated, it is surely worth future efforts to disentangle the relevance of the effects of the overall development level of the knowledge base of a GPT and its composition. To do so, it would surely be conducive to assess the mechanisms behind knowledge diffusion in order to understand which knowledge flows when and with which effect.

9 Impact of Local Knowledge Endowment on Nanotechnology Firm Growth

Picking up the open issue of the nature of knowledge spillovers nurturing innovativeness (Chapter 7) and extending the analysis accomplished in Chapter 8, this chapter investigates the contribution of local knowledge endowment to employment growth in nanotechnology firms. Thereby, the anchorage into the regional knowledge production system as well as the role of the composition of the existing knowledge stock are again be subject to investigation. Yet, the approach is significantly different to the one followed in Chapter 8, since the focus is laid on the influence of the indicated issues on employment growth in firms processing nanotechnology. Hence, the main questions tackled in this chapter are: (i) (How) do firm-specific and location-specific characteristics interact and influence the process of job creation of nanotechnology firms?, and (ii) What is the impact of regional specialisation in this context? Put differently, which characteristic of nanotechnology predominates: its character as a high technology (i.e. being located in a specialised region thereby benefitting from regional knowledge spillovers is of major importance) or the character of a GPT (according to which opportunities aside from already existing specialisations may be more important for firm success)?[1]

9.1 Derivation of Hypotheses

There is a vast literature on firm growth referring to growth in sales, revenues, or employment. Most prominent determinants underlying the analyses are the characteristics of the firm (e.g. size, age, industry affiliation, financing strategy), of firm location (see e.g. Storey (1994) for an overview) or of the entrepreneur (e.g. education, skill distribution). Related theories range from neoclassical considerations on optimal

[1]This chapter relies on joint work with Antje Schimke and Ingrid Ott. Source: Schimke, A., Teichert, N. and Ott, I.: Impact of local knowledge endowment on employment growth in nanotechnology, *Industrial and Corporate Change*, forthcoming. Printed with kind permission of Oxford University Press.

size (Coase 1937), over internal learning-by-doing processes (Penrose 1995) and evolutionary concepts in which the 'fitness' of firms plays a central role (Coad 2007) to the socio-economic view which highlights the importance of resource availability and the competition for these resources (Uhlaner et al. 2007). Empirical findings suggest that there is not one single key determinant driving firm growth but factors are highly context specific and depend upon the interaction of several influencing factors (e.g. Harhoff et al. 1998, Delmar et al. 2003, Coad 2007).

Independent of the studied determinants, country or sector, the literature unambiguously highlights the positive relationship between innovative activity and firm growth (Acs and Audretsch 1988, Del Monte and Papagni 2003, Adamou and Sasidharan 2007, Harrison et al. 2008, Coad and Rao 2008). The studies also stress the overall importance of employment and the availability of qualified labour for innovation (Acs and Audretsch 1990, Pianta 2005, Lopez-Garcia and Puente 2009). Feldman (1994), or more recently Feldman and Kogler (2010), provided evidence that particularly innovative activity tends to cluster thereby pointing to the importance of specialisation; at the same time several studies show that firms in specialised clusters reach higher levels of innovation (Moreno et al. 2004, Fromhold-Eisebith and Eisebith 2005). Of special interest are the characteristics of local knowledge, thereby suggesting that specialised local knowledge has a particularly positive effect on innovation and firm growth (Feldman and Audretsch 1999). Fritsch and Slavtchev (2008, 2010) also confirmed that innovating firms are not isolated, self-sustained entities but rather highly linked to their environment. Location matters since it may provide access to specialised networks of firms, suppliers, institutions, or labour (see also Porter (2000); more critically Martin and Sunley (1998)). Other arguments discussed in the context of clustering include stronger pressure to innovate or lower costs for innovation commercialisation (Ketels 2009). Spillover opportunities and thus the proximity-productivity linkage decrease with distance, as knowledge that is highly contextual most frequently requires interaction and face-to-face contact (see Chapter 2 or (von Hippel 1994)).

However, until recently there are only few studies that analyse the role of location and the proximity-productivity relationship for post-entry performance, i.e. the growth of firms, as was done by e.g. Gabe and Kraybill (2002), Boschma and Weterings (2005), Audretsch and Dohse (2007) and Weterings and Boschma (2009). The concept of regional clusters systematically picks up this proximity-productivity relationship, thereby relying on specific economic activities and has become a popular policy measure. While a cluster always refers to a specialised network of firms and institutions there is no definitely accepted definition of industrial clusters. Porter's considerations however, might be seen as representing the standard concept (Martin and Sunley 2003). Porter (2000, p. 254) defined a cluster as a 'geographically proximate group of inter-connected companies and associated institutions in a particular field that is linked by commonalities and complementarities'. As a positive external knowledge spillover they increase their productivity and economic performance. There is, indeed, evidence that firms in clusters reach higher levels of innovation (Moreno et al. 2004, Fromhold-Eisebith and Eisebith 2005). The basic reasoning behind specialisation or industry-specific advantages being relevant for the efficiency of local innovation activity implies that local agents can share the same particular assets and can benefit from goods and services provided by specialised suppliers as well as from a local labor market pool (Marshall 1890). The cluster environment provides not only a stronger pressure to innovate, but also a richer source of relevant knowledge and ideas as well as lower costs for innovation commercialization (Ketels 2009). Cluster strength is hence considered a determinant of prosperity on a local level. As a clustered industry indicates that there are significant benefits from co-location, the industry's productivity is assumed to increase with the level of specialisation within the cluster. In the light of this, knowledge diffusion will occur when firms are embedded in more specialised environment (Marshallian externalities) or in regions that are more diversified (Jacobian externalities). More precisely, the assumed relevance of clusters hence refers to the characteristics of local knowledge and suggests that specialised local knowledge has a particularly positive effect on innovation and firm growth. This chapter contributes to this literature by extending the basic question of the impact of specialised local knowledge endowment (both amount and composition). In doing so, the analysis focuses on nanotechnology firms' growth. In nanotechnology, given its large scope for improvement, innovation activities are essential firm activities. In Germany, small and medium-sized enterprises (SME) account for more than 80 % of all nanotechnology firms (Schnorr-Bäcker 2009). Due to fragmented R&D and production processes, most of the firms only provide parts of complex value creation chains while being embedded in various networks. As a consequence of their high innovation intensity, the anchorage of the actors within regional specialisations is central. One general expectation concerning the overall role of nanotechnology firms is their contribution to job generation thereby strengthening regional competitiveness. It is reasonable to assume that the characteristics of the economic surrounding feed back to nanotechnology firms' performance and vice versa.

Following the argumentation above, it is natural to expect that location characteristics do affect the growth of firms in nanotechnology. Moreover employment growth in nanotechnology firms should be strongly related to successful innovative activity. Following Feldman (1994), knowledge spillovers (from closely related external factors and knowledge sources) are especially relevant for small firms since the resources necessary in order to maintain the knowledge base are typically beyond their means. Callon (1997) moreover pointed to to the fact that in emergent configuration, a configuration that can be assumed to prevail in emerging nanotechnology, particularly tacit knowledge with a limited geographical range is relevant. Nano-firms hence can be assumed to be particularly dependent on (external) tacit knowledge. The new growth literature finds a propensity for knowledge inputs and spillovers to agglomerate and therefore it can be reasonably assumed that firms that are in fact using knowledge inputs, such as firms in (emerging) high-tech or innovation-intensive industries, will perform better once they are located in a high-density region, as these firms will have better access to knowledge resources and knowledge spillovers. Hence, characteristics of location seem to preserve and even reinforce an innovating firm's growth. However, until recently little effort has been done to analyse the role of location and its economic characteristics for post-entry performance, i.e. the growth of firms (Audretsch and Dohse 2007). The importance of agglomeration and the impact of spatial proximity on firm performance have only been studied recently (Gabe and Kraybill 2002, Audretsch and Dohse 2007, Weterings and Boschma 2009). Following Audretsch and Dohse (2007), who found that regions abundant in knowledge resources provide a particularly fertile soil for the growth of young, technology oriented firms, such an analysis is carried out, also focusing on the special role of locational characteristics for the growth of firms in high-tech, particularly nanotechnology-applying industries. However, the following analysis goes one step further by considering the composition of the local knowledge base. Therefore, it is suggested that the extent to which external knowledge is crucial and can be absorbed differs widely across firm size classes and knowledge intensive sectors. Paying attention to the characteristics of the structure of the region a firm is located in (so-called location characteristics) and the knowledge processing characteristics of the firm itself. The impact of location characteristics on employment growth in nanotechnology is assumed to differ across firm size classes, knowledge intensive sectors and age groups (see description in section 4.3). It is therefore hypothesised that:

Hypothesis 9.1 *Local Knowledge Endowment*
Location characteristics do influence the employment growth of firms in nanotechnology.

Put differently, regions rich in knowledge are supposed to provide a particularly good environment for the growth of technology-oriented, i.e. knowledge intensive firms in emerging configurations.

Picking up the issue of the role of the composition of knowledge, the impact of two economic key characteristics of nanotechnology and its corresponding potential for job creation and growth is addressed: As high technology, the usual arguments in the context of the proximity-productivity relationship of innovation activity as derived in Chapter 2 can be assumed to apply. Especially important are hence not only firm specificities but also an amply specialised surrounding to translate spillovers into actual productivity gains. Key determinants are thus a sufficiently high overlap of firms' activities or put differently and absorptive capacity (Cohen and Levinthal 1990), as well as the availability of qualified labour. Consequently, the agents' regional anchorage and especially the composition of regional labour markets are central determinants of success.

In contrast to this is the general purpose character of nanotechnology, which basically allows for the introduction of the technology in any context. This implies that a certain degree of regional specialisation is not mandatory per se, but, depending upon the state of development of the technology, even the contrary may the case: Too narrow regional specialisation patterns may inhibit the technology's use in a multitude of application fields, thereby possibly suppressing potential opportunities for cross-fertilisation and innovation-enhancing feed-back mechanisms across diverse and so far unrelated value creation chains (see Chapter 3).

Taking hence into account the peculiarities of nanotechnology as GPT and the interaction with the characteristics of location, the relationship between regional specialisation and firm growth is not per se clear in the discussed context. The arguments suggest that the specialisation of the regional knowledge base might not be conducive for the employment growth of firms that are active in the exploration of general purpose nanotechnology since this hampers the inflow of knowledge from other fields and even suppresses positive effects stemming from diversity and nanotechnology's application in a wide variety of fields. Catalysing knowledge recombination and fertilising ideas from other application fields most presumably cannot be processed in an environment with a strong, specialised focus. However, firms experience a tension when they aim to advance and exploit existing knowledge and at the same time explore new fields simultaneously (Leten et al. 2007). Specialisation is necessary to develop sufficiently strong capabilities in particular domains in order to be able to realise economies of scale in technology development while incrementally advancing the technology. Hence, specialisation might have a positive effect on growth in nano-firms: Firms that are not particularly intensive in knowledge are assumed to rather exploit existing knowledge. Consequently, the analysis is separated again. The smaller and the younger a firm is, the more it is assumed to be prone to specialisation externalities due to the fact that small firms are often highly specialised and enter the market via specialised niches (van der Panne 2004). Since the exploration of the field is intensive in knowledge it is moreover assumed that knowledge intensive, exploring firms are particularly benefiting from diversity and hence specialisation might have a negative impact. Given the GPT nature of nanotechnology and the chances that are inherent in diversity and exploration of the field and on the other hand the minimum degree of knowledge in the respective field needed to be able to keep up with leading edge development, too less and too much regional specialisation might negatively influence firm performance in either of the firm classes distinguished (Fritsch and Slavtchev 2010). Hence, it is assumed that local specialisation effects have a negative impact on nanotechnology firm growth. Put another way, the effects of the co-location of the distinct industry the nanotechnology firm belongs to negatively impact the development of the firm since it restrains the growth opportunities across diverse fields that nanotechnology, being a general purpose technology, offers. Having stated this conjecture, it is hypothesised that the feature of nanotechnology being a GPT outweighs the benefits local specialisation is found to inhere for the growth of high-tech firms in general means.

Hypothesis 9.2 *Impact of Local Specialiation*
Local specialisation effects the employment growth of firms in nanotechnology negatively.
(a) While specialisation has a direct negative impact on employment growth in particularly knowledge intensive firms and older firms,
(b) too much local specialisation hampers employment growth in general.

Finally, the robustness of the impact of specialisation and location characteristics on employment growth is considered. Thus, it is investigated whether the yearly changes of the level of specialisation might interfere with the yearly changes in the growth rates. In this context and more technically it is assumed that

Hypothesis 9.3 *Robustness*
Specialisation effects that are related to average employment growth are the same as those that are related to a year-to-year consideration of employment growth.

9.2 Methodology and Data

The analysis in this chapter is most closely related to Audretsch and Dohse (2007) who found that regions abundant in knowledge resources provide a particularly fertile soil for the growth of young, technology-oriented firms. They consider new market firms and point to the need of investigating the relationship between local knowledge endowment and firm performance in other high and emerging technologies. Their main hypotheses are tested in the promising field of nanotechnology relying on unique data on German nano-firms which was composed and collected for this purpose. While Audretsch and Dohse (2007) only elaborated on the influence of the accessible stock – and hence the quantity – of local knowledge, the analysis here extends to the composition and hence the quality of the local knowledge base. Besides, the robustness of the hypotheses is tested by two different econometric approaches and novel measures that expand their explanatory power are introduced.

The focus of the underlying unique data-set is on firms operating in fields that develop or apply nanotechnology. That means that the firms in the sample are concerned with nanotechnology in any possible way, be it basic R&D or the employment of nanotechnology in later stages of the value creation chain, irrespective of whether this is their main field of activity. These firms are not only knowledge intensive by operating in a high-tech sectors, but particularly because nanotechnology is still in a nascent stage of development and hence these firms are intensive in innovation – which is by definition knowledge intensive. However, nanotechnology firms operate across a wide range of industries and are therefore particularly heterogeneous in nature, e.g. referring to $SIZE$, KIS and AGE. This is why on the one hand all firms are investigated together and on the other hand are split in subsamples across these characteristics. The data set of firms consists of records from the 'competence atlas nanotechnology in Germany' (www.nano-map.de), an online database providing information on firms that are concerned with nanotechnology. An online-survey was conducted in 2011, asking the firms for information on employment numbers for different years, profits, year of foundation, zip code and their industry affiliation (i.e. NACE classification of the 2-digit and 3-digit industry affiliation) on the basis of their main products. This is particularly necessary since nanotechnology as GPT does not constitute a single industry, but is present in a wide range of different industries. 216 of 1950 contacted firms answered, which gives a response rate of 11.1%. The non-response bias (respectively t-test) is a commonly used method (e.g. Wooldridge 2002) to ensure whether the firm sample is not prone to sample selection. Running a t-test for the two groups of interest, i.e. early and later answering firms, the latter ones represent the firms that will never provide a response. The corresponding p-values are non-significant for both, the number of employees and the profits, indicating that the firm sample is representative of the entire population. In doing so, the independent samples t-test compares the difference in the means from the two groups to a given value (usually 0). In this vein, the firm sample is split into two groups: (i) response at an early stage (first wave of the survey) and (ii) response at a later time (second wave of survey). The t-test statistics obviously show that there are neither in the case of number of employees nor in the case of profits significant differences between the two groups. The results indicate that there is no statistically

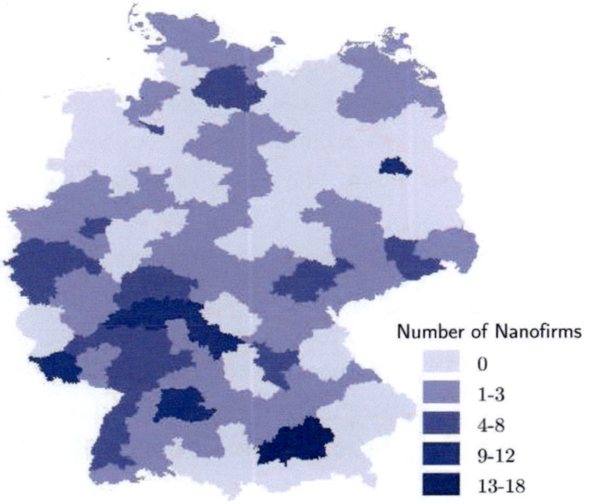

Figure 9.1: Distribution of considered nano-firms across Germany.
Source: own illustration.

significant difference between the mean values for the first wave and the second wave of survey ($t = 1.1866, p = 0.2371 > 0.05$). In other words, the firm sample is not prone to sample selection.

The level of analysis is the geographical level of German planning regions ('Raumordnungsregionen'). Germany consists of 97 planning regions. This level is chosen as it is particularly suited to approximate spatial and functional interrelations between core cities and the corresponding hinterland (BBR 2001). Therefore, they are homogeneous and comparable entities, which are large enough to assume that spillovers are intraregional and hence no connection between the different regions has to be included in the estimations (Audretsch and Dohse 2007). It has to be mentioned that the nano-firms in the sample are not equally distributed: Out of the 97 planning regions, the nanotechnology firms in the sample are located in 62 different regions, some of them hosting a multitude of firms. Figure 9.1 displays this distribution. The data for the regional part of the analyses, i.e. mainly the employment data for the corresponding planning regions comes from the Federal Employment Agency (Bundesagentur für Arbeit), statistics of employees subject to social insurance contributions and from the Federal Office for Building and Regional Planning (BBR, INKAR).

9.2.1 Variables

Dependent Variable

Before starting with the analysis, an operationalization of the term firm growth is necessary. There is a wide range of definitions that deal with firm growth. Garnsey et al. (2006, p. 11) suggested that 'firms' growth can be measured in terms of input (e.g. employees), in terms of value of the firm and in terms of output (e.g. turnover, profit)'. In the following analyses, the growth measure of the growth of employees is employed. Hence, the dependent variables are defined by measuring the log-form of employment growth as the ratio of the year t (respectively 2010) to year $t-1$ (respectively 2006). The variable values for the year of the financial crisis, 2008, were replaced by the average (i.e. mean value) of the other available years' values. More precisely, it might be that the stochastic properties of the growth rates exhibit entirely different growth features as in the other years of the studied time period. In other words, growth events (i.e. growth rates) during the financial crises (respectively 2008) seem to occur with a significantly higher probability to follow extreme growth events. Nevertheless, in some cases number of employees is completely missing for all years, which cannot be replaced accordingly.

Explanatory Variables

Regarding the hypotheses, several independent variables are employed. These variables display firm-specific and location-specific characteristics. The firm-specific variables reflect rather usual factors found to influence employment growth, such as firm size, age and industry affiliation. Location-specific variables by contrast shall reflect the knowledge characteristics that are specific to the environment the firm is located in. An overview of the description of explanatory variables is given in Table 9.1 and the independent variables are discussed as follows:

Firm-specific characteristics The $SIZE$-dummy controls for the size of the firm. Smaller firms more intensively and more frequently rely on knowledge spilling over for generating new knowledge and innovative activity than larger firms (Audretsch 1998). Small and medium-sized firms ($SIZE = 1$) are hence assumed to benefit differently from location-specific characteristics than larger ones ($SIZE = 0$). KIS is an industry-dummy, indicating whether a firm belongs to a particularly knowledge intensive sector within the sample ($KIS = 1$, high-KIS) or not ($KIS = 0$, low-KIS). KIS is constructed by the share of 'knowledge workers' in an industry's labour force, which is measured by the share of employees with a university degree. Sectors with an above-average share of knowledge workers are hence seen as knowledge intensive (Audretsch and Dohse

2007). This dummy is used in order to be able to distinguish between firms that are operating in above average knowledge-intensive industries among the sample of firms and hence especially prone to knowledge spillovers as positive externality raising their productivity. Moreover, high-*KIS* firms should be able to better incorporate, i.e. to use the knowledge that is spilling over as it is widely accepted that firms that are themselves active in knowledge processing and production exhibit a high absorptive capacity (Cohen and Levinthal 1990). Location is hence expected to have a more relevant, positive influence on high-*KIS* firms and also firm age (*AGE*) is investigated as a potential initial trigger for firm growth in nanotechnology. Age is consistently found to be a relevant impact factor on firm performance (Coad 2010). Assuming that the impact of local knowledge characteristics on firm growth depends on firm characteristics, the modal age of the firms in the sample is used as a cut-off point for creating a subsample of younger and older firms each. Hence, *KIS*,*AGE* and *SIZE* of nanotechnology are employed in form of a dummy in order to be able to introduce different subsamples and investigate the particular role of location specific characteristics given differing firm-specific characteristics.

Location-specific characteristics and the nature of the regional knowledge base The location-specific variables refer to the role of locations, particularly to possible knowledge spillovers generated in the region. With *HQ* a region-dummy is introduced that refers to whether a region exhibits a share of highly qualified (*HQ*) employees in the top quartile, measured by employees with university degrees. The *IND* variable, by contrast, displays the absolute number of employees in the firms' industry in its region. In both, the *HQ* and *IND* it is hence implicitly assumed that the regional human capital displays the regional knowledge resources, as commonly done, as knowledge can be considered as incorporated in individuals who are able to process it (Rigby and Essletzbichler 2002). The distinction between these two variables is useful, as the *HQ* dummy is a relatively general measure of knowledge intensity in the region, whereas *IND* is more specialised, pointing to the actual strength of the firm's industry in the considered region. Both are expected to have a positive influence on firm growth. *INDDENS* by contrast is a catch-all region-specific variable catching agglomeration effects in general by displaying the industry density of a region to improve model fit. It measures the number of industry employees subject to social insurance contributions per square kilometre in the respective region. A further standard measure capturing regional knowledge resources is the presence of a university in a region, as universities are at the same time supportive and necessary for regional innovation and economic development (Feldman and Kogler 2010). Research results are open to the public and ready to be exploited as knowledge spillovers. Therefore, the absolute number of students in a region *STUD* is employed. Since it can be expected that knowledge spillovers increase with available knowledge resources, *STUD* should have a positive impact on firm growth. A similar argumentation holds for *R&D*, a variable displaying the share absolute number of employees mainly concerned with *R&D* in a region. The knowledge inherent in and produced by human capital (mainly) concerned with *R&D* is likely to be another source of knowledge spillovers. The specialisation (Location Quotient, *LQ*) variable measures region-specific knowledge-resources and refers to the characteristics of the knowledge within a region. It is constructed using employment data, corresponding to the industry in which the firm operates. *LQ* is calculated by the ratio of the share of employees of a region in the industry into which the nanotechnology firms classified itself, divided by the total share of employees in this very field in the whole country:[2]

$$LQ_{ij} = \frac{E_{i,j}/\sum_i E_{i,j}}{\sum_j E_{i,j} \;/\; \sum_i \sum_j E_{i,j}}, \tag{9.1}$$

with E number of employees, i the region-index and j the industry-index. LQ indices are usual measures for specialisation externalities (Paci and Usai 1999). For the empirical analysis a normalisation is employed, making the index symmetric and easier to interpret by using the formula $LQ(N) = 100 * (LQ^2 - 1)/(LQ^2 + 1)$, which constrains possible values within the interval (-100,100) (Vollrath 1991, Grupp 1994). Values above 0 hence indicate an above average, values below 0 below average specialisation. Following the hypotheses, *LQ* is expected to influence the growth of firms. Table 9.1 pictures the different explanatory variables and a short description of variables, distinguishing between firm-specific and location-specific characteristics.

[2] Note that, for reasons of readability, *LQ* is used instead of $LQ_{i,j}$.

Characteristic	Variable	Description
Firm-Specific	*SIZE*	Small and medium enterprises, defined as those with less than 251 employees (SIZE=1).
	KIS	Firms in sectors with an above-average share of employees with university degree are knowledge intensive (KIS=1).
	AGE	Age of the firm in terms of years since foundation. Cut-off point used to distinguish between young and old firms is modal age.
Location-Specific	*HQ*	Region exhibits a share of highly qualified employees with university degree in the top quartile.
	INDDENS	Measures industry density (employees in industry per km^2) in a region, catchall variable for agglomeration effects.
	IND	Absolute employment in the firms' industry in its region, pointing to the actual strength of the firm's industry in the considered region.
	STUD	Absolute number of students in the considered region.
	R&D	Absolute number of employees in R&D in the considered region.
	LQ	LQ is calculated by the ratio of the share of employees of a region i in industry j, divided by the total share of employees in this very field in the whole country.

Table 9.1: Description of explanatory variables.
Source: own compilation.

9.2.2 Descriptive Statistics and Stochastic Properties

The final database consists of 216 firms. The descriptive statistics for the employed variables are given in Table 9.2. With respect to the different stochastic properties of the entire sample, the variables *KIS*, *SIZE*, *AGE* are hence used to distinguish between the different subsamples. Table 9.3 shows the number of firms differentiated by different firm size classes. Firms classified as SME are defined as those with less than 251 employees (European Commission 2010): Actually, there are more SME than larger firms in nanotechnology. Following Schnorr-Bäcker (2009), however, nano-firms are mostly SMEs and more seldom larger firms, which is why the sample represents the population well. Table 9.3 moreover shows the share of firms differentiated into *KIS* (i.e. the most knowledge intensive sectors) and *AGE* (i.e. younger and older firms). Additionally, Table 9.3 pictures that the sample consists of an above average number of firms active in knowledge intensive sectors (*KIS*). Finally, the sample is distinguished between younger and older firms. The cut-off point in terms of younger and older firms is represented by the modal age of eight years (Fagiolo and Luzzi 2006, Huergo and Jaumandreu 2004). In this vein, the distinction between different age groups provides additional information on the growth process. To sum up, the firm sample operates across a wide range of industries and is therefore particularly heterogeneous in nature, e.g. referring to *SIZE*, *KIS* and *AGE*. Therefore, independent group t-tests are performed to test the different specifications against each other. In the case of the different firm *SIZE* classes, the t-statistic is -2.4202 with 214 degrees of freedom. The corresponding two-tailed p-value is 0.0163, which is less than 0.05. The same is true for the different *AGE* classes, i.e. t-statistic is -2.6107 with 214 degree of freedom and a corresponding two-tailed p-value of 0.0097. Finally, it can be concluded that the difference of means in growth rates between SME/larger firms and younger/older firms is different from 0. Surprisingly, in the case of knowledge intensive sectors ($KIS = 1/KIS = 0$) the mean difference of $KIS = 1$ and $KIS = 0$ is not different from 0 (i.e. $t = 0.0187$; $df = 214$ and p-value$= 0.9851$). Nevertheless, these subsamples can be assumed to operate on different frequencies and are differently influenced by location specific characteristics (Audretsch and Dohse 2007).

Variable	Obs	Mean	StdDev	Min	Max
EMP	216	0.1399	0.4411	-3.6110	1.6337
KIS	236	0.8178	0.3868	0	1
SIZE	236	0.6314	0.4835	0	1
AGE	222	40.4646	53.3503	0	343
HQ	236	0.1151	0.0354	0.0473	0.1845
INDDENS	236	45.4338	39.078	2.1653	165.90
IND	235	10295.4	12475.71	12	70531
STUD	236	38148.5	33889.06	0	134260.4
R&D	236	9112.375	11739.87	140	39879
LQ	234	-5.3429	58.5562	-100	99.4687

Table 9.2: Descriptive statistics.
Source: own calculations.

Category	Subsample	Description	Freq	Share
SIZE	SME	$1 \leq x \leq 250$	144	66.7
	Large-sized	>250	72	33.3
KIS	High-*KIS* (*KIS*=1)	above avg share of R&D EMP	178	82.4
	Low-*KIS* (*KIS*=0)	below avg share of R&D EMP	38	17.6
AGE	Younger	= 8 years (modal age)	42	19.5
	Older	> 8 years (modal age)	174	80.5

Table 9.3: Subsamples w.r.t. firm-specific characteristics.
Source: own calculations.

9.2.3 Regression Approach and Model Fit

First, a regression approach using OLS estimation is set up (see equation 9.2 and 11.6) to analyse the average growth of the firms. As independent variables all the described variables are used. Standard regression approaches are employed since it can be expected that the residuals are approximately normally distributed. There is no evidence for a deviation from a normal distribution in the data. Other problems, such as heteroscedasticity, are not found for the regressions with the logarithm of relative growth as dependent variable, either. Reynolds et al. (1994) and more recently Audretsch and Dohse (2007) developed an estimation approach that includes location-specific determinants of growth which are built on for investigating whether firm growth in nanotechnology is affected by different location-specific characteristics. Again, the average growth effect of these independent variables is analysed. For the investigation the log-level model is employed. In the log-level model, $100 * \alpha_1$ is sometimes called the 'semi-elasticity' of y with respect to x (Wooldridge 2002). First, the impact of indicators on the average growth (from 2007 to 2010) of employment is in focus. In the following equations, *LOCATION* stands for the various measures of location-specific characteristics, in this case *HQ*, *INDDENS*, *IND*, *STUD* and *R&D*. Furthermore, the regressions for subsamples of different firm size classes (*SIZE*), knowledge intensive sectors (*KIS*) and different age groups (*AGE*) all use the following model:

$$\begin{aligned}(log(empl_{2010}) - log(empl_{2007}))_j &= a_0 + \sum_{k=1}^{5} a_k \, LOCATION_{k_j} \\ &+ a_6 \, log(SIZE)_j + a_7 \, log(AGE)_j + a_8 \, KIS + \varepsilon.\end{aligned} \tag{9.2}$$

Equation 9.2 shall preliminarily investigate whether former findings in the literature on the relationship between location characteristics (as discussed above) and employment growth hold for the studied case. The employment of the specialisation effect might catch some of these effects, which is why this basic model is analysed first. However, in equation 9.2 the degree of specialisation of the local knowledge base is still neglected. Since regional specialisation is assumed to have an influence on nano-firm growth, the *LQ* measure is added as well as its squared term LQ^2:

$$\begin{aligned}(log(empl_{2010}) - log(empl_{2007}))_j &= a_0 + a_1 \, LQ_j + a_2 \, LQ_j^2 \\ + \sum_{k=3}^{7} a_k \, LOCATION_{k_j} + a_8 \, log(SIZE)_j &+ a_9 \, log(AGE)_j + a_10 \, KIS + \varepsilon.\end{aligned} \tag{9.3}$$

Third, the robustness of the impact of specialisation and location characteristics on employment growth is analysed. Thus, the perspective is changed from average growth to a year-to-year consideration of growth, investigating whether the yearly changes of the level of specialisation might interfere with the yearly changes in the employment growth rates. This means, if growth in one year depends on an increasing level of specialisation or not, the relationship between current employment growth and previous specialisation might be a direct effect or an indirect effect. As things stand, specialisation effects are only proved for average employment growth. Hence, it is not yet known whether specialisation effects also occur for yearly changes (very short-run consideration). It has also not been proven that year-to-year specialisation effects do exhibit employment growth. To prove this, it would be necessary to disentangle this dynamic effect. Therefore, a cross-sectional time series model is conducted. Hence, firm growth is estimated using cross-sectional time series estimation with fixed effects. In particular, the model shall provide a more detailed insight on individual characteristics that may contribute to the predictor variable and to control for unknown heterogeneity. To decide whether the fixed effects model is suitable (instead of using random effects model), the Hausman test is performed. The null hypothesis can be rejected, leading to the conclusion that the fixed effect model is appropriate ($Prob > chi2$ is significant). To see if time fixed effects are needed when running a fixed effects model, the joint test is performed to see if the dummies for all year are equal to 0 (i.e. if they are not then time fixed effects are needed). The null hypothesis that all year coefficients are jointly equal to zero can be rejected, therefore time fixed effects are needed in the panel specification (i.e. $Prob > F$ is significant). First, one regression set is conducted for all firms together and then two other regressions for each of the $SIZE, KIS$ and AGE subgroups separately:

$$log(empl)_{it} = a_0 + a_1\, LQ_j + a_2\, LQ_j^2 + \sum_{k=3}^{7} a_k\, LOCATION_{k_j} + \varepsilon. \tag{9.4}$$

Finally, it is tested and controlled for multicollinearity (see the correlation matrix in Table F.1 the Appendix G) and endogeneity. Moreover, the first year value in 2007 (or the first available value) of observation is employed as independent variables in the case of H9.1 and H9.2.

9.3 Results and Interpretation

In the following section the main findings of the regression analyses are discussed and interpreted. The regression results are reported in Tables 9.4 - 9.6.

9.3.1 Location Characteristics (H9.1)

Since the main aim is to gain information on the location characteristics that contribute to the growth of nano-firms, the variables differentiate between the characteristics of the structure of the region a firm is located in. Preliminarily it is assumed that location characteristics do influence employment growth of nano-firms (H9.1). The results for the regression analyses are presented in Table 9.4.

First, significant negative coefficients for the *AGE* of firms are found. This especially holds for the subsamples of all firms, smaller firms and both subsamples of *KIS*. Older firms are hence less likely to show higher growth than younger firms, which is in line with the findings of many other scholars before. It can be seen as 'stylised fact' that growth tends to decline with firm age (Audretsch and Dohse 2007). Older firms are characteristically more routinized, more inert and less able to adapt (Coad 2007). In contrast, there is a positive effect of *SIZE* for both knowledge classes and older firms. Against the expectation that firm growth decreases with the size of the firms (which is also a stylised fact), the regression results report a positive coefficient. The positive coefficients suggest that employment growth tends to increase as the firm becomes larger. More important in the context of the hypotheses is the impact of *HQ* representing the knowledge intensity in the region. The positive and significant coefficients of highly qualified employees (*HQ*) in the region on the employment growth of all firms point out that firms exhibit higher growth in regions characterised by a share of highly qualified employees in the top quartile. However, this finding does not hold for all subgroups and varies across different firm size classes, *KIS* and *AGE* groups. Actually, the coefficient of *HQ* is significant and positive in smaller firms but not in larger. Thus, the impact of *HQ* in the region is especially relevant for smaller firms. This might be due to the fact that larger firms are not as much depending on external knowledge and on possible knowledge spillovers stemming from high local endowments in knowledge, since they benefit from internal economies of scale in knowledge production because their own knowledge stock is larger. Looking at the results of firms that belong to a knowledge intensive industry (i.e. $KIS = 1$), a strongly positive significant coefficient is found. This means firms with high knowledge intensity experience higher employment growth in regions with access to highly qualified employees which is very intuitive. Otherwise and in the case of low-knowledge industries ($KIS = 0$) the coefficient shows no longer a significance. This seems similarly plausible since these firms do not rely as much on knowledge activities and hence regional knowledge endowment is not particularly important. Furthermore, another interesting issue concerning the impact of *HQ* (Models 9.VI and 9.VII) is a positive and significant coefficient for firms that are younger than 8 years, but with an insignificant coefficient in case of older firms. This suggests that younger firms experience higher employment growth if they have access to qualified knowledge workers in their region. This finding also goes in line with the general findings by Dosi et al. (1995) and it even more emphasises the relevance of possible knowledge spillovers for new firms that are entering or just entered the nanotechnology-market and its relevance for success in the beginning phase where fundamental knowledge is gained. Interestingly, in the case of low-*KIS* growth is moreover even negatively influenced by the size of the group of employees that work in the same industry they are engaged in (*IND*). As the numbers of employees in the same industry also proxies the strength of regional competition, it might indeed especially affect those firms negatively that do not profit as much as others from the positive effects of this concentration, such as (intra-industry) knowledge spillovers. Looking at the results for the independent variable of *R&D* representing the common share of R&D employees in the region, there is no significant coefficient for most of the models. However, a negative and statistically significant coefficient of *R&D* for low-*KIS* indicates that average employment growth tends to decline with a high share of R&D employees in the region. While this result might be counterintuitive in the first place, it could be a hint to what is investigated in the second hypothesis: It is not knowledge per se that positively influences firm growth, but the influence of knowledge and the potentially resulting spillovers depend on the characteristics of the available knowledge. The kind of R&D processed might, e.g., be too basic or to incoherent to be beneficial for firms that are interested in commercialisation. For instance, Frenken et al. (2007) as well as Boschma and Iammarino (2009) referred to such an issue, when they argue that for knowledge to spill over effectively, and hence contribute positively to a firm's performance, related variety in form of complementarities among industries and their knowledge is necessary. Eventually, H9.1 can be confirmed: Location characteristics do influence the employment growth of nano-firms.

To sum up, the expectations are strongly confirmed by the results, emphasising that location characteristics can stimulate the growth of firms in nanotechnology. Besides typical impact factors such as age and size, the share of highly qualified employees does play a major role. More particularly, this impact of highly qualified employees on firm growth varies across firm size, knowledge intensive industries and age groups. This means, in turn, that the share of highly qualified employees is more important in smaller firms than in larger firms, and seems to be more relevant in firms that are active in particularly knowledge intensive industries. Simultaneously, the impact of local highly qualified employees is more decisive in younger firms. Therefore, more precise hypothesis 9.1 is set up, suggesting that 'while the share of highly qualified employees is more important in smaller and younger firms as well as in firms belonging to a particularly knowledge intensive industry, a high share of R&D employees in the region has no positive impact on non-knowledge-intensive and older firms'. Eventually, the findings in the literature that young, small and knowledge intensive firms with access to a high density of knowledge workers do experience an above average growth (Audretsch and Dohse 2007) are mostly confirmed by these findings. Thus, nanotechnology firms innovate and grow as other highly knowledge intensive firms do, regardless of the peculiarities a GPT implies. Moreover, nanotechnology firms rely as much on knowledge spillovers as other high-tech (but not GPT) firms from other industries. Finally and most

	ALL	SIZE		KIS		AGE	
	MODEL 9.I All firms	MODEL 9.II SME	MODEL 9.III Large firms	MODEL 9.IV KIS=1	MODEL 9.V KIS=0	MODEL 9.VI younger	MODEL 9.VII older
HQ	0.219**	0.198*	0.233	0.250**	-0.0415	0.540*	0.143
	(0.0918)	(0.119)	(0.169)	(0.106)	(0.123)	(0.298)	(0.0906)
INDDENS	0.0002	0.0012	-0.0016	-1.65e-05	0.001	-0.0006	6.25e-05
	(0.0007)	(0.0012)	(0.001)	(0.0009)	(0.0011)	(0.0028)	(0.0006)
IND	-1.85e-07	5.69e-08	-3.69e-07	-1.08e-07	-2.27e-05***	-8.28e-06	-1.55e-07
	(3.20e-07)	(3.48e-07)	(3.56e-07)	(3.13e-07)	(6.99e-06)	(1.63e-05)	(3.37e-07)
STUD	-9.10e-07	-1.21e-06	-1.29e-06	-8.60e-07	-2.38e-06*	-1.84e-06	-9.13e-07
	(8.87e-07)	(1.23e-06)	(1.35e-06)	(9.30e-07)	(2.40e-06)	(3.66e-06)	(8.08e-07)
R&D	-4.48e-06**	-5.30e-06*	-4.84e-06	-4.74e-06**	-3.66e-06	-1.13e-05*	-2.90e-06
	(2.05e-06)	(3.00e-06)	(3.43e-06)	(2.38e-06)	(3.18e-06)	(6.44e-06)	(1.97e-06)
SIZE	0.153***			0.108	0.143	0.345*	0.105*
	(0.0556)			(0.0807)	(0.104)	(0.188)	(0.0610)
KIS	0.00526	-0.026	0.0154			0.0199	0.0111
	(0.0577)	(0.0841)	(0.0572)			(0.186)	(0.0637)
AGE	-0.0010***	-0.0036*	-0.0001	-0.0003	-0.0006		
	(0.0004)	(0.0019)	(0.0005)	(0.0005)	(0.0006)		
Const	-0.0114	0.213**	0.110	0.0289	0.220	-0.128	0.0156
	(0.0668)	(0.0833)	(0.0960)	(0.106)	(0.137)	(0.235)	(0.0668)
Obs	216	134	72	171	35	42	174
R^2	0.063	0.056	0.101	0.060	0.464	0.171	0.033

Table 9.4: Results of OLS regressions of *EMP*.
***Indicates significance at 0.01. Robust standard errors in parentheses.
Source: own calculations.

simply, the location-specific measures indicate that the growth of firms in nanotechnology is affected by their location-specific characteristics.

9.3.2 Specialisation of the Regional Knowledge Base (H9.2)

Remember the supposition that regions that provide knowledge enrich the growth of technology-oriented, i.e. knowledge intensive firms. Since the extent to which external knowledge is crucial and can be absorbed differs widely across different firm size classes and knowledge intensive industries, hypothesis 9.2a states that specialisation has a direct negative impact on employment growth in particularly knowledge intensive firms and older firms. Moreover, a non-linear impact of *LQ* is assumed as H9.2b states that irrespective to the characteristics of a firm, too much specialisation has a negative impact on employment growth of firms in nanotechnology. As can be seen in Table 9.5, the independent variable of interest is *LQ*, representing the extent of regional specialisation. Moreover, LQ^2 is included in order to be able to control for non-linear effects of specialisation. Additionally, the sample is again differentiated into different firm size classes (*SIZE*), knowledge intensity (*KIS*) as well as age groups (*AGE*).

As Model 9.I' in Table 9.5 shows, the coefficient of *LQ* does appear significant with a negative sign. This clearly indicates that specialisation in any application field of general purpose nanotechnology has an overall negative impact on the growth of nano-firms in terms of employment. This is a hint to the fact that specialisation is counterproductive for explorative, knowledge intensive purpose in the GPT field under investigation here. Specialisation suppresses multiple opportunities for nanotechnology as GPT to develop and inhibits possibilities of catalysing effects and cross-fertilisation. The differentiation into different subgroups emphasises that, however, this effect differs across different firm characteristics again: The results for the independent variable of *LQ* are still significantly negative for high-*KIS* and older firms (see Table 9.5: Models 9.IV' and 9.VII'). These are the firms that are especially prone to exploitation activities since they are knowledge-intensive. It might hence be the case that knowledge intensive firms explore the nano-field as their flexibility of thinking might make it more easy for these firms to perceive possibilities of application of old nano-knowledge in new fields. Another issue is that *HQ* shows statistically insignificant coefficients, except in the case of low-*KIS*. An explanation for this issue might be that *HQ* is captured by the specialisation measures. Also, *HQ* and *LQ* are correlated with each other ($r = 0.2296***$) (see Table F.1 in the Appendix F). In the case of low-*KIS*, a significant coefficient with a negative sign is found, which is interpreted as a support for the fact that firms where knowledge is not a crucial driver of growth depend less on highly qualified employees in the region.

	ALL	SIZE		KIS		AGE	
	MODEL 9.I' All firms	MODEL 9.II' SME	MODEL 9.III' Large firms	MODEL 9.IV' *KIS*=1	MODEL 9.V' *KIS*=0	MODEL 9.VI' younger	MODEL 9.VII' older
LQ	-0.0009*	-0.0006	-0.0008	-0.001*	0.0004	-0.0008	-0.0011**
	(0.0005)	(0.0009)	(0.0006)	(0.0006)	(0.0007)	(0.0019)	(0.0006)
LQ^2	-4.61e-06	-3.87e-06	2.41e-06	-7.83e-07	-1.56e-05	-7.17e-06	-4.54e-06
	(8.39e-06)	(1.27e-05)	(9.29e-06)	(1.02e-05)	(1.08e-05)	(2.91e-05)	(8.70e-06)
HQ	0.219**	0.196*	0.246	0.265**	0,00931	0.544	0.138
	(0.0910)	(0.118)	(0.173)	(0.105)	(0.148)	(0.353)	(0.0895)
INDDENS	6.70e-05	0.0011	-0.0017	-0.0002	0.0009	-0.0008	-5.39e-05
	(0.0008)	(0.0012)	(0.0011)	(0.0009)	(0.0010)	(0.0029)	(0.0006)
IND	-1.38e-07	3.81e-08	-2.17e-07	-9.55e-08	-2.38e-05**	-5.63e-06	-1.24e-07
	(2.57e-07)	(4.15e-07)	(3.77e-07)	(2.52e-07)	(9.06e-06)	(1.73e-05)	(2.74e-07)
STUD	-4.40e-07	-8.38e-07	-1.02e-06	-3.43e-07	-2.99e-06	-9.66e-07	-4.63e-07
	(8.98e-07)	(1.37e-06)	(1.31e-06)	(9.75e-07)	(2.46e-06)	(4.18e-06)	(8.20e-07)
R&D	-4.34e-06**	-5.40e-06*	-4.46e-06	-4.54e-06*	-4.78e-06	-1.12e-05	-2.51e-06
	(2.12e-06)	(3.01e-06)	(3.53e-06)	(2.47e-06)	(3.53e-06)	(6.85e-06)	(2.05e-06)
SIZE	0.141**			0.101	0.103	0.346*	0.0903
	(0.0549)			(0.0800)	(0.104)	(0.203)	(0.0596)
KIS	0.0019	-0.0325	0.0251			0.0057	0.0102
	(0.0580)	(0.0835)	(0.0608)			(0.241)	(0.0639)
AGE		-0.0033	-7.73e-05	-0.0002	-0.0006		
		(0.0021)	(0.0005)	(0.0005)	(0.0007)		
Const	-0,00283	0.214**	0,0693	0,0038	0.298**	-0.133	0,0239
	(0.0715)	(0.0880)	(0.113)	(0.112)	(0.140)	(0.243)	(0.0735)
Obs	215	134	71	170	35	42	173
R^2	0.075	0.059	0.130	0.075	0.502	0.176	0.054

Table 9.5: Results of OLS regressions with *LQ* of *EMP*.
***Indicates significance at 0.01. Robust standard errors in parentheses.
Source: own calculations.

The exploration-suppressing impact of specialisation (Greve 2007) might explain the negative influence of specialisation on employment growth. Older firms already survived the critical start-up phase and moreover are more prone to possessing the necessary endowment with resources to further explore the field. For the other subsamples such as differentiation across size and low-*KIS* or younger firms, no significant effect of specialisation can be found. This is contrary to the expectation that especially young and small firm benefit from specialisation since they occupy mostly specialised niches when entering the market. This is why H9.2 can be confirmed and H9.2(a) cannot.

In order to test H9.2(b), the squared form of *LQ* was also included in the model. The results suggest that too much specialisation does not have any influence on the employment growth in firms active in nanotechnology except for the case of low-*KIS* firms where too much specialisation and too little specialisation, in contrast to moderate specialisation is harmful. Although generally specialisation of the regional knowledge base has no impact on a low-*KIS* firm's performance, employment growth declines when the region becomes too specialised. Since this does only hold for one particular case, H9.2(b) cannot be confirmed here. This might be due to the fact that specialisation in general already is counterproductive to the firms' employment growth. This effect does not seem to become more serious with increasing specialisation.

Summarising, it can hence be stated that regional specialisation does have a mostly negative impact on nano-firm employment growth, even though not for all firms similarly but depending on their knowledge processing characteristics. Hypotheses 9.2 can therefore be confirmed in general means.

9.3.3 Robustness of the Impact of Specialisation (H9.3)

In a last step, the robustness of the impact of specialisation and the location characteristics on growth is analysed, trying to highlight the question whether yearly changes of the level of specialisation might interfere with yearly changes in the employment growth rates. This means, if growth in one year depends on an increasing level of specialisation, the relationship between current employment growth and previous specialisation might be a direct effect. To disentangle this dynamic effect, regressions are conducted where the different measures of specialisation LQ, LQ^2 and the different *LOCATION* measures are included. Hence, it is hypothesised that specialisation effects that are related to average employment growth are the same as those that are related to a year-to-year consideration of employment growth. Table 9.6 presents the detailed regression results for the fixed effects model. As already stated in hypothesis 9.1, firms in nanotechnology are affected by location-specific characteristics (e.g. *HQ*, *INDDENS*, *IND*, *STUD*, *R&D*). Hence, most of these indicators are neglected because in this analysis it is beyond the scope to analyse the pure impact of location again. By contrast, the more particular impact of the level of specialisation is considered.

The comparison between the firm characteristics that relate to average growth (H9.2) and the firm characteristics that relate to a year-to-year consideration (H9.3) results in different findings across all subsamples. Obviously, the coefficients for *LQ* never become significant. First, the results for all firms together no longer indicate a negative coefficient for *LQ*. Yet, a significantly negative coefficient for LQ^2 in the overall Model 9.I and the three subsamples of high-*KIS*, small firms and younger firms is found. This can be interpreted as a statistical support for the fact that employment growth tends to decline with very low and very high levels of specialisation.

Put differently, specialisation hampers year-to-year employment growth of local firms if a certain threshold of specialisation is undercut or exceeded. Also in these cases the effect of the average growth path is not confirmed for the year-to-year perspective. For the year-to-year consideration the results suggest that specialisation indeed influences firm employment growth in a non-linear way (see Table 9.6). While the marginal effect of specialisation is initially insignificant, it becomes significant and negative for regions that exhibit extreme values of specialisation. This means although generally specialisation of the regional knowledge base has no impact on a firm's performance, employment growth declines when the region becomes too much or too little specialised. Even though there is no general positive effect for lower levels of specialisation this reminds of an inverted u-shaped relationship between specialisation and performance often found in empirical work on production (Betrán 2011) stating that too much (or to less) specialisation has a negative influence on performance.

Generally spoken, this model does not confirm the results of the OLS regressions (average growth) around hypotheses 9.2. Hence, the results contradict the expectations in hypothesis 9.3, which is why it has to be rejected. The characteristics accompanying average growth are not usually related to occurrence of year-to-year employment growth. The characteristics that come together with average growth are not usually related to occurrence of year-to-year growth. However, an analysis of the year-to-year growth process of nano-firms provides additional information, as discussed above. If the perspective is changed from average growth to year-to-year consideration the findings vary. Hence, the temporal structure of the growth process itself should be considered.

	ALL	SIZE		KIS		AGE	
	MODEL 9.I" All firms	MODEL 9.II" SME	MODEL 9.III" Larger firms	MODEL 9.IV" $KIS = 1$	MODEL 9.V" $KIS = 0$	MODEL 9.VI" Younger	MODEL 9.VII" older
LQ	-0.0023	-0.0029	0.0043	-0.003	0.0037	0.0013	0.0006
	(0.0018)	(0.0021)	(0.0028)	(0.002)	(0.0057)	(0.0081)	(0.0016)
LQ^2	-2.83e-05*	-3.79e-05*	3.24e-05	-3.16e-05*	2.30e-05	-0.0001*	3.36e-06
	(1.64e-05)	(1.98e-05)	(2.37e-05)	(1.75e-05)	(5.99e-05)	(8.53e-05)	(1.46e-05)
INDDENS	-0.0019	-0.0080	-0.0023	-0.0039	-0.0037	-0.0004	-0.0021
	(0.0089)	(0.0134)	(0.0073)	(0.0099)	(0.0233)	(0.0430)	(0.007)
IND	-2.70e-05	-6.34e-05	-3.29e-05	-1.20e-05	-0.000143**	-2.53e-06	-4.24e-05**
	(2.72e-05)	(3.99e-05)	(2.41e-05)	(3.01e-05)	(6.87e-05)	(0.000164)	(2.12e-05)
_*Iyear*_2008	0.106***	0.138***	0.0482***	0.104***	0.132***	0.153**	0.0939***
	(0.0181)	(0.0260)	(0.0160)	(0.0205)	(0.0394)	(0.0749)	(0.0146)
_*Iyear*_2009	0.109***	0.151***	0,0188	0.111***	0.101***	0.191**	0.0841***
	(0.0177)	(0.0245)	(0.0162)	(0.0201)	(0.0368)	(0.0744)	(0.0143)
Const	5.130***	3.576***	9.076***	5.120***	5.824***	3.033	5.753***
	(0.470)	(0.640)	(0.463)	(0.504)	-1.433	-2.496	(0.361)
Obs	652	429	223	538	114	131	521
R^2	0.116	0.158	0.070	0.114	0.192	0.163	0.135
Number of id	222	150	76	184	38	47	175

Table 9.6: Cross-sectional time series analysis (fixed effects incl. time-fixed Effects) for *EMP*.
***Indicates significance at 0.01. Standard errors in parentheses.
Source: own calculations.

9.4 Conclusion

Nanotechnology firms' growth is influenced by the locations that host the firms. More particularly, the analysis in this chapter sets out to examine whether the local endowment with knowledge influences the growth of these firms. As expected in view of nanotechnology firms operating on an innovation and hence in a knowledge intensive high technology field, the performance of these firms is – in general – stimulated by the local access to (high) knowledge. However, the actual impact of knowledge varies across firms with different characteristics. While the share of highly qualified employees never hampers growth (although it seems not to advance it either in e.g. larger firms), the local stock of employees concerned with R&D indeed has a hampering effect. This can be interpreted as a hint to the necessity of the knowledge to be marketable. However, this might also be interpreted as the inefficiency of knowledge transfer from universities to technology. Finally, knowledge is as relevant for nanotechnology firms as for other highly knowledge intensive firms, regardless of the peculiarities a GPT implies: Nanotechnology firms rely as much on knowledge spillovers as other high-tech (but not GPT) firms from other industries. The impact, however, depends on knowledge processing characteristics like it is the case in other industries.

Moreover, the impact of knowledge for nano-firm growth also depends on the characteristics of knowledge itself. The analyses set out to investigate the special influence of specialisation of the regional knowledge base. When analysing average employment growth rates, the impact of specialisation is counterproductive to some firms, it has no effect on growth in others. In the year-to-year consideration, however, regional specialisation only has a negative effect in extreme situations. Although these results differ, it becomes clear that specialisation does not have a positive effect on firm growth in nanotechnology. The relevance of these effects has, however, to be seen in context with the special characteristics of GPTs, which develop their positive and accelerating effect on growth in a setting that is open to exploration and cross-application (which is not supported by specialisation). These findings point to the importance of the study: Although it is popular among policymakers to support the establishment of specialised nano-clusters, the results suggest that this regional specialisation is not conducive for the firms. Moreover, it might even become a burden for the performance of some firms, depending on the local degree of specialisation and the firm's knowledge processing characteristics. However, the findings are relying on a small number of firms in nanotechnology only. Moreover, the indicators on the impact of local knowledge resources, such as *STUD* and *R&D* could be refined (e.g. disentangling relevant *STUD* and *R&D*, such as students in technological fields) in order to be able to further investigate which local knowledge is relevant. Further research should also be accomplished on the effect of specialisation in a larger sample or other (GPT) settings to confirm these results, especially in view of findings that state a positive effect of specialisation for many other, but different circumstances and industries. It moreover lies beyond the scope of this paper to investigate the mechanisms behind the findings. It would be interesting to learn how exactly local knowledge is processed, where spillovers indeed are effective and how specialisation exactly affects innovation in high-technologies.

The conclusion of this chapter remains that local knowledge endowment indeed positively influences firm growth in emerging nanotechnology, while local knowledge specialisation surely is not always positively affecting the growth of individual firms. Although one has to once again consider the emergent character of nanotechnology and the lack of stability and hence predictability, this points to the relevance of the GPT feature of nanotechnology for processing knowledge in firms. And what is most important in terms of the initial questions: There is, in most of the cases, no positive impact of specialisation on the employment growth of nano-firms. Referring to the preponderance of high-tech or GPT features with respect to the relevance of the surrounding, GPT features seem to outweigh high-tech ones – although further empirical investigation needs to be done to disentangle the concrete effects of specialisation on firm growth in the (emerging) high- and nanotechnologies.

Part III.c

Working Package 3: Collaboration and Knowledge Sharing in Networks

10 The Development of Nanotechnology through a Network of Collaboration

Networks of collaborative relationships among innovators have been recognised as an important organisation form of innovative activities allowing for improved knowledge transmission (see Section 2.3). Particularly in high-growth, technology and hence knowledge-intensive industries, networks of collaborative invention can be considered and analysed as organisational devices for the coordination of heterogeneous learning processes by innovators with different sets of accumulated knowledge, skills and (knowledge processing) competencies (Orsenigo et al. 1998). Callon (1997), moreover, argued that particularly in emerging configurations knowledge tends to be tacit. This limits the range of the knowledge and hence its character as a partly local public good. In developing networks, however, knowledge becomes non-exclusive within the networks it circulates in. The main focus of this chapter hence consists in the study of knowledge flows and information exchange among innovators, i.e. in the characterisation of the relations between them. This is done by investigating the German nanotechnology innovation networks.

Networks are assumed to play a more and more important role in innovation activity nowadays. Particularly the increasing complexity of emerging, science-based technologies such as nanotechnology reveals a necessity for joint research and collaboration on the field (Haagedorn 1993): Particularly in emerging technologies, face-to-face interactions in networks of collaboration play a huge role for the success of innovations, since networking is a very important mechanism to exchange tacit knowledge informally. This tacit knowledge is dominating in emergent configurations due to the lack of externalisation mechanisms. The exchange about tacit knowledge is necessary to convert implicit knowledge into explicit knowledge, which constitutes the basis for further innovations. Moreover, (emerging) GPTs are not only knowledge-intensive technologies, but they are in addition applied in a wide range of different sectors, innovation processes in GPTs inherently express the necessity for coordination and collaboration in order to realise cross-fertilisation advantages. Thereby, different, but potentially complementary knowledge can be exchanged resulting in the (faster) generation of new knowledge induced by mutual learning. Moreover, coordination was brought up as a central remedy to resolve market failures in the innovation processes of GPT (see Chapter 3). Subsequently, networking potentially fosters the diffusion and the exchange of knowledge and thereby drives innovative activity.

There has already been detailed empirical work focusing on the network structure of nanotechnology. Most prominently these studies find network-related evidence for the relevance of scientific (basic) research in nanotechnology. Meyer (2006) stressed that around 35% of patent inventors are also publishing scientifically, the relevance of which is confirmed by Bonaccorsi and Thoma (2007), who found that the role of author-inventor patents is central for the development of nano-knowledge. Moreover, also Miyazaki and Islam (2007) found that the regional science pole is actually driving the nano-development. Explainable with respect to the early stage of nanotechnology, these finding can be expected to change over the course of the next few years. Focussing on the role of geography for collaboration in form of co-inventorship in Canada, Schiffauerova and Beaudry (2009) found that more than 60% of the nanotechnology collaborative activity takes place within clusters, while international collaboration constitutes 27% of all cooperation links. This emphasises both, the need for the exchange of knowledge and the need for inflowing knowledge from abroad. However, research on nanotechnology networks still lacks a comprehensive analysis of efficient networks and their evolution coming along with technological advance. This is what is done in the following chapter.

10.1 Derivation of Hypotheses

As discussed already in Section 2.3, the development of high-tech, knowledge-intensive technologies such as nanotechnology becomes more and more complex. This defines the need for the cooperation of actors with different sets of accumulated knowledge and competencies to handle and exploit this knowledge as well as to create new knowledge. Innovators more and more tend to share knowledge and, with the knowledge received from each other, improve their own knowledge levels (Cowan and Jonard 2003). Silicon Valley is frequently instanced as a hub of innovation due to the high level of rapid and unrestrained diffusion of knowledge in the local innovator network (Saxenian 1996).[1]

[1] In this context, particularly the role of ICT and the internet increase in importance. The internet offers a device for spaceless collective invention, generating strikingly large amounts of new knowledge by facilitating knowledge transmission, diffusion and creation. Another recent trend to be mentioned

Knowledge diffusion hence occurs through collaboration, putting an emphasis on the structure of the network through which innovators interact as central impact factor with regard to the extent of diffusion and hence the innovative potential (Cowan et al. 2004). Thus, if one defines innovation as the (commercialisable) recombination of existing and new knowledge which is then spurred by the diffusion of knowledge, the assessment of knowledge flows among innovators and hence networking is a straightforward way to assess innovativeness (Cowan et al. 2004). Putting it different and in a more general way, collaboration and networking should come along with a higher level of innovations. Networking in nanotechnology as an emerging technology, in particular, exhibits rather emerging configurations. In these cases, tacit knowledge dominates and the public good character of knowledge has yet to be developed in networks by becoming non-exclusive through circulation and access to a costly infrastructure, such as technology platforms, necessary for the use and replication of the tacit knowledge (Callon 1997). Note that these networks are subject to continuous change since stable configurations are not yet reached. The fact that nanotechnology converges diverse disciplines tightens the relationship between knowledge sharing in networks and innovativeness since inventors have to be able not only to handle knowledge stemming from very heterogeneous fields, but also to merge and then recombine this diverse knowledge in order to finally develop inventions. In contrast to 'normal' high technologies, inventors hence have to operate on a wider field which results in the need for a much larger and opener network in order to be able to gain access to knowledge stemming from other fields, other regions or other applications. But this opener, wider network, following the above argumentation, has to become closer and more embedded when it comes to the integration of the novel knowledge with view at effectively using it. This aspect is even more important in the early stage nanotechnology is in since available knowledge is still scarce and convergence is still at the beginning. In brief: With growing competencies and interest in the field of nanotechnology the potential to cooperate increases very simply because there are more innovators with the necessary knowledge around. Knowledge becomes less specific and broader (see Chapters 7 and 8 as well as Callon (1997)) which increases the need to teamwork. Networking incentives develop from the 'strategy of interessment' to more concrete knowledge access and stabilisation of positions (Callon 1997). Hence, it is reasonable to assume that collaboration increases.

in this context is the phenomenon of open innovation, particularly prominent in the development of software such as LINUX. Here, users are motivated to develop and integrate their own modifications into the software. Such innovations constitute hence a free improvement of the existing product and an addition to the existing stock of knowledge as basis for new innovations (Cowan and Jonard 2003). Yet, in order to make this 'global scale' of knowledge diffusion via the internet possible, the relevant knowledge has to be codifiable (Cowan et al. 2004). The more codifiable knowledge in an industry hence is, the less important becomes geographic proximity for innovation as discussed in Chapter 2. While these phenomena, given the high degree of tacitness of nanotechnological knowledge, are not tackled in this chapter, they are mentioned for the sake of completeness and rather as an outlook.

Research, by contrast, nevertheless advances the leading edge pointing to the need of a high degree of initial knowledge for innovation. Hence, inventors are particularly dependent on external sources of knowledge, such as constituted by global linkages. National or regional systems of innovation in the field might lack the necessary stock of (specialised) leading edge knowledge. However, the less emerging a GPT is, the less effort concerning the absorption of external knowledge from distant disciplines has to be done since actors gradually fill these niches and the knowledge can be accessed more easily by cooperating with actors that are more proximate or share less diverging knowledge bases. The innovation network of nanotechnology is hence assumed to be characterised by a high degree of international linkages since the local knowledge stock necessary for innovation is only small. These linkages become less important as the local knowledge stock emerges and local competencies develop.

Collaboration can be increased if actors willing to cooperate more easily find a suitable partner. Collaboration is hence assumed to take place where the opportunities are, and, as elaborated above (see Subsection 2.3.1 in particular), this is most presumably the case where geographic and cognitive proximity coincide. Spatial proximity is supposed to increase the chances to find a fitting partner and hence to transfer knowledge efficiently since it fosters face-to-face knowledge exchange and allows for frequent and repeated contact (von Hippel 1994, Audretsch 1998). Geographically proximate partners are even found to form part of a more successful collaborations (Gittelman 2007). Autant-Bernard et al. (2007), however, constrained the role of geography for knowledge spillovers through collaboration mainly to the national level, but they consider geography as an impact factor for the formation of formal relationships. Moreover, they also stressed the role of network effects, i.e. knowledge diffusion properties inside networks for the formation of collaboration.[2] More particularly, research as conducted by Cohen and Levinthal (1990), Boschma and Lambooy (1999) or Boschma and Iammarino (2009) emphasises the need for cognitive proximity for a successful collaboration. In the context of networks, collaboration should hence be more frequent - and increase in their intensity - where cognitive and/or geographic proximity facilitates collaboration.

Hypothesis 10.1 *Collaboration Pattern in Nanotechnology in General*
(a) Over time, collaboration increases.
(b) Over time, the importance of international collaboration decreases.
(c) Collaboration occurs particularly where actors are geographically and cognitively proximate.

[2]This property is picked up again in Chapter 11 in terms of efficiency of collaborations for the development of innovations that are general.

Turning from collaboration in general to network structures caused by collaboration in more particular, the focal point of interest is how knowledge diffusion and hence the efficiency of the network with regard to innovative activity is supported by network structures. The general expectation thus is that the more efficient the network, the more productive the corresponding innovation system. In the context of nanotechnology, an increasingly efficient network of knowledge diffusion can reasonably be conjectured. An in-depth analysis of network characteristics indicating efficiency is however indispensable.

As elaborated in Subsection 2.3.4, the efficiency of a network with respect to knowledge transmission can be assessed by a whole set of different indices: First, efficient knowledge transmission is supported by structural cohesion: The closer actors are interconnected, the more efficient the knowledge transfer should be. Therefore, increasing density of the network would be expected with the development of nanotechnology. Efficient knowledge diffusion, moreover, requires lower levels of fragmentation since knowledge can then be accessed not only directly but also indirectly to a greater extent. Particularly in the context of nanotechnology as converging general purpose technology components might display collaboration in different technological fields. Cross-connection of components is only achieved after a certain threshold-value of convergence is reached. Such a partial overlap, however, constitutes an opportunity for cross-fertilisation, which implies an improved knowledge diffusion. Furthermore, a distinct centre-periphery structure is often instanced as being conducive to rapid knowledge transfers within networks, since they provide rapid and easy connection between diversified and specialised actors anywhere in the network. The most striking approach to assess network efficiency, however, is the concept of a small world network. High degrees of clustering increase the absorptive capacity of a network and support quick flows of knowledge as well as the creation of trust and collaboration in general (Schilling and Phelps 2007), while decreased path lengths improve innovation efficiency due to easier transfer of new knowledge via intermediaries as 'short cuts'. Since the efficiency of the innovation network of nanotechnology can be assumed to increase with the small world property, it is reasonable to expect that the network of nanotechnology develops towards such a small world network structure. At the very beginning of the development, extremes in terms of network topology are expectable, since the network has to be built, while at later stages the development of a general purpose technology should benefit above average from small world properties by connecting subgroups that work on different subdomains of nanotechnology. This argument is also relevant in a more general way: Ter Wal and Boschma (2009) and Graf and Henning (2009) and more recently Tran (2011) pointed to the relevance of a centre-periphery structures of networks, where central actors play the role of important intermediates and 'knowledge brokers', connecting remote actors that only seldom make use of external knowledge. The more established a GPT's network, having already proven to successfully generate innovations, the more should the network hence resemble a small world structure.

Hypothesis 10.2 *Efficiency of the Innovation Network*
The efficiency of the innovation network of nanotechnology increases with its development and over time. This means that
(a) the network becomes less fragmented and more cohesive.
(b) the network becomes more centralised.
(c) the network develops towards a small world.

However, despite of the need for access to more diverse knowledge the knowledge base still has to be somewhat complementary in order for actors to be able to process the knowledge at all: Cohen and Levinthal (1990) stressed the role of absorptive capacity; Feldman and Audretsch (1999) emphasised the need for a common knowledge base and Boschma and Iammarino (2009) quoted related variety when pointing at the importance of a common technological understanding as basis for collaboration. Still, innovators can be specialised in a certain field of knowledge or they can be diversified. The former have a narrower knowledge base resulting in a smaller potential for commonalities (and complementarity) with others, whereas the latter obviously have a diversified knowledge base that overlaps with more actors. Given the relevance of the common knowledge base and the complementarity of knowledge, diversified actors can hence be expected to cooperate with more and more different other actors or, put differently, to occupy a more central position in the network. The more specialised an actor, by contrast, the more probable it is that he is positioned in the periphery (Cantner and Graf 2006). It is reasonable to assume that the network of technological overlap more and more differentiates between diversified and specialised actors, or put differently develops a more distinct centre-periphery structure.

Hypothesis 10.3 *Technological Overlap*
The network of technological overlap of nanotechnology develops from a central structure towards a (more cohesive) center-periphery structure.

10.2 Methodology and Data

As pointed out in Subsection 2.3.1, neither the analysis of the geographic system of innovation nor the analysis of the cognitive system of innovation are on their own capable of explaining technological developments alone, since both the geography as well as the technological particularities are influencing factors: Knowledge flows and diffuses through the network between innovators who are not necessarily placed in the same region. Due to the high degree of complexity of technological knowledge needed for innovation, a certain commonality is needed in order to understand each other. Understanding the specific 'language' makes innovators to members of the technology's community. This community might, contrary to former assumptions about the transfer of tacit knowledge, be geographically dispersed and still offer opportunities to exchange tacit forms of knowledge. In this case, geographical proximity might, to a limited extent, be substituted by cognitive proximity. The technological networks hence do not always require co-location of the innovators for the successful creation of innovations. On the other hand, local players might be integrated into the network due to their geographic proximity to innovators in the technological network – note, however, that this is no causal inclusion. Hence to completely display how innovation is processed one has to consider both, the technological and geographical dimension, tackling the trade-off between geographic networks and technological networks by assessing the largest possible intersection.

With respect to the complex nature of early stage nanotechnology, it should be concluded that it is more than likely that there are different levels of networks that are relevant to its development. Leading-edge basic research is likely to be internationally distributed and hence the links to knowledge might be of a non-local nature as well. It can thus be assumed that networks and connections to external knowledge might play a significant role in the development processes of nanotechnology: Innovators need to gain access to knowledge that is not local and hence to reach beyond provincial channels to absorb knowledge available in surroundings much beyond regional or national boundaries. National or regional networks, on the other hand, are important to share tacit knowledge, which seems to be particularly important for the high-tech, and hence high knowledge demanding innovations in nanotechnology. Moreover, given the general purpose nature of nanotechnology a special feature of local innovation systems might be to bring knowledge from different industrial backgrounds – and hence less coherent knowledge-bases – together.

The chosen level of analysis is hence the technological system of innovation in nanotechnology on the German national level, combining both approaches. Moreover, the investigation is based on different time periods accounting for possible and expected dynamic aspects. As already indicated in Subsection 5.4, the timespan a network connection can be considered as valuable (i.e. valuable knowledge is transferred without renewing the relationship in form of a new joint patent application) for 5 years, which is consistent with a commonly assumed annual depreciation rate of patents around 20% (Leten et al. 2007). This is why the five-year moving time window approach was implemented again to construct the different networks. This results in a split of the German network of nano-innovators into 24 subnetworks, starting in 1980, the year considered as the breakthrough of the feasibility of nanotechnology R&D, and ending in 2007. This means that all networks from 1980-4, 1981-5, ..., 2003-7 were considered separately.[3] For the following analysis, data of German nano-patents with priority application year between 1980 and 2007 are hence employed (see Section 5.1).

All networks reconstructed in the following are based on patent data. Particularly in the emerging stage nanotechnology is in that results is a high domination of scientific and public research (normally published in form of publications), it would have been desirable to also investigate co-author networks as is displayed in publication data. Unfortunately, the available publication data was not in a form that would have allowed in-depth network analyses of this kind. Both, co-inventor and co-applicant networks are then constructed as proposed in Subsection 5.4. While these networks might not all show past direct cooperation (as argued in Subsection 5.4), they both display direct knowledge flows. Therefore, both kinds are included in the analysis. Yet, the inventor networks are assumed more important since applicant networks frequently only express legal rights sharing instead of actual knowledge sharing. Moreover, the following analysis also investigates networks which are constructed in a slightly different way: A network of technological overlap is employed to assess Hypothesis 10.3. Technological overlap is therefore defined as the number of technological classes, again following the ISIC-IPC concordance, in which two actors applied for a patent. Although this measure might seem simplistic, it captures the necessity for a minimal common knowledge in order to be able to benefit from externally flowing knowledge in a very basic way (Cantner and Graf 2006). Since relationships are modelled whenever two actors patent in the same technological class, this network neither displays actual nor past knowledge flows (not even by assumption), but rather a potential for collaboration.

10.3 Analyses and Results

The following section tackles the indicators used to explore the hypotheses as well as the findings for these indicators.

[3]The data handling efforts for such networks are very high. Since it is frequently sufficient to investigate steps, i.e. completely new compositions of networks, some analyses restrain on the intervals 1980-4, 1985-9, 1990-4, 1995-9, 2000-4 and 2003-7.

10.3.1 Collaboration Pattern in General (H10.1)

As the hypothesis to be investigated is split into three subparts its analysis is divided similarly.

Collaboration in General (a)

As Hypothesis 10.1(a) states, collaboration is assumed to increase. This is conjectured to be the case since nanotechnology as GPT combines various different technology fields and hence innovators might benefit from interdisciplinary work in teams. With growing interest in the field of nanotechnology the potential to cooperate moreover increases very simply because there are more innovators with the necessary knowledge around. Also, the incentives to share knowledge increase when more and more knowledge circulates in networks. Figure 10.1 depicts the development patterns of nanotechnology-patents as well as the corresponding innovators. Nanotechnology in Germany obviously follows the international trend of a sharply increasing patenting activity (see Chapter 6). Moreover, the development of the number of distinct innovators, i.e. inventors (a) and applicants (b) is also displayed. It shows that the number of inventors lies above the number of patents. This points to the important role of collaboration among inventors. As displayed in Figure 10.2, the average number of patents per inventor increases only slightly from 0.6 to 0.7, while the average number of inventors per patent increases drastically from 2 in 1980-1984 to 3.2 in 2003-2007. However, the team size dropped slightly over the last 10 periods after a steady increase before. It is sensible to assume that there is a critical mass of inventors on a team that can productively contribute to a single invention, which is counterbalanced by the need for interdisciplinary and diverse knowledge. Therefore, this drop in team size could be explained by increasing preponderance of the former. The case is different with the number of applicants, as it is below the number of patents. This indicates that collaboration is less intense and important among applicants. Presumably, the sector benefits from a critical mass of applicants (in general consisting of firms and institutions). However, collaboration increases here as well, as the average number of applicants per patent increases from 1.1 in 1980-1984 to 1.7 in 2003-2007, despite legally considerably more difficult collaboration of applicants. Obviously, collaboration is indeed important and increases in significance over time.

More particularly, the share of patents that are the result of a collaboration among inventors increases from 59% in 1980-1984 with an average annual growth rate of nearly 14% to 78% in 2003-2007. As with applicants the case is again different: Collaborative patents account for a share of 14% in 1980-1984, which increases by 11% yearly to

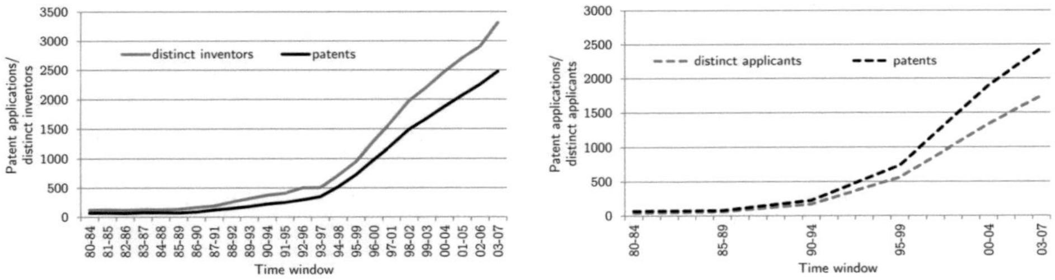

(a) Inventor-based (b) Applicant-based

Figure 10.1: Development of nanotechnology patenting in Germany.
Source: PATSTAT, own search and calculations.

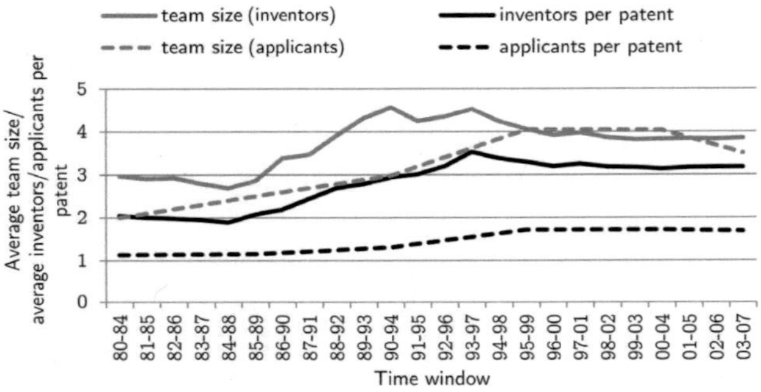

Figure 10.2: Development of the collaboration pattern. Team size is contributors per patent in case of collaboration.
Source: PATSTAT, own search and calculations.

27% in 2003-2007. This points to the fact that the increase in average applicants per patent is not only explained by an increase in the share of collaborations, but rather by an increase in the team size of patents that are jointly applied for (see Figure 10.3(a)).

These figures obviously support Hypothesis 10.1: Collaboration does increase with the development of nanotechnology. In concrete numbers, Table 10.1 displays the correlation coefficient between nanotechnology patenting and share of collaborations. Both for inventors as well as for applicants, the share of collaborations and the number of contributors is significantly (at the 1% level) and highly correlated with the increasing patenting activity. While it is beyond the scope of this chapter to explore the reasons for this, it can be assumed that it is due to the need for complementary, but diverse knowledge in order to create new knowledge for nanotechnology as GPT. The increased interest in nanotechnology that comes along with its technological dynamics obviously offers the opportunities of which the innovators make use in the same vein.

	INVENTORS	APPLICANTS
share collaboration	0.526***	0.7742***
share int collaboration	0.3323*	0.0204
contributors per patent	0.5355***	0.8415***
share interregional collaboration	0.3396*	

Table 10.1: Pearson correlation coefficient of collaboration indicators with number of patents. ***indicates significance at 0.01.
Source: own calculations.

International Collaboration (b)

Part (b) of Hypothesis 10.1 points to a decreasing role of international collaboration. It is conjectured that national actors step by step fill the local knowledge gaps by developing competencies and occupying niches. Therefore, the necessary knowledge can be found within the national system of innovation and resource-demanding international collaboration can be replaced by national collaboration. Figure 10.4 provides two snap-shots of knowledge flowing into the German nanotechnological innovation system. The situation in 1980-1984 is well arranged: The most important collaborative links are to the US, the Netherlands and Switzerland. By contrast and on a first glance, the inflow of knowledge through cooperation in the 2003-2007 period seems to have intensified. Still, the most important partners are the US and Switzerland, followed by France, Austria, the UK and Japan. The conclusions one can draw of the importance of these partners point to both, the need for leading-edge knowledge and the role of proximity. While the US and Japan are certainly not proximate they are leading nations in the field of nanotechnology. Switzerland and Austria, by contrast, are not renowned for providing leading-edge technology, but are geographically and culturally proximate. France and the UK might be regarded as a mixture of both.

However, the picture deceives with respect to the importance of international cooperation as is illustrated by Figure 10.3(b): International collaboration of inventors increases more slowly than does collaboration in general, on average by 9% p.a.. The share of international collaboration of applicants even decreases sharply. Hence, although the share of international collaborations does not decrease as conjectured (Table 10.1 displays a correlation between the increase of international collaborations and the increase in patenting that is significant on the 10% level for inventors and non-significant for applicants), it loses importance vis-à-vis the faster growing rate of collaboration in general (of which the international collaboration is a part). It is hence justifiable to interpret

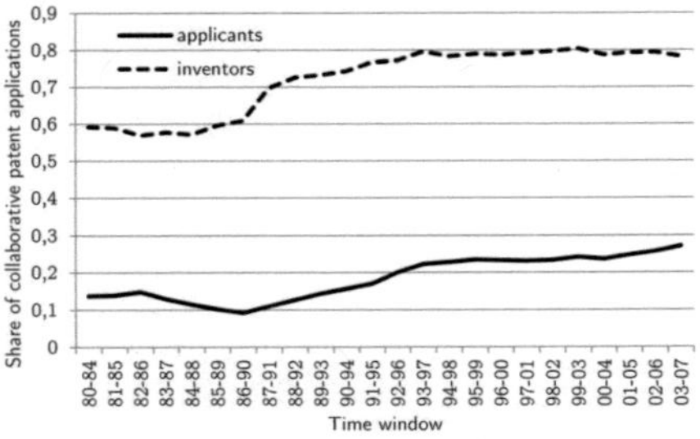

(a) Development of shares of collaborations

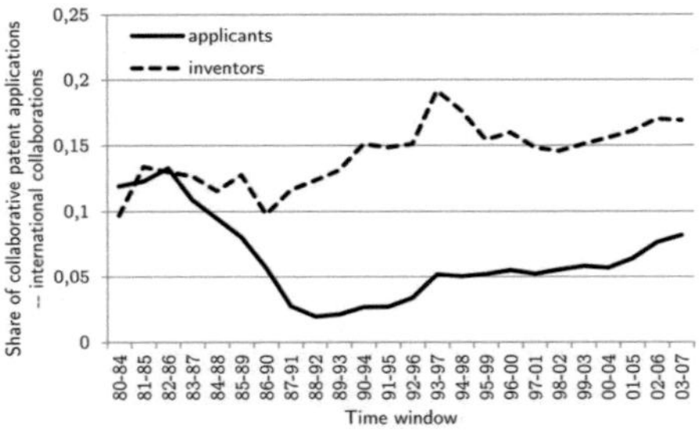

(b) Development of share of international collaborations

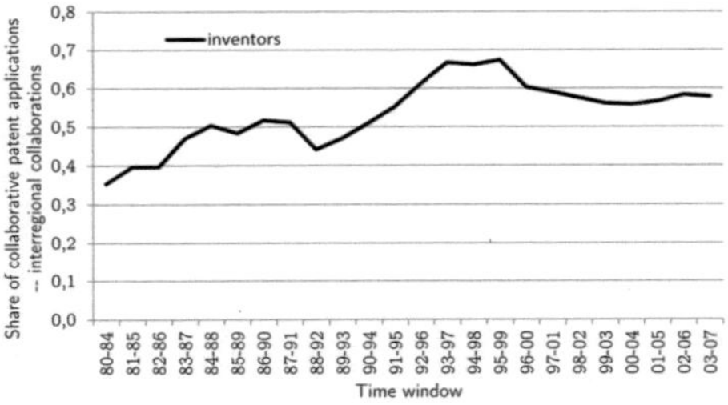

(c) Development of shares of interregional collaborations

Figure 10.3: Development of collaborations.
Source: PATSTAT, own search and calculations.

this development as a slight support for Hypothesis 10.1(b): International collaboration becomes at least less important.

Geographic and Cognitive Proximity (c)

The findings above indicate that collaboration indeed became more important with the development of nanotechnology. This subsection finally explores where collaboration took place within the network. Part (c) now conjectures, that geographically and cognitively proximate actors are more likely to work in teams.[4]

Figure 10.5 sketches the role of cognitive proximity. It shows the three largest components of the networks from 1990-1994[5] and 2003-2007. Vertices are marked in colours according to their technological background in one of the K30 technological fields (see

[4]The assessment in this section focuses on inventors since this is both, more sensible and fruitful – particularly vis-à-vis data-handling issues.

[5]Instead of the first observed time period this network was chosen since it is the first to show any significant interconnection between vertices in components, see Subsection 10.3.2 for further details.

Subsection 5.1.2). An actor was allocated to the technology field where he filed the most patents in.[6] The components are dominated by inventors of one class. Still, there are important vertices that connect one part of the component to the other although

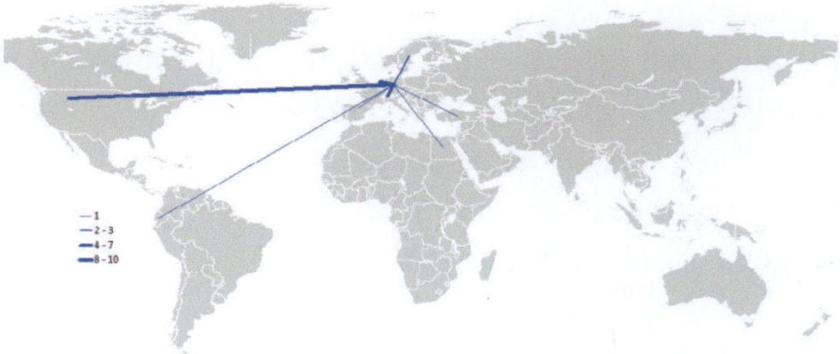

(a) 1980-1984

(b) 2003-2007

Figure 10.4: International patent collaborations of Germany.
Source: PATSTAT, own search, calculation and illustration.

they do not share the same technology – and hence cooperate interdisciplinary. The components that are not shown on the Figure exhibit even less interdisciplinary collaboration. The same picture drawn for the 2003-2007 network looks considerably different: All three largest components are interdisciplinary and contain inventors from various fields. Collaboration in general and interdisciplinary collaboration, which is assumed to be an important cornerstone in the development of general purpose nanotechnology, increased sharply. Having a closer look one can nevertheless observe that there are always several smaller clusters of technologically proximate inventors. Again and although multidisciplinarity increased, collaboration among inventors with the same background is popular. Figures 10.3(c) and 10.6 draw a similar picture for regional proximity. Figures 10.3(c) displays the development of the share of interre-

[6]When actors are listed on only one patent or all patents of an inventor belong to different classes they were omitted.

gional collaboration among all collaborations in German nanotechnology.[7] A collaboration is interregional, when all collaborating actors stem from the same planning region (Raumordnungsregion; (ROR)). The share increases from 35% in 1980-1984 to 58% in recent years. This is significantly (at the 10% level) correlated with the development of nanotechnology as measured in patenting output (see Table 10.1. Hence, geographical proximity seems to decrease in relevance since more collaborations include partners of other regions. By contrast, an ROR is a comparatively small geographical area (between NUTS2 and NUTS3) since it is designed to approximate spatial and functional interrelations between core cities and the corresponding hinterland (BBR 2001). 40% of all collaborations taking place within one such planning region is still emphasising the role geographical proximity.

Figure 10.6 depicts collaboration between different German ROR.[8] The network of 1980-1984 shows that interregional collaboration takes place, but in comparison to the 2003-2007 network only to a very limited extent. However, the interregional collaboration that takes place mainly happens between geographically proximate RORs, such as Unterer Neckar, Rheinhessen/Nahe and Rheinpfalz or Hamburg and Schleswig-Holstein Süd. One component, however, connects regions farther away, among them the metropolitan areas with high innovative output, such as Berlin, Munich or Stuttgart. This obviously indicates that geographical proximity might be a reason for collaboration, but that it is not the only one: Regional players connect to the important regions notwithstanding larger distance. This is most presumably the case since they want to gain access to important, leading-edge or complementary knowledge in the region. This still holds true for the network in 2003-7, although less visible due to the crowding.

Although no systematic measure was employed, this anecdotal evidence supports H10.1 (c) in general, technologically and geographically proximate inventors are more intensively collaborating. The role of technological and geographic proximity, however, seems to decrease with the development of the network. This might have several reasons, e.g. consisting in the higher propensity to collaborate in general emphasising the need for more partners to avoid redundancies, the necessity of complementarity knowledge and perhaps also improved means of codification of tacit knowledge (i.e. the

[7]Note that data that can be used to allocate an innovator to a planning regions is by far not found on all patents. For the calculation of these shares, only patents with such detailed data were considered. Since this was done for both, the number of collaborations as well as the number of interregional collaboration, a possible bias should be kept as low as possible.

[8]Note that collaboration that takes place within one such ROR is not displayed. This part of the hypothesis explores anecdtoally whether there is a tendency for geographically proximate collaboration. A visual way to do so is to depict collaboration within the German network, but between different regions, thereby offering a way to get a feeling for distances.

evolution of tacit knowledge to non-tacit knowledge). In particular, network structure properties, i.e. the diffusion properties of collaboration partners, might shift into focus as supposed by Autant-Bernard et al. (2007), once the networks evolves, thereby substituting geographic effects. The lack of a systematic cross-sectional analysis, however, constrains these ideas to pure conjectures.

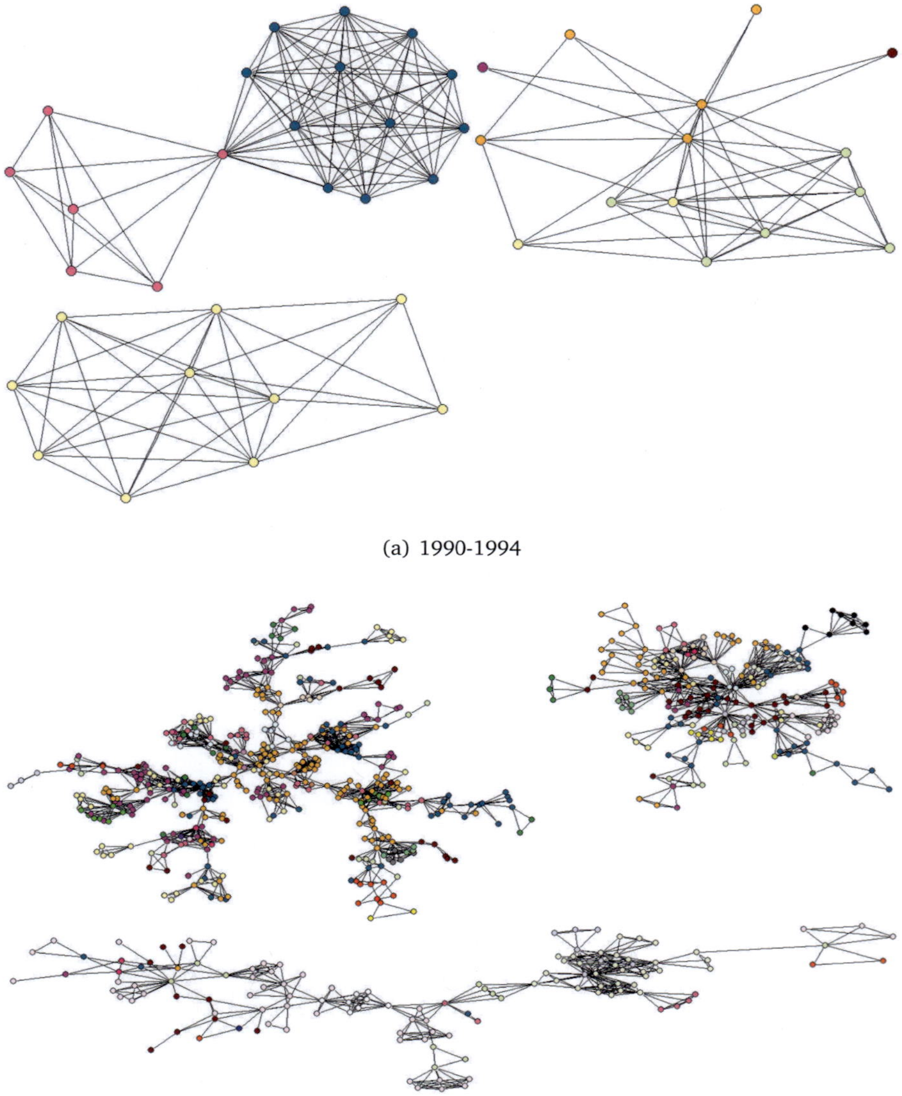

(a) 1990-1994

(b) 2003-2007

Figure 10.5: Development of cognitively proximate collaboration in the nanotechnology inventor networks. Figures display the three largest components each.
Colour of vertices represents a K30 technology field. See Figure G.1 in the Appendix G for the key of the colours to technological fields.
Source: PATSTAT, own search, calculation and illustration.

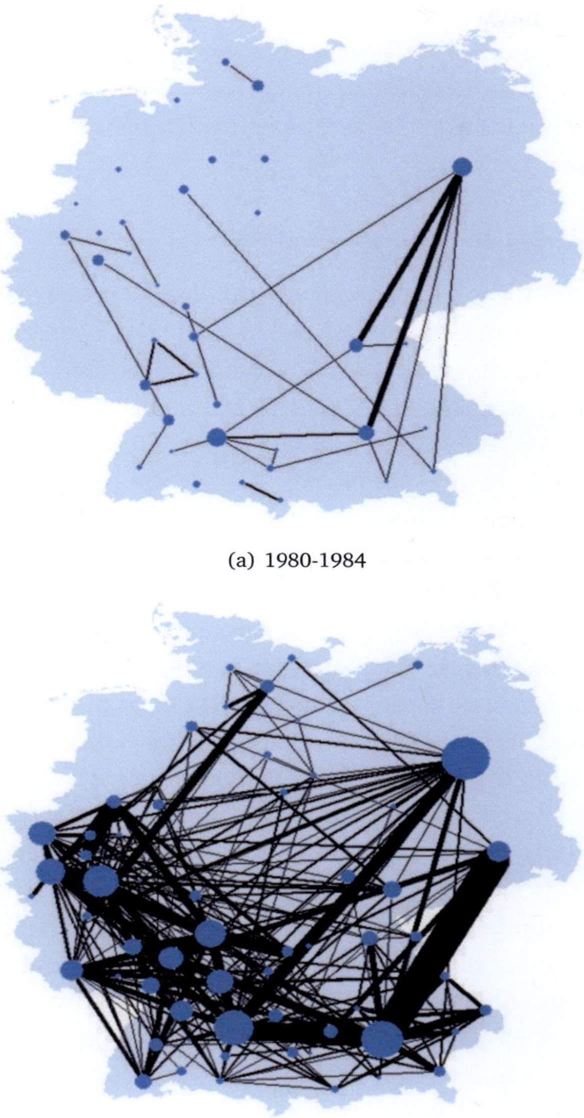

(a) 1980-1984

(b) 2003-2007

Figure 10.6: Development of interregional collaboration patterns in Germany. Size of vertices refers to relative innovative output of the region. Width of edges refers to intensity of collaboration.
Source: PATSTAT, own search, calculation and illustration.

10.3.2 Efficiency of the Innovation Network (H10.2)

Many different kinds of statistical network measures assess the influence of pace and quality of knowledge transmission. This subsection sets out to explore the most important sets of indicators for both, the inventor and the applicant networks of nanotechnology in Germany across the investigated time periods. However, the applicant networks are only considered for comparative and supportive means and hence only snap-shots will be assessed every five years.

Network Fragmentation and Structural Cohesion (a)

The fragmentation of the innovation networks of nanotechnology in Germany can be consulted in order to get a first impression on how well the networks are connected. The number and sizes of the components and isolates are hence used as a first indicator for the collaboration intensity. Table 10.2 contains all indicators calculated in this context and the corrleation coefficient of the indicators when comparing them to the number of patents produced in the relevant period. The average component size steadily increases in the inventor network as well as in the applicant network. Compared with the productivity of the system, a high and significant correlation is found. This points to improved connection within the network and the positive relationship to innovativity. Yet, the numbers are still comparatively low. This might be due to the high numbers in isolates and small components. The share of isolates, however, decreases. That means that inventors more and more connect to the network through cooperation and thereby gain access to important knowledge resources. As was expected, this holds for both the inventor as well as the applicant network, while the applicant network stays less aggregated than the inventor network in these respects. This number moreover is, as conjectured, negatively correlated with the productivity of the system.

Comparing just the numbers of components and isolate does, however, not sufficiently explain a network's connectivity because the importance of large components representing a substantial part of the overall network could be offset by many isolates. Representation shares of the largest component as well as the difference to the second largest component increase, emphasising the role of network aggregation for innovation and knowledge transmission. The better nanotechnology develops, the more the actors seek access to the cumulated knowledge in the network. Interestingly, the applicant network performs even better at the end of the observation period. This might be a hint for the strategic use of networking in case applicants collaborate.

Taking every fragmentation measure into account, it can be concluded that both networks improve in terms of less fragmentation and hence actors gain access to larger shares of the accumulated knowledge. Overall, the inventor networks seem better connected than the applicant networks. This was expected due to lower benefits of applicant collaboration in terms of knowledge transmission (in most cases it's the inventors that need the knowledge for innovation, rather than the applicants) and the higher costs that come along with collaboration in terms of legal complications. Moreover, inventors might collaborate even though they are coming from different disciplines, which might even drive innovations in nanotechnology as GPT. This is not so prominent among applicants, however, since they are mostly companies presumably cooperating with other applicants from the same sector.

	Inventor					Applicant				
period	avg comp size	largest (%)	2nd largest (%)	1st/2nd	isolates (%)	avg comp size	largest (%)	2nd largest (%)	1st/2nd	isolates (%)
80-84	2.0	3.2	3.2	1.00	25.7	1.0	2.9	2.9	1	94.1
81-85	2.1	2.9	2.9	1.00	23.9					
82-86	2.1	6.4	2.6	1.17	23.8					
83-87	2.1	5.9	2.4	1.17	20.5					
84-88	2.1	5.8	2.4	1.17	20.5					
85-89	2.2	6.0	2.7	1.00	18.0	1.1	4.7	2.8	1.67	89.7
86-90	2.3	5.7	2.5	1.00	17.0					
87-91	2.4	5.6	2.3	1.00	16.3					
88-92	2.5	13.4	2.1	2.50	14.9					
89-93	2.6	11.4	3.1	1.43	15.1					
90-94	2.6	8.5	2.7	1.20	16.0	1.2	8.9	5.8	1.54	68.9
91-95	2.7	12.3	2.9	1.56	12.5					
92-96	3.0	13.9	2.3	2.06	12.0					
93-97	3.2	15.9	3.8	1.32	11.1					
94-98	3.2	13.3	2.6	1.59	11.1					
95-99	3.3	26.0	1.9	4.06	10.4	2.3	12.4	4.4	2.78	34.1
96-00	3.4	25.8	1.9	3.98	10.0					
97-01	3.5	27.0	2.8	2.77	9.6					
98-02	3.5	27.8	2.4	3.24	9.5					
99-03	3.6	27.1	2.8	2.64	6.4					
00-04	3.6	15.4	2.7	1.59	9.4	2.6	27.7	2.9	9.56	29.8
01-05	3.7	15.6	2.9	1.46	8.9					
02-06	3.7	17.2	3.2	1.43	8.9					
03-07	3.8	30.2	3.5	2.29	9.2	3.0	36.5	1.5	24.13	25.2
corr[1]	0.798***	0.6237***	0.3478*	0.242	-0.6543***	0.8743**	0.9822***	-0.6491	0.9537***	-0.7628*

Table 10.2: Fragmentation of the innovation networks of nanotechnology.
[1] Pearson correlation coefficient with number of patents.
***Indicates significance at 0.01.
Source: own calculations.

Another measure of connectedness is the cohesion of a network. A cohesive network is assumed to support innovativeness and hence should increase with increasing patent outcome within the network of nanotechnology in Germany. Table 10.3 reports the cohesion measures for the inventor and applicant network and their respective largest components. The average degree, i.e. the number of different other actors one actor is connected to, increases sharply in all networks. It is, as was expected, highly and significantly correlated with the number of patents produced which points to the importance of knowledge sharing for innovativeness. It is considerably higher in the largest component, again playing the importance of lower levels of fragmentation. The density decreases over time and ist negatively (and in case of inventors significantly) correlated with network efficiency. Since the networks grow rapidly over the same period of time, this is only evident since the number of possible lines increases rapidly with the number of vertices, whereas the number of collaborations an individual can maintain is limited (de Nooy et al. 2008). The density hence proves useless as an indicator of cohesion when comparing how network structures evolve in a growing network and is hence only reported for the sake of completeness.

Putting it in a nutshell, the nanotechnology networks become less fragmented and more cohesive over the course of the rapid development on nanotechnological innovations over the last three decades. H10.2(a) can thus be confirmed.

Centre-Periphery Structure (b)

A network with a clear centre-periphery structure exhibits high degrees of centralisation (see Subsection 2.3.3). While the centre of such a network opens opportunities for a more efficient transmission of knowledge and hence for higher degrees of innovativeness, more peripheral inventors are not as well connected and do not have similarly easy access to the knowledge flowing in the network. This structure, in contrast to a network with similar centrality scores for all inventors, points to the degree of development of the innovation network: While established collaborations and important links exist, new inventors or inventors working on a specialised field are less well connected and less important for the overall knowledge transmission in the network. However, vertices that are in the periphery of a network, but connected to at least one intermediary in the centre can get indirect access to all the knowledge flowing in the network, although they do not as much engage in collaboration themselves.

The centre-periphery structure is hence assessed by means of centralisation indicators, i.e. degree and betweenness centralisation. Results for the largest components are displayed in Tables 10.4. They are not as clear as expected for the whole network, which is why they are visualised in Figure 10.7 (exact numbers can still be found in the appendix in Table G.1). This changing structure can be seen as another indication for the still emergent configuration the nanotechnology network is in. Degree centralisation refers to the differences in the degree centrality of the vertices. The degree centrality

	Inventor				Applicant			
	Network		1st Component		Network		1st Component	
period	D	$avg\ d(v_i)$	D	$avg\ d(v_i)$	D	$avg\ d(v_i)$	D	$avg\ d(v_i)$
80-84	0.0091	1.70	1	5	0.0009	0.06	1	1.00
81-85	0.0087	1.78	1	5				
82-86	0.0078	1.80	1	6				
83-87	0.0071	1.76	1	6				
84-88	0.0070	1.76	1	6				
85-89	0.0075	1.95	1	6	0.0028	0.30	1	4.00
86-90	0.0075	2.12	1	6				
87-91	0.0074	2.21	0.6667	4				
88-92	0.0070	2.61	0.4125	8.3				
89-93	0.0061	2.76	0.5069	8.2				
90-94	0.0054	3.00	0.6013	10.22	0.0068	1.72	0.3737	7.10
91-95	0.0050	3.05	0.2460	6.64				
92-96	0.0043	3.39	0.1832	6.59				
93-97	0.0040	3.56	0.1545	6.8				
94-98	0.0028	3.57	0.1181	6.26				
95-99	0.0021	3.62	0.0537	7.36	0.0036	3.28	0.0708	8.00
96-00	0.0016	3.67	0.0397	7.06				
97-01	0.0013	3.79	0.0315	7.03				
98-02	0.0011	3.74	0.0264	7.33				
99-03	0.0009	3.75	0.0227	6.81				
00-04	0.0008	3.74	0.0345	6.58	0.0016	3.46	0.0114	6.76
01-05	0.0007	3.76	0.0305	6.59				
02-06	0.0007	3.76	0.0230	6.02				
03-07	0.0006	3.81	0.0134	6.79	0.0013	3.95	0.0063	6.83
corr[1]	-0.7884***	0.6578***	-0.6392***	0.0313	-0.4638	0.7655*	-0.6767	0.3887

Table 10.3: Structural cohesion of the nanotechnology networks.
[1] Pearson correlation coefficient with number of patents.
***Indicates significance at 0.01.
Source: own calculations.

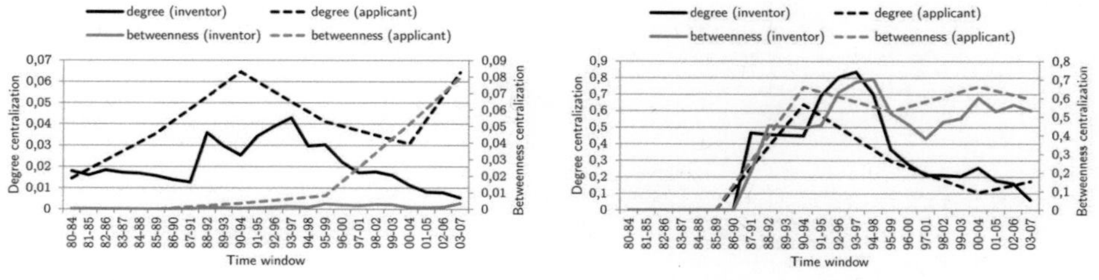

(a) Whole networks

(b) Largest components

Figure 10.7: Centralisation.
Source: PATSTAT, own search and calculations.

is nothing more than the normalised degree. It is hence assessed how different actors are in term of their connectedness. While the degree centrality does not follow a clear trend in the whole network, it decreases after the first increase in the components and is therefore negatively correlated with the productivity of the system. The increase can be explained by the development of a network structure in the components in the first place after 1985. The decrease is caused by a similar increase in average as well as maximum degree centralities, and hence actors tend to have similar numbers of connections to others. However, the lack of a clear development path might point to the emergent setting of the networks that is subject to change since it is not (yet) stable. Betweenness centralisation, by contrast does not decrease. Betweenness centralisation refers to the importance of some vertices as intermediaries for the knowledge flows. The high values might be due to the fact that nanotechnology is a GPT: While not all actors are capable of (re)combining knowledge from different fields, some of the same act as intermediaries between the fields and are hence more important than others for the intra-network knowledge diffusion. This supposition is supported by Figure 10.5, where the nodes with high betweenness centrality are mostly connected to vertices from different technological fields. This centre-periphery structure in the largest component can be tracked in Figure 10.8 for inventors and in Figure 10.9 for applicants. While indeed, degree centralisation cannot be observed it becomes clear that there are some vertices that are important nodes for the cohesion of different parts of the network. Hence, although degree centralisation is decreasing, an increasing centre-periphery structure can be observed for betweenness centralisation with a positive and significant (***) correlation to patenting and hence H10.2(b) can at least not be rejected. Since nanotechnology networks must be assumed to be emergent, this snap shot of development might again change in the next decade when the development towards a stable situation proceeds.

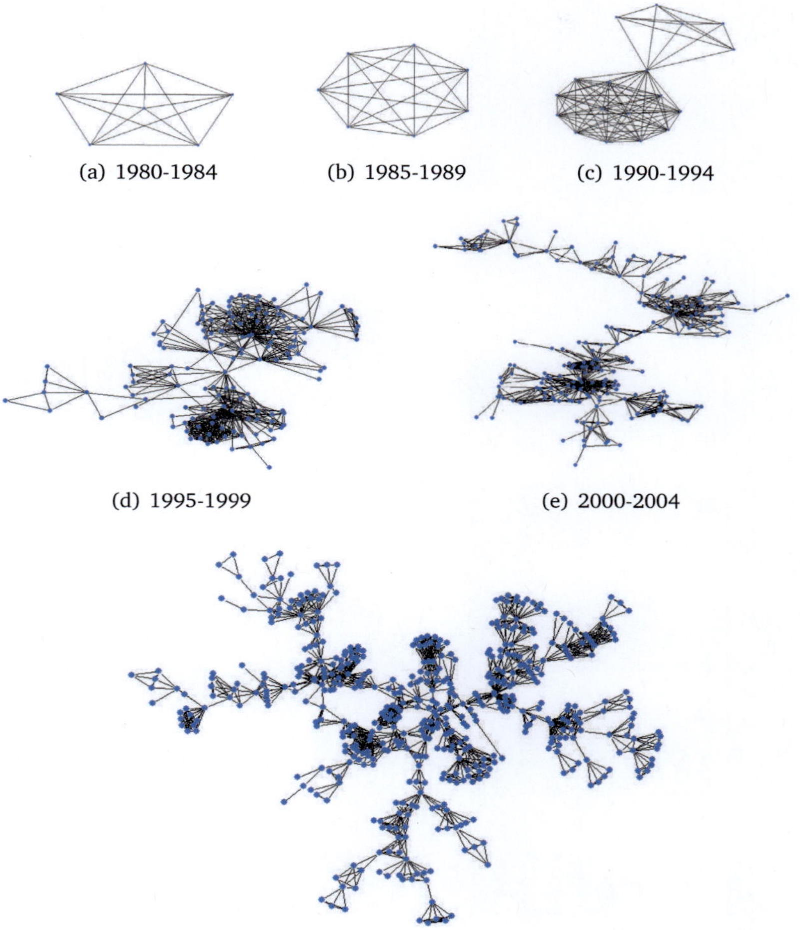

(a) 1980-1984 (b) 1985-1989 (c) 1990-1994

(d) 1995-1999 (e) 2000-2004

(f) 2003-2007

Figure 10.8: Development of the largest component of the inventor-network of nanotechnology. Source: PATSTAT, own search, calculation and illustration.

	Inventor						Applicant					
year	$avgC_B(v_i)$	$maxC_B(v_i)$	C_B	$avgC_D(v_i)$	$maxC_D(v_i)$	C_D	$avgC_B(v_i)$	$maxC_B(v_i)$	C_B	$avgC_D(v_i)$	$maxC_D(v_i)$	C_D
80-84	0	0	0.00	0.00	0	0	-	-	-	-	-	-
81-85	0	0	0.00	0.00	0	0						
82-86	0	0	0.00	0.00	0	0						
83-87	0	0	0.00	0.00	0	0						
84-88	0	0	0.00	0.00	0	0						
85-89	0	0	0.00	0.00	0	0	0	0	0	1	1	0
86-90	0	0	0.00	0.00	0	0						
87-91	0.0667	0.2444	0.2074	0.6667	1.0000	0.4667						
88-92	0.0368	0.4667	0.4524	0.4316	0.8421	0.4561						
89-93	0.0309	0.4543	0.4469	0.5165	0.9211	0.4523						
90-94	0.0249	0.4418	0.4415	0.6013	1.0000	0.4485	0.0386	0.6667	0.6611	0.3737	0.9474	0.6374
91-95	0.0348	0.4732	0.4546	0.2460	0.8889	0.6923						
92-96	0.0255	0.6416	0.6332	0.1832	0.9444	0.8048						
93-97	0.0210	0.6953	0.6897	0.1545	0.9545	0.8372						
94-98	0.0225	0.7142	0.7048	0.1181	0.7925	0.7003						
95-99	0.0165	0.5326	0.5199	0.0537	0.4161	0.3676	0.0196	0.5438	0.5289	0.0708	0.3628	0.2973
96-00	0.0150	0.4722	0.4598	0.0397	0.3146	0.2780						
97-01	0.0137	0.3955	0.3835	0.0315	0.2422	0.2125						
98-02	0.0116	0.4828	0.4730	0.0264	0.2374	0.2126						
99-03	0.0139	0.5040	0.4918	0.0227	0.2267	0.2053						
00-04	0.0232	0.6229	0.6029	0.0345	0.2880	0.2562	0.0106	0.6735	0.6640	0.0114	0.1166	0.1055
01-05	0.0262	0.5528	0.5290	0.0305	0.2083	0.1795						
02-06	0.0220	0.5854	0.5655	0.0230	0.1832	0.1615						
03-07	0.0135	0.5459	0.5334	0.0134	0.0751	0.0619	0.0049	0.6006	0.5963	0.0063	0.1797	0.1737
corr[1]	.	0.528***	0.5433***	-0.7918***	-0.7601***	-0.5931***	0.9723***	0.9985***	0.9984***	-0.4694	-0.3402	0.3579

Table 10.4: Centre-periphery-structure of the largest component of the nanotechnology-networks.
[1] Pearson correlation coefficient with number of patents.
***Indicates significance at 0.01.
Source: own calculations.

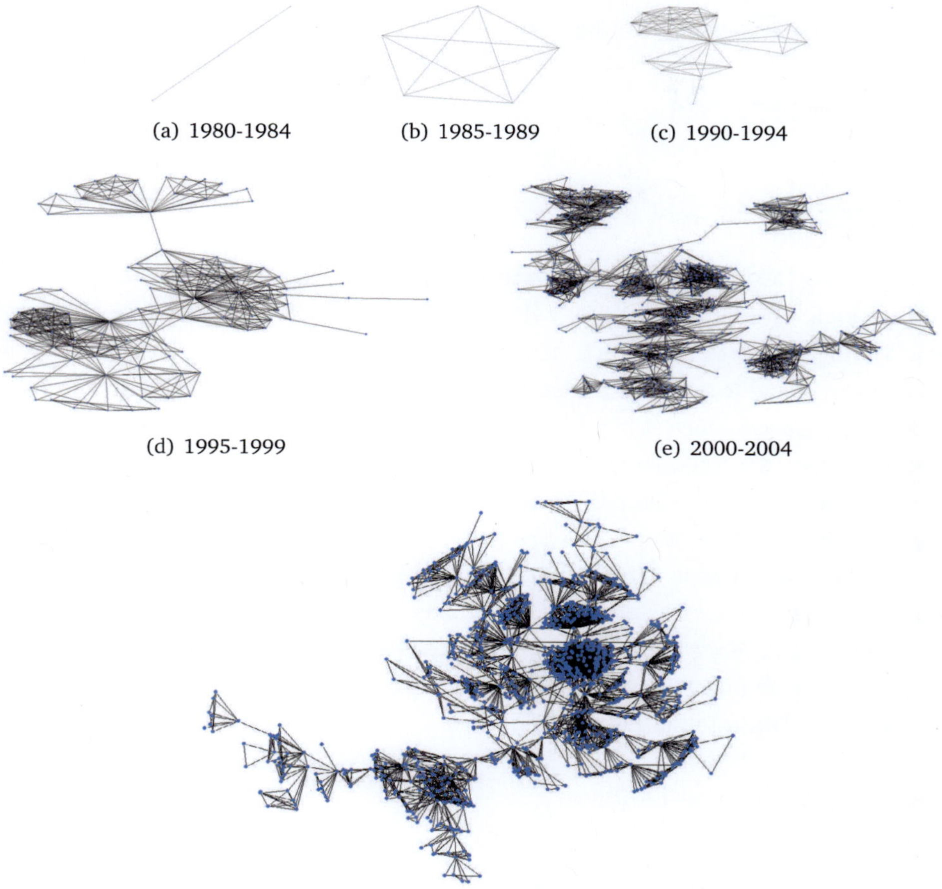

(a) 1980-1984 (b) 1985-1989 (c) 1990-1994

(d) 1995-1999 (e) 2000-2004

(f) 2003-2007

Figure 10.9: Development of the largest component of the applicant-network of nanotechnology. Source: PATSTAT, own search, calculation and illustration.

Small World (c)

The last part of H10.2 refers to small world properties of the largest component of the network, which is assessed in this section. The small world variable assesses the extent to which a network exhibits small world properties. A small world graph is a large-*n*, sparsely connected, decentralised graph, exhibiting a characteristic path length close to that of an equivalent random graph while the clustering coefficient is much greater (Watts 1999). Hence, the number of vertices has to be large compared to the average number of edges, while any vertex can only have a limited number of edges in order to form a decentralised graph. The small world variable hence consists of the characteristic path lengths and the clustering coefficient which are calculated as follows:

Characteristic Path Length

$$L = \frac{\sum_i \sum_j d_{ij}}{2\,n}, \quad L \in [1,\infty), \tag{10.1}$$

with d_{ij} being the geodesic between vertex i and j. The clustering coefficient employed for the small world characteristics calculation is the Watts-Strogatz Clustering Coefficient (Batagelj and Mrvar 2011). It measures the extent to which inventors that are directly connected to a third inventor are also related among each other. This is a measure of cliquishness since it is a property of the network structure which refers to the likelihood that two vertices that are connected to a particular third vertex are also connected to one another. Cliquish networks are prone towards the exhibition of dense neighbourhoods where innovators are better interconnected to each other. This secures a high transmission capacity since knowledge can be diffused easily (Burt 2001). Hence, for each vertex it is observed how many of its connections are also connected. Put differently, for each innovator the connected partners are assessed in terms of their connectedness among each each other. This value is then divided by the number of possible connections in this context (Kogut and Walker 2001):

Watts-Strogatz Clustering Coefficient

$$C = \sum_i \frac{2\,E(G(v_i))}{d(v_i)\,d(v_i - 1)}, \quad C \in [0,1] \tag{10.2}$$

with $E(G(v_i))$ the number of edges among the directly linked neighbours of vertex v_i and $d(v_i)$ its degree.[9] These two measures are then compared to a random network consisting of the same number of vertices and connections per vertex. Watts and Strogatz (1998) calculate limiting values for characteristic path lengths as well as clustering in random networks, which are employed here. For a network with n vertices and average degree d, the average path length is compared to a path length in a random network of $L_{random} = ln(n)/ln(d)$ and a clustering coefficient of $C_{random} = d/n$. For a network to be a small world, the characteristic path length is close to the random network's path length, but the clustering coefficient is substantially larger. This can be expressed in the following quotient (Kogut and Walker 2001).

[9] In case the clustering coefficient is not defined (i.e. the vertex has only direct neighbours) it is omitted from further calculations.

Small World Variable

$$SW = \frac{\frac{C_{actual}}{C_{random}}}{\frac{L_{actual}}{L_{random}}}, \quad SW \in [1, \infty). \tag{10.3}$$

The degree of the small world property increases with the variable. This variable can only be computed in (strongly) connected networks since there would exist infinite path lengths otherwise. This is assured by the fact that only the largest components are assessed similarly. The results are presented in Table 10.5. Note that these results only yield useful results on a relative basis. The small world variable increases clearly over the time periods observed, although not monotonically in case of the inventor network. However, the development of the small world property is significantly and positively correlated with the networks performance in terms of patent output, emphasising the appropriateness of the indicator in terms of efficiency of knowledge transmission. Hence, this can be seen as an indication of the overall increasing efficiency in knowledge transmission in the largest component of the respective networks. While small characteristic path lengths lead to faster knowledge diffusion through the whole network, the high degrees of clustering allow for easy spread of knowledge. Interestingly, the clustering coefficient is relatively high from the beginning pointing to high levels of trust and dense neighbourhoods. Compellingly, the applicant network seems far more efficient than the inventor-network. A possible reason might be the higher cost of connecting for applicants and a correspondingly strategic choice of collaboration partners.

Finally, this indicators show clear evidence for an increasingly efficient network of knowledge for innovation of the German nanotechnology innovators, thereby supporting H10.2(c) in particular and together with the above findings the whole Hypothesis 10.2 in general. Although, due to the emergent character of the technology in general and the networks in particular, the findings have to be constrained to snap-shots, the investigation accomplished in this chapter allows insights into the the development in the last three decades and hence a series of snapshots. What can be concluded is that, on the way of the transition from emergent to more and more stable configurations, the efficiency of the nanotechnology knowledge sharing network increases.

year	Inventor					Applicant				
	representing share	avg $d(v_i)$	L	C	SW	*representing share*	avg $d(v_i)$	L	C	SW
80-84	3.21	5.00	1.00	1.00	1.34	2.94	1	1	-	-
81-85	2.93	5.00	1.00	1.00	1.34					
82-86	6.36	6.00	1.00	1.00	1.27					
83-87	5.93	6.00	1.00	1.00	1.27					
84-88	5.79	6.00	1.00	1.00	1.27					
85-89	5.98	6.00	1.00	1.00	1.27	4.67	4	1	1	1.45
86-90	5.74	6.00	1.00	1.00	1.27					
87-91	5.60	4.00	1.33	0.81	1.49					
88-92	13.42	8.30	1.66	0.89	1.82					
89-93	11.43	8.20	1.66	0.89	1.85					
90-94	8.45	10.22	1.40	0.97	1.51	8.89	7.1	1.69	0.95	2.41
91-95	12.28	6.64	1.90	0.84	3.27					
92-96	13.91	6.59	1.89	0.86	4.91					
93-97	15.90	6.80	1.90	0.88	6.05					
94-98	13.30	6.26	2.17	0.87	7.56					
95-99	26.04	7.36	3.24	0.86	12.26	12.36	8	3.20	0.51	5.23
96-00	25.79	7.06	3.65	0.85	15.74					
97-01	26.99	7.03	4.04	0.86	21.13					
98-02	27.76	7.33	4.21	0.85	21.64					
99-03	27.07	6.81	5.15	0.84	21.39					
00-04	15.38	6.58	5.40	0.85	12.73	27.70	6.76	7.26	0.87	35.27
01-05	15.60	6.59	6.64	0.82	11.65					
02-06	17.23	6.02	6.75	0.82	16.44					
03-07	30.16	6.79	7.84	0.84	25.94	36.49	6.83	6.33	0.89	80.89
corr[1]					0.8112***					0.9692***

Table 10.5: Small world characteristics in the largest component of the respective nanotechnology-networks.
[1] Pearson correlation coefficient with number of patents.
***Indicates significance at 0.01.
Source: own calculations.

10.3.3 Technological Overlap (H10.3)

The last hypothesis expresses the conjecture that the network of technological overlap develops from a rather central structure towards a centre-periphery structure. This hypothesis is assessed for applicants only, since it focuses on the organisational framework (and thereby also encompasses inventors that are mostly very closely related to applicants) and the role of specialisation and diversity as well as the potential of the actors to cooperate and realise cross-fertilisation advantages. Figure 10.10 visualises the German nanotechnology networks of technological overlap from 1980-4 to 2003-7. Table 10.6 presents the most important network statistics. First of all, it is clearly visible that the networks become more cohesive, as the average degree increases drastically and the number of isolates and components decreases (all of them being significantly correlated with the productivity in terms of patent output, average degree positively and isolated and components negatively). This translates into improved possibilities to cooperate for each of the innovators (be it among applicants or inventors). Meanwhile, betweenness centralisation decreases (and is negatively correlated with patent output, significant on the 5% level). This means a drop in the importance of intermediaries. Innovators hence are more or less directly connected to potential cooperation partners, a fact that might be triggered by the small number of technological fields and the increasing number of innovators. Degree centralisation, by contrast increases sharply and is positively related with the yearly patent count. There are some very interdisciplinary innovators at the centre of the network, that exhibit a very high degree centrality. They are thus connected to a large number of actors through technological overlap. It is not surprising that more important applicants in terms of the number of patents are located at the centre of the networks since they can occupy a more diverse technological spectrum than smaller ones. Hence, the German nanotechnology network of technological overlap increases in differentiation between centre and periphery and hence diversity and specialisation. By contrast, centralisation decreases with respect to the distinct role of intermediaries, since actors become nearly equally important for the potential knowledge flow within this network. This translates into more and more well-developed opportunities for the actors to collaborate interdisciplinarily and eventually realise cross-fertilisation effects. Note however, that in case of decreased cognitive proximity (as is the case when actors with different technological backgrounds collaborate) other forms of proximity have to act as substitutes in order to facilitate transfers of tacit knowledge. Most easily, this might be realised through geographic proximity. Hence, a more regional perspective instead of the national perspective would shed further insights on how these multiple opportunities could indeed be realised.

However, so far hypothesis 10.3 can be supported. The network of technological overlap becomes more cohesive and opens opportunities for collaboration and cross-fertilisation exceeding the frontiers of disciplines. This is particularly interesting in the light of nanotechnology being a general purpose technology that moreover merges knowledge of different classical disciplines. However, since intermediaries become less prominent, the centre-periphery structure only intensifies with respect to degree and hence direct (potential) links.

year	components	largest(%)[1]	isolates(%)[1]	$avg\ d(v_i)$	C_D	C_B
1980	3	87	13	4.4	0.46	0.33
1981	3	67	8	2.5	0.38	0.24
1982	7	57	43	2	0.45	0.17
1983	6	50	19	2.13	0.3	0.11
1984	6	76	14	4.21	0.26	0.27
1985	7	57	22	4.09	0.39	0.07
1986	2	90	5	3	0.41	0.56
1987	5	65	8	3.38	0.16	0.17
1988	5	35	5	3.5	0.15	0.04
1989	7	40	5	1.7	0.19	0.07
1990	3	88	3	4.67	0.18	0.34
1991	1	100	0	8.42	0.3	0.12
1992	4	90	2	9.6	0.33	0.08
1993	3	92	0	10.88	0.29	0.12
1994	3	97	1	28.27	0.42	0.15
1995	6	90	6	21.38	0.54	0.15
1996	2	29	1	35.79	0.43	0.07
1997	2	98	0	49.27	0.4	0.06
1998	3	99	0	63.51	0.45	0.04
1999	1	100	0	115.56	0.57	0.05
2000	1	100	0	103.2	0.56	0.05
2001	1	100	0	115.43	0.56	0.06
2002	1	100	0	136.23	0.56	0.03
2003	1	100	0	124.5	0.66	0.04
2004	1	100	0	144.87	0.58	0.07
2005	1	100	0	161.79	0.7	0.05
corr[2]	-0.6741***	0.5416***	-0.4442**	0.9876***	0.7956***	-0.4767**

Table 10.6: Network of technological overlap.
[1] Percentage refers to share of vertices in the network.
[2] Pearson correlation coefficient with number of patents.
***Indicates significance at 0.01.
Source: own calculations.

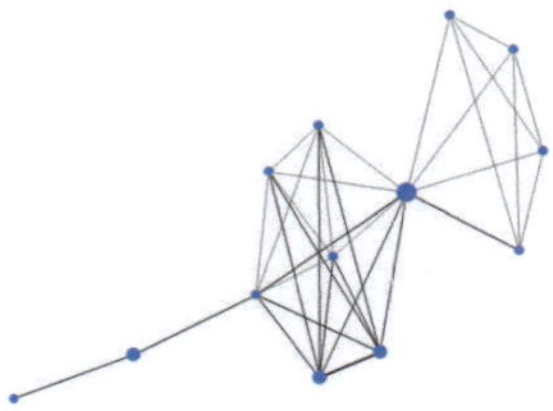

(a) 1980

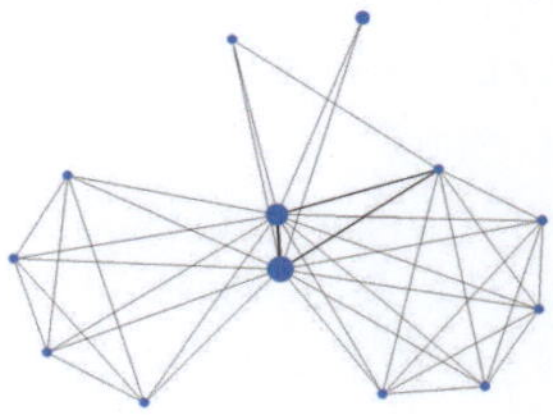

(b) 1985

(c) 1990

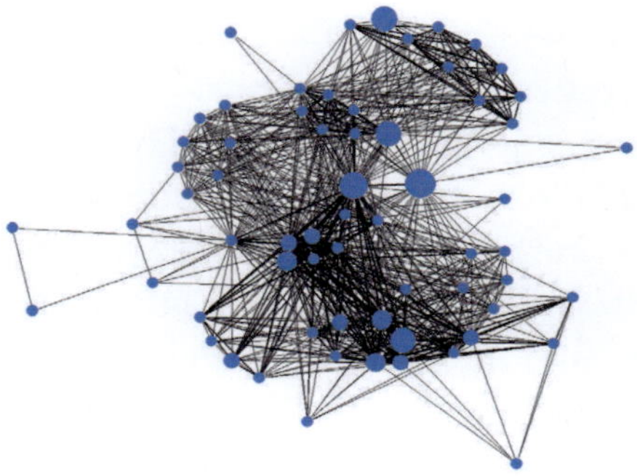

(d) 1994

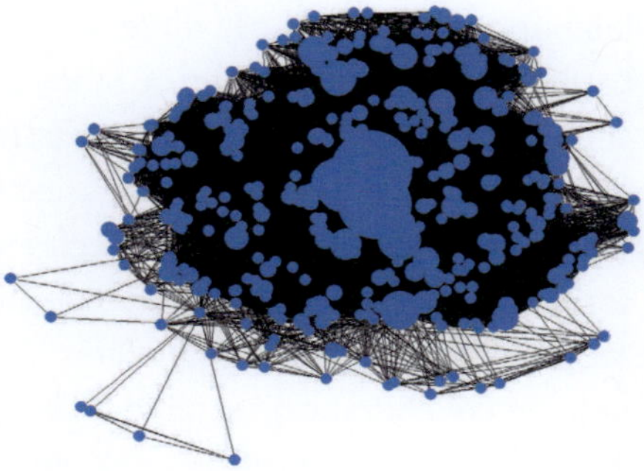

(e) 2000

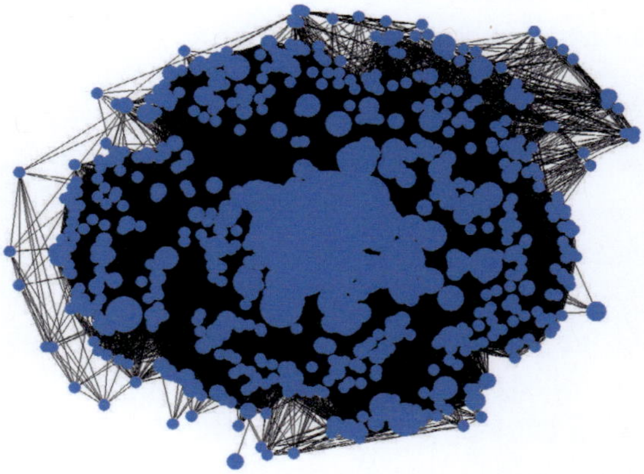

(f) 2005

Figure 10.10: Development of the network of technological overlap of applicants. Size of vertices proportional to the number of filed patents, width of edges proportional to the number of overlapping technology fields.
Source: PATSTAT, own search, calculation and illustration.

10.4 Conclusion

The aim of this chapter is to conduct a comprehensive analysis of the evolution of the German nanotechnology innovation network with respect to the dynamics of collaboration in general, the efficiency of knowledge transmission and the potential for cross-fertilisation. In particular, the emergent character of nanotechnology had to be kept in mind for the interpretation of the results. The analysis was accomplished by an explorative data analysis focused on three main conjectures: The increase of collaboration, the increase of efficiency and the organisation of collaboration opportunities into a centre-periphery structure.

Collaboration indeed clearly increased with the development of nanotechnology. This concerns the average number of innovators that contribute to a patent, the share of patents that are the result of collaboration as well as the team size in this case. It is assumed that this is due to the increased need for complementarity and diverse knowledge particularly relevant in high-tech and general purpose nanotechnology. There is, by contrast, evidence for a tendency of innovators to co-operate with geographically and cognitively proximate candidates. In line with this is the decreasing trend of international collaboration. Although the share of international collaboration increases, the importance of international linkages can be stated to decrease in importance since this share grows less than the one of collaborations in general. The reason is seen in the development of a national knowledge base that offers the access to relevant (niche) knowledge within the national borders.

The focus in this chapter is put on the efficiency of knowledge transmission within these growing networks of innovators in nanotechnology in Germany. The networks not only become larger, but also less fragmented and denser. Less fragmented networks offer larger neighbourhoods of direct, but above all indirect relations to other innovators and hence facilitate the access to more, more relevant and more diverse knowledge. Denser networks refer to the number of (different) direct ties an innovator has and hence to increasing habits of knowledge exchange with more partners. The most important indicator in the context of efficient knowledge transmission is the small world variable. It relates average path length, i.e. the distance to other innovators, to random average path length and clustering, i.e. the density of the neighbourhood, to random clustering. Thereby, the importance of dense neighbourhoods that create trust and facilitate knowledge exchange and the importance of short cuts that provide fast access to rather remote knowledge are both accounted for. The analyses of this chapter unravelled that the efficiency of knowledge transmission indeed increased over the last decades.

Last, the potential for cooperation and cross-fertilisation in form of networks of technological overlaps was investigated. In brief, this network of opportunities became larger and more efficient and now exhibits a structure coined by diversified actors with a large potential for cooperation and cross-fertilisation in the centre and rather specialised, less connected actors in the periphery. Through the network, they nevertheless have the opportunity to access diverse knowledge if they intend to.

This chapter hence shows that knowledge is more and more efficiently shared in the course of the development of innovations in nanotechnology. Although one might argue that in such emergent network configuration no definitive conclusion could be drawn about the development path of nanotechnology networks, the study of the network characteristics over many periods allows for a plausible analysis of the trends. Moreover, the comparison of the recent snap-shot to early snap-shots allows for a comparison of extremely emergent and ever more stable configurations. Extrapolating the trends, it can reasonably be expected that this knowledge-sharing continues and advances in the future. The findings describe the development of the network features and their correlation with the patenting output. It was, however, beyond the scope of the chapter to find clear causal relationships. It can reasonably be assumed that the improved network structures caused the increase in innovative output, but it might, at least partly, be the other way around. Successful innovations, for instance, might have seduced the actors to more risky cooperation that eventually substantially contributed to improved networking. It would hence be worthwhile to investigate the mechanisms that are at work more deeply. Studies such as conducted by Gao et al. (2011) that investigate the causal relationships of network efficiency and patenting might help to assess these issues. It is moreover not clear how and why cooperation in nanotechnology begins and what the distinct incentives are. The analyses find a hint for the role of geographic and cognitive proximity on the one hand and the huge necessity countervailed by a large potential for cross-fertilisation and multidisciplinary collaboration on the other hand. More cooperation and more cross-fertilisation might be beneficial, since the development of nanotechnology as GPT is driven by multipurpose applications and hampered by a lack of coordination. Further research on how to support collaboration across fields and how to use the unravelled potential for cross-fertilisation could hence help to improve the development of this growth-driving technology.

11 What Drives Generality? Assessing the Mechanisms of Knowledge Creation

The development of nanotechnology as a general purpose technology depends on and triggers a wide range of innovations; most of them in high-tech industries. While this does not distinguish the innovation processes at work from other high tech innovations alone, general purpose technologies typically occupy a wide range of fields. GPTs merge different, in other means separate disciplines (Wood et al. 2003, Ott et al. 2009). This feature was also found to be true for nanotechnology (see H6.5 in Chapter 6). In other words, nanotechnology as a GPT overlaps with research in almost any scientific discipline, with physics, chemistry and biology being some examples (Meyer and Persson 1998). Moreover, nanotechnology as GPT has the potential to become applied in a particularly wide range of fields: One and the same innovation can be applied and relevant in life sciences, engineering or information technologies similarly. Given the assumption that one inventor can only handle a limited amount of (leading-edge) knowledge, collaboration should be an important factor for the development of innovations in nanotechnology. More particularly, collaboration should positively influence the *generality*, i.e. the multitude of possible applications of the inventions produced – and thereby support the development of pervasiveness as a constituting feature of a GPT. This, on the other hand, implies that inventors and innovators have to be able not only to handle knowledge stemming from very heterogeneous fields, but also to merge this diverse knowledge in order to eventually develop innovations or incrementally advance applications in the various fields. They hence have to be able to handle knowledge from fairly wider fields than innovators in traditional high tech branches, resulting in the need for a much larger and opener network of accessible (incorporated) knowledge, ensuring access to this diverse knowledge. This aspect is even more important in the early stage of a GPT's development, as it is the case in the example of nanotechnology, where the body of knowledge in the field is still scarce and convergence is still at the beginning. Therefore, early innovators (particularly such as newly established firms, see Baum et al. (2000)) are even more dependent on external sources of knowledge. Basic research, in particular, is often even characterised by a high degree of global distribution and international collaboration. Given the complexity of nanotechnology in particular and GPTs in general, early stage development is therefore especially dependent on external linkages. Resources are constraint and moreover, even respective regional or national systems of innovation in the field still lack the necessary stock of knowledge. Collaboration can therefore be assumed to impact the value of inventions in nanotechnology in multiple ways.

Since nanotechnology gains its fundamental economic importance through its generality of purpose, i.e. the possibility to apply nanotechnology in a wide range of fields, one way to assess the economic value of a nanotechnology-patent is to consider the value of this invention for the GPT's impact on overall innovativeness and value-creation. This could hence be assessed in terms of its generality. For a patent to become as general as possible, (interdisciplinary) collaboration seems of outmost importance. The investigation of the factors around collaboration that might lead to a 'general' invention is the scope of this chapter. Therefore, aspects of most of the preceding chapters are tackled, such as the generality of patents (Chapters 3 and 6), the access to knowledge and the role of collaboration (Chapters 2, 7 and 10), the impact of experience (Chapters 2 and 8) as well as the composition of knowledge (Chapters 6, 7, 8 and 9). This chapter hence not only constitutes the second part of Working Package 3, but also concludes this thesis by providing something similar to a catchall-analysis.

11.1 Derivation of Hypotheses

Collaboration in general is found to have a positive influence on the value of patents in nanotechnology (Beaudry and Schiffauerova 2011). However, 'value' here refers to the usefulness in general, i.e. the extent to which an innovation might create economic value added in which field whatsoever. This is commonly measured by the number of citations (Trajtenberg 1990), the size of the patent family (Lanjouw et al. 1998), patent renewal data (Wang et al. 2010) or the number of claims (Lanjouw and Schankerman 2004). The latter is the measure Beaudry and Schiffauerova (2011) chose. However, these definitions of value do not discriminate between a preferably wide set range of application fields and therefore do not take into account a GPT's special feature of generality. Since the effect of nanotechnology on economic growth depends crucially on the general applicability in a wide range of fields, the investigation of where this generality stems from seems therefore particularly worthwhile. It can be assumed that collaboration does not only have a positive effect on the sheer number of innovations and their general value, but collaboration might also trigger generality in a narrower sense. By opening up the opportunity for the integration of at least to a minor extent different knowledge and in the best case possible cross-fertilisation, collaboration supports the creation of new and general ideas in a field as wide as nanotechnology. Collaboratively developed inventions are therefore assumed to be more relevant in a wider range of fields. Furthermore, displaying (in the best case diverse but complementary) accumulated and simply a larger amount of knowledge, the number of inventors per patent (i.e. the size of the collaborating group) should impact the generality of a patent positively. This, again, is found to be true for the impact of research outcomes in general: The more contributors and the larger the collaborating group, the more important the outcome (Lewison and Cunningham 1991). Widening this assumption to the generality (and therefore an impact as broad as possible) of patents it can be argued that the more inventors there are, the more (different) incorporated knowledge is accessible for the development of a new idea. Moreover, given the nascent stage of the development of nanotechnology, knowledge stemming from international R&D contexts can be assumed to be an important input for the generation of new nanotechnological knowledge. Referring to scientific research, the internationality of research teams is found to influence the impact of the resulting paper positively (Narin and Whitlow 1990, van Raan 1998). Since international collaboration, in general and hence also in a more technological context, is assumed to enrich the (diversity of the) knowledge background of local inventors with complementary resources (otherwise costly international cooperation would hardly take place), it is reasonable to expect that the generality of a patent developed in the course of an international collaboration is higher than the one of a patent developed locally.

Hypothesis 11.1 *Role of Collaboration in General*
(International) Collaboration increases the generality of a patent.

Based on the concept of collective invention, the dynamics of knowledge sharing can be assessed through various innovation networks. Here, the network of inventors as an interpersonal network of individuals, who collaborate and exchange information to produce innovations and scientific knowledge is in focus. It is believed that social networks, both informal friendship and formal collaboration networks, contribute to innovation by facilitating information, knowledge and technology diffusion (Hertzum 2008). In this vein, a relevant assumption is made and investigated: A better network position of inventors can be hypothesised to have a positive impact on the generality of their inventions. Two dimensions impact this relationship: The closer an inventor is to other inventors and their knowledge, the shorter is the way knowledge has to travel. Subsequently, more and more differing knowledge can be assessed by the individual in a central network position – with an increasing probability of diversity among the incorporated knowledge. Moreover, this inventor is more prone to be indeed capable of integrating this presumably diverse knowledge into his work. The high level of incorporated knowledge he is connected to is likely to be correlated with a higher degree of absorptive capacity (Cohen and Levinthal 1990).

Hypothesis 11.2 *Impact of the Access to (New) Knowledge*
An inventor in a more central position in the network of inventors contributes to an invention of higher generality.

However, the well-positioned, central inventors are not necessarily the most productive inventors. By contrast, most inventive output in nanotechnology is produced by only a small proportion of inventors. An experienced inventor is presumed to be able to resort to a well-developed experience in successfully integrating knowledge and developing relevant nano-knowledge thereof. Advancing the role of experience, so called 'star-inventors', i.e. inventors that contributed to a certain threshold number of patents, can be put into focus.[1] In terms of general impact, Beaudry and Schiffauerova (2011) showed that the value of a patent increases when a star-inventor contributes to its production since these star-inventors exhibit high levels of absorptive capacity due to a well developed experience, resulting in an ability to convert accessible knowledge into inventions well above the average. Heinze and Bauer (2007) moreover found that more productive scientists in nanotechnology are also more creative, addressing a broad disciplinary spectrum in their work. Therefore, they could be seen as drivers of a group of inventors, leading them to a successful exploitation of given and diverse knowledge resources: When collaborating groups are provided not only with fresh knowledge from distinct research environments, but also with an experienced and successful researcher with a high absorptive capacity (with their higher ability to effectively communicate with their colleagues and their broad work spectrum (Heinze and Bauer 2007)), this should lead to an increased opportunity for creative recombination of this accessible knowledge and thus enhance generality.

Hypothesis 11.3 *Impact of Experience*
The experience of an inventor increases the generality of an invention.

Finally, and most importantly, the respective knowledge that forms the combined knowledge base of the collaborating inventors impacts the generality of an invention. Under-

[1] This concept of star-inventors is adopted from the 'star-scientists' that have been discussed e.g. by Zucker and Darby (1996) and more specifically for nanotechnology also by Heinze and Bauer (2007).

standing collaboration in a cognitive approach requires the valuation of the technological background of innovators (Meyer et al. 2011), relying on the fact that the cognitive background of each individual strongly influences the ability to integrate further knowledge. Cognitive constraints of inventors arise because of different intellectual complexities and ways of knowledge transfer. Therefore, innovators will keep close to their original knowledge background to search for new knowledge because similar knowledge is easier to process (Cohen and Levinthal 1990, Boschma 2005). Transferring these findings to networking, collaborations are frequent with partners who belong to the same or at least similar technological trajectory because they share the same knowledge base. On the one hand, a certain degree of commonality in the technological understanding constitutes a basis for successful collaboration (Feldman and Audretsch 1999, Boschma and Iammarino 2009). Yet, GPTs in general and nanotechnology in particular (as found for H6.5 in Chapter 6) typically merge different, in other means separate disciplines. Inventors hence have to be able not only to handle knowledge stemming from very heterogeneous fields, but also to merge this diverse knowledge in order to eventually develop inventions usable in a wide range of fields. They hence have to operate on a fairly wider field than inventors in traditional high tech branches. This has consequences on the exploration part of the innovation process, namely the need for a much larger and opener network in order to be able to gain access to knowledge stemming from other fields (and not only from actors within the same disciplines but on different tracks). On the other hand, collaboration with inventors that share exactly the same knowledge base does not bring any new knowledge into the team. In such cases, collaboration produces at best the opportunity for labour sharing, which is not assumed to be the main driver of knowledge creation. Frenken et al. (2007) therefore referred to the term of 'related variety', capturing the complementarity of knowledge given a certain extent of relatedness. Particularly in the context of the creation of inventions as general as possible, the role of the complementarity of the knowledge base has to be emphasised. In the cases under consideration, the investigation of filed patents, the relatedness of knowledge can be, more or less, assumed to be given: When a collaboration culminates into a patent application, it should be fair to suppose that the knowledge of the inventors is sufficiently related. Hence, it is finally hypothesised

Hypothesis 11.4 *Impact of the Technological Background*
The less the knowledge background of the (individual) inventors in a group is coherent, the more general is the resulting invention.

11.2 Methodology and Data

In the following analysis, it is built on German nanotechnology priority patent applications in order to build the network of inventors as discussed in Subsection 5.4. Therefore, all patents from the nano-database (described in Subsection 5.3.1) were selected with at least one inventor allocated in Germany. These will be called German nano-patents henceforth. The approach of the social network analysis introduced in Section 2.3.3 was then employed to evaluate the connections between the inventors in the German nanotechnology network. As also already indicated in Subsection 5.4, the timespan a network connection is assumed to be valuable (i.e. valuable knowledge is transferred without renewing the relationship in form of a new joint patent application) amounts to five years. This is why, once again, the five-year moving time window approach was used to construct the different networks. This results in a split of the German network of nano-inventors into 22 subnetworks, starting in 1980 and ending in 2005. This means that the networks from 1980-4, 1981-5, ..., 2001-5 were considered separately. However, only patent applications from 1984 – 2005 were considered for the assessment of the role of collaboration for the generality of patents. This is due to the fact that in order to determine the network position of an inventor in year t, the network of the precedent 5 years of collaboration, i.e. the network from year $t-4$ to year t is considered. Considering only the patents applied for in one particular year to construct the network would not capture the relationships created before and maintained throughout this particular year.

11.2.1 Variables

Dependent Variable

Aiming at assessing the impact of collaboration on the multipurpose of a patent, the *GENERALITY* indicator is employed. As already introduced in Chapter 6, this indicator identifies valuable GPT-inventions as patents that are cited by a wide range of different industries. To measure this, Trajtenberg et al. (1997) employed the Hirschman-Herfindahl index which was further developed by Moser and Nicholas (2004) and Hall and Trajtenberg (2006) as generality index G_i,

$$\widetilde{G_i} = \frac{N_i}{N_i - 1}\left(1 - \sum_{j}^{n_i} s_{ij}^2\right), \quad \widetilde{G_i} \in [0,1], \tag{11.1}$$

where s_{ij} denotes the percentage of citations received by patent i assigned to patent class j, out of n_i technological classes; with N_i being number of citations observed. Thus, if the knowledge of an invention benefited subsequent inventions in a wide range of technological fields, this measure is close be to one, whereas if most citations are concentrated in a few fields it is close to zero. Due to the small forward time window in the field of emerging technologies s_{ij} is biased downwards as not all the citations are yet observed, a lag effect which is counterbalanced by the term $\frac{N_i}{N_i-1}$ (Hall 2002).

Explanatory Variables

In order to assess H11.1, variables displaying whether a patent is the result of a collaboration, how many inventors contributed and whether the collaboration is an international collaboration are necessary. Very basically, the dummy *COLL* captures this, taking the value of 1 in case of a collaborative invention, i.e. an invention with more than one inventor, and 0 otherwise. *EXCOLL* is similarly constructed, taking the value 1 in case of a collaboration with at least one inventor from outside Germany in the team and vanishing otherwise. *INV* is a count variable, most simply counting the number of inventors on a patent application. It is included in order to assess the role of the team-size.

H11.2 refers to the access to knowledge the collaborating team has. It thereby relies on the network position of an inventor and hence on the degree of connection of an inventor to other inventors. Therefore, various different variables are included that contain information on the centrality of an inventor in the respective German nanotechnology network. Basically, two main indicators displaying network centrality exist: The degree centrality, $C_D(v_i)$ displays the number of different co-inventors (in all patent applications over the last 5 years) an inventor has, relative to the possible connections he could have in the given network. A high degree centrality hence refers to an inventor important for the knowledge transmission in a network via direct connections to others. Since degree centrality, however, does not account for the importance of an inventor for the knowledge flow in a network in terms of the quality of his connections, also betweenness centrality $C_B(v_i)$ is included. It captures the intermediary role of inventors for the knowledge transfer between inventors that are not directly connected. For instance an inventor might be the single connection between important subgroups, i.e. components, of the network. Hence, very relevant and presumably new knowledge might flow via this inventor. Assuming that the connections in the networks, or, put differently, the social relations, are the channels that transmit information and knowledge between people, central inventors are hence those who either have good access to the knowledge flowing in the network or who are able to control the flow of knowledge (see Section 2.3.3 for further details). Inventors in good networking positions hence gain access and control the flow of intentionally as well as unintentionally transferred knowledge, the latter commonly known as knowledge spillovers. As for the integration into the regressions, the average as well as the maximum centralities of the group of inventors contributing to a patent are included, offering the possibility to disentangle whether a single, well connected inventor or the average connectedness of the whole team is (more) important. This finally gives four variables, i.e. $MAX\ C_D(v_i)$, $AVG\ C_D(v_i)$, $MAX\ C_B(v_i)$ and $AVG\ C_B(v_i)$.

In order to tackle the role of experience as assumed to impact generality in H11.3, three different variables are included (see e.g. Beaudry and Schiffauerova (2011) who already employed similar indicators): While the average number of patents per inventor *AVG_PATS_P_INV* in an R&D team shall display the overall experience and similarly the absorptive capacity of a team. The dummy for the integration of a star inventor *STAR* tackles the role of a single, outstandingly experienced and successful inventor. The number of stars *#STARS* counts their number and shall investigate whether a larger number of stars can still increase the generality value of an innovation.

Last, the technological backgrounds of the individual inventors who contributed to a patent are subject to investigation in H11.4. Every inventor should have a specific technological background, either due to his education or due to his experience. For the following analysis it is assumed that every inventor has only one distinctive (main) technological background. Petrie (1976) acknowledged that for most individuals it is hard even to master one discipline given time and energy constraints. Matching inventors to their technological background is a complicated task, most of all due to the fact that the discipline of an inventor is not included in patent information. A feasible approach to integrate the technological background of an inventor nonetheless is the use of the IPC classes and the corresponding technology classes (following the ISIC-concordance, see Subsection 5.1.2) a patent is classified into. However, patents often have more than one technological class and inventors can have contributed to many patents, which results in the fact that inventors can have contributed to patents that belong to many different technologies. Still, the technological background of a single inventor has to be approximated as adequate as possible. Moreover, the results from interdisciplinary team work have to be disentangled, where knowledge from one technology is incorporated into another or where technologies are combined. For this reason the inventors are allocated to the technological class that occurred most frequently amongst their individual patent portfolio. Then, in case of a collaboration, the qualitative technological coherence of the different technological backgrounds of the inventors is calculated, again based on the technological relatedness matrix introduced in Chapter 6: To calculate the coherence of a portfolio of technological background of a group of inventors, the measure of the degree of relatedness is determined for each pair of technology classes. Commonly, this measure is constructed using co-occurrences of technological classes that are associated (directly or via citations) to a patent (Breschi et al. 2003, Leten et al. 2007). Subsequently, two technology classes are considered as technologically related if patents associated to one technology class often cite patents classified in the other technology class and vice versa. Based on the matrix containing the individual values for each class, the coherence *COH* of the portfolio of technological backgrounds of the inventors on a patent is then calculated. However, this coherence indicator cannot be computed for technology portfolios that only consist of one technological class. Instead, the variety *VAR*, i.e. the inverse of *COH*, is employed, which is a straightforward measure for how 'different' technological backgrounds are: $VAR = 1/COH$, with $VAR = 0$ by definition for all single inventors or teams of inventors with the same technological background. Although this might underestimate the role of diversity within one technological field, this seems at least a feasible way to tackle this kind of individual background at all. Yet, this approach turns the focus to a considerably high basic degree of diversity which might indeed become a problem, if the assumption of given relatedness once a team collaborates is not fair. However, assuming it is fair, the expectation according to H11.4 then is: The more technological variety a technology portfolio of a collaborating group exhibits, the higher the extent to which the inventors bring together complementarities and the higher the degree of generality, accordingly. Hence, a positive relationship is to be expected.

The above proposed *GENERALITY* indicator implemented as the dependent variable is an indicator relying on forward citations and their technological classification. This indicator, however, can also be used to measure the generality of backward citations. Backward citations indicate the prior technological knowledge the actual invention is relying on, regardless of the inventors and their networks and hence without directly referring to the actual collaboration on the patents. Yet, backwards generality *BW_GEN* refers to the composition of the knowledge base possibly used to create new knowledge. The knowledge constituting the base for the creation of new knowledge has to have been incorporated in the inventors somehow or the inventors at least have to have been able to process this knowledge, which finally culminated into a successful invention. For this reason, it might be insightful to implement this *BW_GEN* indicator as well when aiming to find out the role of the background of the inventors. It might be a fair assumption to suppose that a higher level of convergence of the invention, or, put differently, a sensible combination of knowledge from more different fields, results in a better applicability in terms of generality of the current invention. Hence, backwards generality can be assumed to induce (forward) generality – or, more generally speaking, interdisciplinarity produces pervasiveness.

Last, the number of citations (*CITATIONS*) each individual patent receives is included. While the number of citations is not assumed to have a causal effect on generality, several of the variables described above might influence the value in terms of applicability of a patent positively (see e.g. Beaudry and Schiffauerova 2011). Since the scope of this chapter is to go one step further and investigate the factors that impact generality, i.e. the applicability of patents in a multitude of fields, the implementation of the *CITATIONS* variable shall serve as a robustness check: If the variables only have an effect on the number of citations (and not on the generality in a broader sense) these effects should be controlled for in the regressions once the *CITATIONS* variable is included. The *CITATIONS* variable shall hence on the one hand improve the model fit and on the other hand allow for disentangling the effects on value in a broader and generality in a narrower sense. Table 11.1 provides an overview on the different variables employed.

Characteristic	Variable	Description
dependent	*GENERALITY*	inverse concentration index of patent forward citations across different technological fields
collaboration	*INV*	number of inventors involved
	COLL	collaboration: at least two contributing inventors (dummy)
	EXCOLL	external collaboration: at least two contributing inventors from at least two different countries (dummy)
access to knowledge	$MAX\ C_D(v_i)$	max degree centrality of contributing inventors
	$AVG\ C_D(v_i)$	avg degree centrality of contributing inventors
	$MAX\ C_B(v_i)$	max betweenness centrality of contributing inventors
	$AVG\ C_B(v_i)$	avg betweenness centrality of contributing inventors
experience	*STAR*	at least one star inventor contributed to the patent
	#STARS	number of stars that contributed to the patent
	AVG_PATS_P_INV	average number of patents field by the contributing inventors
background	*VAR*	variety, i.e. non-coherence of technological backgrounds of contributing inventors
	BW_GEN	generality of backwards citations
control	*CITATIONS*	number of forward citations a patent receives

Table 11.1: Description of variables.
Source: own compliation.

11.2.2 Descriptive Statistics

In order to get a clear picture of the underlying data set that exceed the descriptive statistics as presented in Table 11.2, Chapter 10 should be referenced. The underlying dataset of the analysis accomplished there is very similar to the data employed in this chapter. However, since the variables employed differ, the data is once again presented.

Although this chapter does not gear towards a thorough and focused analysis of the relationship between generality and the evolution over time, the consideration of the development path of nanotechnology given in this subsection might help to gain fundamental insights into the data.

As Figure 11.1(a) depicts, the number of patents as well as the number of inventors increases sharply during the considered time period. The stronger increase of inventors compared to the number of patents indicates that the role of collaboration increases. In Figure 11.1(b), the variables included for the assessment of the role of collaboration in general are displayed. The share of patents that are developed collaboratively increases similarly to the number of inventors per patent, indicating that the increase in the number of inventors per patent also translates into a higher share of collaborations and not only into larger group sizes. Together with the findings from Chapter 10 it can be stated that German inventors collaborate more intensely, thereby exchanging their knowledge and building larger networks of knowledge diffusion. The share of international collaborations, however, only increases to a very small extent – which might be due to the fact that knowledge external to the German nanotechnology inventor network is relatively more important at the beginning of the nano development.

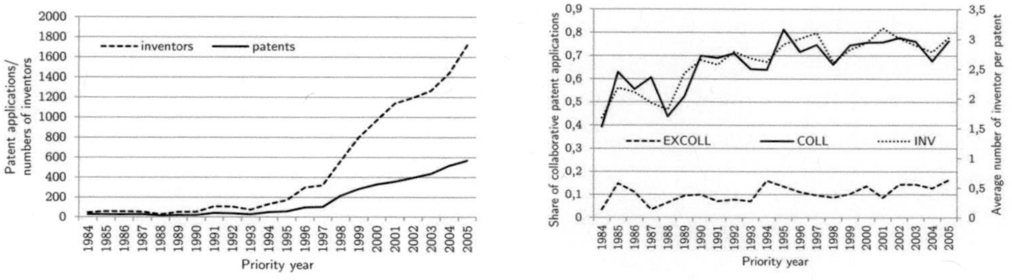

(a) Patents and Inventors (b) *INV*, *COLL*, *EXCOLL*

Figure 11.1: Development of collaboration in nanotechnology patenting. Source: PATSTAT, own search and calculations.

Figure 11.2 displays the development of network positions as indicating the access to knowledge of a team of researchers. While both the average as well as the maximum degree centrality measure clearly decrease over the course of the years, the respective betweenness centrality measures increase. As concerning the decreasing value of degree centrality, this could be explained by the crowding of the network and specialisation within components (and hence less central positions in terms of direct collaborations) with simultaneous disappearance of highly centralised inventors who are active across the whole field of nanotechnology. The increasing value of betweenness centrality emphasises that, despite a lower number of direct connections on average, intermediaries gain in importance. This fits into the picture, since the tendency towards component occupation and the general increase in network size is counterbalanced by more and more central intermediaries.

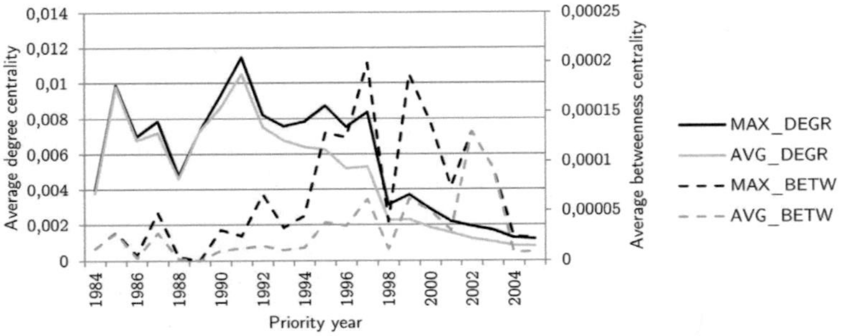

Figure 11.2: Development of network positions of individual inventors.
Source: PATSTAT, own search and calculations.

Most naturally, the experience as displayed in Figure 11.3 increases with the development of nanotechnology. This manifests itself in the average number of patents per inventor as well as in the sheer number of star-inventors that contribute to a nanotechnology patent. However, by far not every team benefits from the absorptive capacity of such an experienced inventor, even more so the share of patents that are co-developed by a patent seems to have stagnated over the last ten years observed (while the collaborating stars increase). Whether this supports the development of nanotechnology as GPT or not is investigated in the following section.

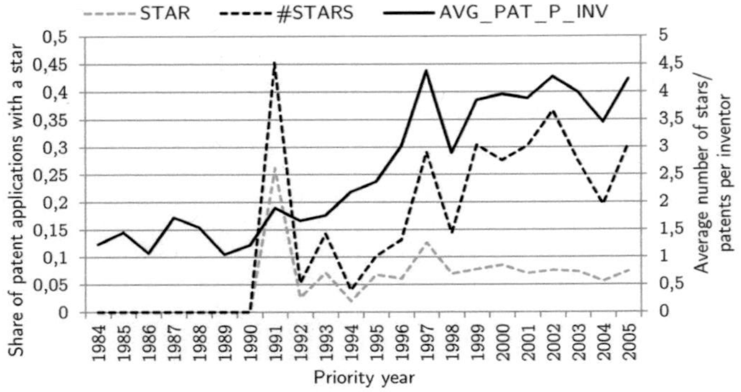

Figure 11.3: Experienced inventors.
Source: PATSTAT, own search and calculations.

The technological background shall be assessed by the generality of backwards citations and the variety of technological portfolios. The former is relatively constant over time while the latter increases slightly. First of all, the constant value of *BW_GEN* indicates that nanotechnology inventions still rely on a wide range of different technology fields. This emphasises the need for the ability to cope with the need for a diverse set of knowledge and competencies by the group of inventors, the achievement of which might be the reason for the decreasing coherence of the technological backgrounds in a team of inventors. Put differently: There is an unbowed necessity for the integration of diverse knowledge, which is accounted for by an increasing interdisciplinarity in innovation.

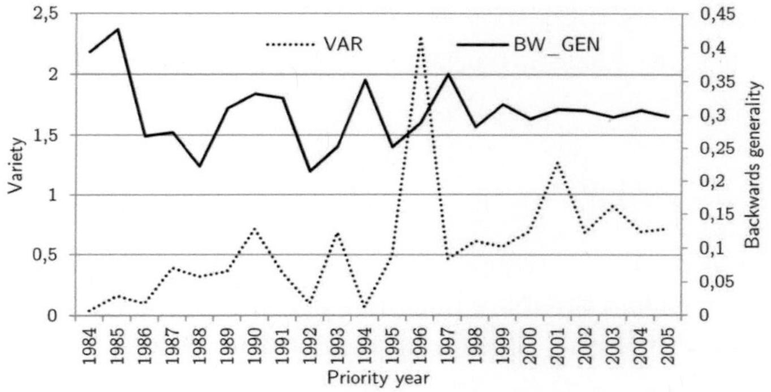

Figure 11.4: Technological backgrounds of inventors.
Source: PATSTAT; own search and calculations.

Variable	Obs	Mean	StdDev	Min	Max
GENERALITY	3691	0.2446	0.3006	0	0.9033
INV	3691	2.887	1.9252	1	16
COLL	3691	0.7302	0.444	0	1
EXCOLL	3691	0.1249	0.3306	0	1
MAX $C_D(v_i)$	3691	0.003	0.0061	0	0.0608
AVG $C_D(v_i)$	3691	0.0022	0.0039	0	0.0423
MAX $C_B(v_i)$	3691	0.0001	0.0004	0	0.0037
AVG $C_B(v_i)$	3691	0.0002	0.0005	0	0.006
STAR	3691	0.0707	0.2564	0	1
#STARS	3691	0.2525	0.8036	0	10
AVG_PAT_P_INV	3691	3.673	5.1157	1	66.5
BW_GEN	3691	0.3031	0.3091	0	0.9053
VAR	3691	0.7552	5.7942	0	100
CITATIONS	3691	2.8353	5.82	0	114

Table 11.2: Descriptive statistics.
Source: own calculations.

11.2.3 Regression Approach

Since the dependent variable is a variable with values in the interval $[0,1]$, the variable can be treated as a fraction. An OLS estimation approach would be misspecified in so far as the predicted variable might lie outside this interval. Moreover, OLS implies that a ceteris paribus unit increase in each independent variable affects the dependent variable to the same extent regardless of its initial value. This cannot be the case, since this would necessarily result in values exceeding the range of this interval (Wooldridge 2002). An approach to modelling fractional dependent variables is fractional logit, as developed by Papke and Wooldridge (1996). Fractional logit models are similar to familiar logit models except for the restriction on yielding predictions between 0 and 1 inclusive and not just its boundaries. It models the conditional expected value of the dependent variable y as a logistic function (Wooldridge 2002):

$$E(y|x) = \frac{exp(x\beta)}{[1+exp(x\beta)]} \tag{11.2}$$

The predicted values of y are thereby also be in the interval $[0,1]$ while the effect on $E(y|x)$ of any independent variable x decreases with increasing $x\beta$. The model is based on maximum quasi-likelihood estimations, since y is not restricted to 0 or 1. Wagner (2001) showed that the fractional logit approach is superior to other possible methods that can be used to estimate models with dependent variables that are (like) proportions.

The interpretation of the coefficients yielded by fractional logit estimations is, however, not straightforward. The coefficients of the fractional logit model are of similar nature as coefficients in standard logit or probit regression: They do not hold the effects of other explanatory variables constant since they do not equate to the first partial derivatives, which makes the derivation of the second derivatives a non-trivial task (Greene 1993). Therefore, marginal effects are computed at means for all variables with 0 to 1 change for dummies. Finally, it is tested and controlled for multicollinearity (see the correlation matrix in the Appendix H), which is why some of the variables have to be included into distinct models.

The following models are estimated for the assessment of the four hypotheses stated:

MODEL 11.I – H11.1

$$\widetilde{G}_i = a_0 + a_1\, INV_i/COLL_i + a_2\, EXCOLL_i + a_3\, BW\_GEN_i + a_k\, YEAR_k + \varepsilon \tag{11.3}$$

MODEL 11.II – H11.2

$$\widetilde{G}_i = a_0 + a_1\, NETWORK\ POS_i + a_2\, COLL_i + a_3\, EXCOLL_i + a_4\, BW\_GEN_i + a_k\, YEAR_k + \varepsilon \quad (11.4)$$

MODEL 11.III – H11.3

$$\widetilde{G}_i = a_0 + a_1\, EXPERIENCE_i + a_2\, COLL_i + a_3\, EXCOLL_i + a_4\, BW\_GEN_i + a_k\, YEAR_k + \varepsilon \quad (11.5)$$

MODEL 11.IV – H11.4

$$\widetilde{G}_i = a_0 + a_1\, VAR_i + a_2\, COLL_i + a_3\, EXCOLL_i + a_4\, BW\_GEN_i + a_k\, YEAR_k + \varepsilon \quad (11.6)$$

11.3 Results and Interpretation

The results of the accomplished regression analyses confirm the derived hypothesis in most of the cases as can be seen in Tables 11.3 and 11.5 as well as in Tables 11.4 and 11.6. The latter present the results of the models where *CITATIONS* as a control variable is included (see Subsection 11.2.1), in the following denoted with a prime. The description and interpretation of the results follows in the rest of this section.

11.3.1 Collaboration (H11.1)

Remember that hypothesis 11.1 stated the conjecture that collaboration is conducive to the generality value of a patent. Models 11.I(a) and 11.I(b) (as well as 11.I'(a) and 11.I'(b)) investigate this hypothesis in particular, the results of which can be taken from Table 11.3 (11.4, respectively). The results of the fractional logit analyses of the two models clearly support this hypothesis: Collaboration indeed has a significantly positive influence on the generality of a patent. This is true for all the employed variables (*INV*, *COLL*, *EXCOLL*). As derived in Model 11.I(a), a patent resulting from collaboration, in general, has a higher generality than a patent from one single inventor, keeping all other variables constant at mean. More particularly, every unit increase in the number of inventors increases the generality of a patent (see Model 11.I(b)) in an economically and statistically significant way. The same is true for the effect of international collaboration. Yet, once the number of citations is included, as done so in the models 11.I'(a) and 11.I'(b), the significance of the effect of external collaboration vanishes. This indicates that international collaboration affects one part of the generality aspect, namely the sheer quantity effect, but does not have an effect on the isolated effect of breadth in application. The significance of the impact of external collaboration might hence at least be considered with doubts. However, since the effect of collaboration in general has proven significant and positive, H11.1 stays validated: As expected, a patent that is the result of a collaboration exhibits higher degrees of generality, i.e. it is applicable in a wider range of fields. This discrete yes-or-no-relationship can even be extended into a more continuous one: The more inventors contribute to the patent, the more general the patent becomes.[2]

11.3.2 Access to (New) Knowledge (H11.2)

To assess hypothesis 11.2, it shall be tested whether the access to knowledge, proxied by a good network position, has a positive effect on the generality. Therefore, four different models, 11.II(a)-(d) (see Table 11.3), have been estimated since the variables employed could not be included in one model for multicollinearity reasons. The results strongly confirm the hypothesis: All employed variables for network positions that indicate the extent of access to knowledge (i.e. $MAXC_D(v_i), AVGC_D(v_i), MAXC_B(v_i), AVGC_B(v_i)$) are positive and significant. It does not matter wether average or maximum centralities are included, all of the variables yield impressively significant results. Concerning degree centrality this means, generally spoken, that better connected inventors contribute to more general patents. More particularly, both seems important and conducive: a well connected team on average as well as a very well connected individual within one team. According to the results, the former situation is even more helpful. Put differently, it is more important that all individuals are well connected than that one individual is very well connected. This might be due to the fact that degree centrality refers to direct connections and hence very direct access to knowledge, offering the possibility for each individual to directly incorporate knowledge and learn through experience. Larger individual knowledge processing abilities and knowledge stocks indeed should be more conducive than, strinkingly spoken, one intelligent and several fools. Concerning betweenness centrality and hence the intermediary position of an inventor in the German nanotechnology innovation network, again both, the team average as well as the maximum value are significant and with positive correlation. In this case, however, maximum betweenness has a larger impact compared to the average group value. This seems plausible since betweenness centrality refers to indirect connection and hence one well connected intermediary already offers the whole team the necessary access to different kinds of knowledge in different other fields of the network, which can then be processed jointly. The more inventors in the group exhibit high betweenness centralities the better, however, with the confinement that this increases the probability of redundancy which in turn does not constitute additional benefits. The results obtained are indeed very similar to the ones found by Beaudry and Schiffauerova (2011)

[2]It is beyond the scope of this chapter to test for the impact of extreme values. I.e. it is imaginable that the number of inventors has a decreasing effect on generality once a certain threshold value is reached, as crowding might inhibit effective work.

for the pure value of patents. It is, however, not straightforward that the result for the quantitative valuation of 'usefulness' of a patent yields such similar results. In order to further disentangle the different forces that lead to broad applicability in contrast to massive applicability regardless of the breadth of the fields, the *CITATIONS* measure was included as test of robustness of the results (11.II'(a)-(d), Table 11.4). If this good access to knowledge transmitted via the network was only boosting the value in the sense of applicability in what field whatsoever, the *CITATIONS* variable as a value proxy should catch these effects and the network position variables should no longer show any significance. Indeed, the implementation of *CITATIONS* weakens the extent to which these variables impact patent generality, however, all results stay as highly significant as before. Hypothesis 11.2 is therefore impressively confirmed: The better the access to knowledge transferred in the network of nanotechnology-inventors, directly or indirectly, the better the performance in terms of generality of a patent.

11.3.3 Experience (H11.3)

Hypothesis 11.3 expresses the conjecture that experience enhances the generality of the patent outcome of an innovation process, since experience improves absorptive capacity and hence knowledge processing abilities. This hypothesis is tested by the implementation of the experience variables *STAR*, *#STARS* and *AVG_PAT_P_INV* in Models 11.III(a)-(c) (Table 11.5). The results obviously support this hypothesis: Both, *STAR* as well as *#STARS* impact generality positively and significantly. Star-inventors feature high degrees of experience with successful innovation and hence with knowledge recombination. Besides, they can be assumed to have a large knowledge stock incorporated. With the size also the probability of diversity within this knowledge stock increases. The larger marginal effect of the star-dummy in comparison to the effect of the number of stars indicates that it is more important that at least one experienced inventor is in the team. Although more experienced inventors contribute to more generality, this effect is smaller than the latter one. This seems plausible: One experienced team-member can help to absorb the knowledge that is gained access to and knows how to recombine this knowledge. An additional member with such high knowledge-processing capabilities does bring additional benefit, but less than the step from 0 to 1 star-inventor on the team. The importance of experience is supported by the significant result of *AVG_PAT_P_INV*. Not only experience beyond a certain threshold value, but on a very basic level translates into a better performance with respect to a general innovation result. Beaudry and Schiffauerova (2011) find, by contrast, that this lower level of experience does not have an impact on the (quantitative) value of a patent.

	MODEL 11.I(a)		MODEL 11.I(b)		MODEL 11.II(a)		MODEL 11.II(b)		MODEL 11.II(c)		MODEL 11.II(d)	
	Coeff	dy/dx[1]	Coeff	dy/dx[1]	Coeff	dy/dx[1]	Coeff	dy/dx[1]	Coeff	dy/dx[1]	Coeff	dy/dx[1]
INV			0.1042***	0.0182***								
			(0.0140)									
$MAX\ C_D(v_i)$					46.1643***	8.0389***						
					(3.9079)							
$AVG\ C_D(v_i)$							65.0067***	11.3221***				
							(7.6426)					
$MAX\ C_B(v_i)$									547.5201***	95.2411***		
									(59.7281)			
$AVG\ C_B(v_i)$											412.1007***	71.6165***
											(56.3216)	
COLL	0.4240***	0.07***			0.2228***	0.0377***	0.226***	0.0382***	0.3678***	0.06099***	0.3687***	0.061***
	(0.0671)				(0.0686)		(0.0694)		(0.0671)		(0.0675)	
EXCOLL	0.2495***	0.0457***	0.2089***	0.038***	0.2373***	0.0433***	0.2314***	0.0422***	0.2531***	0.0463***	0.246***	0.0449***
	(0.0776)		(0.0797)		(0.0786)		(0.0788)		(0.0778)		(0.0776)	
BW_GEN	1.457***	0.2541***	1.4594***		1.4654***	0.2552***	1.4557***	0.2535***	1.4637***	0.2546***	1.4511***	0.2522***
	(0.0880)		(0.0881)		(0.0876)		(0.0873)		(0.0877)		(0.0877)	
YEARS	yes		yes		yes		yes		yes		yes	
Const	-2.7041***	(0.1094)	-2.6937***		-2.6025***		-2.5951***		-2.6750***		-2.6593***	
			(0.3234)		(0.1084)		(0.1085)		(0.1094)		(0.1092)	
Obs	3691		3691		3691		3691		3691		3691	
R^2	0.1595		0.1631		0.1884		0.1785		0.1834		0.1732	

Table 11.3: Results of fractional logit estimations, models 11.I-11.II.
***Indicates significance at 0.01. Robust standard errors in parentheses.
[1] Marginal effects evaluated at means for all variables with 0 to 1 changes for dummies.
Source: own calculations.

	MODEL 11.I'(a)		MODEL 11.I'(b)		MODEL 11.II'(a)		MODEL 11.II'(b)		MODEL 11.II'(c)		MODEL 11.II'(e)	
	Coeff	dy/dx[1]	Coeff	dy/dx[1]	Coeff	dy/dx[1]	Coeff	dy/dx[1]	Coeff	dy/dx[1]	Coeff	dy/dx[1]
INV			0.0674***	0.012***								
			(0.0133)									
MAX $C_D(v_i)$					32.5277***	5.6865***						
					(4.17)							
AVG $C_D(v_i)$							41.2854***	7.2196***				
							(8.187)					
MAX $C_B(v_i)$									412.395***	72.0447***		
									(55.5139)			
AVG $C_B(v_i)$											320.227***	55.8847***
											(51.3315)	
COLL	0.2641***	0.0447***			0.1364**	0.0234**	0.1502**	0.0258**	0.227***	0.0385***	0.2215***	0.0376***
	(0.0649)				(0.0657)		(0.0661)		(0.0649)		(0.0652)	
EXCOLL	0.0861	0.0153	0.056	0.0106	0.0837	0.0149	0.0799	0.0142	0.0885	0.0158	0.083	0.0147
	(0.081)		(0.0829)		(0.0819)		(0.0819)		(0.0812)		(0.0809)	
BW_GEN	1.2286***	0.2151***	1.2311***	0.2155***	1.2415***	0.2170***	1.2354***	0.2160***	1.236***	0.2159***	1.2271***	0.2142***
	(0.0869)		(0.0869)		(0.0868)		(0.0867)		(0.0871)		(0.0868)	
CITATIONS	0.1456***	0.0255***	0.1447***	0.0253***	0.1392***	0.0243***	0.1411***	0.0247***	0.1405***	0.0246***	0.1422***	0.0248***
	(0.0142)		(0.0142)		(0.0142)		(0.0142)		(0.0142)		(0.0141)	
YEARS	yes		yes		yes		yes		yes		yes	
Const	-2.6219***		-2.6209***		-2.5582***		-2.5615***		-2.5984***		-2.5848***	
	(0.1025)		(0.0987)		(0.102)		(0.1021)		(0.1025)		(0.1024)	
Obs	3691		3691		3691		3691		3691		3691	
R^2	0.3201		0.3213		0.3304		0.3257		0.3291		0.3254	

Table 11.4: Results of fractional logit estimations, models 11.I'-11.II' (with *CITATIONS*).
***Indicates significance at 0.01. Robust standard errors in parentheses.
[1] Marginal effects evaluated at means for all variables with 0 to 1 changes for dummies.
Source: own calculations.

These results show they do contribute to a better applicability in a wider range of fields, although to a smaller extent than do highly experienced inventors. These findings are weakened but still consistent with the findings from the models that included the *CITATIONS* measure (Models 11.III'(a)-(c), Table 11.6), which definitely points to their robustness. Hypothesis 11.3 is hence fully supported: Experience of inventors drives the generality of nanotechnology patents, most presumably via two channels: increased absorptive capacity and a larger (and more diverse) stock of knowledge incorporated.

11.3.4 Technological Background (H11.4)

Last, hypothesis 11.4 points to the positive impact of the non-relatedness of the technological backgrounds of the inventors, which is assessed by the implementation of *VAR* and *BW_GEN* in Model 11.IV (Table 11.5). The empirical literature finds evidence for the need for related variety for innovations. In the course of deriving the hypotheses, it was argued above that the relatedness of the background could fairly be assumed when innovative efforts culminated into a patent. Given this precondition, variety of backgrounds should contribute positively to a particularly wide scope on innovations as needed for a GPT to become effective. However, the findings here do not support this, i.e. *VAR* is not significant. There might be two reasons for this: First, the variety produces indeed difficulties in mutual understanding within the process of knowledge creation and hence the assumption of the given threshold in relatedness needed for a successful cooperation is not fair. Second, this measure might simply be too abrasive, meaning that the variety of technological backgrounds goes too far when one measures it in terms of qualitative difference between K30 technology fields and neglects differences and hence variety within one technological field. The second variable that assesses H11.4, by contrast, supports the conjecture: *BW_GEN* has been implemented in each of the models estimated and never proves to be insignificant. The more diverse the knowledge underlying, again measured in terms of K30 generality, but this time without any direct link to the inventors that incorporate the knowledge, the more general the invention gets. This might appear straightforward at the first glance. At the second glance, there is more beyond the obvious. First, this also implies information on the inventors: In order to be able to process this diverse knowledge and produce one coherent invention, inventors do have to have the capacity and ability to absorb the relevant knowledge from their surrounding (e.g. via collaboration and good access to knowledge in their network), to combine it with their own previously existing stock of knowledge and finally to process all this information, knowledge and competencies to a valuable innovation, both in terms of quantity and in terms of quality. Second, and this is neither as obvious as the first, the convergence of knowledge definitely happens when

	MODEL 11.III(a)		MODEL 11.III(b)		MODEL 11.III(c)		MODEL 11.IV	
	Coef.	dy/dx[1]	Coef.	dy/dx[1]	Coef.	dy/dx[1]	Coef.	dy/dx[1]
STAR	0.8816***	0.1821***						
	(0.0855)							
#STARS			0.3218***	0.0558***				
			(0.0372)					
AVG_PAT_P_INV					0.0681***	0.0117***		
					(0.0061)			
VAR							-0.0046	-0.0008
							(0.0045)	
COLL	0.3705***	0.0612***	0.3202***	0.0533***	0.3059***	0.0507***	0.4287***	0.0707***
	(0.0668)		(0.068)		(0.0675)		(0.0672)	
EXCOLL	0.2589***	0.0473***	0.2686***	0.0492***	0.2975***	0.0545***	0.2492***	0.0457***
	(0.0780)		(0.0788)		(0.0773)		(0.0776)	
BW_GEN	1.4473***	0.2510***	1.4283***	0.2478***	1.4108***	0.243287***	1.4593***	0.2545***
	(0.0877)		(0.0874)		(0.0871)		(0.0881)	
YEARS	yes		yes		yes		yes	
Const	-2.7424***		-2.7389***		-2.9332***		-2.7055***	
	(0.1084)		(0.1097)		(0.1126)		(0.1095)	
Obs	3691		3691		3691		3691	
R^2	0.1815		0.1876		0.2071		0.1597	

Table 11.5: Results of fractional logit estimations, models 11.III-11.IV.
***Indicates significance at 0.01. Robust standard errors in parentheses.
[a] Marginal effects evaluated at means for all variables with 0 to 1 changes for dummies.
Source: own calculations.

	MODEL 11.III'(a)		MODEL 11.III'(b)		MODEL 11.III'(c)		MODEL 11.IV'	
	Coef.	dy/dx[1]	Coef.	dy/dx[1]	Coef.	dy/dx[1]	Coef.	dy/dx[1]
STAR	0.7376***	0.1494***						
	(0.0846)							
#STARS			0.2689***	0.0468***				
			(0.0359)					
AVG_PAT_P_INV					0.0558***	0.0097***		
					(0.0056)			
VAR							-0.0011	-0.0002
							(0.0043)	
COLL	0.2245***	0.038***	0.18***	0.0306***	0.1736***	0.0294***	0.2652***	0.0448***
	(0.0647)		(0.0657)		(0.0651)		(0.0651)	
EXCOLL	0.0967	0.0171	0.1052	0.0187	0.1322*	0.0235*	0.0861	0.0153
	(0.0809)		(0.0811)		(0.0803)		(0.0809)	
BW_GEN	1.2241***	0.2132***	1.2088***	0.2105***	1.1977***	0.2075***	1.2291***	0.2151943***
	(0.0867)		(0.0865)		(0.0864)		(0.0870)	
CITATIONS	0.1414***	0.0246***	0.1401***	0.0244***	0.1360***	0.0235***	0.1455***	0.0254***
	(0.0140)		(0.0139)		(0.0138)		(0.0142)	
YEARS	yes		yes		yes		yes	
Const	-2.6575***		-2.6491***		-2.6491***		-2.6221***	
	(0.0558)		(0.1025)		(0.1047)		(0.1025)	
Obs	3691		3691		3691		3691	
R^2	0.3310		0.3346		0.3432		0.3201	

Table 11.6: Results of fractional logit estimations, models 11.III'-11.IV' (with *CITATIONS*).
***Indicates significance at 0.01. Robust standard errors in parentheses.
[1] Marginal effects evaluated at means for all variables with 0 to 1 changes for dummies.
Source: own calculations

one innovation is created that builds on knowledge from a diverse set of technologies. However, it is far from trivial that this convergence translates into generality directly. These results show that it does, to a high degree and robustly across pure quantity effects. It is, most presumably, the result of the 'related variety'-background of the people behind the innovation. Otherwise, i.e. with a narrow technological background, backwards generality would not translate into forward generality, but into a specialised (niche) innovation – or in no innovation at all. Although not as impressive as the last validations, H11.4 should hence be seen at least as non-rejectable.

11.4 Conclusion

This chapter intends to shed light on the factors that impact the generality of nanotechnological innovations within the innovation processes. A special focus is laid on the role of knowledge processing, i.e. collaboration, access to knowledge, experience and technological background of inventors. The analysis is accomplished by the assessment of four corresponding hypotheses, most of which could be validated completely. The interplay of the four hypothesis is illustrated in Figure 11.5. To put each of them in a nutshell:

Collaboration does support the generality of a nanotechnology innovation. The more people collaborate, the more (diverse) knowledge they bring together and the more their innovations outreach their individual knowledge frontier. Possibilities for knowledge sharing, mutual learning, cross-fertilisation and also unintended (positive) knowledge externalities in form of technological knowledge spillovers might occur. While these are not measured isolatedly (and are, if at all, extremely difficult to measure), the positive effect of collaboration on the generality of patents should incorporate all of them to a certain extent.

Networking is a beneficial source of (new) knowledge and good networking positions help to increase the generality of a patent, regardless of their reference to direct or rather indirect and hence intermediary linkages. It is hence not only intra-group collaboration that drives generality of innovations, but also the use of knowledge resources external to the group but internal to the innovation system.

Moreover, to be able to absorb the knowledge stemming from any sources whatsoever and translate it into innovative generality, experience proves elementary. Both, highly experienced star-inventors as well as marginally experienced multiple inventors contribute positively to the generality of a patent. It can be assumed that this is due to two aspects, one being higher stock of accumulated and incorporated knowledge, the other one being rather process-related and referring to the absorptive capacity. However, the mechanisms were not tested and are still an open point for further research – a central one given the scope of the effect experience showed. Last, the investigation of the role of the technological backgrounds is the only hypothesis that cannot be supported directly. While variety does not show a significant effect (which was supposed to be the result of a too broad definition of variety in backgrounds), the backwards generality and thereby the variety in the knowledge the innovation is based on has a fairly significant and positive effect on the generality. These findings show that the variety in the underlying knowledge does have an effect on the innovative generality outcome. Yet, since the reference to how this is processed by the inventor(s) could not be made, further research is needed, again with respect to the underlying mechanisms.

It remains to be stated that the assessment of the factors impacting generality is a worthwhile task, particularly in delineation to (i) other, more quantity-based and hence less information containing value indicators and (ii) in the special context of a general purpose technology. In this case, generality of inventions vitally contributes to a GPT's scope for growth and economic development. The analyses accomplished here indicate that the support of collaboration across diverse technological and experience backgrounds does not only constitute a nutrient medium for a network wherein knowledge can be transmitted, but also reinforces generality directly via this very network activity and the improvement of the accessibility of knowledge.

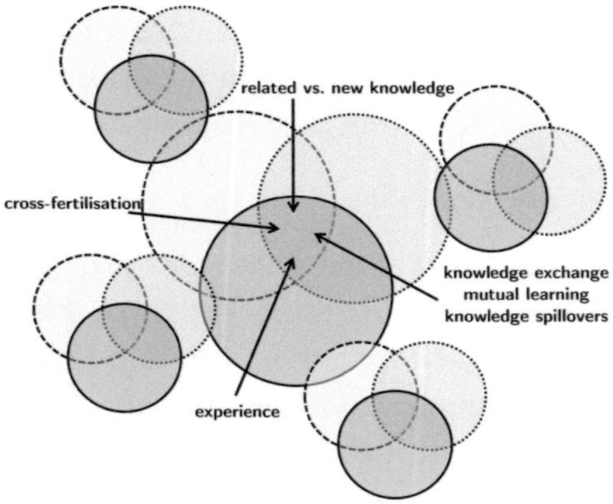

Figure 11.5: Interplay of the dimensions investigated:
Each circle represents an inventor, the boundaries of which represent the different level of experience, the filling represents the technological background and the smaller sets of circles schematise the network relations.
Source: own illustration.

Part IV

FINAL CONCLUSION

12 Conclusion and Policy Implications

General purpose technologies are argued to be the 'engines of innovation' or even 'engines of growth'. By follow-up innovations across a wide range of fields and due to the inherent innovational complementarities, a set of radical break-through innovations can impact the economic development of a whole era. This impact stands and falls with the availability and the efficient use of knowledge for the creation of innovations. Knowledge, however, is a particular input, since it is at least partially a public good. In modern theories of economic growth, this feature constitutes the basis for long-term economic growth. Knowledge has a stock-character, is non-rival and not (always) fully excludable, which results in huge opportunities for the employment of knowledge in innovation. Knowledge, once created, can be re-used and re-employed in other contexts and develop additional economic value at lower additional costs or even at no additional costs at all. Yet, given the particular relevance of tacit knowledge for technological innovations, the accessibility and the diffusion of knowledge are dependent on geographical space: (Tacit) Knowledge does not travel frictionlessly. The efficiency of (tacit) knowledge sharing depends on the distance between source and recipient of the knowledge and hence geographical proximity is crucial. Innovation-intensive technologies can therefore benefit extraordinarily well from knowledge, if the (local) organisation of knowledge access and knowledge sharing is ensured. Since GPTs are particularly intensive in innovation and since innovation is steadily reinforced through the GPT's inherent dual inducement mechanism, knowledge access and knowledge sharing should be of similar importance for their development. Moreover, GPTs develop their huge effect on economic growth due to their applicability in a wide range of fields. This introduces the relevance of cross-fertilisation, i.e. the employment of knowledge from one context into a completely different one that, at the end, benefits innovations in both fields. This puts an emphasis not only on the stock of available knowledge, but also on its complementarity and its composition. Last, the huge effect of GPTs on economic growth is curbed by sub-optimally low levels of innovation that arrive too late. This is due to externalities and uncertainty. The coordination of the use of knowledge is instanced as a remedy for these market-failures, another way in which the organisation of the employment of knowledge would enhance the development of a GPT.

12.1 Findings and Summary of Results

The common thread running throughout the empirical analyses of this paper is the investigation of the interaction of knowledge and the particular features of a GPT with respect to the promising effects on economic growth. Therefore, the development of nanotechnology as key technology of the future and showcase GPT is studied in depth. More particularly, the research accomplished in this thesis intends to shed light on two major sets of questions. First, the impact of the composition of knowledge and the corresponding localised knowledge spillovers is subject to investigation. In this context, spillovers are treated as abstract as done in most of the literature on spillovers and no concrete mechanisms, but rather the potential for spillovers, is analysed. The second set of questions puts the focus the other way around: The concrete mechanisms of knowledge transmission, in which spillovers are assumed to be inherent, are analysed rather than the composition of knowledge, which is mainly abstracted from.

The empirical analyses of this thesis are subdivided in three working packages, the results of which are summarised separately in the following (for a summary on the set-up and contributions of each analysis see Subsection 4.2).

12.1.1 Building Blocks – Working Package 1

Working Package 1 constitutes the building block for the rest of the empirical analyses. It is thus first of all investigated whether the characteristics of nanotechnology are in line with the typical features of a GPT. The second part of the first working package consists in developing hypotheses and exploring the topic around (local) knowledge, innovation and GPTs by studying the case of nanotechnology in Hamburg, Germany.

The analysis in Chapter 6 reveals that nanotechnology can indeed be considered as an emerging GPT. Nanotechnology was not unambiguously considered to be a GPT before. But by offering a coherent and systematised analysis based on patent and publication data that altogether expanded the set of the existing studies, the analysis accomplished in this chapter strongly proves the point. Moreover, evidence is supported that nanotechnology is a merging technology. This is important since the convergence-character often comes along with the GPT character, but has important implications for the processing of knowledge that reaches beyond the impact of the GPT characteristics: Individuals need to be able to combine knowledge from different fields already in the process of innovation creation. Then the diffusion of these innovations across a wide range of fields ensures the development of the GPT characteristics.

The analysis in Chapter 7 with the aim of revealing relevant issues in the context of knowledge, location and innovation in GPTs, is of rather explorative nature: Hypothesis are tested, indicators are explored, developed and employed and anecdotal evidence is searched for. This case study, besides exploring the concrete situation of Hamburg, hence offers the basis for the rest of the empirical research accomplished by pointing at the need for systematisation of the issues related to the two working packages to follow: The development of nanotechnology is assumed to anchor into existing industrial specialisation patterns. Moreover, specialisation and diversity and with them the Marshall-Jacobs controversy are indicated to be an important and non-neglectable aspect in the context of the localised development of nanotechnology (referring to Working Package 2). Furthermore, collaboration occurs, which bears knowledge sharing and the very probable possibility of positive knowledge externalities to become effective since it is a central mechanism for knowledge transfers (Working Package 3).

12.1.2 Knowledge Composition and Localised Knowledge Spillovers – Working Package 2

The analyses in the preceding chapters provide strong evidence for the importance of knowledge composition and localised knowledge spillovers for innovation in general purpose technologies, which is why Working Package 2 investigates the issues in more depth.

Chapter 8 employs patent applications as proxies for the technological knowledge base of German regions to investigate the impact of its characteristics and the assumed corresponding knowledge spillovers on subsequent knowledge creation, again approximated by new patent filings. Four sets of characteristics are then analysed by the means of negative binomial regression analysis: The role of the anchorage, the impact, and the dynamics of specialisation and diversity and the diffusion from scientific to technological innovations. It is found that the fitness of the NKB to the regional specialisation patterns influences new knowledge creation positively, as well as specialisation and diversity do. This is in line with the expectations, since nanotechnology as a GPT potentially benefits from both, industry-specific externalities from specialisation (as instanced to be conducive to leading-edge innovation in high-technologies) as well as city-specific externalities from diversity (as necessary for the deployment of the generality feature of nanotechnology). The availability of scientific knowledge drives technological innovations, too, pointing to the necessity of technology transfer. However, no clear results are obtained for the temporal structure of the relative importance. The findings suggest, in contrast to the hypothesis, that specialisation is particularly relevant in later stages, which might indicate the need for specialised knowledge in exploitation-related phases of the development of nanotechnology.

In Chapter 9, a different approach to explore a similar issue is pursued: The central question is again how the composition of knowledge influences the development of nanotechnology. Here, employment data and data from a survey designed exclusively for this purpose are employed to analyse the effect of local knowledge characteristics on firm growth in nanotechnology. Moreover, the research question is narrowed, aiming to disentangle the preponderance of nanotechnology as a high-technology with the necessity of specialisation externalities or nanotechnology as a GPT, pointing to the role of city-specific diversity externalities. Again, it is no surprise that the OLS regressions employed found that local knowledge endowment indeed positively influences firm growth in nanotechnology. This points to the importance of access to knowledge and to potential knowledge spillovers. Local knowledge specialisation, by contrast, surely is not always positively affecting the growth of individual firms. Put in another way, in most of the cases, no positive impact of specialisation on the employment growth of nano-firms was found in the OLS and panel analysis conducted. Referring to the preponderance of high-tech or GPT features with respect to the relevance of the surrounding, GPT features seem to outweigh high-tech ones.

The main findings of this Working Package 2 can hence be summarised as follows: The assumption that the development of nanotechnology anchors into existing industrial specialisation patterns is supported by both, the analysis in Chapter 7 and the analysis in Chapter 8. Moreover, specialisation and diversity of the nano-knowledge base both prove to be driving the development of the technology, although no clear dynamic impact pattern can be disentangled. Hence regional assets do play a role for innovation in GPTs. Regional knowledge bases, therefore, can be seen as a suitable entity to design proper innovation policies. Furthermore, Marshall as well as Jacobs made a point in the context of GPT innovations. Industry-specific externalities can be assumed to support leading-edge innovations in distinct application fields, while city-specific externalities drive the development of nanotechnology as a multipurpose technology, e.g. by inducing spillovers and offering access to complementary knowledge. Both kinds of spillovers, following the results of the accomplished analyses, can be seen as important in the innovation processes of GPTs by offering opportunities for knowledge-sharing and at the same time providing an incentive to innovate within regions. Thereby, innovative activity can be increased and speeded up. With the view on the preponderance of specialisation and hence high-tech characteristics versus multipurpose GPT-features, specialisation within one industry does not always support the employment growth of nanotechnology firms, thereby pointing, once again, to the relevance of the consideration of particular GPT features for designing innovation policies in this context.

12.1.3 Collaboration and Knowledge Sharing in Networks – Working Package 3

Working Package 3 intends to shed light on how knowledge is transmitted in networks, is processed for innovation and how this contributes to the development of nanotechnology as a general purpose technology. In contrast to Working Package 2, where knowledge transfers are assumed to occur and the composition of knowledge is in focus, this Working Package focuses on the afore neglected mechanisms of transfer. To be precise, an emphasis is put on collaboration and networking as central mechanisms for knowledge transmission, very probably including knowledge spillovers. Collaboration is pointed out to be of particular importance for the development of GPTs in general and nanotechnology in particular. The organisation of knowledge-sharing in networks is suggested to trigger spillovers that reduce the (social) cost of innovation by re-employing already gained knowledge several times in different contexts. Moreover, networking could result in cross-fertilisation effects that boost both, direct innovations as well as indirect innovations through the enhancement of the applicability of the GPT and thereby elevate its effects on aggregate economic growth.

The analysis in Chapter 10 is conducted by constructing co-inventorship networks in German nanotechnology. These networks are then assessed and evaluated in terms of their effectiveness by means of social networks analysis. The assessment shows that collaboration increases with the productivity of the technological system of innovation. The number of distinct inventors in the system, the share of collaborations and the team-size increase, while the relative importance of international collaboration decreases. More particularly, the organisation of collaboration in the networks of the different periods becomes more and more efficient. Hence, not only the opportunities and the conversion of knowledge sharing improves, but also the network properties develop towards a more fertile and productive system of knowledge transmission. Last, the analysis reveals a large potential for knowledge sharing across disciplinary boundaries. This network of technological overlap, moreover, develops towards a centre-periphery structure with diversified innovators in the centre and specialised innovators in the periphery. Chapter 10 hence points to the importance, the opportunities and the use of coordination and cooperation in the network of innovators in Germany. It thus provides resilient evidence that collaboration indeed drives innovation. Moreover, coordination and cooperation were instanced as a remedy for the market failures that occur on the horizontal as well as on the vertical level of a GPT's various value creation chains. Collaboration in networks seems to be a sensible mechanism to internalise some of the arising market failures into networks and thereby raise the level of innovations as well as speed up the innovation processes through sharing of relevant pre-adoption knowledge.

The results of Chapter 10 suggest that networking can still be improved in terms of expansion and efficiency. Particularly and on a more regional scale, opportunities for cross-disciplinary collaborations exist that can be exploited. Chapter 11 more precisely zooms in on how generality and thereby the degree of the 'generality of purpose', which is strongly correlated with the (potential) impact of a GPT on economic development, is reached and enhanced. Fractional logit regression analyses are employed to disentangle the different factors that might impact the generality of purpose, i.e. the applicability across a wide range of fields particularly in contrast to the mere applicability in any one field. First of all, collaboration proves to be of outmost importance by bringing together different sets of acquired knowledge. Then, particularly the network position and hence the access to diverse sources of (locally) existing knowledge is conducive as well as the team's ability to incorporate knowledge received in this manner. Another crucial aspect is the extent to which the processed knowledge is diverse and 'general'. Hence, the creation of a 'better' in terms of 'broader' and hence 'more impacting' GPT can be fostered by collaboration of the right innovators with a suitable composition of knowledge, skills and meta-competencies.

The findings of Working Package 3 are hence clear: The productivity of the nanotechnology innovation network increases with intensity and the efficiency of collaboration in networks, suggesting a strong causal relationship. Factors impacting collaboration are diverse and include geographic proximity, technological proximity, technological complementarity, overall knowledge composition, experience, strategic network positions and much more. Since collaboration in networks is regarded as a powerful and well-oiled mechanism for knowledge sharing, in particular for knowledge transfers and knowledge spillovers, it can be assumed to boost innovation in GPTs. More precisely, knowledge externalities occur, knowledge production can be coordinated and hence the arising market-failures in the innovation processes of a GPT can be met. Moreover, collaboration of centrally positioned, experienced innovators who incorporate to some extent complementary and new knowledge is found to enhance the level of generality and thereby a GPT's impact on the overall economic development.

12.2 Main Conclusion

In brief, this thesis investigates how the access, composition and transmission of knowledge impacts the development of a GPT; more precisely the development of nanotechnology as an emerging GPT. The literature revised in the theoretical part of this thesis suggests that general purpose technologies act as an engine of growth through innovation. Innovation, by contrast, is strongly relying on knowledge. The particular features of knowledge as a partially public good open up huge opportunities for boosting the innovativeness in GPTs and thereby its economic impact. The innovation processes of GPTs are, in turn, hampered by similarly occurring externalities on the horizontal and vertical level of the value creation chain that lower the total level of innovations as well as by uncertainties that decelerate the pace of innovations. The empirical analyses in this thesis, first of all, show that nanotechnology is a suitable example for an emerging GPT. Location is found to be an important dimension due to the fact that tacit knowledge only diffuses to an extent limited by spatial proximity.

The analysis around the role and the composition of the local nano-knowledge base as well as the corresponding knowledge spillovers provides evidence that the local knowledge base is important for the development of innovations in nanotechnology. Most presumably this is the case due to knowledge transfers that are not invariant to distance and due to arising knowledge spillovers. Moreover, not only the access to *any* knowledge, but also the composition of nanotechnological knowledge is of importance for innovative activity and hence for a GPT's impact on growth. The regional specialisation pattern, for instance, influences the development of nanotechnology insofar, as the degree of fitness of nanotechnological applications with the regional specialisation pattern has a positive impact on innovativeness. Also in this context, Marshall as well as Jacobs spillovers can be considered conducive on a regional scale. Both kinds of spillovers seem to support the development of both characteristics inherent in nanotechnology, the ones of a knowledge-intensive high-technology and the ones of a widespread general purpose technology. The latter seem to outbalance the former on the level of the individual firm.

Concerning the role of knowledge sharing and collaboration in networks more concretely, the analyses identify several strategies to boost the impact a GPT can have on economic growth by more precisely investigating the important knowledge transmission mechanisms of collaboration and networking. The performance of a GPT can be enhanced through collaboration by offering efficient means for the organisation and coordination of knowledge sharing and knowledge spillovers. Arising externalities can be internalised into the network and eventually foster an increase in the technology's generality level due to knowledge sharing in teams and networks. Collaboration in networks hence is rightly seen as means of innovation enhancing knowledge sharing, even more so in the context of a GPT.

This thesis sets out to investigate how the development of GPTs as engines of growth can be sustained by the access to knowledge. Due to the wide scope of this question it has to be narrowed substantially. To be able to finally find a qualified answer the question is constrained on the role of the composition of knowledge as well as the impact of knowledge sharing. Both are found to be relevant for the development of a GPT, in particular of nanotechnology. *Knowledge hence gains when it is shared,* particularly when knowledge of the right composition is shared and complemented. Knowledge sharing drives innovation in manifold manners and thereby impacts GPTs as engines of innovation in a multiplicative way: Knowledge sharing operationalizes the re-use and re-employment of knowledge in different contexts, which lowers the costs and increases the productivity of innovations in general. Knowledge sharing induces cross-fertilisation and thereby enhances the wide applicability as well as the dual inducement feedback mechanism within the innovation processes of a GPT. Knowledge sharing directly impacts the generality of innovation and thereby the scope of a GPT and its impact on economic growth. Knowledge sharing offers mechanisms of coordination and reduces uncertainty and thereby increases innovative activity in GPTs in particular. Providing well-designed framework conditions for the development of a supportive knowledge base and the intensification of knowledge sharing are therefore suggested to be able to sustainably support the working principles of the engine of growth GPT.

Concerning the indicated threefold contribution of this dissertation to the state of the art, it can be concluded that the findings delineated above comply with the promise: With the contribution to the Marshall-Jacobs controversy and the role of networking for innovation, the understanding of the working principles behind knowledge, knowledge transfers and innovation in general are enhanced. Even more compellingly, all of the results enrich the comprehension of how innovative activity in GPTs contributes to its effects on economic growth. Last, the policy implications derived from the state of the development of nanotechnology in the light of the findings on innovation-inducing factors are yet to follow below.

12.3 Limitations and Future Research

There is a number of limitations that restrict the findings and therefore have to be kept in mind when discussing the results of the preceding analyses. Yet, there are even more issues beyond the scope of this thesis that are nevertheless of huge importance for the understanding of the role of knowledge sharing for innovation in general purpose technologies. The former have already been instanced throughout the course of this work, yet, they are summarised for the sake of completeness and to avoid overestimation of the results.[1] The latter is introduced in form of future research propositions.

12.3.1 Limitations

The main limitation to the interpretability of the results obtained is that nanotechnology is still an emerging GPT. On the one hand, it was chosen as showcase particularly because of the importance to understand innovation processes in this field in order to be able to support them and ensure optimal effects on economic growth. On the other hand, emergence implies change. This means that all the results obtained have to be regarded as snap-shots of the development up to today. Since the configuration of nanotechnology's innovation system is not yet stable, a straightforward interpolation of past trends into the future should only be dared with extreme caution. Yet, the analysis of the past points to relevant issues and offers explanations for the development nanotechnology has taken. Moreover, it traces the path of the technology's transition towards a stable situation, whereby more recent configurations are already more stable than former ones. Thereby, the analyses allow for insights in how the technology *could* develop and how it *could* be supported. Note, however, that findings are not mandatory, there is no path dependency in the development of an emerging technology that becomes stable over time. However, the importance of the ex-ante analysis of a GPT underway, its development, the relevant issues and possible policy measures that support its impact on economic growth outweighs the instable character of results and predictions, which is why nanotechnology still is the best choice as a showcase example.

Another issue when discussing the limitations of this thesis is the underlying data. Given the emergent state nanotechnology is in, basic research is still very important. This research commonly culminates in publications rather than patents. However, particularly for the network analyses, the relevant publication data to build up networks could not be accessed. Therefore, the second part of the thesis mostly relies on patent data, keep in mind that application-related research in nanotechnology is even more

[1] Note, that only the main structural limitations will be mentioned again. For minor limitations see the corresponding analysis itself.

emergent than scientific research. Furthermore, working with patent data is fruitful due to the excellent availability of the data and the huge amount of corresponding information. On the other hand, the nano-patent database, in most cases the basis for the accomplished analyses, depicts only an imperfect picture of actual nano-innovations. Not all innovations are patentable, not all nano-patents are contained in the database and others are that are not nano-related. Needless to say that similar analyses to the ones conducted above with a notional database concluding all nano-innovations could possibly lead to other results. However, the probability that all the deducted results would not hold in such a case is extremely small.

Moreover, another methodological drawback is the lack of traceability of the transmission of tacit knowledge, notably knowledge spillovers through (common) indicators. This issue is approached by two evasions. Innovations in form of patents are understood as including also the tacit dimension – not necessarily by the information on the patent itself (since this is mostly textbook codified knowledge), but by the tacit knowledge needed to create such an innovation in the first place. By dispensing with concrete traceability at all, an approach chosen in Working Package 2 around the composition of knowledge, knowledge spillovers were simply assumed to occur. Thereby, it is relied on empirical evidence for the high probability of their occurrence in knowledge contexts. Using this approach, particular emphasis is put on how knowledge stocks are characterised. Another way is to build on the findings that tacit knowledge needs proximity and at best face-to-face contacts to be transferred. This approach does not distinguish systematically between intentional knowledge transfers and unintentional spillovers since the latter is assumed to arise with the former. It is employed when the concrete mechanism is in focus. Another possible way to trace transfers with patent-data is the in depth-analysis of patent citations. Yet, these operationalizations stay indirect and hence are far from being perfect. Therefore the deducted results have to be treated with care.

12.3.2 Future Research

The empirical work accomplished in this thesis often is pioneering work. As stated in the motivation for the research on this topic, the precise relationship of knowledge, innovation, location and GPT characteristics has not been subject to investigation before. Therefore, each of the conducted analysis could be refined, re-tested and verified. There is thus no doubt that there is plenty of room for further research. Next to performing similar analyses with different data, several empirical extensions seem particularly worthwhile.

First of all it has to be stated that this thesis started with the interest in the role of knowledge for innovation in general purpose technologies. However, to operationalize the issues the analyses are conducted using the showcase example of nanotechnology after having provided evidence for this technology to be an emerging GPT. Therefore, a replication is necessary in order to confirm the results deducted for this particular case for other context. Particularly due to the emerging character of nanotechnology and the inherent pressure of change, it would be insightful to replicate the analysis with a GPT in a more stable configuration. This would be particularly worthwhile for a comparative scope. It would, moreover, allow for detecting whether the discovered factors impacting the development of nanotechnology are generalizable. Moreover, strengths and weaknesses in the German nanotechnology environment could be revealed, or the performance of nanotechnology as well as the predicted opportunities could be evaluated and related to the corresponding framework conditions.

Moreover, the network analyses could be narrowed down to a regional level. Then, framework conditions and performances of different regions could be compared and the most important network structures for the efficient transmission of knowledge on a regional scale could be disentangled systematically. It is imaginable that productive regions become best-practise examples for weaker regions; the diagnosis for their weaker performance could be delivered by network structure analysis of multiple agent networks. Particularly the network of technological overlap is interesting for regions since it depicts a map of potential cooperation partners who could create substantially important innovations if they collaborate. The analytical benchmarking of actual regional collaborations against the potential for innovations or the benchmarking of the network efficiencies against actual economic performance could be insightful in this respect.

Another concrete idea in the context of the extension of this thesis would be to connect the input into GPT innovations to the output in terms of concrete growth. Such an analysis would allow for the investigation of the growth-promoting frameworks through the direct mechanisms that are at work when the GPT impacts growth. Variables to include could be, following the above deducted results, R&D expenditure for the GPT, knowledge background of the agent, experience, knowledge composition in the region, spillovers at work, network position of the agent, network structure of the region, etc.. In this context, it would be particularly insightful to identify gatekeepers and brokers of knowledge. These could be the local repository of knowledge able to recombine existing ideas from various resources. Thus, they should be extraordinarily well-performing and enhance the productivity of the system by connecting regions with external knowledge.

The role and evolution of electronic communications versus direct face-to-face communication is widely excluded in this thesis. The argument for doing this is that the transfer of embodied knowledge needs direct contact between individuals to flow successfully. Yet, electronic communication increases in importance and can occur instantaneously at any distance with no decay. Gaspar and Glaeser contended in 1997 that the interpersonal dimension can be hidden in electronic communication and the content of what is communicated can be much more strategic. While it is true that electronic communication was restricted in so far that direct contact still allowed individuals to exchange way more than information this might be subject to change at present. With the 'web 2.x' and social media, channels to transport more than information via new media have emerged. In this vein, electronic and face-to-face communications might evolve from complements (Henderson 2007) to substitutes. A large area for future research is hence the investigation of the possibilities of information and communication technologies for the transmission of tacit knowledge and the correspondingly renewed discussion of the role of geographic proximity at present and above all in future.

Another important aspect in the same vein is the impact of open innovation. This new paradigm is frequently discussed in the context of networking, innovation and technology and hence directly related to the issues assessed in this thesis. Open innovation thereby refers to the use of purposive inflows and outflows of knowledge to accelerate firm-internal innovation and expand the markets for the external use of the innovation. Within this paradigm, R&D is treated as an open system, where knowledge from the outside and from the inside are both employed to develop innovations (Chesbrough 2008). The difference to the approach pursued in the current thesis is the notion of the 'system' of openness, which expands the idea of networks of collaboration considered here far beyond the occasional exchange of knowledge for innovation. Due to both, the emergence of the knowledge economy as well as the high levels of the state of the art in industrialised economies in conjunction with the already mentioned predominance of the internet, the investigation of this phenomenon, its propositions, institutional underpinnings and the corresponding consequences might be important to understand the relationships around GPT as engines of growth as tackled in this thesis in the future.

12.4 Policy Implications and Recommendations

This thesis investigates how new knowledge is created, accumulated and shared, thereby contributing to innovation in GPTs. Interested in how the particular features of GPTs impact these processes and how these processes impact the development of GPTs in turn, the empirical analyses are accomplished in the context of nanotechnology as a showcase example. Given the results obtained, sensible policy implications can only be derived for this particular GPT, whereas its emerging and therefor snapshot character has to be kept in mind. More research would be necessary to derive policy implications for the support of growth-sustaining GPTs in general. Yet, even in the context of nanotechnology, implications and recommendations for economic policy can only be tentatively derived and given, since nanotechnological development is only at its beginning and data is still very scarce. Hence, the implementation of policy instruments should go along with continuous observation and analysis of nanotechnology's status quo and its development. Being aware of all the limitations inherent in the accomplished analyses, some preliminary implications can be derived that build on the following aims of European and German economic policy with respect to nanotechnology.

European and German policy towards the development of nanotechnology are closely geared. On the European level, the recently expired nano strategy in the context of the seventh framework program (FP-7) (European Commission 2004, 2009) is actually becoming redesigned with, among others, the aim of maximising the contribution of nanotechnology to sustainable development and cross-cutting and enabling R&D (BMBF 2011b). Foci of the EU nanotechnology policy, however, include international collaboration, interdisciplinary collaboration and networking. Policy instruments aim to create arrangements that institutionalise the development of internationally and institutionally diverse research networks, e.g. by improving the mobility of researchers and supporting long-term research collaborations (Pandza et al. 2011). The German federal government further itemises these goals in the 'action-plan 2015' (BMBF 2011a). There it is stated that potentials of nanotechnology shall be exploited and nanotechnology shall contribute to growth and innovation in Germany. The federal government sees an already existing network of infrastructure which shall be extended. Three supposed instruments are of further interest in the context of this thesis: So called 'alliances for innovation' (Innovationsallianzen) shall develop a leverage effect on economic growth by setting-up long-term R&D strategies as well as a pre-defined division of labour, time and budgets. Moreover, regional cluster ('Spitzencluster') policies shall promote strategic partnerships of firms, research institutes and other regional actors in order to support the development of commercialisable high-technologies. Last, Germany's top-position in the international development of nanotechnology is to be advanced through international cooperation (BMBF 2011a). With respect to the goals of the European/German nanotechnology policy in terms of economic growth and taking into account the proposed policy instruments, the following preliminary policy implications can be deducted from the results of this thesis.

First of all, the investment of (public) R&D into nanotechnology seems to be promising. Nanotechnology can be considered as a GPT, thereby potentially contributing heavily to economic growth. The theoretical models on GPTs show that due to only imperfect appropriability and occurring uncertainties, innovation in GPT arrive too late and to a too little extent, in principle legitimating governmental intervention. The support of nanotechnological R&D is, due to positive externalities, an obvious way to advance the technology. This is already done (as sketched in Chapter 6): In recent years, the German government spent around 15 million Euros annually, complemented with more than a billion (in 2007/8) from the EU. However, the output of these investments is assumed to be still way below its potential. The results of this thesis go one step further since they include some findings on how public and private investments can become as efficient as possible.

The analyses on the role of knowledge composition and localised knowledge spillovers brought up evidence for the importance of compatibility of nanotechnological knowledge with the overall regional knowledge base as well as for the impact of both, specialisation and diversity. These findings suggest that a one-size-fits-all cluster policy might not bring the intended results for the development of nanotechnology. By contrast, isolated nano-clusters might even be counterproductive with view on the preponderance of nanotechnology's GPT features. Specialisation, however, is conducive to nanotechnological development if diversity is not suppressed. Hence, a policy recommendation would be to thoroughly investigate each and every regional specialisation pattern and the opportunities for nanotechnological application within these specialisation patterns when aiming at setting up cluster policies. Moreover, framework conditions should encourage local agents to choose a not too narrow scope: Research should touch upon diverse technological fields in order to possibly enable and trigger manifold starting points for other agents from at best other technological fields to involve in cross-cutting R&D in nanotechnology. This, in turn, exposes the necessity for agents to be able to build up the specific capabilities to manage innovation in such diverse and interdisciplinary networks. Policy measures to support the development of such 'absorptive capacities' seem sensible in this respect, thinking about the creation of multidisciplinary study programmes to educate researchers in cross-border thinking or leadership workshops that bring together different researchers from different disciplines.

The importance of the role of collaboration and networking is also particularly highlighted. Hence, even more with the need for diversity, the opportunities of cross-fertilisation and the corresponding impacts on the generality of innovation the support of regional collaboration seems promising. Therefore, institutions of technology transfer, technology platforms or distinct cluster institutions and other local players might act as connecting device for bringing local agents with similar but complementary interests, knowledge and competencies together. Picking up the instrument of 'alliances for innovation', the role of such alliances could hence be to develop region-wise strategies that set up research programmes, link agents, enable cross-fertilisation and thereby support both specialisation as well as diversity. The envisaged support of international collaboration seems sensible in order to connect to world-wide leading-edge research. However, the results of this thesis indicate that the inter- and intra-regional collaboration is even more crucial.

These policies do not have to start from scratch. By contrast, it can be built on existing policy measures and best-practise examples. However, in some case modifications or special care might be necessary: There are several attempts to build up nanotechnology clusters in Germany that, in most of the cases, do support the development of a particular field of nanotechnology depending on the local structures. The initiative 'networking for innovation' (Kompetenznetze Deutschland), for instance, points to the existence of clusters with the topic micro-nano-opto, such as 'cc NanoBioNet', 'Cluster Nanotechnologie', 'Kompetenznetz für Materialien der Nanotechnologie' and the 'Nanotechnologie-Kompetenzzentrum Ultradünne funktionale Schichten'. Yet, in order to avoid counterproductive and lock-in effects of such cluster policies, the openness and support of interdisciplinary cooperation seems of importance. To account for the necessity of compatibility, specialisation and diversity, existing nano-clusters should somehow become connected to the regional strengths, thereby paying attention to all possible connections with a particular eye on diversity. Imaginable instruments could be public research funding, creation of institutions of technology transfer, public private partnerships, research prizes, etc. that allow to direct a focus towards the integration of new fields. Another example for implemented policy measures that are worth to be pursued and extended is the example of the 'Centre for applied nanotechnology (CAN)' in Hamburg (see Chapter 7). This public private partnership ensures the tying into the regional specialisation patterns by acting as an interface of technology transfer and connection of competencies at the same time with a focus on the previously existing local economic structure with a specialisation in life sciences. Such institutions could become a best-practise example for institutions that coordinate cooperation and help agents to find suitable partners, thereby enabling cross-fertilisation. With regard to the emerging character of nanotechnology and the corresponding high costs for knowledge production due to necessary technology platforms, such institutions are of particular importance: They can offer access to the costly infrastructure and to the tacit knowledge flowing in the network at the same time. This is not even constrained to one field, but the platform can be accessible for researchers from any discipline thereby constituting an interface for the establishment of cross-fertilisation.

As it appears from the results of this thesis, framework conditions should hence be set in such a way that the given regional strengths and weaknesses are taken into account when promoting both, specialisation and diversity of nano-knowledge for the development of nanotechnology in regions. Moreover, the framework for collaboration should be as open and encouraging as possible, since collaboration enables the efficient sharing of knowledge and supports the generality, the applicability and subsequently the impact nanotechnology has on economic growth. By positioning the regional nano-knowledge bases similarly, a sustainable nutrient medium for innovation and growth could eventually be established.

References

Abernathy, W.: 1991, *The Productivity Dilemma*, John Hopkins University Press, Baltimore.

Acemoglu, D., Aghion, P. and Zilibotti, F.: 2006, Distance to frontier, selection, and economic growth, *Journal of the European Economic Association* **4**(1), 37–74.

Acs, Z. and Audretsch, D.: 1988, Innovation and firm size in manufacturing, *Technovation* **7**, 197–201.

Acs, Z. and Audretsch, D.: 1990, *Innovation and Small Firms*, MIT Press, Cambridge, MA.

Acs, Z., Audretsch, D. and Feldman, M.: 1994, R&D spillovers and recipient firm size, *Review of Economics and Statistics* **76**(2), 336–340.

Adamou, A. and Sasidharan, S.: 2007, The impact of R&D and FDI on firm growth in emerging-developing countries: Evidence from Indian manufacturing industries, *Madras School of Economic Policy Working Paper* **37**.

Aghion, P. and Howitt, P.: 1992, A model of growth through creative destruction, *Econometrica* **60**, 155–173.

Aghion, P. and Howitt, P.: 1998, *Endogenous Growth*, MIT Press, Cambridge, MA.

Aghion, P. and Howitt, P.: 2009, *The Economics of Growth*, MIT Press, Cambridge, MA.

Agrawal, A., Kapur, D. and McHale, J.: 2008, How do spatial and social proximity influence knowledge flows? Evidence from patent data, *Journal of Urban Economics* **64**, 258–269.

Ahuja, G.: 2000, Collaboration networks, structural holes, and innovation: a longitudinal study, *Administrative Science Quarterly* **45**, 425–455.

Airbus S.A.S.: 2007, Flying by nature, Blagnac.
URL: www.airbus.com/store/mm_repository/pdf/att00011423/media_object_file_gmf_2007.pdf

Allen, R.: 1983, Collective invention, *Journal of Economic Behaviour and Organization* **4**, 1–24.

Almeida, P.: 1996, Knowledge sourcing by foreign multinationals: Patent citation analysis in the U.S. semiconductor industry, *Strategic Management Journal* **17**, 155–165.

Almeida, P. and Kogut, B.: 1999, Localization of knowledge and the mobility of engineers in regional networks, *Management Science* **45**(7), 905–917.

Amir, R., Evstigneev, I. and Wooders, J.: 2003, Noncooperative versus cooperative R&D with endogenous spillover rates, *Games and Economic Behavior* **42**, 184–207.

Anselin, L., Varga, A. and Z. Acs, .: 1997, Local geographic spillovers between university research and high technology innovations, *Journal of Urban Economics* **24**, 422–448.

Antonelli, C.: 2008, Pecuniary knowledge externalities: The convergence of directed technological change and the emergence of innovation systems, *Industrial and Corporate Change* **17**(5), 1049–1070.

Arrow, K. J.: 1962, The economic implications of learning by doing, *Review of Economic Studies* **29**, 155–172.

Aschhoff, B., Crass, D., Cremers, K., Grimpe, C. and Rammer, C.: 2010, European competitiveness in key enabling technologies, Final Report to the European Commission.

Asheim, B. and Gertler, M.: 2005, Regional innovation systems and the geographical foundations of innovation, *in* J. Fagerberg, D. Mowery and R. Nelson (eds), *The Oxford Handbook of Innovation*, Oxford University Press, Oxford, pp. 291–317.

Ashton, W. and Sen, R.: 1989, Using patent information in technology business planning-II, *Research Technology Management* **32**(2), 36–42.

Audretsch, D.: 1998, Agglomeration and the location of innovative activity, *Oxford Review of Economic Policy* **14**(2), 18–29.

Audretsch, D. and Dohse, D.: 2007, Location: A neglected determinant of firm growth, *Review of World Economics* **143**(1), 79–107.

Audretsch, D. and Feldman, M.: 1996, R&D spillovers and the geography of innovation and production, *The American Economic Review* **86**(3), 630–640.

Audretsch, D. and Feldman, M.: 2004, Knowledge spillovers and the geography of innovation, *in* H. J. and T. J. (eds), *Handbook of Regional and Urban Economics: Cities and Geography*, Vol. 4, Elsevier, Amsterdam, pp. 2713–2739.

Audretsch, D., Lehman, E. and Warning, S.: 2005, University spillovers and new firm location, *Research Policy* **34**, 1113–1122.

Autant-Bernard, C., Billand, P., Frachisse, D. and Massard, N.: 2007, Social distance versus spatial distance in R&D cooperation: Empirical evidence from European collaboration choices in micro and nanotechnologies, *Papers in Regional Science* **86**(3), 495–519.

Avenel, E., Favier, A., Ma, S., Mangematin, V. and Rieu, C.: 2007, Diversification and hybridization in firm knowledge bases in nanotechnologies, *Research Policy* **36**, 864–870.

Balconi, M., Breschi, S. and Lissoni, F.: 2004, Networks of inventors and the role of academia: An exploration of Italian patent data, *Research Policy* **33**, 127–145.

Barabasi, A. and Albert, R.: 1999, Emergence of scaling in random networks, *Science* **286**, 509–512.

Barro, R.: 1991, Economic growth in a cross-section of countries, *The Quarterly Journal of Economics* **106**, 407–443.

Barro, R. and Sala-i-Martin, X.: 2003, *Economic Growth*, MIT Press, Cambridge, MA.

Batagelj, V. and Mrvar, A.: 2011, Pajek program for analysis and visualization of large networks: Reference manual. Version 2.05.

Bathelt, H. and Glückler, J.: 2005, Resources in human geography: From substantive concepts to a relational perspective, *Environment and Planning A* **37**(9), 1545–1563.

Bathelt, H., Malmberg, A. and Maskell, P.: 2002, Clusters and knowledge: Local buzz, global pipelines and the process of knowledge creation, *DRUID Working Paper*, number 02 in *12*.

Baum, J., Calabrese, T. and Silverman, B.: 2000, Don't go it alone: alliances network composition and startups' performance in Canadian biotechnology, *Management Journal* **21**, 267–294.

Baum, J., Shipilov, A. and Rowley, T.: 2003, Where do small worlds come from?, *Industrial and Corporate Change* **12**, 697–725.

Baumol, W.: 2002, *The Free-market Innovation Machine*, Princeton University Press, Princeton.

Bawa, R.: 2004, Nanotechnology patenting in the US, *Nanotechnology Law & Business* **1**, 31–50.

BBR: 2001, *Aktuelle Daten zur Entwicklung der Städte, Kreise und Gemeinden*, Bundesamt für Bauwesen und Raumordnung, Bonn. Band 8.

Beaudry, C. and Schiffauerova, A.: 2009, Who's right, Marshall or Jacobs? The localization versus urbanization debate, *Research Policy* **38**(2), 318 – 337.

Beaudry, C. and Schiffauerova, A.: 2011, Impacts of collaboration and network indicators on patent quality: The case of Canadian nanotechnology innovation, *European Management Journal* **29**(5), 362–376.

Bengisu, M. and Nekhili, R.: 2006, Forecasting emerging technologies with the aid of science and technology databases, *Technology Forecasting & Social Change* **73**, 835–844.

Benner, M. and Tushman, M.: 2003, Exploitation, exploration and process management: The productivity dilemma revisited, *Academy of Management Review* **28**, 238–56.

Bercovitz, J. and Feldman, M.: 2011, The mechanisms of collaboration in inventive teams: Composition, social networks, and geography, *Research Policy* **40**(1), 81–93.

Bergmann, E. and Maier, G.: 2009, Network central: Regional positioning for innovative advantage, *Annals of Regional Science* **43**, 615–644.

Berkun, S.: 2007, *The Myths of Innovation*, O'Reilly Media Inc., Sebastopol.

Bernstein, J. and Nadiri, M.: 1988, Interindustry R&D spillovers, rates of return, and production in high-tech industries, *American Economic Review* **78**, 429–434.

Betrán, C.: 2011, Regional specialization and industry location in the long run: Spain in the US mirror (1856-2002), *Cliometrica* **5**, 259–290.

BMBF: 2009, nano.DE-Report 2009.
URL: http://www.bmbf.de/de/nanotechnologie.php

BMBF: 2011a, Aktionsplan Nanotechnologie 2015.
URL: http://www.bmbf.de/pub/aktionsplan_nanotechnologie.pdf

BMBF: 2011b, nano.DE-Report 2011.
URL: http://www.bmbf.de/pub/nanoDE-Report_2011.pdf

Boje, A., Ott, I. and Stiller, S.: 2010, Metropolitan cities under transition: The example of Hamburg/Germany, *Managing Global Transitions* **8**(4), 327–352.

Bonaccorsi, A. and Thoma, G.: 2007, Institutional complementarity and inventive performance in nano science and technology, *Research Policy* **36**, 813–831.

Bosch, K.: 1998, *Statistik-Taschenbuch*, Oldenbourg Verlag, Oldenbourg.

Boschma, R.: 2005, Proximity and innovation. A critical assessment, *Regional Studies* **39**(1), 61–74.

Boschma, R. and Iammarino, S.: 2009, Related variety, trade linkages, and regional growth in Italy, *Economic Geography* **85**, 289–311.

Boschma, R. and Lambooy, J.: 1999, Evolutionary economics and economic geography, *Journal of Evolutionary Economics* **9**, 411–429.

Boschma, R. and Weterings, A.: 2005, The effect of regional differences on the performance of software firms in the Netherlands, *Journal of Economic Geography* **5**, 567–588.

Bottazzi, L. and Peri, G.: 2003, Innovation and spillovers in regions: Evidence from European patent data, *European Economic Review* **47**, 687–710.

Brakman, S., Garretsen, H. and van Marrewijk, C.: 2009, *The New Introduction to Geographical Economics*, Vol. 2, Cambridge University Press, Cambridge, UK.

Breschi, S., Cassi, L., Malerba, F. and Vonortas, N.: 2009, Networked research: European policy intervention in ICTs, *Technology Analysis & Strategic Management* **21**(7), 833–857.

Breschi, S. and Lissoni, F.: 2001a, Knowledge spillovers and local innovations systems: A critical survey, *Industrial and Corporate Change* **10**, 975–1005.

Breschi, S. and Lissoni, F.: 2001b, Localised knowledge spillovers vs. innovative milieux: Knowledge 'tacitness' reconsidered, *Papers in Regional Science* **80**, 255–273.

Breschi, S. and Lissoni, F.: 2003, Mobility and social networks: Local knowledge spillovers revisited, *CESPRI working paper* **142**.

Breschi, S. and Lissoni, F.: 2004, Knowledge networks from patent data: Methodological issues and research targets, *in* W. Glaänzel, H. Moed and U. Schmoch (eds), *Handbook of Quantitative S&T Research*, Kluwer Academic Publishers, Dordrecht.

Breschi, S. and Lissoni, F.: 2005, 'cross-firm' inventors and social networks: Localised knowledge spillovers revisited, *Annales d'Economie et de Statistique* **79/80**, 189–209.

Breschi, S., Lissoni, F. and Malerba, F.: 2003, Knowledge-relatedness in firm technological diversification, *Research Policy* **32**, 69–87.

Breschi, S. and Malerba, F.: 2001, The geography of innovation and economic clustering: Some introductory notes, *Industrial and Corporate Change* **10**(4), 817–833.

Bresnahan, T.: 2010, General purpose technologies, *in* B. Hall and N. Rosenberg (eds), *Handbook of Economics of Innovation*, Vol. 2, Elsevier, Amsterdam.

Bresnahan, T. and Gambardella, A.: 1998, The division of labor and the extent of the market, *in* E. Helpman (ed.), *General Purpose Technologies and Economic Growth*, MIT Press, Cambridge, MA, pp. 253–281.

Bresnahan, T. and Trajtenberg, M.: 1992, General Purpose Technologies: 'Engines of growth'?, *NBER working paper series*, Vol. 4148.

Bresnahan, T. and Trajtenberg, M.: 1995, General Purpose Technologies: 'Engines of growth'?, *Journal of Econometrics* **65**, 83–108.

Bürgerschaft FHH: 2008, Bericht über die Evaluierung der Centrum für Angewandte Nanotechnologie (CAN) GmbH sowie erforderliche Haushaltsveränderungen 2009ff, Drucksache 19/182.
URL: www.hamburgische-buergerschaft.de/get_download.php?download=2300

Burt, R.: 1992, *Structural holes. The social structure of competition*, Harvard University Press, Cambridge, MA.

Burt, R.: 2001, Bandwidth and echo: Trust, information, and gossip in social networks, *in* A. Casella and J. Rauch (eds), *Networks and Markets: Contributions from Economics and Sociology*, Russel Sage Foundation, New York.

Burt, R.: 2004, Structural holes and good ideas, *American Journal of Sociology* **110**, 349–399.

Cairncross, F.: 1997, *The death of distance*, Harvard Business School Press, Watertown, MA.

Calero, C., Buter, R., Cabello Valdas, E. and Noyons, E.: 2006, How to identify research groups using publication analysis: An example in the field of nanotechnology, *Scientometrics* **66**(2), 365–376.

Callon, M.: 1997, Analysis of strategic relations between firms and university laboratories, Paper prepared for the Conference on the Need fro New Economics of Science, University of Notre Dame, 13-16 March, 1997.

Caniëls, M.: 2000, *Knowledge Spillovers and Economic Growth. Regional Growth Differentials across Europe*, Edwar Elgar, Cheltenham.

Cantner, U. and Graf, H.: 2006, The network of innovators in Jena: An application of social network analysis, *Research Policy* **35**, 463–480.

Cantwell, J. and Janne, O.: 1999, Technological globalization and innovative centres: The role of corporate technological leadership and locational hierarchy, *Research Policy* **28**, 119–144.

Carlaw, K. and Lipsey, R.: 2006, GPT-driven endogeneous growth, *The Economic Journal* **116**, 155–174.

Chen, Z. and Guan, J.: 2010, The impact of small world on innovation: An empirical study of 16 countries, *Journal of Informetrics* **4**, 97–106.

Chesbrough, H.: 2008, Open innovation: A new paradigm for understanding industrial innovation, *in* H. Chesbrough, W. Vanhaverbeke and J. West (eds), *Open Innovation. Researching a New Paradigm*, Oxford University Press, Oxford.

Cincera, M.: 2003, Special issue on the economics of knowledge spillovers: Introduction and overview, *Brussels Economic Review - Cahiers Economiques de Bruxelles* **46**(3), 5–10.

Coad, A.: 2007, Understanding the processes of firm growth – a closer look at serial growth rate correlation, *Review of Industrial Organization* **31**, 69–82.

Coad, A.: 2010, Investigating the exponential age distribution of firms, *Economics: The Open-Access, Open-Assessment E-Journal* **4**, 2010–2017.

Coad, A. and Rao, R.: 2008, Innovation and firm growth in high-tech sectors: A quantile regression approach, *Research Policy* **27**(4), 633–648.

Coase, R.: 1937, The nature of the firm, *Economica* **4**, 386–405.

Cohen, W. and Levinthal, D.: 1990, Absorptive capacity: A new perspective on learning and innovation, *Administrative Science Quarterly* **35**(1), 128–152.

Coleman, J.: 1988, Social capital in the creation of human capital, *American Journal of Sociology* **94**, 95–120.

Combes, P.: 2000, Economic structure and local growth: France, 1984-1993, *Journal of Urban Economics* **47**, 329–355.

Cooke, P.: 1992, Regional innovation systems: Competitive regulation in the new Europe, *Geoforum* **23**, 365–382.

Cooke, P.: 2009, The knowledge economy, spillovers, proximity and specialisation, *in* D. Pontikakis, D. Kyriakou and R. van Bavel (eds), *The Question of R&D Specialisation. Perspectives and Policy Implications*, European Commission, pp. 29–39.

Cowan, R. and Foray, D.: 1997, Quandaries in the economics of dual technologies and spillovers from military to civilian research and development, *Research Policy* **24**, 851–868.

Cowan, R. and Jonard, N.: 2003, The dynamics of collective invention, *Journal of Economic Behaviour and Organization* **52**, 513–532.

Cowan, R. and Jonard, N.: 2004, Network structure and the diffusion of knowledge, *Journal of Economic Dynamics and Control* **28**(8), 1557–1575.

Cowan, R., Jonard, N. and Özman, M.: 2004, Knowledge dynamics in a network industry, *Technological Forecasting and Social Change* **71**, 469–484.

Cowan, R., Jonard, N. and Zimmermann, J.-B.: 2005, Bilateral collaboration and the emergence of innovation networks, *Management Science* **53**, 1051–1067.

Csikszentmihalyi, M.: 1997, *Creativity, Flow and the Psychology of Discovery and Invention*, Harper Perennial, New York.

Dahl, M. and Pedersen, C.: 2004, Knowledge flows through informal contacts in industrial clusters: Myth or reality?, *Research Policy* **33**, 1673–1686.

Daim, T., Rueda, G., Martin, H. and Gerdsri, P.: 2006, Forecasting emerging technologies: Use of bibliometrics and patent analysis, *Technological Forecasting & Social Change* **73**, 981–1012.

Dasgupta, P. and David, P.: 1994, Towards a new economics of science, *Research Policy* **23**, 487–521.

David, P.: 1990, The dynamo and the computer: A historical perspective on the modern productivity paradox, *American Economic Review* **80**(2), 355–360.

David, P.: 1991, Computer and dynamo: The modern productivity paradox in a not-too-distant mirror, *Technology and Productivity: The Challenge for Economic Policy* pp. 315–347.

David, P. and Wright, G.: 1999, General purpose technologies and surges in productivity: Historical reflections on the future ot the ICT revolution, Paper presented to the International Symposium on 'Economic Challenges of the 21st Century in Historical Perspective', Oxford, UK.

de Bondt, R.: 1996, Spillovers and innovative activities, *International Journal of Industrial Organization* **15**, 1–28.

de Groot, H., Poot, J. and Smit, M.: 2008, Agglomeration externalities, innovation and regional growth: Theoretical perspectives and meta-analysis, *University of Waikito Working Paper in Economics* **01/08**.

de Jong, J. and Freel, M.: 2010, Absorptive capacity and the reach of collaboration in high technology small firms, *Research Policy* **39**, 47–54.

de Nooy, W., Mrvar, A. and Batagelj, V.: 2008, *Exploratory Social Network Analysis with Pajek*, Cambridge University Press.

Del Monte, A. and Papagni, E.: 2003, R&D and the growth of firms: Empirical analysis of a panel of Italian firms, *Research Policy* **32**(6), 1003–1014.

Delmar, F., Davidsson, P. and Gartner, W.: 2003, Arriving at the high-growth firm, *Journal of Business Venturing* **18**(2), 189–216.

Desrochers, P.: 2001, Local diversity, human creativity, and technological innovation, *Growth and Change* **32**, 369–394.

Desrochers, P. and Leppälä, S.: 2010, Opening up the 'Jacobs spillovers' black box: Local diversity, creativity and the processes underlying new combinations, *Journal of Economic Geography* pp. 1–21.

D'Este, P., Guy, F. and Iammarino, S.: 2011, Shaping the formation of university-industry research collaborations: What type of proximity does really matter?, *Papers in Evolutionary Economic Geography (PEEG)* **1106**.

Dittrich, K. and Kijkuit, B.: 2004, Exploration and exploitation clusters in the internet industry, DRUID Summer Conference.

Dixit, A. and Stiglitz, J.: 1977, Monopolistic competition and optimum product diversity, *American Economic Review* **67**, 297–308.

Dohse, D.: 2001, Knowledge creation, knowledge diffusion and regional growth, *in* J. Bröcker and H. Herrmann (eds), *Spatial Change and Interregional Flows in the Integrating Europe. Essays in Honour of Karin Peschel*, Physica, Heidelberg.

Döring, T. and Schnellenbach, J.: 2006, What do we know about geographical knowledge spillovers and regional growth? A survey of the literature, *Regional Studies* **40**, 375–395.

Dosi, G.: 1988, The nature of the innovation process, *in* G. Dosi, C. Freeman, R. Nelson, G. Silverberg and L. Soete (eds), *Technical Change and Economic Theory*, Pinter, London.

Dosi, G., Marsili, O., Orsenigo, L. and Salvatore, R.: 1995, Learning, market selection and the evolution of industrial structures, *Small Business Economics* **7**(6), 411–436.

Duranton, G. and Puga, D.: 2000, Diversity and specialization in cities: Why, where and when does it matter?, *Urban Studies* **37**(3), 533–555.

Duranton, G. and Puga, D.: 2005, From sectoral to functional urban specialization, *Journal of Urban Economics* **57**(2), 343–370.

European Commission: 2004, Auf dem Weg zu einer europäischen Strategie für Nanotechnologie .
URL: http://eur-lex.europa.eu/LexUriServ/LexUriServ.do?uri=COM:2004:0338:FIN:DE:PDF

European Commission: 2009, Nanowissenschaften und Nanotechnologien: Aktionsplan für Europa 2005-2009, Zweiter Durchführungsbericht.
URL: http://eur-lex.europa.eu/LexUriServ/LexUriServ.do?uri=COM:2009:0607:FIN:DE:PDF

European Commission: 2010, Green paper: Unlocking the potential of cultural and creative industries, *COM (2010)* **183**.

European Patent Office: 2010, Data catalog EPO worldwide patent statistical database - EPO PATSTAT.

European Patent Office: 2011, Nanotechnology and patents.
URL: http://documents.epo.org/projects/babylon/eponet.nsf/0/623ECBB1A0FC13E1C12575AD0035EFE6/$File/nanotech_brochure_en.pdf

Fagiolo, G. and Luzzi, A.: 2006, Do liquidity constraints matter in explaining firm size and growth? Some evidence from the Italian manufacturing industry, *Industrial and Corporate Change* **15**(1), 1–39.

Fallah, M. and Ibrahim, S.: 2004, Knowledge spillovers and innovation in technological clusters, *IAMOT* .

Feldman, M.: 1999, The new economics of innovation, spillovers and agglomeration: A review of empirical studies, *Economics of Innovation and New Technology* **8**, 5–25.

Feldman, M. and Audretsch, D.: 1999, Innovation in cities: Science-based diversity, specialization and localized competetion, *European Economic Review* **43**, 409–429.

Feldman, M. and Desrochers, P.: 2003, The evolving role of research universities in technology transfer: Lessons from the history of Johns Hopkins University, *Industry and Innovation* **10**, 5–24.

Feldman, M. and Kogler, D.: 2010, Stylized facts in the geography of innovation, *in* B. Hall and N. Rosenberg (eds), *Handbook of the Economics of Innovation*, Elsevier, Oxford.

Feldman, M. P.: 1994, *The Geography of Innovation*, Springer, Boston.

Feynman, R.: 1959, Plenty of room at the bottom, Transcript of a talk presented at the American Physical Society, Pasadena.

Finardi, U.: 2011, Time relations between scientific production and patenting of knowledge: The case of nanotechnologies, *Scientometrics* **89**, 37–50.

Fischer, M., Scherngell, T. and Jansenberger, E.: 2009, Geographic localisation of knowledge spillovers: Evidence from high-tech patent citations in europe, *Annals of Regional Science* **43**, 839–858.

Fleming, L., King, C. and Juda, A.: 2006, Small worlds and regional innovation, *SSRN Working Paper* .
URL: http://papers.ssrn.com/sol3/Delivery.cfm/SSRN_ID892871_code237033.pdf?abstractid=892871&mirid=1

Fleming, L., King, C. and Juda, A.: 2007, Small worlds and regional innovation, *Organization Science* **18**(6), 938–954.

Fleming, L. and Sorenson, O.: 2001, Technology as a complex adaptive system: Evidence from patent data, *Research Policy* **30**, 1019–1039.

Freeman, L.: 1979, Centrality in social networks: I. conceptual clarification, *Social Networks* **1**, 215–239.

Frenken, K., van Oort, F. and Verburg, T.: 2007, Related variety, unrelated variety and regional economic growth, *Regional Studies* **41**(5), 685–697.

Frietsch, R., Köhler, F. and Blind, K.: 2008, Weltmarktpatente - Strukturen und deren Veränderungen, Studie zum deutschen Innovationssystem 07-2008.

Frietsch, R., Schmoch, U., Neuhäusler, P. and Rothengatter, O.: 2011, Patent applications – structures, trends and recent development, Studie zum deutschen Innovationssystem Nr. 9-2011.

Fritsch, M. and Franke, G.: 2004, Innovation, regional knowledge spillovers and R&D cooperation, *Research Policy* **33**, 245–255.

Fritsch, M. and Slavtchev, V.: 2007, Universities and innovation in space, *Industry and Innovation* **14**, 201–218.

Fritsch, M. and Slavtchev, V.: 2008, Industry specialization, diversity and the effiency of regional innovation systems, *in* C. van Beers, A. Kleinknecht, R. Ortt and R. Verburg (eds), *Determinants of Innovative Behaviour. A firm's internal practices and its external environment*, Palgrave Macmillan, New York, pp. 272–293.

Fritsch, M. and Slavtchev, V.: 2010, How does industry specialization affect the efficiency of regional innovation systems?, *The Annals of Regional Science* **45**, 87–108.

Fromhold-Eisebith, M. and Eisebith, G.: 2005, How to institutionalize innovative clusters? Comparing explicit top-down and implicit bottom-up approaches, *Research policy* **34**, 1250–1268.

Fujita, M. and Thisse, J.: 2002, Does geographical agglomeration foster economic growth? And who gains and looses from it?, *CEPR Discussion Paper* **3135**.

Gabe, T. and Kraybill, D.: 2002, The effect of state economic development incentives on employment growth of establishments, *Journal of Regional Science* **42**, 703–730.

Gambardella, A., Giuri, P. and Luzzi, A.: 2007, The market for patents in Europe, *Research Policy* **36**(8), 1163 – 1183.

Gao, X., Guan, J. and Rousseau, R.: 2011, Mapping collaborative knowledge production in China using patent co-inventorships, *Scientometrics* **88**, 343–362.

Garcia-Vega, M.: 2006, Does technological diversification promote innovation? An empirical analysis for European firms, *Research Policy* **35**, 230–246.

Garnsey, E., Stam, E. and Heffernan, P.: 2006, New firm growth: Exploring processes and paths, *Industry and Innovation* **13**(1), 1–20.

Gaspar, J. and Glaeser, E.: 1997, Information technology and the future of cities, *Journal of Urban Economics* **43**, 136–156.

Geng, H. and Zhou, L.: 2005, How semiconductor chips are made, *in* H. Geng (ed.), *Semiconductor Manufacturing Handbook*, McGraw Hill, New York.

Gertler, M.: 2003, Tacit knowledge and the economic geography of context, or the undefinable tacitness of being (there), *Journal of Economic Geography* **3**, 75–99.

Gilsing, V., Nooteboom, B., Vanhaverbeke, W., Duysters, G. and van den Oord, A.: 2008, Network embeddedness and the exploration of novel technologies: Technological distance, betweenness centrality and density, *Research Policy* **37**, 1717–1731.

Gittelman, M.: 2007, Does geography matter for science-based firms? Epistemic communities and the geography of research and patenting in biotechnology, *Organization Science* **18**(4), 724–741.

Glaeser, E.: 1996, Economic growth and urban density: A review essay, *Cities and the New Global. Economy Conference Proceedings*, Vol. 1, Government of Australia. Printing Office, Melbourne, pp. 227–246.

Glaeser, E., Kallal, H., Scheinkman, J. and Shleifer, A.: 1992, Growth in cities, *Journal of Political Economy* **100**(6), 1126–1152.

Glänzel, W., Meyer, M., du Plessis, M., Thijs, B., Magerma, T., Schlemmer, K., Debackere, K. and Veugelers, R.: 2003, Nanotechnology – analysis of an emerging domain of scientific and technological endeavour, *Steuntpunt O&O Statistieken* .

Graf, H. and Henning, T.: 2009, Public research in regional networks of innovators: A comparative study of four East-German regions, *Regional Studies* **43**(10), 1360–0591.

Graham, S. and Iacopetta, M.: 2009, Nanotechnology and the emergence of a General Purpose Technology.
URL: *http://papers.ssrn.com/sol3/papers.cfm?abstract_id=1334376*

Granovetter, M.: 1973, The strength of weak ties, *American Journal of Sociology* **78**, 1360–1380.

Granstrand, O.: 1998, Towards a theory of the technology-based firm, *Research Policy* **25**(5), 467–491.

Greene, W.: 1993, *Econometric Analysis*, Macmillan, New York.

Greunz, L.: 2003, The impact of industrical specialisation and diversity on innovation, *Brussels Economic Review* **46**(3), 11–33.

Greunz, L.: 2004, Industrial structure and innovation – evidence from European regions, *Journal of Evolutionary Economics* **14**(5), 563–592.

Greve, H.: 2007, Exploration and exploitation in product innovation, *Industrial and Corporate Change* **16**, 945–975.

Griliches, Z.: 1979, Issues in assessing the contribution of research and development to productivity growth, *Bell Journal of Economics* **10**(1), 92–116.

Griliches, Z.: 1990, Patent statistics as economic indicators: A survey, *Journal of Economic Literature* **28**, 1661–1707.

Griliches, Z.: 1998, The search for R&D spillovers, *in* Z. Griliches (ed.), *R&D and Productivity: The Econometric Evidence*, University of Chicago Press, Chicago.

Grimpe, C. and Patuelli, R.: 2008, Knowledge production in nanomaterials: An application of spatial filtering to regional systems of innovation, *ZEW Discussion Paper* **08-064**.

Grossmann, G. and Helpman, E.: 1990, Comparative advantage and long-run growth, *American Economic Review* **80**, 796–815.

Grossmann, G. and Helpman, E.: 1991, Trade, knowledge spillovers, and growth, *European Economic Review* **35**, 517–526.

Grupp, H.: 1990, The concept of entropy in scientometrics and innovative research, *Scientometrics* **18**, 219–239.

Grupp, H.: 1994, The measurement of technological performance of innovations by technometrics and its impact on established technology indicators, *Research Policy* **23**, 175–193.

Grupp, H.: 1996, Spillover effects and the science base of innovations reconsidered: An empirical approach, *Evolutionary Economics* **6**, 175–197.

Grupp, H.: 1998, *Foundations of the Economics of Innovation. Theory, Measurement and Practice*, Edward Elgar, Cheltenham, UK.

Grupp, H., Fornahl, D., Tran, C., Stohr, J., Schubert, T., Malerba, F., Montobbio, F., Cusmano, L., Bacchiocchi, E. and Puzone, F.: 2010, National specialisation and innovation performance, Final report.

Grupp, H., Jungmittag, A., Schmoch, U. and Legler, H.: 2000, *Hochtechnologie 2000: Neudefinition der Hochtechnologie für die Berichterstattung zur technologischen Leistungsfähigkeit Deutschlands*, Fraunhofer ISI.

Grupp, H., Münt, G. and Schmoch, U.: 1996, Assessing different types of patent data for describing high-technology export performance, *in* OECD (ed.), *Innovation, Patents and Technological Strategies*, OECD.

Gulati, R. and Gargiulo, M.: 1999, Where do interorganizational networks come from?, *American Journal of Sociology* **104**, 1439–1493.

Haagedorn, J.: 1993, Understanding the rationale of strategic technology partnering: Interorganizational modes of cooperation and sectoral differences, *Strategic Management Journal* **14**(5), 371–385.

Hagemann, H., Christ, J., Erber, G. and Rukwid, R.: 2011, Die Bedeutung von Innovationsclustern, sektoralen und regionalen Innovationssystemen zur Stärkung der globalen Wettbewerbsfähigkeit der baden-württembergischen Wirtschaft, Final project report.

Hall, B.: 2002, A note on the bias in the Herfindahl based on count data, *in* A. Jaffe and M. Trajtenberg (eds), *Patents, Citations, and Innovation*, MIT Press, Cambridge, MA.

Hall, B. and Trajtenberg, M.: 2004, Uncovering GPTs with patent data, *NBER Working Paper* **10901**.

Hall, B. and Trajtenberg, M.: 2006, Uncovering GPTs with patent data, *in* B. Hall and M. Trajtenberg (eds), *New frontiers in the economics of innovation and new technology: Essays in honor of Paul A. David*, Edward Elgar, Northhampton, MA.

Handelskammer Hamburg: 2006, Eckpunkte für eine Industriepolitik in Hamburg. Cluster richtig auswählen und entwickeln, Hamburg.
URL: www.hk24.de/servicemarken/branchen/industrieplatz_hamburg/anlagen/eckpunkte_fuer_eine_industriepolitik_in_Hamburg.pdf

Hansen, M.: 1999, The search-transfer problem: The role of weak ties in sharing knowledge across organization subunits, *Administrative Science Quarterly* **44**, 82–111.

Hargadon, A.: 2003, *How Breakthroughs Happen: The Surprising Truth About How Companies Innovate*, Harvard Business School Press, Boston.

Harhoff, D., Stahl, K. and Woywode, M.: 1998, Legal form, growth and exit of west German firms – empirical results for manufacturing, construction, trade and service industries, *Journal of Industrial Economics* **46**(4), 453–488.

Harrison, R., Jaumandreu, J., Mairesse, J. and Peters, B.: 2008, Does innovation stimulate employment? A firm-level analysis using comparable micro-data from four European countries, *NBER Working Paper* **14216**.

Heckman, J. and Borjas, G.: 1980, Does unemployment cause future unemployment? Definitions, questions, and answers from a continuous time model of heterogeneity and state dependence, *Econometrica* **48**, 247–283.

Heinze, T.: 2004, Nanoscience and nanotechnology in Europe: Analysis of publications and patent applications including comparisons with the United States, *Nanotechnology Law & Business* **1**(4), 427–445.

Heinze, T. and Bauer, G.: 2007, Characterizing creative scientists in nano-S&T: Productivity, multidisciplinarity, and network brokerage in a longitudinal perspective, *Scientometrics* **70**(3), 811–830.

Helpman, E. and Trajtenberg, M.: 1998a, Diffusion of general purpose technologies, *in* E. Helpman (ed.), *General Purpose Technologies and Economic Growth*, MIT Press, Cambridge, MA.

Helpman, E. and Trajtenberg, M.: 1998b, A time to sow and a time to reap, *in* E. Helpman (ed.), *General Purpose Technologies and economic growth*, Cambridge, pp. 55–83.

Henderson, J.: 2007, Understanding knowledge spillovers, *Regional Science and Urban Economics* **37**(4), 497–508.

Henderson, R., Jaffe, A. and Trajtenberg, M.: 1998, Universities as a source of commercial technology: A detailed analysis of university patenting, *The Review of Economics and Statistics* **LXXX**, 119–127.

Henderson, V.: 1997, Medium size cities, *Regional Science and Urban Economics* **27**, 583–612.

Henderson, V., Kuncoro, A. and Turner, M.: 1995, Industrial development in cities, *The Journal of Political Economy* **103**(5), 1067–1090.

Henn, S.: 2008, Formierung und Wirkungsgefüge regionaler Technologiecluster: Das Beispiel Nanotechnologie im Saarland und in Berlin-Brandenburg, *Zeitschrift für Wirtschaftsgeographie* **52**(213), 95–113.

Hertzum, M.: 2008, Collaborative information seeking: The combined activity of information seeking and collaborative grounding, *Information Processing and Management* **44**, 957–962.

Hessen Agentur: 2008, Einsatz von Nanotechnologien im Energiesektor, Hessisches Ministerium für Wirtschaft, Verkehr und Landesentwicklung, Wiesbaden.

Hicks, D.: 1995, Published papers, tacit competencies and corporate management of the public/private character of knowledge, *Industrial and Corporate Change* **4**, 401–424.

Hinze, S., Reiss, T. and Schmoch, U.: 1997, Statistical analysis on the distance between fields of technology, Report for European Commission TSER Project.

Hinze, S. and Schmoch, U.: 2004, Opening the black box. Analytical approaches and their impact on the outcome of statistical patent analyses, *in* H. Moed, W. Glänzel and U. Schmoch (eds), *Handbook of Quantitative Science and Technology Research*, Vol. 2, Kluwer, Dordrecht.

Hoekman, J., Frenken, K. and van Oort, F.: 2009, The geography of collaborative knowledge production in Europe, *Annals of Regional Science* **43**, 721–738.

Howells, J.: 2002, Tacit knowledge, innovation and economic geography, *Urban Studies* **39**, 871–884.

Huang, C., Notten, A. and Rasters, N.: 2010, Nanoscience and technology publications and patents: A review of social science studies and search strategies, *Journal of Technology Transfer* .

Huber, F.: 2011, Do clusters really matter for innovation practices in information technology? Questioning the significance of technological knowledge spillovers, *Journal of Economic Geography* pp. 1–20.

Huergo, E. and Jaumandreu, J.: 2004, How does probability of innovation change with firm age?, *Small Business Economics* **22**(3), 193–207.

Hullmann, A.: 2006, The economic development of nanotechnology - an indicator-based analysis, European Commission, DG Research.

Hullmann, A.: 2007, Measuring and assessing the development of nanotechnology, *Scientometrics* **70**(3), 739–758.

Ibrahim, S., Fallah, M. and Reilly, R.: 2009, Localized sources of knowledge and the effect of knowledge spillovers: An empirical study of inventors in the telecommunications industry, *Journal of Economic Geography* **9**, 405–431.

IVAM: 2010, Micro/nano atlas of Germany, Dortmund.

Jacobs, J.: 1969, *The economy of cities*, Random House, New York.

Jaffe, A.: 1986, Technological opportunity and spillovers of R&D: Evidence from firms' patents, profits and market value, *American Economic Review* **76**(5), 984–1001.

Jaffe, A.: 1989, Real effects on acacemic research, *American Economic Review* **79**(5), 957–970.

Jaffe, A., Trajtenberg, M. and Fogarty, M. S.: 2000, Knowledge spillovers and patent citations: Evidence from a survey of inventors, *American Economic Review* **90**(2), 215–218.

Jaffe, A., Trajtenberg, M. and Henderson, R.: 1993, Geographic localization of knowledge spillovers as evidenced by patent citations, *The Quarterly Journal of Economics* **108**(3), 577–598.

Jansen, D., Wald, A., Franke, K., Schmoch, U. and Schubert, T.: 2007, Drittmittel als Performanzindikator der wissenschaftlichen Forschung, *Kölner Zeitschrift für Soziologie und Sozialpsychologie* **59**, 125–49.

Jorde, T. and Teece, D.: 1990, Innovation and cooperation – implications for competition and antitrust, *Journal of Economic Perspectives* **4**, 75–96.

Jovanovic, B. and Rousseau, P.: 2002, Moore's law and learning by doing, *Review of Economic Dynamics* **4**, 346–375.

Jovanovic, B. and Rousseau, P.: 2005, General purpose technologies, *in* P. Aghion and S. Durlauf (eds), *Handbook of Economic Growth*, Vol. 1B, Elsevier, Amsterdam.

Kahnert, R.: 1998, Wirtschaftsentwicklung, Sub- und Desuburbanisierung, *Informationen zur Raumentwicklung* **24**, 509–520.

Kamien, M., Eitan, M. and Israel, Z.: 1992, Research joint ventures and R&D cartels, *American Economic Review* **82**(5), 1293–1306.

Karlsson, C. and Manduchi, A.: 2001, Knowledge spillovers in a spatial context – a critical review and assessment, *in* M. Fischer and J. Fröhlich (eds), *Knowledge, complexity and innovation systems*, Springer, Berlin.

Katz, M.: 1986, An analysis of cooperative research and development, *Rand Journal of Economics* **17**, 527–543.

Katz, M. and Ordover, J.: 1990, R&D cooperation and competition, *Brookings Papers on Economic Activity – Microeconomics* pp. 137–203.

Keilbach, M.: 2000, *Spatial Knowledge Spillovers and the Dynamics of Agglomeration and Regional Growth*, Physica, Heidelberg.

Keller, W.: 2002, Geographic localization of international technology diffusion, *American Economic Review* **92**, 120–142.

Ketels, C.: 2009, Clusters, cluster policy, and Swedish competitiveness in the global economy, *The Globalisation Council Expert Report* **30**.

Knudsen, B., Florida, R., Gates, G. and Stolarick, K.: 2007, Urban density, creativity and innovation.

URL: *http://creativeclass.com/rfcgdb/articles/Urban_Density_Creativity_and _Innovation.pdf*

Kogut, B. and Walker, G.: 2001, The small world of Germany and the durability of national networks, *American Sociological Review* **66**(3), 317–335.

Kondratieff, N. and Stolper, W.: 1935, The long waves in economic life, *The Review of Economics and Statistics* **17**(6), 105–115.

Krugman, P.: 1991a, *Geography and Trade*, MIT Press, Cambridge, MA.

Krugman, P.: 1991b, Increasing returns and economic geography, *Journal of Political Economy* **99**, 483–499.

Krugman, P.: 1995, *Development, Geography and Economic Theory*, MIT Press, Cambrigde, MA.

Lambooy, J.: 2010, Knowledge transfers, spillovers and actors: The role of context and social capital, *European Planning Studies* **18**(6), 873–891.

Lanjouw, J., Pakes, A. and Putnam, J.: 1998, How to count patents and value intellectual property. The uses of patent renewal and application data, *Journal of Industrial Economics* **46**, 405–432.

Lanjouw, J. and Schankerman, M.: 2004, Patent quality and research productivity: Measuring innovation with multiple indicators, *The Economic Journal* **114**, 441–465.

Laredo, P.: 2003, University research activities. On-going transformations and new challenges, *Higher Education Management and Policy* **15**(1), 138–163.

Lawson, C. and Lorenz, E.: 1999, Collective learning, tacit knowledge and regional innovative capacity, *Regional Studies* **33**(4), 305–317.

Leten, B., Belderbos, R. and van Looy, B.: 2007, Technological diversification, coherence and performance of firms, *Journal of Product Innovation Management* **24**(6), 567–579.

Lewison, G. and Cunningham, P.: 1991, Bibliometric studies for the evaluation of transnational research, *Scientometrics* **21**, 325–342.

Lipsey, R., Bekar, C. and Carlaw, K.: 1998, What requires explanation?, *in* E. Helpman (ed.), *General Purpose Technologies and economic growth*, MIT Press, Cambridge, MA, pp. 15–54.

Lipsey, R., Carlaw, K. and Bekar, C.: 2005, *Economic Transformations: General Purpose Technologies and Long Term Economic Growth*, Oxford University Press, Oxford.

Lopez-Garcia, P. and Puente, S.: 2009, What makes a high-growth firm? A probit analysis using Spanish firm level data, *Banco de Espana Working Paper* **0920**.

Lucas, R.: 1988, On the mechanics of economic development, *Journal of Monetary Economics* **22**, 3–42.

Lundvall, B.: 1992, *National Systems of Innovation: Towards a Theory of Innovation and Interactive Learning*, Pinter, London.

Lundvall, B.: 1996, The social dimension of the learning economy, *DRUID Working Paper* **96.1**.

Lux Research: 2006, *The Nanotech Report*, 4 edn, Lux Research, New York.

Lux Research: 2008, *The Nanotech Report*, 5 edn, Lux Research, New York.

Malecki, E.: 2010, Everywhere? The geography of knowledge, *Journal of Regional Science* **50**(1), 293–513.

Malerba, F.: 2002, Sectoral systems of innovation and production, *Research Policy* **31**, 247–264.

Malmberg, A. and Maskell, P.: 2006, Localized learning revisited, *Growth and Change* **37**, 1–18.

Mangematin, V. and Errabi, K.: 2012, The determinants of the science-based cluster growth: The case of nanotechnology, *Environment and Planning C: Government and Policy* **30**(1), 128–146.

March, J.: 1991, Exploration and exploitation in organizational learning, *Organization Science* **2**(1), 71–87.

Mariani, M.: 2000, Networks of inventors in the chemical industry, *Research Memoranda* **014**.

Marlet, G. and van Woerkens, C.: 2004, Skills and creativity in a cross-section of Dutch cities, *Tjalling C. Koopmans Research Institute Discussion Paper Series* **04-29**.

Marshall, A.: 1890, *Principles of Economics*, Macmillan, London.

Martin, R.: 2011, Differentiated knowledge bases and the nature of innovation networks, Paper to be presented at the DRUID Academy 2012.

Martin, R. and Sunley, P.: 1998, Slow convergence? The new endogenous growth theory and regional development, *Economic Geography* **74**, 201–27.

Martin, R. and Sunley, P.: 2003, Deconstructing clusters: Chaotic concept or policy panacea?, *Journal of Economic Geography* **3**(1), 5–35.

Massard, N. and Mehier, C.: 2010, Proximity and innovation through an 'accessibility to knowledge' lens, *Regional Studies* **43**(1), 77–88.

Maurseth, P. and Verspagen, B.: 2002, Knowledge-spillovers in Europe, *Scandinavian Journal of Economics* **104**(4), 531–545.

Menz, N. and Ott, I.: 2011, On the role of general purpose technologies within the Marshall-Jacobs controversy: The case of nanotechnologies, *KIT Working Paper Series in Economics* **18**.

Meyer, M.: 2006, Are patenting scientists the better scholars? An exploratory comparison of inventor-authors with their non-inventing peers in nano-science and technology, *Research Policy* **35**, 1646–1662.

Meyer, M.: 2007, What do we know about innovation in nanotechnology? Some propositions about an emerging field between hype and path dependency, *Scientometrics* **70**, 779–810.

Meyer, M. and Bhattacharya, S.: 2004, Commonalities and differences between scholarly and technical collaboration. An exploration of co-invention and co-authorship analyses, *Scientometrics* **61**(3), 443–456.

Meyer, M., Libaers, D. and Park, J.-H.: 2011, The emergence of novel science-related fields: Regional or technological patterns? Exploration and exploitation in United Kingdom nanotechnology, *Regional Studies* **45**(7), 935–959.

Meyer, M. and Persson, O.: 1998, Nanotechnology – interdisciplinarity, patterns of collaboration and differences in application, *Scientometrics* **42**(2), 195–205.

Michels, C. and Schmoch, U.: 2012, The growth of science and database coverage, *Scientometrics* (Online First).

Milgram, S.: 1967, The small world problem, *Psychology Today* **1**, 61–67.

Miyazaki, K. and Islam, N.: 2007, Nanotechnology systems of innovation – an analysis of industry and academic research activities, *Technovation* **27**, 661–675.

Mogoutov, A. and Kahane, B.: 2007, Data search strategy for science and technology emergence: A scalable and evolutionary query for nanotechnology tracking, *Research Policy* **36**, 893–903.

Moreno, R., Paci, R. and Usai, S.: 2004, Geographical and sectoral clusters of innovation in Europe, *Working Paper CRENoS* **15**.

Morone, P. and Taylor, R.: 2004, Knowledge diffusion dynamics and network properties of face-to-face interactions, *Journal of Evolutionary Economics* **14**(3), 327–351.

Morrison, A., Rabelotti, R. and Zirulia, F.: 2011, When do global pipelines enhance knowledge diffusion in clusters?, *Papers in Evolutionary Economic Geography (PEEG)* **1105**.

Moser, P. and Nicholas, T.: 2004, Was electricity a general purpose technology? Evidence from historical patent citations, *American Economic Review, Papers and Proceedings* **94**(2), 388–394.

Mowery, D., Oxley, J. and Silverman, B.: 1998, Technological overlap and interfirm cooperation: Implications for the ressource-based view of the firm, *Research Policy* **27**, 507–523.

Narin, F. and Whitlow, E.: 1990, Measurement of scientific cooperation and coauthorship in CEC-related areas of science.

National Nanotechnology Initiative: n.d., What is nanotechnology?
URL: *http://www.nano.gov/html/facts/whatIsNano.html*

Nelson, R. and Phelps, E.: 1966, Investment in humans, technological diffusion and economic growth, *American Economic Review* **56**, 69–75.

Nelson, R. and Winter, S.: 1982, *An evolutionary theory of economic change*, Oxford University Press, New York.

Nesta, L.: 2008, Knowledge and productivity in the world's largest manufacturing corporations, *Journal of Economic Behavior & Organization* **67**, 886–902.

Newman, M.: 2001, Scientific collaboration networks II. Shortest paths, weighted networks and centrality, *Physical Review E* **64**.

NEWMEX Consulting GmbH: 2004, Entwicklungsstrategie Nanotechnologie für Hamburg und Schleswig-Holstein, Innovationsstiftung Hamburg/ Innovationsstifung Schleswig Holstein.
URL: www.i-sh.org/ish/NINa-Initiative/Dateien/Nano_Ergebnisbericht.pdf

Nikulainen, T.: 2007, Identifying nanotechnological linkages in the Finnish economy - an explorative study, *ETLA Discussion Paper* **1101**.

Nonaka, I. and Takeuchi, H.: 1995, *The Knowledge-Creating Company: How Japanese Companies Create the Dynamics of Innovation*, Oxford University Press, Oxford.

Nonaka, I., Toyama, R. and ByosiÃ¨re, P.: 2003, A theory of organizational knowledge creation: Understanding the dynamic process of creating knowledge., *in* M. Dierkes, A. B. Antal, J. Child and I. Nonaka (eds), *Handbook of Organizational Learning and Knowledge*, Oxford University Press, Oxford, pp. 491–517.

Nooteboom, B.: 2000, *Learning and Innovation in Organizations and Economies*, Oxford University Press, Oxford.

Noyons, E., Buter, R., Raan, A., Schmoch, U., Heinze, T., Hinze, S. and Rangnow, R.: 2003, Mapping excellence in science and technology across Europe. Nanoscience and nanotechnology. Report to the European Commission.

OECD: 2009, Patents as statistical indicators of science and technology, *OECD Patent Statistics Manual*, OECD, Paris, chapter 2.

Oinas, P. and Malecki, E.: 2002, The evolution of technologies in time and space, *International Regional Science Review* **25**, 102–131.

Orsenigo, L., Pammolli, F., Riccaboni, M., Bonaccorsi, A. and Turchetti, G.: 1998, The evolution of knowledge and the dynamics of an industry network, *Journal of Management and Governance* **1**, 147–175.

Ott, I., Papilloud, C. and Zülsdorf, T.: 2009, What drives innovation? Causes of and consequences for nanotechnologies, *Managing Global Transitions* **7**(1), 5–26.

Owen-Smith, J. and Powell, W.: 2003, The expanding role of university patenting in the life sciences: Assessing the importance of experience and connectivity, *Research Policy* **32**, 1695–1711.

Owen-Smith, J. and Powell, W.: 2004, Knowledge networks as channels and conduits: The effects of spillovers in the Boston biotechnology community, *Organization Science* **15**(1), 5–21.

Paci, R. and Usai, S.: 1999, Externalities, knowledge spillovers and the spatial distribution of innovation, *GeoJournal* **49**, 381–390.

Paci, R. and Usai, S.: 2007, Knowledge flows across European regions, *Working Paper CRENoS* **200704**.

Palmberg, C., Dernis, H. and Miguet, C.: 2009, Nanotechnology: An overview based on indicators and statistics, *OECD STI Working Paper* **2009/7**.

Palmberg, C. and Nikulainen, T.: 2006, Nanotechnology as a general purpose technology of the 21st century? – An overview with focus on Finland, *DIME Working Paper Series*.

Pandza, K., Wilkins, T. and Alfoldi, E.: 2011, Collaborative diversity in a nanotechnology innovation system: Evidence from the EU Framework Programme, *Technovation* **31**, 476–489.

Papke, L. and Wooldridge: 1996, Econometric methods for fractional response variables with an application to 401(k) plan participation rates, *Journal of Applied Econometrics* **11**, 619–632.

Pavitt, K.: 1985, Patent statistics as indicators of innovative activities: Possibilities and problems, *Scientometrics* **7**(1-2), 77–99.

Penrose, E.: 1995, *The Theory of the Growth of the Firm*, Oxford University Press, Oxford.

Peri, G.: 2002, Knowledge flows and knowledge externalities, *CESifo Working Paper* **765**.

Persson, O., Danell, R. and Schneider, J.: 2009, How to use bibexcel for various types of bibliometric analysis, *in* F. Aström, R. Danell, B. Larsen and J. Schneider (eds), *Celebrating scholarly communication studies: A Festschrift for Olle Persson at his 60th Birthday*, International Society for Scientometrics and Informetrics, Leuven, pp. 9–24.

Petrie, H.: 1976, Do you see what I see? The epistemology of interdisciplinary inquiry, *Educational Researcher* **5**(2), 9–15.

Pianta, M.: 2005, Innovation and employment, *in* J. Fagerberg, D. Mowery and R. Nelson (eds), *The Oxford Handbook of Innovation*, Oxford University Press, Oxford, pp. 568–598.

Plum, O. and Hassink, R.: 2011, On the nature and geography of innovation and interactive learning: A case study of the biotechnology industry in the Aachen technology region, Germany, *European Planning Studies* **19**(7), 1141–1163.

Polanyi, M.: 1966, *The tacit dimension*, Doubleday, New York.

Porter, A. and Rafols, I.: 2009, Is science becoming more interdisciplinary? Measuring and mapping six research fields over time, *Scientometrics* **81**(3), 719–745.

Porter, A., Youtie, J., Shapira, P. and Schoeneck, D.: 2008, Refining search terms for nanotechnology, *Journal of Nanoparticle Research* **10**, 712–728.

Porter, M.: 1990, *The Competitive Advantage of Nations*, Macmillan, London.

Porter, M.: 1998, Clusters and competetion, *On Competetion*, Harvard Business Review, Boston, pp. 197–287.

Porter, M.: 2000, Locations, clusters and company strategy, *in* G. Clark, M. Feldman and M. Gertler (eds), *The Oxford Handbook of Economic Geography*, Oxford University Press, Oxford, pp. 253–274.

Ranft, A. and Lord, M.: 2000, Acquiring new knowledge: The role of retaining human capital in acquistions of high-tech firms, *The Journal of High Technology Management Research* **11**(2), 295–319.

Reynolds, P., Storey, D. and Westhead, P.: 1994, Cross-national comparisons of the variation in new firm formation rates, *Regional Studies* **28**(4), 443–456.

Rigby, D. and Essletzbichler, J.: 2002, Agglomeration and productivity differences in US cities, *Journal of Economic Geography* **2**, 407–432.

Robinson, D., Rip, A. and Mangematin, V.: 2007, Technological agglomeration and the emergence of clusters and networks in nanotechnologies, *Research policy* **36**, 871–879.

Roco, M.: 2007, The NNI: Past, present and future, *in* W. Goddard, D. Brenner, S. Lyshevski and G. Iafrate (eds), *Handbook on Nanoscience, Engineering and Technology*, CRC Press, London.

Romer, P.: 1986, Increasing returns and long-run growth, *Journal of Political Economy* **94**, 1002–1037.

Romer, P.: 1990, Endogenous technological change, *Journal of Political Economy* **98**(5), S71–S102.

Runkwid, C. and Christ, J.: 2011, Quantitative Clusteridentifikation auf Ebene der deutschen Stadt- und Landkreise (1999-2008).

Saha, A., Love, H. and Schwart, R.: 1994, Adoption of emerging technologies under output uncertainty, *Agricultural & Applied Economics Association* **76**(4), 836–846.

Sala-i-Martin, X.: 2002, 15 years of new growth economics: What have we learnt?, *UPF Economics and Business Working Paper* **620**.

Saxenian, A.: 1996, *Regional Advantage: Culture and Competition in Silicon Valley and Route 128*, Harvard University Press, Cambridge, MA.

Schankerman, M. and Pakes, A.: 1986, Estimates of the value of patent rights in European countries during the post-1950 period, *Economic Journal* **96**, 1052–1077.

Scheidegger, N.: 2008, Die Wirkung struktureller Löcher auf den Karriereerfolg im Management: Eine kontingente Betrachtung, *in* C. Stegbauer (ed.), *Netzwerkanalyse und Netzwerktheorie. Ein neues Paradigma in den Sozialwissenschaften*, VS Verlag für Sozialwissenschaften, Wiesbaden, pp. 503–516.

Schiffauerova, A. and Beaudry, C.: 2009, Canadian nanotechnology innovation networks: Intra-cluster, inter-cluster and foreign collaboration, *Journal of Innovation Economics* **4**, 119–146.

Schiffauerova, A. and Beaudry, C.: 2012, Collaboration spaces in Canadian biotechnology: A search for gatekeepers, *Journal of Engineering and Technology Management* **29**, 281–306.

Schilling, M. and Phelps, C.: 2007, Interfirm collaboration networks: The impact of large-scale network structure on firm innovation, *Management Science* **53**(7), 1113–1126.

Schimke, A., Teichert, N. and Ott, I.: 2013, Impact of local knowledge endowment on employment growth in nanotechnology, *Industrial and Corporate Change* **forthcoming**.

Schmoch, U.: 2003, *Hochschulforschung und Industrieforschung. Perspektiven der Interaktion*, Campus Verlag, Frankfurt/Main.

Schmoch, U., Grupp, H., Mannsbart, W. and Schwitalla, B.: 1988, *Zur Einschätzung zukünftiger industrieller Trends bei Industrierobotern, Lasern, Solargeneratoren und immobilisierten Enzymen*, Verlag TÜV Rheinland.

Schmoch, U., Laville, F., Patel, P. and Frietsch, R.: 2003, Linking technology areas to industrial sectors, Final Report to the European Commission, DG Research.

Schmoch, U., Michels, C., Schulze, N. and Neuhäusler, P.: 2012, Performance and structures of the German science system 2011, *Studien zum deutschen Innovationssystem* **09**.

Schmoch, U. and Thielmann, A.: 2012, Cyclical long-term development of complex technologies – premature expectations in nanotechnology?, *Research Evaluation* **21**, 126–135.

Schnorr-Bäcker, S.: 2009, Nanotechnologie in der amtlichen Statistik, *Statistisches Bundesamt, Wirtschaft und Statistik* **3**, 209–215.

Schrader, S.: 1991, Informal technology transfer between firms: Cooperation through information trading, *Research Policy* **20**, 153–170.

Schroeder, R., van den Ven, A., Scudder, G. and Polley, D.: 1989, The development of innovation ideas, *in* A. van den Ven, H. Angle and M. Poole (eds), *Research on the management of innovation: The Minnesota studies*, Harper and Row, New York, pp. 107–134.

Schultz, L. and Joutz, F.: 2010, Methods for identifying ermerging general purpose technologies: A case study, *Scientometrics* **85**, 155–170.

Schumpeter, J.: 1912, *Theorie der wirtschaftlichen Entwicklung*, Duncker & Humblot.

Schumpeter, J.: 1946, *Kapitalismus, Sozialismus und Demokratie*, Bern.

Shapira, P. and Youtie, J.: 2008, Emergence of nanodistricts in the United States: Path dependency or new opportunities?, *Economic Development Quarterly* **22**, 187.

Shea, C., Grinde, R. and Elmslie, B.: 2011, Nanotechnoogy as general-purpose technology: Empirical evidence and implications, *Technoogy Analysis & Strategic Management* **23**(2), 175–192.

Singh, J.: 2005, Collaborative networks as determinants of knowledge diffusion patterns, *Management Science* **51**(5), 756–770.

Singh, J.: 2008, Distributed R&D, cross-regional knowledge integration and quality of innovative output, *Research Policy* **38**(1), 77–96.

Smith, A.: 1776, *The Wealth of Nations*, Modern Library, New York.

Smolny, W.: 2000, *Endogenous Innovations and Knowledge Spillovers. A Theoretical and Empirical Analysis*, Physica, Heidelberg.

Snijders, T.: 2001, The statistical evaluation of social network dynamics, *in* M. Sobel and M. Becker (eds), *Sociological methodology*, Blackwell, Cambridge.

Solow, R.: 1956, A contribution to the theory of economic growth, *Quarterly Journal of Economics* **70**(1), 65–94.

Solow, R.: 1957, Technical change and the aggregate production function, *Review of Economics and Statistics* **39**(3), 312–320.

Sonn, J. and Storper, M.: 2008, The increasing importance of geographical proximity in knowledge production: An analysis of US patent citations 1975-1997, *Environment and Planning A* **40**(5), 1020–1039.

Sorenson, O.: 2004, Social networks, informational complexity and industrial geography, *in* D. Fornahl, C. Zellner and D. Audretsch (eds), *The Role of Labour Mobility and Informal Networks for Knowledge Transfer*, Kluwer, Dordrecht.

Sorenson, O. and Stuart, T.: 2001, Syndication networks and the spatial distribution of venture capital investments, *American Journal of Sociology* **106**(6), 1546–1588.

Statistische Ämter des Bundes und der Länder: 2008, *Volkswirtschaftliche Gesamtrechnungen der Länder*.
URL: *http://www.vgrdl.de/Arbeitskreis_VGR/tbls/tab01.asp*

Stigler, G.: 1951, The division of labour is limited by the extent of the market, *The Journal of Political Economy* **59**(3), 185–193.

Storey, D.: 1994, *Understanding the Small Business Sector*, Thomson Business Press, London.

Storper, M. and Venables, A.: 2005, Buzz: Face-to-face contact and the urban economy, *in* S. Breschi and F. Malerba (eds), *Clusters, Networks and Innovation*, Oxford University Press, New York, pp. 319–342.

Suzuki, J. and Kodama, F.: 2004, Technological diversity of persistent innovators in Japan. Two case studies of large Japanese firms, *Research Policy* **33**, 531–549.

Tappeiner, G., Hauser, C. and Walde, J.: 2008, Regional knowledge spillovers: Fact or artifact?, *Research Policy* **37**, 861–874.

Teece, D.: 1986, Profiting from technological innovation: Implications for integration, collaboration, licensing and public policy, *Research Policy* **15**, 285–305.

Ter Wal, A. and Boschma, R.: 2009, Applying social network analysis in economic geography: Framing some key analytic issues, *Annals of Regional Science* **43**, 739–756.

Thompson, P.: 2006, Patent citations and the geography of knowledge spillovers:eevidence from inventor- and examiner-added citations, *The Review of Economics and Statistics* **88**(2), 383–388.

Tödtling, F., Lehner, P. and Trippl, M.: 2006, Innovation in knowledge intensive industries: The nature and geography of knowledge links, *European Planning Studies* **14**(8), 1035–1058.

Trajtenberg, M.: 1990, A penny for your quotes: Patent citations and the value of innovations, *RAND Journal of Economics* **21**, 172–187.

Trajtenberg, M., Jaffe, A. and Henderson, R.: 1997, University vs. corporate patents: A window on the business of innovations, *Economics of Innovations and New Technology* **5**(2), 19–50.

Tran, C.: 2011, *Role and dynamics of 'Late-comers' in the global technology competition*, KIT Scientific Publishing, Karlsruhe.

Uhlaner, L., Wright, M. and Huse, M.: 2007, Private firms and corporate governance: An integrated economic and management perspective, *Small Business Economics* **29**(3), 225–241.

Uzzi, B. and Spiro, J.: 2005, Collaboration and creativity: The small world problem, *American Journal of Sociology* **111**(2), 447–504.

van der Panne, G.: 2004, Agglomeration externalities: Marshall vs. Jacobs, *Journal of Evolutionary Economics* **14**, 593–604.

van der Panne, G. and van Beers, C.: 2006, On the Marshall - Jacobs controversy: It takes two to tango, *DRUID Working Paper* **06-23**.

van Raan, A.: 1998, The influence of international collaboration on the impact of research result, *Scientometrics* **42**, 423–428.

Vanhaverbeke, W., Duysters, G. and Beerkens, B.: 2007, Technological capability building through networking strategies within high-tech industries, *UNU-MERIT Working Paper Series* **018**.

Venables, A. J.: 2006, Shifts in economic geography and their causes, *CEP Discussion Paper 767*.

Verspagen, B. and Duysters, G.: 2004, The small worlds of strategic technology alliances, *Technovation* **24**, 563–571.

Verspagen, B. and Schoenmakers, W.: 2000, The spatial dimension of knowledge spillovers in europe: Evidence from firm patenting data, *Eindhoven Center for Innovation Studies (ECIS) working paper series* **00.07**(016).

Verspagen, B., van Moergastel, T. and Slabbers, M.: 1994, MERIT concordance table: IPC-ISIC (rev. 2).

Veugelers, R.: 1998, Collaboration in R&D: An assessment of theoretical and empirical findings, *De Economist* **146**, 419–443.

Vollrath, T.: 1991, A theoretical evaluation of alternative trade intensity measures of Revealed Comparative Advantage, *Review of World Economics* **127**(2), 265–280.

von Hippel, E.: 1987, Cooperation between rivals: Informal know-how trading, *Research Policy* **16**, 291–302.

von Hippel, E.: 1994, Sticky information and the locus of problem solving: Implications for innovation, *Management Science* **40**, 429–439.

Vonortas, N.: 1994, Inter-fim cooperation in imperfectly appropriable research, *International Journal of Industrial Organisation* **12**, 413–435.

Wagner, C. and Leydesdorff, L.: 2005, Network structure, self-organisation, and the growth of international collaboration in science, *Research Policy* **34**, 1608–1618.

Wagner, J.: 2001, A note on the firm size-export relationship, *Small Business Economics* **17**(4), 229–237.

Walker, G., Kogut, B. and Shan, W.: 1997, Social capital, structural holes and the formation of an industry network, *Organization Science* **8**(2), 109–125.

Wang, J.-C., Chiang, C.-H. and Lin, S.-W.: 2010, Network structure of innovation: Can brokerage or closure predict patent quality?, *Scientometrics* **84**, 735–748.

Wassermann, S. and Faust, K.: 2009, *Social Network Analysis. Methods and Applications*, Cambridge University Press, Cambridge.

Watts, D.: 1999, Networks, dynamics, and the small-world phenomenon, *American Journal of Sociology* **105**(2), 493–527.

Watts, D. and Strogatz, S.: 1998, Collective dynamics of 'small-world' networks, *Nature* **393**(6684), 440–442.

Weterings, A. and Boschma, R.: 2009, Does spatial proximity to customers matter for innovative performance? Evidence from the Dutch software sector, *Research Policy* **38**(5), 746–755.

Wilkinson, F. and Moore, B.: 2000, Concluding reflections: Some policy implications, *in* D. Keeble and F. Wilkinson (eds), *High-Technology Clusters, Networking, and Collective Learning in Europe*, Ashgate, Hampshire, pp. 230–259.

Wong, P., Ho, Y. and Chan, C.: 2007, Internationalization and evolution of application areas of an emerging technology: The case of nanotechnology, *Scientometrics* **70**(3), 715–737.

Wood, S., Jones, R. and Geldhart, A.: 2003, The social and economic challenges of nanotechnology, Economic and Social Research Council.
URL: http://sei.nnin.org/doc/resource/esrc%20paper.pdf

Wooldridge, J.: 2002, *Econometric Analysis of Cross Section and Panel Data*, MIT Press, Cambridge, MA.

Wößmann, L.: 2003, Specifying human capital, *Journal of Economic Surveys* **17**(3), 239–270.

Wu, W.: 2005, Dynamic cities and creative clusters, *World Bank Policy Research Working Paper* **3509**.

Youtie, J., Iacopetta, M. and Graham, S.: 2008, Assessing the nature of nanotechnology: Can we uncover an emerging general purpose technology?, *Journal of Technology Transfer* **33**, 315–329.

Zhang, J., Baden-Fuller, C. and Mangematin, V.: 2007, Technological knowledge base, R&D organization structure and alliance formation: Evidence from the biopharmaceutical industry, *Research Policy* **36**, 515–528.

Zitt, M., Barre, R., Sigogneau, A. and Laville, F.: 1999, Territorial concentration and evolution of science and technology activities in the European Union: A descriptive analysis, *Research Policy* **28**, 545–562.

Zucker, L. and Darby, M.: 1996, Star scientists and institutional transformation: Patterns of invention and innovation in the formation of the biotechnology industry, *Proceedings of the National Academy of Sciences* **93**, 12709–12716.

Zucker, L., Darby, M. and Brewer, M.: 1998, Intellectual human capital and the birth of U.S. biotechnology enterprises, *American Economic Review* **88**(1), 290–306.

Zucker, L., Darby, M., Furner, J., Liu, R. and Ma, H.: 2007, Minerva unbound: Knowledge stocks, knowledge flows and new knowledge production, *Research Policy* **36**, 850–863.

Part V

APPENDIX

A General Purpose Technologies

To put this dual inducement mechanism more formally and strictly following Bresnahan and Trajtenberg (1995), a given GPT with a quality z is provided to the application sectors for the price w. The profit decreases when w increases. The technology level T_a can be chosen by the downstream sectors by controlling their R&D-activity. T_a correlates positively with the profit of the application sectors, as well as with z. The application sectors act profit-maximising when

$$\max_{T_a} \pi^a(w,z,T_a) - C^a(T_a) \tag{A.1}$$

where C^a denotes costs for innovation in application sectors and π^a are the gross private returns to technological advance. With the innovational complementarities given by

$$\pi^a{}_{zT_a} = \frac{\delta^2 \pi^a(w,z,T_a)}{\delta z \delta T_a} \geq 0 \tag{A.2}$$

it follows that the marginal value of enhancing the application sectors' technology increases with z. The technology investment function

$$T_a = R^a(z,w) \tag{A.3}$$

follows from the first order condition for (A.1). With $\frac{d^2 C^a}{d^2 T_a} > 0$ and the second order condition ($\frac{\delta^2 C^a}{\delta^2 T_a} < 0$), R^a is upward sloping in z. This implies that a technological improvement of the GPT results in complementary improvements in the downstream sectors.

Modelling the profit-maximising behaviour of the GPT sector yields

$$\max_{z} \pi^g(z,T_A,c) - C^g(z) \tag{A.4}$$

with $C^g(z)$ denoting the innovation costs (with $\frac{dC^g(z)}{dz} > 0$ and $\frac{d^2 C^g(z)}{d^2 z} > 0$), c is the constant marginal production cost for the good embodying the GPT and T_A the aggregate technological level of all application sectors.

Assumed $\pi^g(z, T_A, c) \equiv \max_w (w-c) \sum_a X^a(w, z, T_a)$, whereas $\sum_a X^a(w, z, T_a)$ is the (conditioned) input-demand of all application sectors, with the first order condition this gives

$$z = R^g(T_A, c) \tag{A.5}$$

Because z depends on T_A and therefore on every single T_a, the GPT-firm reacts on changes in T_a in the following way:

$$\frac{\delta R^g(T_A, c)}{\delta T_a} = \frac{\frac{\delta^2 \pi^g(z, T_A, c)}{\delta z \delta T_a}}{-\frac{\delta^2 \pi^g(z, T_A, c)}{\delta^2 z} + \frac{d^2 C^g(z)}{d^2 z}} \tag{A.6}$$

It is assumed that each application sector behaves as if $\delta w(z, T, c)/\delta T_a = 0$, i.e. the application sectors do not account for the price change in the GPT that is induced by a technology improvement (Bresnahan and Trajtenberg 1992). The innovational complementarities (see A.1), from which $\frac{\delta^2 \sum_a X^a(w,z,T_a)}{\delta z \delta T_a} > 0$ follows, lead to $\frac{\delta^2 \pi^g(z,T_A,c)}{\delta z \delta T_a} > 0$. The second order condition gives $\frac{\delta^2 \pi^g(z,T_A,c)}{\delta^2 z} < 0$. Thus

$$\frac{\delta R^g(T_A, c)}{\delta T_a} > 0 \tag{A.7}$$

Hence R^g is upward sloping in T_A. Thus private return to investment in z increases with T_A.[1] The incentive to innovate for the GPT sector is interrelated with the behaviour of the application sectors since innovations in the GPT sector raise the return to innovations in each application sector and vice versa. The choice of the quality of the GPT z and the technology level T_A are therefore complements.

[1] For a more detailed modelling of application sectors and the GPT sector see Bresnahan and Trajtenberg (1995).

B Methodology and Data

B.1 European Patent Application

(19) Europäisches Patentamt / European Patent Office / Office européen des brevets

(11) **EP 2 168 737 A1**

(12) **EUROPEAN PATENT APPLICATION**
published in accordance with Art. 153(4) EPC

(43) Date of publication:
31.03.2010 Bulletin 2010/13

(21) Application number: **07803638.1**

(22) Date of filing: **23.07.2007**

(51) Int Cl.:
B27K 3/08 (2006.01) *A01N 25/00* (2006.01)
B27K 3/52 (2006.01)

(86) International application number:
PCT/ES2007/000451

(87) International publication number:
WO 2009/013361 (29.01.2009 Gazette 2009/05)

(84) Designated Contracting States:
AT BE BG CH CY CZ DE DK EE ES FI FR GB GR HU IE IS IT LI LT LU LV MC MT NL PL PT RO SE SI SK TR
Designated Extension States:
AL BA HR MK RS

(71) Applicant: **Tramat, S.L.**
Pol. Ind Valle de Güimar
Parcela 10, manzana 1
38509 Candelaria- Santa Cruz de Tenerife (ES)

(72) Inventor: **GONZALO PEREZ, Antonio**
E-38509 Candelaria- Santa Cruz de Tenerife (ES)

(74) Representative: **Pons Ariño, Angel**
Glorieta Ruben Dario 4
28010 Madrid (ES)

(54) **METHOD FOR OBTAINING A FINISHED WOOD PRODUCT, USING NANOTECHNOLOGY**

(57) The invention relates to a method for obtaining a finished wood product, using an autoclave including a chamber (1). According to the invention, sheets of dry wood (2) having a moisture content of less than 25 % are introduced into the chamber of the autoclave and an initial vacuum is applied in order to extract the air from inside the chamber and the wood. Subsequently, a preservative (3) to be absorbed by the wood is introduced into the chamber without altering the vacuum and when the chamber has been filled with said preservative a pressure is applied until the wood is saturated. The excess preservative solution is then returned to a tank and a final vacuum is applied to re-establish the internal pressure of the wood and to dry same. The invention is **characterised in that** the preservative to be absorbed by the wood is an emulsion (3) formed by a mixture of a water-soluble preservative with added nanoparticles or an oil-soluble preservative with added nanoparticles, preferably carbon nanotubes, clay nanotubes or similar. The system can also be brought to atmospheric pressure, after the autoclave has been flooded, and a second vacuum can be applied to remove the excess preservative solution.

Figure B.1: European patent application.
Source: EPO.

B.2 PATSTAT diagram

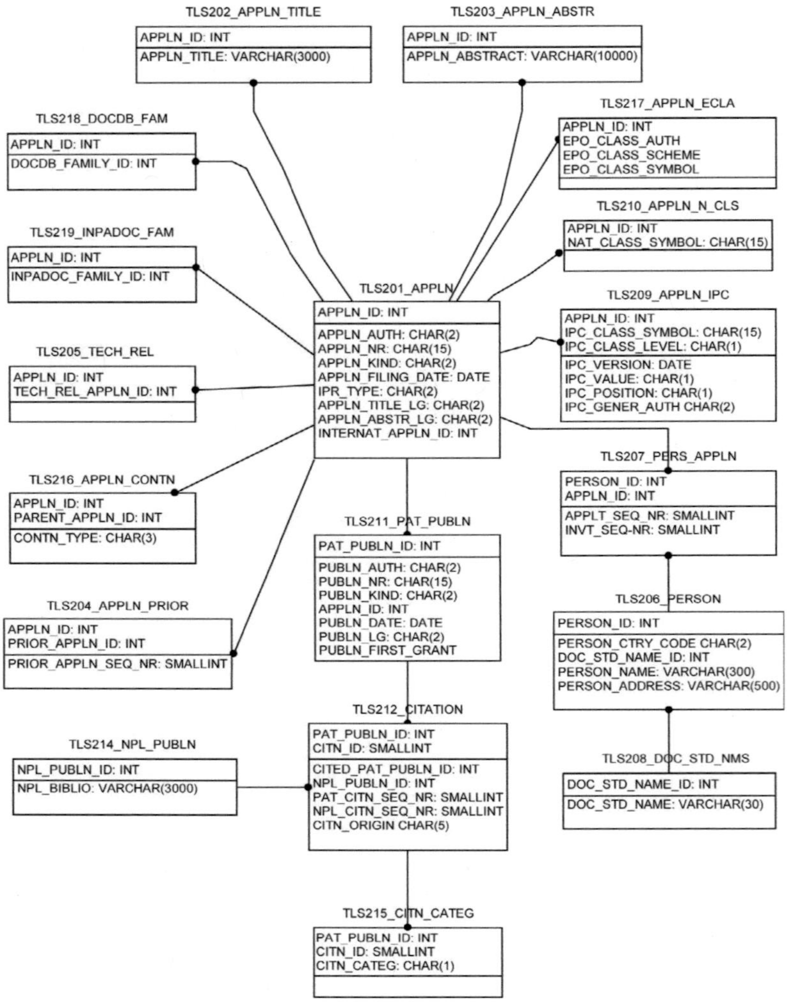

Figure B.2: PATSTAT Diagram, September 2010.
Source: European Patent Office (2010).

B.3 Search Terms

B.3.1 Nano-Patent Search Term

The query that identified nano-patents was generated searching for the following terms in title and abstract (referring to Mogoutov and Kahane (2007), Glänzel et al. (2003) and Porter et al. (2008)):

nano; carbon tube; mechanical resonator; quantum dot; low dimensional system; semiconductor structure; li batter; solar cell; carbon composite; carbon fiber; field emitter; crystal memory; emission propert; thin film; carbon film; film deposit; gold catalyst; tube modified; gold particle; plga particle; heterogeneous catalyst; composite powder; tribological propert; composite coating; composite coating; silicate, composite; clay composite; polymer composite; composite prepared; coating deposited; lipid particle; al2o3 composite; coating produced; sol method; semiconducting material; diamond film; mesoporous material; soft magnetic material; primordial protein; block copolymer; hydrogen storage material; zinc compound; clay composite; walled carbon; metallic carbon; semiconducting carbon; single carbon; surface plasmon; finite-difference time-domain method; chemisorption; atomistic simulation; tio2 solar; sensitized tio2; dye solar; sensitized solar; electrochemical performance; induced deposition; field emission; vapor deposition; crystalline diamond; chemical vapor; ion implantation; plasma chemical; magnetic fluid; crystalline silicon; crystal morphology; laser ablation; laser deposition; beam epitaxy; sputtering; molecular beam epitaxy; mesoporous silica; solid lipid; drug carrier; enhanced raman; co oxidation; direct electrochemistry; electrode modified; raman scattering; immunosensor based; resonance light; modified glassy; glucose biosensor; biosensor based; electrochemical biosensor; drug delivery; modified electrode; amorphous alloy; delivery system; surface chemistry; ball milling; drug release; heterogeneous catalysis; spark plasma; supramolecular chemistry; gene delivery; severe plastic; gel method; mechanical alloy; plasma sintering; gold electrode; situ polymerization; carbon electrode; single-molecule; biosensor; oligomeric silsesquioxane; metallic glass; poly methacrylate; block copolymer; grain growth; plastic deformation; sintering; microstructural evolution; microstructure superplasticity; surface plasmons; electrostatic force microscopy; transmission electron microscopy; quantum rings; chemical vapor deposition; graphitic carbon; dye-sensitized solar cell; magnetization reversal; porous carbon; supercapacitor; growth from solutions; diamond-like carbon; mesoporous; self-assembly; surface-enhanced raman; mechanical alloying; spark plasma sintering; ball milling; montmorillonite; organoclay; electrospinning; amorphous alloy

and excluding the following words:

nano2; nano3; nano4; nano5; nano liter; nano second,

always in-/excluding different orthographic versions and words with differing suffixes.

B.3.2 ICT Patent Search Term

Identifying ICT patents, patents from the following IPC classes were extracted, referring to the 8th edition of the IPC:

Telecommunications:
G01S; G08C; G09C; H01P; H01Q; H01S; H1S5; H03B; H03C; H03D; H03H; H03M; H04B; H04J; H04K; H04L; H04M; H04Q;
Consumer Electronics:
G11B; H03F; H03G; H03J; H04H; H04N; H04R; H04S;
Computers, Office Machinery:
B07C; B41J; B41K; G02F; G03G; G05F; G06; G07; G09G; G10L; G11C; H03K; H03L;
Other ICT:
G01B; G01C; G01D; G01F; G01G; G01H; G01J; G01K; G01L; G01M; G01N; G01P; G01R; G01V; G01W; G02B6; G05B; G08G; G09B; H01B11; H01J; H01L

B.4 Publication Identification - Search Terms and Subject Areas

B.4.1 Nano Publication Search Term

Based on a combination of different search queries, again relying on Mogoutov and Kahane (2007), Glänzel et al. (2003) and Porter et al. (2008) but, due to WOS database restrictions, shorter than the patent equivalent, nano-publications were identified using the following query:

(SO=(nano*) OR TS=(nano* NOT(nano2, nano3, nano4, Nano5, nanosecon*, nanoliter*)) OR TS=("quantum dot*" OR "quantum wire*" OR "beam epitaxy*" OR "molecul* engineer*" OR "carbon tub*" OR "fulleren*" OR "self assembl* monolayer*" OR "self assembl* dot*" OR "molecul* self assembl*" OR "single carbon*" OR "single molecule*" OR "atom* force microscop*" OR "tunnel* microscop*" OR "drug delivery" OR "walled carbon" OR "composite* coating" OR "thin film" OR "microstructure*" OR "semiconducting material*" OR "singe electron*" OR "atomic(w)layer" OR "molecular manipulation" OR "quantum wire?" OR "quantum devic*" OR "molecul* manufactur*" OR "molecular motor" OR "drug carrier" OR "single electron* tunneling" OR "supramolecular chemistry" OR "molecular templates" OR "soft lithograph*" OR "tube* modified" OR "vapor deposition" OR "ball milling"))

B.4.2 ICT Publication Search Term

To identiy ICT-publications, it was suffificient to search for the following Thomson ISI subject areas (according to Schmoch 2011, personal communication):

'Computer Science' and 'Telecommunications'

B.4.3 CE Publication Search Term

The search term that identified relevant CE-publications was developed by a team at the Chair in Economic Policy at the Karlsruhe Institute of Technology:

(SO=("combustion engine*") OR TS=("combustion engine*" OR "CI engine*" OR "compression ignition engine*" OR "combustion motor" OR "combustion product" OR "combustion-product" OR "otto engine*" OR "otto cycle*" OR "diesel engine*" OR "diesel cycle*" OR "two-stroke engine*" OR "two stroke engine*" OR "four-stroke engine*" OR "four stroke engine*" OR "six-stroke engine*" OR "six stroke engine*" OR "wankel engine*" OR "wankel rotary engine*"))

B.5 Concordances

IPC at 4-digit-level (K30 and K44 with concordance developed by Hinze et al. (1997) and Schmoch et al. (2003) respectively, based upon NACE and ISIC)

K30	FIELD	IPC
1	ELECTRICAL ENGINEERING	F21H; F21K; F21L; F21M; F21P; F21Q; F21W; F21Y; F21S; F21V; G05F; H01B; H01C; H01F; H01G; H01H; H01J; H01K; H01M; H01R; H01T; H02B; H02G; H02H; H02J; H02K; H02M; H02N; H02P; H05B; H05C; H05F; H05K
2	AUDIOVISUAL TECHNOLOGY	G09F; G09G; G11B; H03F; H03G; H03J; H04N; H04N; H04N; H04N; H04N; H04N; H04R; H04S
3	TELECOMMUNICATIONS	G08C; H01P; H01Q; H03B; H03C; H03D; H03H; H03K; H03L; H03M; H04B; H04H; H04J; H04K; H04L; H04M; H04N; H04N; H04N; H04Q
4	INFORMATION TECHNOLOGY	G06C; G06D; G06E; G06F; G06G; G06J; G06K; G06M; G06T; G10L; G11C
5	SEMICONDUCTORS	B81B; B81C; H01L
6	OPTICS	G02B; G02C; G02F; G03B; G03C; G03D; G03F; G03G; G03H; H01S
7	CONTROL TECHNOLOGY	G01B; G01C; G01D; G01F; G01G; G01H; G01J; G01K; G01L; G01M; G01N; G01P; G01R; G01S; G01V; G01W; G04B; G04C; G04D; G04F; G04G; G05B; G05D; G07B; G07C; G07D; G07F; G07G; G08B; G08G; G09B; G09C; G09D; G12B
8	MEDICAL TECHNOLOGY	A61B; A61C; A61D; A61F; A61G; A61H; A61J; A61L; A61M; A61N; A61Q
9	NUCLEAR ENGINEERING	C07C; G01T; G21B; G21C; G21D; G21F; G21G; G21H; G21J; G21K; H05G; H05H
10	ORGANIC CHEMISTRY	C07D; C07F; C07H; C07J; C07K
12	PHARAMCEUTICS	A61K; A61P
13	BIOTECHNOLOGY	C07G; C12M; C12N; C12P; C12Q; C12R; C12S
14	FOOD CHEMISTRY	A01H; A21D; A23B; A23C; A23D; A23F; A23G; A23J; A23K; A23L; C12C; C12F; C12G; C12H; C12J; C13D; C13F; C13J; C13K
18	MATERIALS	B22C; B22D; B22F; B82B; C01B; C01C; C01D; C01F; C01G; C03C; C04B; C21B; C21C; C21D; C22B; C22C; C22F; C22K
17	SURFACE TECHNOLOGY	B05C; B05D; B32B; C23C; C23D; C23F; C23G; C25B; C25C; C25D; C40B; C25F; C30B
11	POLYMERS	C08B; C08F; C08G; C08H; C08K; C08L; C09D; C09J
15	BASIC MATERIALS CHEMISTRY	A01N; C05B; C05C; C05D; C05F; C05G; C07B; C08C; C09B; C09C; C09F; C09G; C09H; C09K; C10B; C10C; C10F; C10G; C10H; C10J; C10K; C10L; C10M; C11B; C11C; C11D
16	CHEMICAL ENGINEERING	B01B; B01D; B01F; B01J; B01L; B02C; B03B; B03C; B03D; B04B; B04C; B05B; B06B; B07B; B07C; B08B; F25J; F26B
19	MATERIALS PROCESSING	A41H; A43D; A46D; B28B; B28C; B28D; B29B; B29C; B29D; B29K; B29L; B31B; B31C; B31D; B31F; C03B; C08J; C14B; C14C; D01B; D01C; D01D; D01F; D01G; D01H; D02G; D02H; D02J; D03C; D03D; D03J; D04B; D04C; D04G; D04H; D05B; D05C; D06B; D06C; D06G; D06H; D06J; D06L; D06M; D06P; D06Q; D21B; D21C; D21D; D21F; D21G; D21H; D21J
20	HANDLING	B25J; B41B; B41C; B41D; B41F; B41G; B41J; B41K; B41L; B41M; B41N; B65B; B65C; B65D; B65F; B65G; B65H; B66B; B66C; B66D; B66F; B67B; B67C; B67D
21	FOOD PROCESSING	A01B; A01C; A01D; A01F; A01G; A01J; A01K; A01L; A01M; A21B; A21C; A22B; A22C; A23N; A23P; B02B; C12L; C13C; C13G; C13H
22	ENVIRONMENTAL TECHNOLOGY	A62D; B01D; B01D; B01D; B01D; B01D; B01D; B01D; B01D; B09B; C02F; F01N; F23G; F23J
23	MACHINE TOOLS	B21B; B21C; B21D; B21F; B21G; B21H; B21J; B21K; B21L; B23B; B23C; B23D; B23F; B23G; B23H; B23K; B23P; B23Q; B24B; B24C; B24D; B26D; B26F; B27B; B27C; B27D; B27F; B27G; B27H; B27J; B27K; B27L; B27M; B27N; B30B
24	ENGINES	F01B; F01C; F01D; F01K; F01L; F01M; F01P; F02B; F02C; F02D; F02F; F02G; F02K; F02M; F02N; F02P; F03B; F03C; F03D; F03G; F03H; F04B; F04C; F04D; F04F; F23R
25	THERMAL PROCESSES	F22B; F22D; F22G; F23B; F23C; F23D; F23H; F23K; F23L; F23M; F23N; F23Q; F24B; F24C; F24D; F24F; F24H; F24J; F25B; F25C; F27B; F27D; F28B; F28C; F28D; F28F; F28G
26	MECHANICAL ELEMENTS	F15B; F15C; F15D; F16B; F16C; F16D; F16F; F16G; F16H; F16J; F16K; F16L; F16M; F16N; F16P; F16S; F16T; F17B; F17C; F17D; G05G
27	TRANSPORT	B60B; B60C; B60D; B60F; B60G; B60H; B60J; B60K; B60L; B60M; B60N; B60P; B60Q; B60R; B60S; B60T; B60V; B61B; B61C; B61D; B61F; B61G; B61H; B61J; B61K; B61L; B62B; B62C; B62D; B62H; B62J; B62K; B62L; B62M; B63B; B63C; B63H; B63J; B64B; B64C; B64D; B64F
28	SPACE TECHNOLOGY	B63G; B64G; C06B; C06C; C06D; C06F; F41A; F41B; F41C; F41F; F41G; F41H; F41J; F42B; F42C; F42D
29	CONSUMER GOODS	A24B; A24C; A24D; A24F; A41B; A41C; A41D; A41F; A41G; A42B; A42C; A43B; A43C; A44B; A44C; A45B; A45C; A45D; A45F; A46B; A47B; A47C; A47D; A47F; A47G; A47H; A47J; A47K; A47L; A62B; A62C; A63B; A63C; A63D; A63F; A63G; A63H; A63J; A63K; B25B; B25C; B25D; B25F; B25G; B25H; B26B; B42B; B42C; B42D; B42F; B43K; B43L; B43M; B44B; B44C; B44D; B44F; B68B; B68C; B68F; B68G; D04D; D06F; D06N; D07B; F25D; G10B; G10C; G10D; G10F; G10G; G10H; G10K
30	CIVIL ENGINEERING	E01B; E01C; E01D; E01F; E01H; E02B; E02C; E02D; E02F; E03B; E03C; E03D; E03F; E04B; E04C; E04D; E04F; E04G; E04H; E05B; E05C; E05D; E05F; E05G; E06B; E06C; E21B; E21C; E21D; E21F

Table B.1: Concordance IPC K30.
Source: Hinze et al. (1997).

K44	NACE	FIELD	IPC
1	15	FOOD, BEVERAGES	A01H; A21D; A23B; A23C; A23D; A23F; A23G; A23J; A23K; A23L; A23P; C12C; C12F; C12G; C12H; C12J; C13F; C13J; C13K
2	16	TOBACCO PRODUCTS	A24B; A24D; A24F
3	17	TEXTILES	D04D; D04G; D04H; D06C; D06J; D06M; D06N; D06P; D06Q
4	18	WEARING APPAREL	A41B; A41C; A41D; A41F
5	19	LEATHER ARTICLES	A43B; A43C; B68B; B68C
6	20	WOOD PRODUCTS	B27D; B27H; B27M; B27N; E07G
7	21	PAPER	B41M; B42D; B42F; B44F; D21C; D21H; D21J
8	22	PUBLISHING, PRINTING	
9	23	PETROLEUM PRODUCTS, NUCLEAR FUEL	C10G; C10L; G01V
10	24.1	BASIC CHEMICAL	B01J; B09B; B09C; B29B; C01B; C01C; C01D; C01F; C01G; C02F; C05B; C05C; C05D; C05F; C05G; C07B; C07C; C07F; C07G; C08B; C08C; C08F; C08G; C08J; C08K; C08L; C09B; C09C; C09D; C09K; C10B; C10C; C10H; C10J; C10K; C12S; C25B; F17C; F17D; F25J; G21F
11	24.2	PESTICIDES, AGRO-CHEMICAL PRODUCTS	A01N
12	24.3	PAINTS, VARINISHES	B27K
13	24.4	PHARMACEUTICALS	A61K; A61P; C07D; C07H; C07J; C07K; C12N; C12P; C12Q
14	24.5	SOAPS, DETERGANTS, TOILET PREPARATIONS	C09F; C11D; D06L
15	24.6	OTHER CHEMICALS	A62D; C06B; C06C; C06D; C08H; C09G; C09H; C09J; C10M; C11B; C11C; C14C; C23F; C23G; D01C; F42B; F42D; G03C
16	24.7	MAN-MADE FIBRES	D01F
17	25	RUBBER AND PLASTIC PRODUCTS	A45C; B29C; B29D; B60C; B65D; B67D; E02B; F16L; H02G
18	26	NON-METALLIC MINERAL PRODUCTS	B24D; B28B; B28C; B32B; C03B; C03C; C04B; E04B; E04C; E04D; E04F; G21B
19	27	BASIC METALS	B21C; B21G; B22D; C21B; C21C; C21D; C22B; C22C; C22F; C25C; C25F; C30B; D07B; E03F; E04H; F27D; H01B
20	28	FABRICATED METAL PRODUCTS	A01L; A44B; A47H; A47K; B21K; B21L; B22F; B25B; B25C; B25F; B25G; B25H; B26B; B27G; B44C; B65F; B82B; C23D; C25D; E01D; E01F; E02C; E03B; E03C; E03D; E05B; E05C; E05D; E05F; E05G; E06B; F01K; F15D; F16B; F16P; F16S; F16T; F17B; F22B; F22G; F24J; G21H
21	29.1	ENERGY MACHINERY	B23F; F01B; F01C; F01D; F03B; F03C; F03D; F03G; F04B; F04C; F04D; F15B; F16C; F16D; F16F; F16H; F16K; F16M; F23R
22	29.2	NON-SPECIFIC PURPOSE MACHINERY	A62C; B01D; B04C; B05B; B61B; B65G; B66B; B66C; B66D; B66F; C10F; C12L; F16G; F22D; F23B; F23C; F23D; F23G; F23H; F23J; F23K; F23L; F23M; F24F; F24H; F25B; F27B; F28B; F28C; F28D; F28F; F28G; G01G; H05F
23	29.3	AGRICULTURAL AND FORESTRY MACHINERY	A01B; A01C; A01D; A01F; A01G; A01J; A01K; A01M; B27L
24	29.4	MACHINE-TOOLS	B21D; B21F; B21H; B21J; B23B; B23C; B23D; B23G; B23H; B23K; B23P; B23Q; B24B; B24C; B25D; B25J; B26F; B27B; B27C; B27F; B27J; B28D; B30B; E21C
25	29.5	SPECIAL PURPOSE MACHINERY	A21C; A22B; A22C; A23N; A24C; A41H; A42C; A43D; B01F; B02B; B02C; B03B; B03C; B03D; B05C; B05D; B06B; B07B; B07C; B08B; B21B; B22C; B26D; B31B; B31C; B31D; B31F; B41B; B41C; B41D; B41F; B41G; B41L; B41N; B42B; B42C; B44B; B65B; B65C; B65H; B67B; B67C; B68F; C13C; C13D; C13G; C13H; C14B; C23C; D01B; D01D; D01G; D01H; D02G; D02H; D02J; D03C; D03D; D03J; D04B; D04C; D05B; D05C; D06B; D06G; D06H; D21B; D21D; D21F; D21G; E01C; E02D; E02F; E21B; E21D; E21F; F04F; F16N; F26B; H05H
26	29.6	WEAPONS AND AMMUNITION	B63G; F41A; F41B; F41C; F41F; F41G; F41H; F41J; F42C; G21J
27	29.7	DOMESTIC APLLIANCES	A21B; A45D; A47G; A47J; A47L; B01B; D06F; E06C; F23N; F24B; F24C; F24D; F25C; F25D; H05B
28	30	OFFICE MACHINERY AND COMPUTERS	B41J; B41K; B43M; G02F; G03G; G05F; G06C; G06D; G06E; G06F; G06G; G06J; G06K; G06M; G06N; G06T; G07B; G07C; G07D; G07F; G07G; G09D; G09G; G10L; G11B; H03K; H03L
29	31.1	ELECTRIC MOTORS, GENERATORS, TRANSFORMERS	H02K; H02N; H02P
30	31.2, 31.3	ELECTRIC DISTRIBUTION, CONTROL, WIRE, CABLE	H01H; H01R; H02B
31	31.4	ACCUMULATORS, BATTERY	H01M
32	31.5	LIGHTENING EQUIPMENT	F21H; F21K; F21L; F21M; F21S; F21V; H01K
33	31.6	OTHER ELECTRICAL EQUIPMENT	B60M; B61L; F21P; F21Q; G08B; G08G; G10K; G21C; G21D; H01T; H02H; H02M; H05C
34	32.1	ELECTRONIC COMPONENTS	B81B; B81C; G11C; H01C; H01F; H01G; H01J; H01L
35	32.2	SIGNAL TRANSMISSION, TELECOMMUNICATIONS	G09B; G09C; H01P; H01Q; H01S; H02J; H03B; H03C; H03D; H03F; H03G; H03H; H03M; H04B; H04J; H04K; H04L; H04M; H04Q; H05K
36	32.3	TV & RADIO RECEIVERS, AV ELECTRONICS	G03H; H03J; H04H; H04N; H04R; H04S
37	33.1	MEDICAL EQUIPMENT	A61B; A61C; A61D; A61F; A61G; A61H; A61J; A61L; A61M; A61N; A62B; B01L; B04B; C12M; G01T; G21G; G21K; H05G
38	33.2	MEASURING INSTRUMENTS	F15C; G01B; G01C; G01D; G01F; G01H; G01J; G01M; G01N; G01R; G01S; G01W; G12B
39	33.3	INDUSTRIAL PROCESS CONTROL EQUIPMENT	G01K; G01L; G05B; G08C
40	33.4	OPTICAL INSTRUMENTS	G02B; G02C; G03B; G03D; G03F; G09F
41	33.5	WATCHES, CLOCKS	G04B; G04C; G04D; G04F; G04G
42	34	MOTOR VEHICLES	B60B; B60D; B60G; B60H; B60J; B60K; B60L; B60N; B60P; B60Q; B60R; B60S; B60T; B62D; E01H; F01L; F01M; F01N; F01P; F02B; F02D; F02F; F02G; F02M; F02N; F02P; F16J; G01P; G05D; G05G
43	35	OTHER TRANSPORT EQUIPMENT	B60F; B60V; B61C; B61D; B61F; B61G; B61H; B61J; B61K; B62C; B62H; B62J; B62K; B62L; B62M; B63B; B63C; B63H; B63J; B64B; B64C; B64D; B64F; B64G; E01B; F02C; F02K; F03H
44	36	FURNITURE, CONSUMER GOODS	A41G; A42B; A44C; A45B; A45F; A46B; A46D; A47B; A47C; A47D; A47F; A63B; A63C; A63D; A63F; A63G; A63H; A63J; A63K; B43K; B43L; B44D; B62B; B68G; C06F; F23Q; G10B; G10C; G10D; G10F; G10G; G10H

Table B.2: Concordance IPC K44.
Source: Schmoch et al. (2003).

C Nanotechnology as an Emerging General Purpose Technology

C.1 Technological Relatedness and Coherence

The technological relatedness matrix was constructed as follows (for further details see Leten et al. (2007)): Let O_{ij} be the observed number of cited patents of technology class j citing patents of technology class i, with $O_i = \sum_j O_{ij}$. A certain technology class has a higher random probability to be cited if many patents are classi?ed in that technology class, where N_j is the total number of patents classified in technology class j, with $T = \sum_j N_j$. This results in the expected number of cited patents of technology class j citing patents of technology class i

$$E_{ij} = O_i \times \frac{N_j}{T} \tag{C.1}$$

The matrix of the measures of technological relatedness between class i and j, R_{ij} is then calculated as follows:

$$R_{ij} = \frac{O_{ij} + O_{ji}}{E_{ij} + E_{ji}} \tag{C.2}$$

If $R_{ij} > 1$, technologies i and j are more related than could be expected on a random basis.

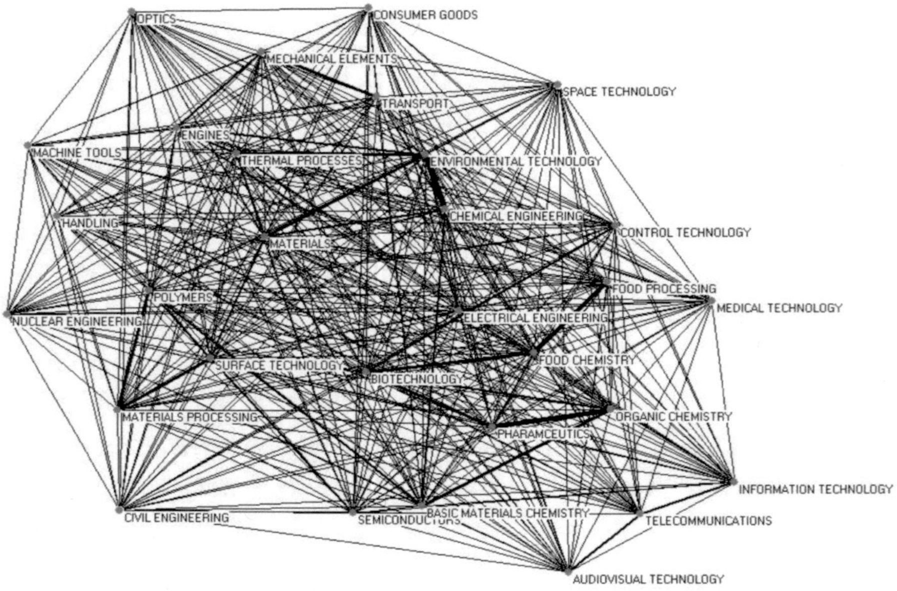

Figure C.1: Network of related technological Fields. Widths of edges proportional to the degree of relatedness.
Source: own calculations.

	1	2	3	4	5	6	7	8	9	10	11	12	13	14	15	16	17	18	19	20	21	22	23	24	25	26	27	28	29	30
1																														
2	0,58																													
3	0,50	2,10																												
4	0,35	1,43	2,13																											
5	1,15	0,46	0,35	0,75																										
6	0,55	1,29	0,64	0,36	1,04																									
7	0,60	0,49	0,84	1,39	0,47	0,50																								
8	0,14	0,13	0,06	0,22	0,05	0,25	0,52																							
9	1,12	0,44	0,23	0,34	0,84	0,74	0,98	1,10																						
10	0,04	0,05	0,00	0,01	0,03	0,36	0,29	0,07	0,03																					
11	0,33	0,18	0,01	0,01	0,20	0,90	0,07	0,51	0,05	1,14																				
12	0,01	0,01	0,00	0,01	0,01	0,04	0,27	0,74	0,08	4,86	0,65																			
13	0,01	0,01	0,01	0,03	0,02	0,04	1,68	0,30	0,07	2,44	0,27	2,56																		
14	0,07	0,00	0,00	0,01	0,01	0,01	0,08	0,19	0,02	0,68	0,46	1,86	3,26																	
15	0,17	0,16	0,00	0,01	0,15	0,71	0,12	0,26	0,73	2,77	2,07	1,18	0,91	1,19																
16	0,23	0,06	0,02	0,11	0,28	0,16	0,74	0,57	0,59	1,41	0,88	0,40	0,67	0,93	1,70															
17	0,91	0,45	0,04	0,06	1,67	0,73	0,19	0,57	0,94	0,14	1,98	0,08	0,07	0,19	0,70	1,08														
18	0,90	0,13	0,03	0,01	0,88	0,45	0,13	0,17	1,28	0,34	0,96	0,21	0,07	0,14	1,21	2,18	2,41													
19	0,30	0,22	0,02	0,08	0,14	0,49	0,21	0,59	0,15	0,18	2,69	0,16	0,13	0,29	1,05	1,02	2,61	1,00												
20	0,24	0,31	0,14	0,32	0,21	0,74	0,70	0,38	0,16	0,05	0,43	0,05	0,05	0,43	0,21	0,72	1,19	0,15	1,07											
21	0,10	0,05	0,03	0,07	0,02	0,02	0,31	0,24	0,02	0,05	0,17	0,14	0,32	4,40	0,43	0,72	0,29	0,07	0,34	0,54										
22	0,18	0,02	0,01	0,01	0,04	0,08	0,22	0,26	1,05	0,30	0,44	0,10	0,59	0,48	1,31	6,41	0,82	2,78	0,48	0,12	0,39									
23	0,47	0,07	0,03	0,11	0,54	0,28	0,37	0,27	0,86	0,02	0,14	0,02	0,01	0,12	0,25	0,44	1,08	1,30	1,01	0,80	0,53	0,33								
24	0,46	0,02	0,05	0,07	0,11	0,02	0,51	0,21	0,16	0,01	0,02	0,00	0,00	0,02	0,08	0,55	0,34	0,42	0,11	0,13	0,09	2,14	0,45							
25	0,73	0,03	0,04	0,06	0,34	0,10	0,51	0,16	0,60	0,02	0,06	0,01	0,05	0,39	0,46	1,38	0,41	1,83	0,35	0,19	0,52	2,89	0,75	1,76						
26	0,44	0,10	0,04	0,07	0,08	0,08	0,41	0,31	0,23	0,01	0,13	0,00	0,01	0,03	0,08	0,31	0,51	0,30	0,58	0,47	0,37	0,44	0,99	1,74	0,63					
27	0,52	0,10	0,17	0,19	0,05	0,13	0,53	0,09	0,05	0,01	0,23	0,00	0,00	0,01	0,04	0,11	0,33	0,13	0,44	0,33	0,29	0,29	0,30	0,86	0,59	2,65				
28	0,22	0,11	0,28	0,17	0,19	0,35	0,87	0,05	0,13	0,05	0,14	0,03	0,03	0,03	0,12	0,23	0,60	0,45	0,20	0,18	0,13	0,19	0,19	0,35	0,34	0,31	1,12			
29	0,27	0,36	0,09	0,28	0,23	0,19	0,37	0,71	0,10	0,01	0,22	0,06	0,02	0,37	0,10	0,40	0,86	0,12	0,72	0,77	0,50	0,22	0,73	0,13	0,92	0,55	0,58	0,43		
30	0,23	0,10	0,12	0,09	0,05	0,08	0,36	0,06	0,17	0,02	0,21	0,01	0,03	0,02	0,27	0,35	0,65	0,50	0,40	0,29	0,53	0,61	0,61	0,26	0,46	1,40	0,78	0,43	0,68	

Table C.1: Technological relatedness matrix.
Source: Leten et al. (2007).

C.2 Results

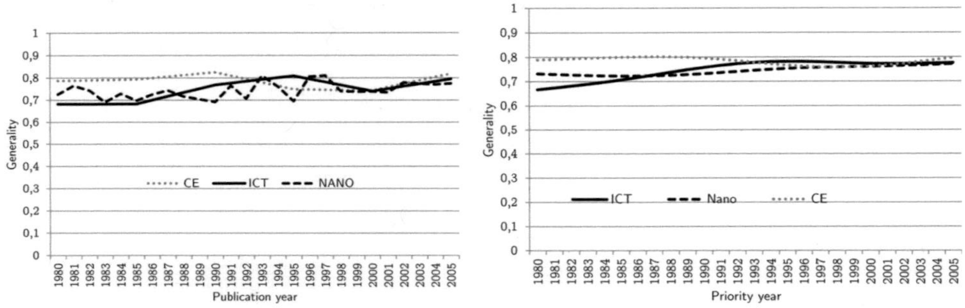

(a) World (b) EU27

Figure C.2: Forward average generalities of Top10 publications (SA) in the World.
Source: WOS, own search and calculations.

GEN	Obs	Mean	StdDev	ICT	CE
NANO	26	0.74	0.04	-0.1465	-2.6157**
ICT	6	0.75	0.05		-1.4996
CE	6	0.79	0.03		

Table C.2: t-Tests (unpaired) of forward average generalities for ICT-, Nano- and CE-publications in the world across the years. ***Indicates significance at 0.01.
Source: own calculations.

D Localised Nanotechnology: The Case of Hamburg

Code	Thomson Reuters Subject Area
BIO1	biochemical research methods
BIO2	biochemistry & molecular biology
BIO3	biophysics
CHE1	chemistry, analytical
CEL	cell biology
CHE5	chemistry, multidisciplinary
CHE7	chemistry, physical
CHR	crystallography
ENG3	engineering, chemical
ENG5	engineering, electrical & electronic
INS	instruments & instrumentation
MAT2	materials science, ceramics
MAT4	materials science, coatings & films
MAT5	materials science, composites
MAT6	materials science, multidisciplinary
MET1	metallurgy & metallurgical engineering
NAN	nanoscience & nanotechnology
NUC	nuclear science technology
OPT	optics
PHA	pharamcology & pharmacy
PHY1	physics, applied
PHY2	physics, atomic, molecular & chemical
PHY3	physics, condensed matter
PHY6	physics, multidisciplinary
POL	polymer science
SPE	spectroscopy

Table D.1: Coded Thomson Reuters subject areas (top 25).
Source: own codification.

Code	IPC Class
A01	agriculture; forestry; animal husbandry; hunting; trapping; fishing
A23	foods or foodstuffs; their treatment, not covered by other classes
A61	medical or veterinary science; hygiene
B01	physical or chemical processes or apparatus in general
B05	spraying or atomising in general; applying liquids or other fluent materials to surfaces, in general
B23	machine tools; metal-working not otherwise provided for
B29	working of plastics; working of substances in a plastic state in general
B32	layered prodcuts
B64	aircraft, aviation; cosmonautics
B81	micro-structural technology
B82	nano-technology
C01	animal of vegetable oils, fats, fatty substances or waxes; fatty acids therefrom; detergents; candles
C02	treatment of water, waste water, sewage or sludge
C03	glass; mineral or slag wool
C04	cements, concrete; artificial stone; ceramics; refractories
C07	organic chemistry
C08	organic macromolecular compounds; their preparation or chemical working-up; compositions based thereon
C09	dyes; paints; polishes; natural resins; adhesives compositions not otherwise provided for; applications of materials not otherwise provided for
C11	micro-structural technology
C12	biochemistry; beer; spirits; wine; vinegar; microbiology; enzymology; mutation or genetic engineering
C23	coating metallic material; coating material with metallic material; chemical surface treatment; diffusion treatment of metallic material; coating by vacuum evaporation, by sputtering, by ion implantation or by chemical vapour deposition in general; inhibiting corrosion of metallic material or incrustation in general
G01	measuring; testing
G02	optics
H01	basic electric elements
H02	generation, conversion, or distribution of electric power

Table D.2: Coded IPC classes (top 25).
Source: WIPO.

	1	2	3	4	5
1 *DEPTH_pub*	1				
2 *BREADTH_pub*	0.19	1			
3 *DEPTH_pat*	-0.08	-0.72	1		
4 *BREADTH_pat*	0.29	0.43	-0.55	1	
5 *GDP/Capita*	-0.16	0.67	-0.64	0.29	1

Table D.3: Correlation matrix ad Chapter 7.
Source: own calculations.

E The Impact of the Knowledge Composition on the Innovation Outcome: Specialisation vs. Diversity

	1	2	3	4	5	6	7	8	9
1 *PUB_SPEC*	1								
2 *PUB_COMP*	-0.2	1							
3 *PUB_DIV*	-0.33	0.14	1						
4 *PUB_SIZE_NKB*	-0.71	0.18	0.22	1					
5 *PAT_SPEC*	0.35	-0.28	-0.17	-0.66	1				
6 *PAT_COMP*	-0.06	0.17	0.09	0.07	-0.23	1			
7 *PAT_DIV*	-0.38	0.26	0.34	0.48	-0.61	0.19	1		
8 *PAT_SIZE_NKB*	-0.39	0.24	0.18	0.73	-0.85	0.18	0.53	1	
9 HQ_T-1	-0.42	0.00	0.05	0.51	-0.54	0.2	0.41	0.53	1

Table E.1: Correlation matrix ad Chapter 8.
Source: own calculations.

F Impact of Local Knowledge Endowment on Nanotechnology Firm Growth

	1	2	3	4	5	6	7	8	9	10	11
1 *EMP*	1										
2 *HQ*	0.06	1									
3 *INDDENS*	0.05	0.37	1								
4 *IND*	-0.03	-0.08	-0.06	1							
5 *STUD*	0.02	0.63	0.45	-0.09	1						
6 *R&D*	-0.05	0.59	0.1	0.01	0.24	1					
7 *LQ*	-0.11	0.23	0.02	0.00	0.19	0.23	1				
8 LQ^2	-0.02	-0.12	-0.02	-0.08	0.04	-0.05	-0.41	1			
9 *SIZE*	0.16	-0.11	-0.13	-0.02	-0.12	-0.11	-0.07	-0.06	1		
10 *KIS*	0.16	0.16	0.02	-0.01	-0.01	0.22	0.06	0.11	0.15	1	
11 *AGE*	-0.19	-0.02	-0.06	0.07	0.01	0.05	0.05	0.03	-0.14	0.01	1

Table F.1: Correlation matrix ad Chapter 9.
Source: own calculations.

G The Development of Nanotechnology through a Network of Collaboration

	Inventor						Applicant					
year	$avgC_B(v_i)$	$maxC_B(v_i)$	C_B	$avgC_D(v_i)$	$maxC_D(v_i)$	C_D	$avgC_B(v_i)$	$maxC_B(v_i)$	C_B	$avgC_D(v_i)$	$maxC_D(v_i)$	C_D
80-84	0	0.0002	0.0003	0.0091	0.0241	0.0179	0	0	0	0.0009	1	0.0145
81-85	0	0.0003	0.0003	0.0086	0.0245	0.0161						
82-86	0	0.0002	0.0002	0.0078	0.0261	0.0184						
83-87	0	0.0002	0.0002	0.0071	0.0242	0.0172						
84-88	0	0.0001	0.0001	0.007	0.0237	0.0169						
85-89	0	0.0001	0.0001	0.0075	0.0231	0.0157	0	0	0	0.0028	0.0377	0.0356
86-90	0	0.0003	0.0003	0.0075	0.0213	0.0139						
87-91	0	0.0003	0.0003	0.0074	0.02	0.0127						
88-92	0	0.0011	0.0011	0.007	0.0427	0.0359						
89-93	0	0.0008	0.0008	0.0061	0.0357	0.0297						
90-94	0	0.0006	0.0006	0.0054	0.0307	0.0254	0	0.0035	0.0035	0.0068	0.0709	0.0646
91-95	0	0.0009	0.0009	0.005	0.0392	0.0343						
92-96	0	0.0013	0.0013	0.0043	0.0431	0.0389						
93-97	0	0.0016	0.0016	0.004	0.0467	0.0428						
94-98	0	0.0012	0.0012	0.0028	0.0324	0.0297						
95-99	0	0.0032	0.0032	0.0021	0.0323	0.0303	0	0.0081	0.0081	0.0036	0.0445	0.0410
96-00	0	0.0027	0.0027	0.0016	0.0237	0.0222						
97-01	0	0.0023	0.0023	0.0013	0.0184	0.0171						
98-02	0	0.003	0.0030	0.0011	0.0186	0.0176						
99-03	0	0.0028	0.0028	0.0009	0.0169	0.0159						
00-04	0	0.0011	0.0011	0.0008	0.0122	0.0113	0.0002	0.0515	0.0513	0.0016	0.0322	0.0307
01-05	0	0.001	0.0010	0.0007	0.0088	0.0081						
02-06	0	0.0012	0.0012	0.0007	0.0084	0.0078						
03-07	0	0.0035	0.0035	0.0006	0.006	0.0054	0.0002	0.0798	0.0796	0.0013	0.0655	0.0643

Table G.1: Centre-periphery-structure of the nanotechnology-networks.
Source: own calculations.

Figure G.1: Colourkey for colours of vertices.
Source: own illustration.

H What Drives Generality? Assessing the Mechanisms of Knowledge Creation

	1	2	3	4	5	6	7	8	9	10	11	12	13	14
1 *GENERALITY*	1													
2 *INV*	0.14	1												
3 *COLL*	0.12	0.6	1											
4 *EXCOLL*	0.07	0.27	0.23	1										
5 *MAX* $C_D(v_i)$	0.27	0.37	0.26	0.06	1									
6 *AVG* $C_D(v_i)$	0.25	0.37	0.28	0.07	0.90	1								
7*MAX* $C_B(v_i)$	0.19	0.2	0.11	0.02	0.64	0.39	1							
8 *AVG* $C_B(v_i)$	0.11	0.24	0.15	0.05	0.28	0.16	0.6	1						
9 *BW_GEN*	0.27	0.05	0.05	0.02	0.03	0.04	0.02	0.03	1					
10 *STAR*	0.18	0.13	0.10	0.01	0.43	0.34	0.4	0.30	0.03	1				
11 *#STARS*	0.19	0.32	0.17	0.02	0.37	0.28	0.4	0.37	0.06	0.67	1			
12 *AVG_PAT_P_INV*	0.24	0.17	0.15	0.00	0.47	0.35	0.59	0.47	0.07	0.69	0.72	1		
13 *VAR*	0.00	0.07	0.08	0.02	0.02	0.02	0.01	0.02	0.03	0.00	0.00	0.00	1	
14 *CITATIONS*	0.45	0.12	0.10	0.09	0.28	0.29	0.12	0.03	0.14	0.09	0.08	0.10	-0.01	1

Table H.1: Correlation matrix ad Chapter 11.
Source: own calculations.